Graham Shaw

THE COST OF AUTHORITY

Manipulation and Freedom in the
New Testament

FORTRESS PRESS   PHILADELPHIA

Library of Congress Cataloging in Publication Data

Shaw, Graham, 1944–
    The cost of authority.

        1. Authority (Religion)—Biblical teaching.
        2. Freedom (Theology)—Biblical teaching.
        3. Bible.   N.T. Epistles of Paul—Criticism,
    interpretation, etc.   I. Title.
BS2655.A8S53   1983   262'.8   82–48545
ISBN 0–8006–1707–X (Fortress Press : pbk.)

9612K82   Printed in the United Kingdom   1-1707

CONTENTS

Contents

PREFACE

For much of Christian history it would have been quite natural for a theologian to present his work in the form of commentary on the New Testament. Today that seems a rash, almost foolhardy approach, for the Christian texts are now surrounded by a specialist literature of daunting complexity. The recent explosion of post-graduate research has created such a wealth of material that a lifetime of scholarship is hardly adequate to master it. The slight reference in what follows to contemporary New Testament study does not imply indifference to that enterprise, far less any fundamentalist repudiation of it. It is rather that the questions with which this book is concerned have not received close attention, and those questions have themselves suggested a distinctive method of understanding the New Testament. Instead of defending this method by contrasting it with a more conventional approach, I thought it best simply to use the method and leave others to make the appropriate comparisons. I will be surprised if all my suggestions find ready agreement; but I hope that impatience with any particular conclusions will not obscure the importance of the questions I have raised and the necessity of devising some method to answer them.

I have tried to write in a way that is accessible to the general reader and yet has some interest for the student. I have been encouraged in that hope by the kindness and criticism of two scholars, whose knowledge of the texts is far greater than mine. I would like to thank the Rev. John Fenton, Canon of Christ Church, for his unstinting generosity of time and attention. If a writer of my obstinacy can be preserved from gross error that is entirely his achievement. I must also acknowledge my debt to Professor J. D. M. Derrett, whose Wilde Lectures on religious freedom and discipline provided a fascinating stimulus and counterpoint to my own thought.

This book is an attempt to learn from experience. Its origins are pastoral and personal; it derives from my observation as a parish clergyman and a college chaplain. The style of criticism I have adopted may seem almost ruthless, but it cannot be dismissed as formulating purely academic questions. Nearly all the inconsistencies, which I have explored in the New Testament, I have first encountered as discrepancies and misgivings in pastoral experience. Why is the church more effective in conveying guilt rather than communicating forgiveness? Why is Christianity resented as a burden rather than welcomed as an opportunity? The criticism of authority in the New Testament has demanded an analysis of my own ministry – the preoccupation with buildings and public observance, an awareness of the subtleties of prestige and the flattery of others, the self-knowledge that comes from looking at parish accounts and acknowledging the economic basis of a clergyman's existence. It has also demanded an attempt to see honestly the communities I have served – the confused expectations of luck, good health, security or married happiness that lie behind so much religious practice, and the disappointment of those expectations; the antagonism and aggression which often accompany belief; faith as an alibi for intellectual dishonesty, a means not of facing the truth about oneself but of hiding from it. Such disturbing experiences have not driven me to disillusion; but they have compelled me to revise my own faith to take account of them.

Far from closing the New Testament I began to read it more avidly, but with new questions. The process has proved exciting and painful. The most helpful guides have not been the German giants of modern theology, but the great Russian novelists of the last century, Dostoyevsky and Tolstoy. Many of the assumptions which lie behind this book are derived from Ivan Karamazov's poem of the Grand Inquisitor, who chides Jesus with wanting to go into the world 'empty handed, with some promise of freedom, which men in their simplicity and their innate lawlessness cannot even comprehend, which they fear and dread'. Faced by a Jesus who has come again the Inquisitor gives this account of himself: 'We have corrected your great work and have based it on miracle, mystery and authority', and defends his work of 'correction' as the only means of bringing about a universal happiness. Ivan describes his poem as 'absurd', which in one sense it is, for the returning Jesus establishes his identity by performing exactly the kind of miracles, which the Inquisitor will claim as his own. Moreover Ivan writes as an atheist, so that the Christian identity of his poem is ambiguous; nevertheless it provides the most haunting exposition of Jesus as the messenger of freedom:

> Instead of taking possession of men's freedom you multiplied it and burdened the spiritual kingdom of man with its sufferings for ever.

You wanted man's free love so that he should follow you freely, fascinated and captivated by you. Instead of the strict ancient law, man had in future to decide for himself with a free heart what is good and what is evil, having only your image before him for guidance (Dostoyevsky, *The Brothers Karamazov*, Penguin, Vol. 1, p. 299).

In the poem the only answer the Inquisitor receives is an enigmatic kiss. That is doubtless the path of artistic wisdom, but the Inquisitor's objections to a gospel of freedom deserve attention. In the poem he assumes that only miracle, mystery and authority can bring about human peace. In this book I shall argue that they are intrinsically divisive, and must inevitably destroy the peace they promise. More crucially the poem assumes that Jesus and his message of freedom can be distinguished from the context of miracle, mystery and authority, with which he has been associated. The poet may not need to face the embarrassment that the New Testament itself is quite as plausibly the work of his Inquisitor as of his Jesus. If the theologian is not to lapse into sentimentality he cannot turn his back on that contradiction. The poem of the Grand Inquisitor is the work of a fictional character, and Dostoyevsky's own attitude to his creation is far from clear. To speak of the poem as conveying Dostoyevsky's own religious beliefs is to oversimplify, but the questions raised within the poem by the Inquisitor, and by the poem's assumptions may help to clarify in the mind of the reader the central questions of this book.

In trying to answer those questions I have repeatedly turned to the much more explicit religious writing of Tolstoy. His eye for the uses of religious doctrine by individuals and by institutions was astonishingly shrewd, particularly his refusal to allow the reader to detach religious doctrines from the interests of those who preach them. His account of the prison service in *Resurrection* is savage, but also salutary:

The priest performed his functions with an easy conscience because he had been brought up from childhood to believe that this was the one true faith which had been held by all the saints that had ever lived and was held now by the spiritual and temporal authorities. He did not believe that the bread became flesh, or that it was good for the soul to pronounce a great number of words, or that he had really devoured a bit of God – no one could believe that – but he believed that one ought to believe it. But the main thing that confirmed him in this faith was the fact that, in return for fulfilling the demands of this faith, for eighteen years now he had been drawing an income which enabled him to support his family, and send his son to a high-school and his daughter to a school for the daughters of clergy.

The same incident is used to illustrate the way in which social prestige and deeply confused expectations make much religious practice plausible:

> The majority of the prisoners (with the exception of a few who saw through the deception practiced on those who adhered to this faith, and laughed at it in their hearts) – the majority of them believed that these gilded ikons, candles, chalices, vestments, crosses, repetitions of incomprehensible words, 'Jesu most sweet' and 'Have mercy', possessed a mystic power by means of which a great many comforts might be obtained, in this life and in the life to come. Though most of them had made several attempts – by means of prayers, special services, candles – to get the goods of this life, and their prayers had remained unanswered, each of them was firmly convinced that their lack of success was accidental and that the establishment, approved by learned men and by archbishops, must be a thing of the greatest importance, and indispensable, if not for this life, at any rate for the hereafter (Tolstoy, *Resurrection*, Penguin, pp. 185, 186).

It is perhaps not surprising that this passage brought about the excommunication of its author; although intended as Christian criticism of religious practice, it found a more ready echo in Marxist minds.

Tolstoy developed a subversive understanding of the Christian gospel, and his analysis of the anarchistic implications of the kingdom of God deserves much more attention than it has received from contemporary theologians. Nevertheless his positive use of Jesus' teaching is in many ways naive, and involved Tolstoy in insuperable intellectual and personal contradictions, which have been seized upon by writers as diverse as D. H. Lawrence, Lenin and Isaiah Berlin. Yet the very difficulties of his own eventual position served to highlight for me those contradictions in the New Testament itself, to which I have tried to attend. His most valuable constructive contribution is the attempt to define Christianity not in apostolic terms, but in terms of discipleship. Critically this led him to repudiate the whole complex of ideas based on apostolic authority: authoritative priesthood, dogma and infallible Bible. Instead he adopted the role not of the prophet, but of the disciple, and tried to develop an appropriate understanding of religious truth and its relation to human freedom. Instead of involving some unique and privileged statement, Christianity becomes a kind of learning. He articulates this most powerfully in *The Kingdom of God*:

> Man is not fixed in relation to truth. As he passes through life, each individual man and humanity in general gains knowledge of a greater and greater degree of truth and frees himself more and more from error.

And therefore men are always in a threefold relation to truth. They have already so assimilated some truths that these have become an unconscious basis for their actions; other truths are only beginning to be perceived by them; and a third group, though not yet assimilated, have revealed themselves with sufficient clearness to compel recognition in one way or other – they must either be acknowledged or rejected.

And it is in the recognition or rejection of such truths that man is free (Tolstoy, *The Kingdom of God*, The World's Classics, p. 425).

Tolstoy never pretends that such freedom is easy to exercise, but at least the lie can be avoided. He was fully aware of the contradictions between his own profession and practice, and quite modest about the extent to which they could be resolved:

I do not say that if you are a landowner you are bound immediately to give your land to the poor; if you are a capitalist to give your money or your factory to the workpeople; if you are a tsar, minister, official, judge or general, that you should at once renounce your advantageous position; or if you are a soldier (if that is to say, you occupy the position on which all violence is based) that you should immediately refuse military service despite all danger of doing so.

Were you to do this you would be doing the very best thing possible, but it may be, as is most likely, that you have not the strength. You have ties; a family, dependents, and superiors; you are under such powerful influences that you are not strong enough to shake them off. But to recognize the truth as a truth and to avoid lying about it is a thing you can always do. It is always in your power to cease asserting that you remain a landowner, a manufacturer, a merchant, an artist or a writer, because that is useful to mankind; that you are a governor, a public prosecutor or tsar, not because it is agreeable to you and you are used to it, but for the public good; that you continue to be a soldier not from fear of punishment but because you consider the army necessary for the security of people's lives. It is always in your power, to stop lying like that to yourself and to others, and you not only can but should do this, because in this alone – in freeing yourself from falsehood and confessing the truth – lies the sole welfare of your life (*The Kingdom of God*, p. 441).

Tolstoy does not here address the clergy – perhaps he had despaired of their response – but those words provoked this study, which is my attempt to avoid lying and recognize the truth.

Exeter College, September 1982

AUTHORITY AND THE SIGNIFICANCE OF CONTRADICTION IN THE NEW TESTAMENT

(a) The embarrassment of Christian history

An immediate task before the Christian church is to acknowledge its own unacceptable face. For on that act of honesty, the plausibility of the Christian message depends. A call to repentance does not deserve attention if it comes from an institution which cannot submit itself to the discipline it demands of others. This is not done simply by appropriating the words of the confession: 'We acknowledge and bewail our manifold sins and wickedness, which we from time to time most grievously have committed, by thought, word and deed, against Thy divine majesty, provoking most justly Thy wrath and indignation against us.' This emphasizes the shortcomings of the individual, but it carefully leaves the prestige of the institution untarnished. Instead, the self-abasement of the sinner only serves to exalt the source of forgiveness. Because the attention of the believer has been concentrated on his own failings, the collective failures of the church have proved difficult to recognize or remedy. To be a Christian obviously involves learning to take responsibility for one's own life, acknowledging one's own sins, gaining a new realism about oneself; but being a Christian must also involve taking responsibility for a particular religious tradition, acknowledging its dangers and mistakes, and learning from that experience without evasion. Personal repentance must be accompanied by religious revision; otherwise the repentance is only partial, the honesty too selective to be convincing.

Christianity cannot claim to be a new religion. For the individual it may represent a new awareness, a fresh discovery, but the religion itself is no longer a novelty. Millions have tried to shape their lives by it, and whole societies have embarked on experiments in Christian faith and obedience. If Christianity was still untried, the mere comparison of one's own inadequacies with its promise of deliverance and new life might lead one to grasp them boldly; but today the promises of Christianity cannot be divorced from the performance which they have fostered. The historical record of two thousand years of Christian endeavour inevitably affects the plausibility of its promises. Does Christianity bring freedom? Is the new life really any different from the old? In the first century such questions might have seemed speculative, an escape from the challenge of the new faith. Twenty centuries later they cannot be avoided. To speak in the style of G. K. Chesterton of Christianity as untried is glib deceit. It gains its plausibility from the guilty awareness in all believers of the distance between profession and life, but if true it would be a devastating verdict on Christianity. Few ideals have so preoccupied the imagination of men, or inspired more utter devotion. If therefore the ideals are still untried, it may well be that they are inadequate to guide men through the complexities of life. The same simplicity which gives them their imaginative power to haunt and obsess may also condemn them to ineffectiveness in actual life.

The attractiveness of G. K. Chesterton's position is that it by-passes all the embarrassments of historical experience; the same motive often leads the religious to cultivate a deliberately selective vision. The edifying chapters of Christian history and the noble aspects of Christian people receive the spotlight, while the rest remains in shadow. The role of Christians in the abolition of slavery masks the centuries of Christian connivance at that institution. The viewpoint of Christian Socialists or the early Franciscans is celebrated; the reinforcement of bourgeois property rights by Christian teaching is overlooked. The church exploits the beauty of the great mediaeval cathedrals, but prefers to forget the immense concentrations of landed wealth and social privilege which made them possible. The use of gold and silver in the liturgy needs and justifies the prisons which protect it. The *ersatz* peace and goodwill of Christmas is not allowed to touch the real antagonisms of life, as the soldiers in the trenches of the First World War quickly discovered.

This highly selective vision of Christian historical experience has its counterpart in the personal dimension. The exaltation of trust easily connives at credulity. Dependence and patience provide ready excuses for cowardice. Aggression, which the Christian sensibility finds difficult to accommodate, is only allowed illicit or unacknowledged expression. The cost of obedience in terms of frustration and immaturity is overlooked. The cult of innocence, which underlies much teaching on poverty and chastity, burdens experience with guilt and nostalgia. Above all, the self-assertion of so much religious conviction is neither acknowledged nor criticized. However consoling the note of the self-congratulation, it is inevitably precarious. It is continually threatened by the very honesty which Christianity advocates. It is disturbing, therefore, that much religious practice is designed to reinforce the selective vision, not to criticize it. The veneration of the saints, for instance, distracts us from the sinners, and illustrates the way in which such a vision entails a divisive stance within society. Thus the Christian is not encouraged to brood too long or too often on those who are outside: the Muslim, the Hindu, or the atheist. Instead he is urged to concentrate on the love, poverty, suffering and obedience of Christ: the divisiveness, wealth and self-assertion of his followers are then less easily perceived. Worship may open the mind to mystery and complexity; it may integrate experience without repudiation or suppression. It would, therefore, be unfair to portray all worship as simply the reinforcement of a selective vision, but that description exactly fits much that passes for worship. 'All things bright and beautiful' hardly prepares children for adult reality. The formalized focus on particular holy texts inevitably narrows the perceptions of those who submit to it. The sinners and the atheists seldom answer back, and are never allowed the last word. This deliberate selectivity is difficult to reconcile with honesty, and in so far as it predominates, worship is transformed into propaganda.

A more sophisticated way of evading the embarrassment of Christian history is the resort to relativism. All moral condemnation of patterns of behaviour in the past is condemned as hasty and anachronistic – an imposition of standards and values on a world where they are either inappropriate or unacknowledged. Such a 'solution' makes it almost impossible to learn from any historical experience. Moreover, the argument is easily reversed to prevent us applying moral norms derived from the past in a present to which they are alleged to be alien. This makes impossible any kind of moral judgment except a purely momentary and intuitive one. There is also a danger that by learning arguments which seem to justify or condone cruelty, fanaticism and oppression in the past, we may find it easier to condone or connive at them in the present. The sophistication and implicit scepticism of this position has never made the resort to historical relativism particularly appealing to religious people. A small group of liberal academic theologians may find it attractive, but it lacks religious power. It is too obviously a half-way house to unbelief.

The third way of avoiding the discipline of Christian history has probably been the most powerful – the distancing device of claiming that whatever offends 'is not really Christian'. Much of the strength of denominational distinctions comes from this function. They are a means of continuing to assert a Christian identity without having to take responsibility for the whole of Christian history. For instance, in England a

Roman Catholic can distance himself from the Erastianism and strong class affiliations of the Church of England. The Anglican can distance himself from the authoritarian tendency of Roman Catholicism and the fundamentalism of much non-conformity. The Free Churches can distance themselves from the formality and laxity of the Established Church. The vitality of the denominational distinctions derives from the repudiation of embarrassing history which they make possible. Such a strategy has two weaknesses. It encourages a collective self-righteousness, which easily rubs off on to individuals. It also makes further revision very difficult, as it has equated such revision with repudiation. The search for a true Christianity which transcends the failures of the past is a necessary task, unless we are to identify ourselves complacently with some existing institution; but the failures of the past must not simply be repudiated. They belong to us as much as the successes. It is only by acknowledging them as Christian and yet submitting them to careful analysis and moral scrutiny that we can transform a source of embarrassment into one of maturity and strength.

It is not surprising that religious people should succumb to impatience with history, because part of the attraction of Christianity lies precisely in putting the past behind one, and so transcending its limitations. Christianity offers a new beginning. That is a heady promise which can easily seem compromised by insisting that the record be examined. It is a temptation both to those seeking a Christian identity and to those who transmit it. For the Christian leader there is some attraction in diverting attention from the record to himself. In that way much evidence which might discredit his claims is concealed. Moreover, the living have a natural interest in elevating their authority at the expense of the dead. The religious seeker may well respond warmly to such a claim. It rescues him from the ambiguities and uncertainties of the past, with their disconcerting requirements of criticism and judgment. It is much simpler and apparently more conclusive to recognize that the historical uncertainties with their competing claims cannot be determined. Instead, the decision is made on the assessment of a living believer who is at least accessible and knowable with an immediacy which the past necessarily lacks. In this way teacher and student connive in order to avoid looking at the past too closely. On this view, it is enough that today the Christian community to which one belongs is not oppressive or bigoted, is socially aware and personally sensitive – if there have been failures in the past, to err is human, and present practice proves that they have been recognized and put right. It seems ungentlemanly to grub around for skeletons in the Christian family cupboard. The difficulty with this apparently common-sense solution is its cost in terms of self-righteousness and rigidity, so that all three ways of disposing of the past make unacceptable demands. The reinforcement of a selective vision is inherently unstable, depending as it does on consistent self-deception which cannot be sustained indefinitely; while the path of historical relativism threatens to undermine any consistent moral judgment.

(b) Oppressive and divisive authority in Christian history

The difficulty may seem exaggerated until some specific examples of Christianity's record have been examined, or there is a danger of prejudging the outcome. By some kind of moral calculation the good might clearly outweigh the evil, and so justify Christian commitment. There are two objections to such a solution. The first is the extreme difficulty of assessing the whole contribution of Christianity on any moral calculus. The difficulty of the procedure makes arbitrary results very probable. The second objection is more fundamental, for the real difficulty is not whether on balance Christianity has been 'a good thing'. The difficulty of the historical record is more precise and more specifically related to the claims of Christianity. Christianity is not simply a programme for human reform. It is a gospel of freedom, deliverance and reconciliation. It proclaims Jesus as the Saviour. It offers men the opportunity of new life and brotherhood. The fundamental challenge of the historical experience is that it directly contradicts that claim. Repeatedly in the church's history the message of freedom and deliverance has only served to sanctify a new system of social control, buttressed by bitterly divisive social attitudes.

In this respect Christian experience has a disconcerting similarity to many modern secular ideologies. The moral earnestness to abolish slavery established the British Empire. The French pursuit of freedom, equality and fraternity brought first the Terror and then the Empire. The search for social regeneration in Italy and Germany established Fascism. Most pervasively, the Marxist dreams of a new humanity have sanctioned systematic oppression and the uncritical concentration of power. These secular gospels have all promised a fresh start, and have often directly appealed to aspirations for freedom and fraternity. Repeatedly such rhetoric has only served to sanction the replacement of one tyranny by another, and provided ancient antagonisms with new sanctions. Some features of Christian history suggest disturbing parallels.

For instance, throughout Christian history there has been a tendency to sectarian attitudes and organization. The attraction of such a stance is the strong sense of group identity which it makes possible. It has always proved attractive in times of acute social dislocation. To the rootless, the powerless and the lonely it offers a secure social context in which to achieve significance. The sense of release that such security can give should not be underestimated, particularly for the first generation which has experienced the transition. The difficulty for succeeding generations is that the security and social context are taken for granted, while the prohibitions and restrictions which are its condition are perceived as unwarranted restraint. The promises of sectarian religion are usually very bold: new life, holiness, in the words of Scripture, the sense of being 'a royal priesthood', specially chosen by God. The vitality, expressed in confidence and aggression, of sectarian religion is a tribute to the freedom it initially conveys. Its converts have a sense of deliverance from the constraints and esteem of surrounding society, and an escape from their own unsatisfactory past. They can easily appropriate the history of the Exodus, its sense of decisive change, of being the special concern of God, its repudiation of Egypt, its delight in being possessed of the promised land; but the cost of this exhilaration is heavy. It derives much of its excitement from the alienation from surrounding society which it articulates, and it can only be preserved by inflexible internal discipline which sustains the group identity by exclusion. Within a few generations sectarian religion has been repudiated as intolerable, or revised to remove its more oppressive features, or it has become an inherited piety, sanctioned by parents and family. To retain that identity is no longer to achieve freedom, but to revere ancestors. Formally the doctrines and practices of the group may well remain unchanged, but their function has been transformed. The words of grace and freedom, of election and deliverance, may still be used, but what continues to be communicated is obedience and conformity to the traditions of the family.

Within the sect love is interpreted as conformity to the group, which demands strict obedience to its discipline and is reinforced by alienation from the surrounding world. This sectarian profile fits most of the early church, and some groups of Christians in every age. High Church exponents of the virtues of the primitive community tend to forget that the episcopate emerged as the most effective means of securing sectarian cohesion. The church in the generation preceding Constantine was not a vigorously expanding and vital community. Most of its members were the children of Christian parents, with attitudes of superiority and distance from surrounding society, marked by the obstinacy of their convictions and the effectiveness of their internal discipline. From this stagnation they were rescued by the unlooked-for recognition of the Emperor. Those who decry the impact of Constantine and the creation of Christendom forget that the conversion of the Empire was in some sense the salvation of the church, and could quite plausibly appear to many of those who witnessed it as such.

The opportunities of this sudden reversal were immense, even if it was accompanied by much disorientation. As prestige could no longer be secured by martyrdom, ascetic practice and miraculous claims became the mark of the new élite. As the gulf between church and state diminished, it was replaced by a growing social distance between clergy and laity. Within Roman society the church exchanged an alienated for a conservative position: the price was a revolutionary identification with the institutions of secular power. In the East the identification became uncritical. The emperor was greeted as the vicegerent of Christ, and the church both provided a legitimation of that authority and benefited from its fruits. In the West the vigour of the papacy, unchecked either by ecclesiastical competitors or by imperial control, evolved claims which eventually embraced all secular sovereignty. In both East and West the bishops exchanged a sectarian role, whose sanction was exclusion, for a public role using the laws and powers of the state to control the laity, reserving to themselves the discipline of the clerical caste.

It is difficult to describe the resulting conditions as the liberation of man. In a lucid if sobering passage the mediaeval historian R. W. Southern points out that the obligations of serfdom could be eased or evaded with more success than those of baptism:

> The Church was a compulsory society in precisely the same way as the modern state is a compulsory society . . . In baptism the godparents made certain promises on behalf of the child which bound him legally for life. From a social point of view a contractual relationship was established between the infant and the Church from which there was no receding. For the vast majority of members of the Church baptism was as involuntary as birth, and it carried with it obligations as binding and permanent as birth into a modern state, with the further provision that the obligations attached to baptism could in no circumstances be renounced. Baptism was not the only involuntary tie which bound a mediaeval man: secular serfdom, if he was so unfortunate as to be born into this condition, was another. Serfdom, however, could be revoked by purchase, or flight or free gift; and the higher forms of secular ob-ligation were all in some degree voluntary – a man could take them up, and in certain conditions renounce them. But the obligations assumed in baptism were there for ever, and they brought secular obligations and penalties in their train no less than spiritual ones (*Western Society and the Church in the Middle Ages*, Penguin 1970, pp. 17, 18).

The end of the sectarian social position did not therefore immediately give men freedom. Rather, secular authority sought to buttress an unstable position by allying with the church, precisely because it was perceived as cohesive and self-disciplined, and the church authorities found in the state a welcome source of wealth and judicial power with which to extend their control over society. Neither emperor nor bishop is a convincing guardian of the freedom of man.

Not only was the gain to freedom slight; the divisive sectarian stance towards society remained little changed. The antagonism and repudiation which had previously been directed ineffectually and therefore harmlessly at the powerful majority were now turned towards minorities which lacked the power to defend themselves. Internally Jews and heretics received the full force of Christian hostility, and the rise of Islam provided a new external enemy to replace the heathen gods. In sectarian times Christian leaders had gained prestige from persecution, and played a crucial role in defining their communities in opposition to society. With the recognition of the state, they then proved their zeal by persecuting minorities, and later strengthened the cohesion of society by inflaming hatred of the infidel. The symbiotic relationship between religious authority and social alienation was not significantly changed.

All this seems comfortably remote from the chastened churches of the modern world, living in predominantly pluralist societies, and largely confined to a private and therefore marginal role in deliberately secular states. A sense of impotence and ineffectiveness is more likely to haunt the modern clergyman than any guilt about the price and dangers of power. The experience of being peripheral to the interests and decisions of the surrounding world is deeply depressing. Some have understandably turned their backs on Christendom, treating it as a term of abuse, and have instead returned to an aggressively sectarian stance. As there is much in the New Testament and the early church which legitimizes this, it is easily represented as a return to primitive simplicity. The cost in arbitrary authority and social divisiveness is not easily recognized, and will presumably have to be rediscovered. Another response to the churches' loss of influence is reassertion, by which the national churches have sought to become more all-embracing, and Roman Catholics more self-consciously papal. The implications of such reassertions are usually hidden by the triumph of indifference; but enthusiasts for identifying church and state, or as it is now more euphemistically described 'community', should not forget the smothering conformity and persistent manipulation which this has always bred when successful. Those who are loyal to the papal monarchy would do well to reflect on the benefits they derive in personal freedom from all those social forces which counterbalance the sovereignty of Saint Peter. Every Roman Catholic practising birth control is exercising a freedom which is dependent upon the constraints on papal power. The acceptable face of the Papacy in modern times is directly related to the successful repudiation of its authority and jurisdiction. One can afford to be affectionate when the power to threaten has been removed.

Sectarianism, the identification of the church and the community, and the claims of the papal monarchy are still with us, and a Christian has to take responsibility for them. He cannot consign them to a remote past, and if Christendom and the Papacy now appear benign, that is not so much because the claims involved have changed, but because they have ceased to be effective. Furthermore Protestant Christianity, which has proved so successful in disrupting Christendom and curtailing papal power, has failed either to sustain freedom or to promote reconciliation. The sense of freedom certainly accompanied the process of transition. The élan of No-Popery celebrated a feeling of liberation. The exclusion of the clergy from secular power, and their integration with the laity by permitting marriage, gave a new self-respect to the laity, and to the clergy a new domesticity to comfort them for their diminished control of society. With marriage came also a greater resistance to internal ecclesiastical discipline: the bishop had, so to speak, met his match in the vicar's wife. Moreover, some aspects of Protestantism defeated the control not only of the papacy but also of the state. In America particularly, the pursuit of the godly society in opposition to corrupting secular power created the conditions for the ultimate separation of church and state. In all these changes the gain to freedom seemed real at the time, but was then undermined by its own consequences.

Protestantism was everywhere marked by a decline in the dominance of the clergy, and their greater integration with the laity. It quickly became apparent that the vacuum of power which their demotion created was to be filled by the educated and wealthy classes, so that an aristocratic or bourgeois society replace the priestly one. The gap between layman and clergyman was lessened, but it was only of a certain class of layman that this was true. Deprived of religious authority, the clergy allied themselves with the educated and wealthy in society, and used this identification to buttress their threatened status. Most of the Protestant clergy tried to replace the magic of the mass with the prestige of education. The churches of the Protestant world became increasingly affiliated to the middle classes, and shared the alienation of that class from the pre-industrial poor and the modern working class. The use of sexual inhibition which had buttressed the separate identity of the clergy was now transferred to a particular class in society, and sanctified and legitimized their precarious social superiority. Thus freedom for the privileged children of the middle classes has not been mediated by Christianity, but by a rejection of sexual prohibitions and a romantic identification with the working class from which those prohibitions were intended to distinguish them. In these circumstances the cross was replaced as a sign of freedom by something which conveyed both explicit sexuality and a proletarian origin – ubiquitous jeans. The poor correctly perceived bourgeois Christianity to be indifferent to their interests – at best a vehicle of guilty condescension by a deviant minority of the middle-class – and replied with massive and disconcerting indifference. For the poor, repudiation of Christianity, a refusal to be blinded by the use of its prestige in the interests of a particular class, proved the first step to liberation and self-respect.

If the class affiliations of Protestant Christianity reflect the erosion of the priestly caste, the elevation of the authority of Scripture was both the means of challenging papal authority and the substitute for that authority. The legitimation it gave for challenging the institutions of late mediaeval Christendom proved explosive; moreover it was accessible to all who could read. Protestant ministers might insist that it required a knowledge of the ancient languages, which incidentally ensured their own necessity, but the principle of *sola scriptura* gave a new self-respect and independence to all who were literate. This was only threatened by the growth of science and of historical method. For the emphasis on an infallible Bible, which had at first proved a means of liberation, became itself a source of anxiety which could only be allayed by repression. Challenged by evolution in its cosmology, and by historical criticism in its insistence on the miraculous, it could only defend itself by a vigorous repudiation of such disruptive approaches. As the threat to biblical infallibility came no longer from the Pope but from scientists and historians, the reassertion of the uniqueness of the Bible became more shrill. This new anxiety was expressed in fundamentalist Christianity by an emphasis on faith as uncritical conformity to the fundamentalist group, which could only be maintained by separation from its critics. Its fragile basis provides a strong impulse to reassure the members by communicating it to others. The aggressively missionary stance betrays the need of the faithful to convince themselves.

The repressive and conflict-laden aspects of Christianity are many and varied. They are difficult to recognize and impossible to repudiate. The detachment of the writer as chaplain of an Oxford college is entirely illusory. Such a position is the direct beneficiary of the wealth and social status acquired by close identification of church and state. Freedom from the distraction of a large church building has not been purchased by dispensing with such buildings and the prestige they confer. It is made possible only by the continuing adequacy of the endowment which originally created such edifices. A certain independence of episcopal control is achieved by a total dependence on the very secular power of a governing body. The beauty of the building and the choral liturgy imposes itself on generations of undergraduates. They remain little conscious of its economic basis, and only confusedly aware of the contradiction between the institution they see and the teachings it propagates. If a chaplain can afford to be tolerant towards dissent, that at least in part reflects the confidence and the arrogance of established wealth. Significantly, the use of the chapel by the servants of the college is rare and occasional. It is correctly seen as being the preserve of an educated and cultured élite.

(c) *The responsibility of a religion for its history*

This picture of Christianity may seem unduly sombre; it neglects the many positive contributions which the church has made to society and to individuals. All that has been pointed out is the cost of such benefits; nor are the drawbacks accidental, they are an integral part of the Christian tradition. The pious response to such a description will be to impute it to human sin. The religion is good, but it respects human freedom and therefore one must expect sinful human beings to distort it. If Christianity was simply a religion of resignation, reconciling man to his limitations but not challenging the limitations themselves, that defence would be plausible, and it is fair to recognize that many who try to defend Christianity in this way regard their religion as just such a matter of despairing pessimism. Recognition of reality is certainly a part of Christianity, but the gospel also promises change: deliverance, freedom and reconciliation. Christianity is a message not about the inevitability of evil and sin, but about the possibility of new life and holiness. It is specifically the promise of Christianity which is challenged by the actual record, not least because the repression and the alienation seem directly related to the moral conviction and social vitality of the religion in all its forms. To plead the sinfulness of man as an adequate explanation is to evade the painful process of religious revision. The prestige of Christianity is preserved unsullied while the individual is preoccupied with his personal inadequacies; but the believer is as responsible for his religion as for his life. Both religion and life demand realistic reappraisal. Such a defence also serves to discredit freedom by suggesting that man's misuse of it is at fault and should be remedied by obedience. An alternative explanation would place the blame on the denial of freedom to others and the refusal to exercise one's own freedom.

The traditional Protestant response to the problem has been to appeal from a corrupted church to an uncorrupted Bible. The pure religion is to be found in the pages of scripture, and then re-emerges uncontaminated to validate whichever Protestant community is speaking. However, this has not succeeded in casting off an authoritarian and divisive inheritance; it has only given it new forms. This can only mean that the origins of the problem lie in the New Testament. As long as the New Testament remains fundamentally uncriticized, it will function as a carrier of those destructive attitudes which have surfaced repeatedly in Christian history.. The first objective must therefore be to outline an appropriate critical method, and then to apply it to the earliest New Testament texts.

(d) Is religious authority necessarily oppressive and divisive?

Christian history raises questions about the exercise of any religious authority. Is all religious authority of its nature oppressive, evading criticism by divisive social attitudes? Is the Christian gospel inherently self-contradictory, promising freedom but enforcing obedience, promising reconciliation but sanctioning division? Is the language of Christianity a device for disguising the exercise of power? The heart of the problem is to be found in the preconditions for freedom. Any exercise of freedom demands an act of imagination by which certain constraints in reality are transcended. Confronted by sickness we imagine the possibility of healing. Confronted by actual injustice we imagine what a just society might look like. Confronted by unhappy and discontented individuals we dare to imagine bliss. Without such a critical and creative use of the imagination to transcend the limits of the actual, there is no possibility of change or freedom; and this inevitably involves a temporary suspension of disbelief. If the imagination is to be effective, it demands free play at least for a while. The danger inherent in the religious use of the imagination is that it will demand a permanent immunity from criticism. Religious authority then becomes a continuous exercise of fantasy, refusing to be checked by the constraints of actual experience. Though men die, it will obstinately continue to speak of eternal life. Though the environment remains stubbornly unresponsive to human wishes, it will cling to belief in the efficacy of prayer. Though men remain bound by economic and sexual needs, it will perpetuate standards of absolute poverty and chastity. The flight of imagination which is used to transcend limitation, and hence to change and exercise freedom, must be temporary. Having transcended reality it must then return to it, and submit the dream to the test of actual experience and action. Only in that way can limited creatures explore their opportunities for freedom, limited but real. Never to dream is the path of passive accommodation, but to refuse to turn from dream to reality is equally ineffectual. It deprives men of the power to act and discover their freedom as surely as the most hidebound common sense.

The use of imagination to attain freedom inevitably distances human beings from one another. Conformity to the expectations of family or school or social class can be only avoided by distancing ourselves in imagination from these groups to which we belong. The adolescent, for instance, imagines himself apart from his family in order to acquire a new freedom. Because freedom challenges social conformity, it carries potential for conflict, and a temporary distancing can become a permanent repudiation. The danger to which religious people seem particularly prone is that once they have distinguished themselves from others to acquire a new freedom, to explore different possibilities of living, the alienation becomes irreconcilable. This is not to say that the use of the imagination which is a precondition of freedom is always arbitrary and alienating; it is only to point out that it can easily become so, as Christian history has amply proved. The two questions, therefore, which the New Testament raises are these. Is the authority it claims compatible with the freedom it promises? Does the new identity it bestows on the believer alienate or reconcile?

(e) *The criticism which the New Testament invites*

To ask such questions is not to impose an alien sociological criticism but to take seriously the claims that the New Testament makes about itself. To a generation of critics brought up on the axiom that 'Christianity is a historical religion', it will certainly suggest a change of emphasis. Christianity is primarily a religion of salvation: it claims to bring deliverance and peace, and the examination of those claims deserves a central place in any study of the New Testament. Moreover, it implies a rather different understanding of the faith with which the texts must be approached. No prior positions need to be taken on the existence of God or the possibility of revelation. No special pleading is required to rehabilitate the miraculous, far less a commitment to some version of infallibility. It is enough that the reader admits the possibility of human freedom and of reconciliation between men, and does not regard those possibilities as mutually incompatible. Such a faith cannot be taken for granted. We do at times despair of the possibility of freedom, and resign ourselves to submission. We do at times treat the antagonisms in which we are involved as being resolvable only by violence and death. It often seems impossible to reconcile the demands of personal freedom and social harmony. If such faith was not continually threatened, the New Testament would not be good news, but platitude. It is because the gospel evokes and sustains such faith that it deserves its name.

The approach to the New Testament adopted here involves two tasks. The first is to recognize the crucial part the texts play in asserting and exercising Christian authority. The second and more difficult task is to appraise that authority. This is not simply critical in a negative way – it must also define how authority is to be authenticated and used legitimately. Without such a positive criterion the result would be to trivialize and debunk in an irresponsible way. Much of what follows will be abrasive but the force of the criticism is not nihilistic; it derives from a positive commitment to the freedom and unity of man.

(i) *The recognition of authority*

The function of the Christian texts in asserting and exercising authority has received slight attention. In part this reflects the preoccupations of the readers. Christian scholars with doctrinal beliefs about the historical Jesus or the early church have tended to treat them as so much historical evidence, and non-Christian scholars have followed that emphasis even when challenging their conclusions. The lay religious reader has usually come to the New Testament with one of two interests. He may wish to reassure himself about the relevance of his religion, and so will welcome almost any perceived correspondence between the New Testament and the twentieth-century world, with little concern or ability to criticize the New Testament attitude. He is merely grateful that here religion can be applied to everyday life. Otherwise he is likely to be reading the Bible to reinforce and develop a Christian position which he has already adopted, and which he looks to the Bible to confirm. Again the correspondences between the New Testament and his beliefs will be sufficient, without criticizing the basis of those attitudes in the New Testament. The scholar sees the authority of the New Testament in terms of its historical reliability, and thus finds it difficult to perceive the other ways in which the New Testament is an authority. The religious layman is so used to the authoritative stance of modern Christian communities that he fails to perceive how tendentious is the original assertion of that authority in the texts. Furthermore, the preoccupation of the readers is abetted by the art of the writers. Even where the exercise of authority is obvious, as in the Pauline letters, it is made plausible with great subtlety, and with a skill of which the writer was only partly conscious. In the Gospels the assertion of authority is yet more oblique and more effective.

Some readers may be repelled by any suggestion of a political element in the New Testament. Politics are felt to be dirty, and political manoeuvres particularly dirty, but such an attitude only invites deception. To point to a political element in the New Testament is not necessarily to discredit it. Such awareness makes possible criticism, but it does not prejudge the outcome of that criticism. Christians who have experienced the contradictions of allying the church with secular power, and have repudiated that alliance are deluding themselves if they believe that any actual Christian community has ever existed that has not been concerned with power. The status of Jesus as Messiah may have been open to misrepresentation, but his execution by the Romans was not entirely a mistake. He represented a real challenge to the power relationships of the ancient world. Authority is always a bid for power over other human beings, and Jesus' style of authority, while different from its Jewish and Roman competitors, was no less subversive for not depending on a holy Temple or imperial legions. To refuse to be aware of the political dimension of Christianity is either to connive at one's own manipulation or to adopt a version of Christianity which is indistinguishable in practice from disbelief. The first way refuses to take responsibility for the manner in which power is exercised in and by the Christian community by resolutely denying its existence. In such a view holiness prohibits criticism. The church distinguishes itself from surrounding society precisely by being the area within which politics are not practised. The second course, by denying to Christianity any sovereignty in this life, but confining it to some hypothetical future state, equates Christian commitment with practical atheism. This may partially explain the surprising *modus vivendi* of Russian Orthodoxy and the Communist party.

The task of recognizing claims to authority in Christian texts looks deceptively easy. Paul, for instance, speaks directly about his apostolic authority, and large sections of his letters are rulings on particular issues. Jesus is called Christ and Lord; he commands and promises; his authority is explicitly noted in the Gospels. To that extent the New Testament is quite straightforward, but a full awareness of that assertion of authority is more disturbing. For instance, the way in which a group perceives its relation to the surrounding society is closely connected with the way in which authority is exercised within the group. Thus arbitrary authority and divisive social attitudes reinforce each other. Similarly, the promises and privileges which give a group identity and distinguish it from others, at first sight appear quite unconnected with the Lordship of Christ or the authority of an apostle. Not until the relationship has been made clear has a full awareness of the structure of authority within the texts been achieved. Secondly, the appeal to God distracts attention from the human speaker. Heaven is silent, and when men's attention is directed towards it, we easily fail to notice that human lips are moving. This is not to dismiss all talk of God as deceit, but it does suggest that we fix our eyes most carefully on the human speaker, and treat with caution any confusion of identity between man and God. Wherever a man cannot speak in his own name, but buttresses his speech with divine authorship, suspicion is certainly in order. Is the human speaker benefiting by this device, and if so, how?

Is such suspicion appropriate? There is a danger of that cheap and irritating reversal of statement so much loved by the amateur psychologist: 'You said this, but what you really meant . . .' If no positive criterion of authentic authority was offered, such distrust would be excessive. The use of suspicion is not intended to subvert all authority, but to clarify what is legitimate. The approach can be justified on three grounds. First, it is mistaken to think that words are used only to communicate meaning: every conjuror knows that they are also used to conceal. It is therefore entirely proper to ask whether a text is diverting attention, and this is particularly appropriate wherever authority is being claimed. Authority and trickery often accompany each other, and not simply in the magic of the shaman. The pomp and magnificence of monarchy distracts attention from its dependence on the connivance of those who are ruled, as the myth of the social contract cloaks elements of violence and compulsion in existing communities. Secondly, we know that the vehemence of an assertion is no guarantee of its truth. Consciousness of truth is more often associated with a confidence that the truth can be left to speak for itself. That is not to condemn all utterance as anxiety, but it does justify caution towards exaggerated language and bold paradox. Finally, if a certain suspicion towards texts which assert authority over the reader is legitimate, that is much strengthened when the text contains contradictions of attitude. Such tensions suggest a significance in the text which transcends the author's conscious meaning, and which is not to be equated with his explicit message. Only by looking closely at such features can we be sure that they are not creating confusion and bewilderment which then become sanctified as mystery.

(ii) The appraisal of authority

Becoming conscious of the subtle ways in which authority is asserted in the New Testament is not easy, but the appraisal of that authority is even more difficult. All authority tends to evoke alternations between resentment and uncritical submission, and religious authority is no different. Sniggering anti-clericalism and passionate atheism are the natural complement to the assertions of dogmatic or scriptural infallibility. A fair appraisal of the way authority is being used requires the recognition of two unavoidable circumstances. First, the exercise of power is unavoidable. Any human being who speaks or acts cannot avoid exercising some influence over the words and deeds of others. We may be frightened by the possibilities of such power; we may wish to deny our responsibility for it; but we possess it, and as long as we live we cannot abdicate it. It is not, therefore, a proper objection to any New Testament writing to detect the exercise of power within it; it is the use made of authority that has to be carefully assessed. Secondly, life is inherently unstable. All its accommodations are temporary, and security is inevitably short-lived. The same impermanence of life which makes dreams of permanence so attractive, condemns them to unreality. The response to this consciousness of death crucially affects the way power is used. In the present we know that we have real power, but we also know that we will die. The anticipation of death can make us sulk and repudiate the power which we actually have, but such a response is as illusory as the refusal to anticipate death at all.

The oppressive use of authority derives from the determination to perpetuate a position of power which is threatened by an instability it cannot ultimately evade. Moreover the same instability which will eventually terminate the whole situation may in the short term accentuate the disequilibrium in which a particular position of power is grounded. Thus the poor get poorer and the rich get richer. The determination to perpetuate power easily welcomes further accumulations of power without realizing their self-destructive implications. Self-perpetuating authority can defend itself from dissolution only by oppression, and the New Testament contains many examples of that ruthless self-defence at work.

In the first place, the determination to perpetuate power fosters illusion. It must conceal from itself and from others its own mortality. Its vigorous assertion depends on repressing the anticipation of death, because its prestige depends on hiding that weakness from those over whom it exercises power. In secular terms, the creations of such fantasy are obvious. Monumental buildings from the pyramids to Stalin's palaces of culture, exaggerated public rhetoric, association with the ancient (which is mistaken for the eternal), military display and musical manipulation all give an illusory impression of permanence. The New Testament is marked by not dissimilar illusions. Jesus lives. Christ is declared to be the same, yesterday, today and for ever. Jesus is represented as saying that 'heaven and earth shall pass away, but my words shall not pass away'. The eternity and unchangeability may be attributed to God, but his human representatives easily appropriate to themselves something of the same qualities. Such illusions are always insecure, and authority which depends upon them cannot quiet its own anxiety.

This insecurity breeds an intolerance of criticism. The carefully orchestrated vision must not be disturbed by any dissenting voices. The explicit form of this intolerance is prohibition, which imposes silence and practises censorship. The insistent demand for attention, the nervous warnings against false prophets and the exclusion of critics by anathema are the New Testament equivalents of this. With greater subtlety the critic is discredited, his motives are impugned, but his arguments are not given the courtesy of a reply. Jewish and Gentile critics of the faith are sometimes dealt with in a way which is prophetic of Marxist repudiation of bourgeois criticism. Moreover authority can make itself almost immune to criticism by basing its claims in such a way that they defy examination. The Marxist appeal to an indefinite future state has only secularized the dishonesty of Jewish and Christian eschatology. The appeal to immediate revelation of a charismatic kind may be totally repudiated, but short of that it is very difficult to criticize. The paranoid delight in persecution can exploit deep resources of self-pity, and produce an invincible obstinacy. Moreover an authority which refuses to listen to others will be afraid to criticize itself publicly. Because it already possesses the truth, it can admit neither development nor mistake. In making the most surprising *volte-face* it must continue to assert its unchanging identity. Thus in modern times we have witnessed the curious spectacle of the Roman Catholic Church repressing the very Mass for which its priests had once died. The history is too embarrassing a commentary on new claims, especially when these are made with the old arrogance. In the New Testament there is a similar embarrassment about the novelty of the Gentile mission.

To foster illusion and silence criticism requires a clearly defined or gathered group. It must be possible to disown the critic, and keep at bay disturbing experience. Such insecure authority depends on the existence of the 'other' from which it so vociferously dissociates itself. In that way it encourages the anxieties which it allays. There has always, for instance, been a streak in Christianity which communicates guilt in order to appreciate forgiveness; but there must be no shadow of connivance. As Paul nervously asks, 'Shall we persist in sin, so that there may be all the more grace?' That connivance can only be convincingly repudiated if those who do not conform are excluded, and this demands an element of visibility. Accent and skin-colour, dress or table-manners provide social visibility; its political equivalents are identity-cards and passports. In religious terms, ritual and religious observance are crucial in maintaining the same divisive identity. The New Testament contains passages of venomous hostility towards outsiders, and a stress on sacramental forms of visibility, especially baptism, which effectively defines outsiders. These clear indications of insecure and therefore arbitrary authority are associated with an emphasis on obedience and a fondling of the sanctions which enforce it. In terms of secular politics the apparatus of the police-state is a partial admission of failure. In the New Testament some passages exalt uncritical obedience, which is then enforced by the immediate sanction of social exclusion, and by the ultimate if unusable deterrent of the last judgment.

Insecure power is not only incapable of recognizing its temporal limitation; it is also very reluctant to acknowledge its present basis. Rhetoric and ritual disguise the precise political and economic arrangements on which it depends. Middle-class democracies hide behind constitutional monarchies. The rhetoric of American individualism and freedom conceals the corporate domination of the political process. Responsibility becomes difficult to perceive and therefore easy to evade. Individual assertions of authority are disguised by grandiose or misleading identifications. Thus the Party claims to be the proletariat or the people; Louis XIV and de Gaulle use the egoism of the nation to cloak their own. In religious terms the speaker identifies himself with God, or apparently more modestly with Christ or the Holy Spirit. The failure to speak in one's own person, and the resulting confusion of identity, is often found in the New Testament and is always ground for caution.

How does any system of authority which is oppressive in its effects and ultimately self-destructive nevertheless perpetuate itself? Why is it not overthrown by those it dominates, or radically modified by those who operate it? Those whom it dominates reconcile themselves to their lot by regarding it as inevitable, and thus excuse themselves from the suffering which change and freedom would entail. Moreover, those who have reconciled themselves to oppression and disowned their freedom, compensate themselves by insisting on their right to oppress in turn. Those who submitted to their elders and betters and told themselves that their submission was inevitable will in their turn undermine the freedom and commitment to change of those who came after them. Freedom is not simply an absence of constraint; it has to be won and exercised amid many forces that threaten it. Thus we cannot acquire freedom without courage, nor can we confer freedom on those who lack courage.

Although the exercise of power cannot be avoided, the use to which that power is put can be assessed, and is largely determined by attitudes towards mutability and death. An awareness of the temporary nature of all positions of power and an honest recognition of the inevitability of death are the necessary conditions for a use of the power which we actually have that is neither self-perpetuating nor oppressive. Because it is not committed to a doomed enterprise, power which recognizes the inevitability of its own dissolution need not try to sustain the impossible by the illusory. The New Testament contains a great deal of teaching which reminds us of the impermanence of wealth and power. Jesus is represented as anticipating his death in his baptism, in his teaching and at the last supper. From this realism about his own death that he derives the freedom to give himself, in contrast to the fears and hesitations of his disciples. While those who seek to perpetuate power greedily snatch at every possible accumulation of power, he is content to use the power which he actually has. Because he has recognized death, he can use that power with self-discipline and ultimately in self-surrender. It is that use of power which the New Testament celebrates as creative and liberating.

Authority which has come to terms with the prospect of its own extinction finds a certain security in such realism. Freed from the pursuit of the impossible, it can attend to more modest and therefore attainable objectives. It has no need to hide the truth in fantasy. Beside much illusion, the New Testament also contains merciless realism. Jesus, for example, punctures the reverence that insecure power demands: he dismisses Herod as 'that fox', and points out that not one stone of the Temple will be left standing. Nor is such realism directed only negatively. The carefully concealed and cultivated mystery at the heart of Jewish life is replaced by Jesus' cruelly exposed body as the veil of the Temple is rent in two. His weakness and nakedness on the cross mock the alleged miracles which seek to make him more palatable. The New Testament is no stranger to the desire for an almighty and all-knowing Jesus from whom we might derive the kind of security we vainly seek in competing authorities. The cry of dereliction and the anxiety of Gethsemane provide an effective antidote to such dreams. The most ruthless and rationalistic critic of the Gospel narratives is not necessarily distorting the text, for at least in part it supports him. It was not by denying his death but by anticipating it that Jesus was free to use his power, without needing either to increase it or defend it.

Authority which has recognized its own temporary nature need not repress criticism, but can listen to it. The recognition of its own mortality is the fundamental act of self-criticism, a truth which is implicit in Jesus' baptism at the beginning of his ministry. Nevertheless the New Testament is often defensive towards criticism. The Gospels love to give Jesus the last word in dispute; at first the Pharisees, and in St John's Gospel the Jews as a whole, are deliberately discredited, but there are contrary indications. Against the little know-all in the Temple, there must be counted the adult religious teacher who learns from the Syro-Phoenician woman, and is surprised by a Gentile's faith. While much of the dialogue is contrived, Jesus is immersed in conflict and debate. His utterances are greeted with less respectful silence than the average sermon, and because so much of his teaching emerges from meetings with other people, he not only speaks, he also listens. He lives surrounded by questioners and dies to a background of abuse. This is not the only picture of Jesus which the Gospels give, but it is sufficiently prominent to question the adequacy and even the appropriateness of the authoritarian alternative. In the same way eschatological immunity, immediate revelation and paranoia towards persecutors are all attributed to Jesus in the New Testament, but there are also signs of a confidence in communication and an appeal to common experience. His use of parables does not look to another world for vindication. It invites assent from the listeners' experience of a world which is common to speaker and audience alike. The Anglican writers who saw in the Gospels nothing but their own common sense may have overlooked much else that was inconvenient, but they also saw something which was there. The emphasis on the neighbour, on the public fruits of religion as well as its secret motives, the confidence in everyday perceptions as a guide to religious truth, are all important correctives to the esoteric and privileged tendencies of much New Testament teaching. For unlike the esoteric and privileged versions of that teaching, they facilitate criticism rather than evade it.

Authority which recognizes the temporary nature of its position of power is not threatened by the outlook and experience of others. It can therefore adopt a much more open and inclusive social stance because it knows that its own identity cannot be preserved indefinitely. It has no need to foster antagonism or insecurity. Instead it can use its power to encourage the autonomy of others, while respecting their integrity. In religious terms, it can sit loosely to all forms of visibility because it does not need continually to draw attention to itself. There is much in the New Testament which reflects this. Jesus' eating with publicans and sinners deliberately questions the rigid distinctions of contemporary religion, and the church's openness to Gentiles is only an extension of the same attitude. The teaching on forgiveness is subversive of all legal distinctions, and the criticism of sabbath observance, circumcision and food laws all repudiate a divisive visibility. The teaching on rank, reinforced by the parable of Jesus washing the feet of his disciples, extends this teaching to religious authority itself – the distinction between disciples and master is deliberately confused. In one sense the whole insistence on incarnation is the culmination of this liberating reversal. Orthodox stress on the otherness of God tends to legitimate social alienation. In the New Testament it is replaced by a radical identification of God and man. I John correctly sees this as the legitimation of the inclusive, forgiving love which is one of the distinguishing marks of the New Testament: 'For God is love; and his love was disclosed to us in this, that he sent his only Son into the world to bring us life. The love I speak of is not our love for God, but the love he showed to us in sending his Son as the remedy for the defilement of our sins. If God thus loved us, dear friends, we in turn are bound to love one another (4.9–11)'.

A use of power which encourages the independence of others, and an exercise of authority which seeks the response of others rather than their silence, does not stress obedience but opportunity. Often Jesus' parables are in terms of invitation, and the beatitudes replace commandments by blessings. This gracious use of authority looks for the free response of others, which produces a dual emphasis on the grace of God and the freedom of man. These are not, as Augustinian theology implies, in tension; they are the correlates of each other. Man's freedom is created by and exercised in the opportunities which God chooses to provide. The replacement of the command by the invitation expresses this, even if the invitation is sometimes accompanied by such menacing imagery that the difference between grace and law is undermined. The stress on judgment cannot be ignored, but it is connected by an element of surprise and unpredictability. The images of judgment are further modified by the natural analogies which often accompany them. Here the stress is not on the decision of the judge to punish, but on the orderliness of the world. The sanction is no external vengeance, but integral to the structures of reality which are to be changed. On this account the invitations of God demand an attention to reality, not to foster submission, but to inform and make possible its transformation.

An authority which bases and disciplines its position by reference to truth not only anticipates its revision but can recognize and admit its present basis. It does not have to conceal this by the use of ritual and rhetoric. Thus Jesus can speak in his own person – he is free to say 'I'. Thus he can take responsibility for his own judgment, so that he acknowledges change: 'They were told . . . but what I tell you.' This reflects a radical freedom towards Scripture and tradition incompatible with other elements in the New Testament which turn to the Old Testament for legitimation or try to conceal the new by dressing it up in the old. Moreover, he appeals to the individual judgment of his disciples: 'Who do you say that I am?' In the stories of healing he attributes the cure not to his own faith, but to the faith of the person who has made the request. Those who are restored do not remain dependent on Jesus; they are released to freedom and autonomy. The freedom with which he expresses himself recognizes the integrity and independence of others.

Those who want an infallible guide in the New Testament will seek to reconcile all these contradictions. I do not believe that such an infallible guide is available, or that such reconciliation is convincing – it only produces a desperate attempt to save appearances. However, the real objection to such an attempt is not theoretical but practical. The attempt to reconcile these contradictions has led to the repeated betrayal of freedom and solidarity by arbitrary and divisive authority. It is only by identifying the witness in the New Testament to authentic authority which both frees and reconciles, and using that as a criterion for interpreting the New Testament as a whole, that we may hope not to repeat the old mistakes of Christian history. In the last resort it is better to insist on the contradictions in the text and reconcile mankind than to achieve a reconciliation of the texts which baptizes our antagonisms.

Before I attempt to practise the kind of criticism which I have outlined, one further objection should be heard: this approach may seem unduly polemical, for there is a strong vein of negative criticism in what follows. I identify more readily with the awkwardness of Protestantism and tend to equate catholicism with complacency. I believe, however, that Christianity is inherently critical. It has its origins in a critical and courageous revision of Judaism. Its positive values emerged in the process of polemic and cannot be understood apart from it, nor can its affirmations be deprived of their daring. Christianity exhibits its vitality and validity, not by safely reiterating infallible truth, but by having the courage to learn, a process in which each approximation to the truth is the product of free and vigorous criticism, and itself invites such criticism. The polemic should not conceal the positive commitment to freedom and reconciliation. Instead, it serves to remind us of their cost.

(f) Paul and Mark: the selection of the texts

This study begins with a close examination of the Pauline letters, because they are the earliest Christian documents we possess. It would, however, be deeply misleading to confine this study to Paul, for this is not one more attack on the influence of Paul, a reversion to the favourite liberal charge of the nineteenth century that Paul perverted the religion of the Jesus of the Gospels. The real importance of the Pauline letters is exactly the reverse: the study of Paul enables us to see the Gospels in a new and better light. The great merit of Paul is that he makes explicit what would otherwise be a matter of conjecture. By comparison a Gospel has an appearance of objectivity. Authority is asserted obliquely in the portrayal of Christ. As an author Mark is largely invisible. He conceals the particular aims of the hierarchy he serves and affects a universal audience. Without the Pauline letters we might suspect that the Gospels were concerned with power, that with the divine claims there was a subtle counter-point of human authority and control, but in the absence of any independent evidence that would not have been easy to demonstrate. The Pauline letters supply that deficiency.

It is not merely that the Pauline letters display a direct concern with the assertion, defence and exercise of his authority. Indeed the fact that they are so explicitly concerned with the writer's own position, while the Gospels seem impervious to such considerations, might suggest that an analysis of Paul's letters has no relevance to the Gospel material. Moreover the marked discrepancy in literary form and history between the letters and the Gospels does not facilitate comparison. In the place of one author defending himself, the Gospel materials have often been worked at by many hands, and are the product of a complex oral tradition. This may have been ordered and revised by the evangelist, but it is not his creation in the sense that Paul's letters seem to be.

The points of contact between these two very different literary phenomena lie in the strategies for consolidating power which they share. There is no parallel in any Gospel for Paul's direct defence of his apostolate, but many of the means he uses to conduct that defence are present, and so are some of his distinctive contradictions. The manipulation of eschatological anxiety, and the offer of privilege in another world; the divisive emphasis on divine judgment to provide sanctions to control behaviour, the stress on secrecy which gives to the initiates a special status, the prestige derived from persecution, and explanations of dissent, which render it harmless; accounts of the relation to secular power, which are both dismissive yet acquiescent, a stress on internal unity at the cost of external antagonism, the fusion of the crucified identity with asceticism, the legitimation of the New Testament by reference to the Old, the exploitation of the social impact of prayer; above all a continuity in the conception of the Christian privilege, as sonship, inheritance, election, and the possession of the Spirit. All these bind together the Pauline epistles and the four Gospels. Furthermore such strategies for defending authority are accompanied by the same high cost in terms of contradictory attitudes. There is a similar ambivalence towards the audience, and an identical distrust of the world. Cosmic dualism and the unresolved conflict between flesh and spirit mark the Gospels as deeply as the epistles. Both sets of documents assert the miraculous.

The presence of the same strategies in two very different literary traditions suggests that the Gospels are as concerned with the elaboration of authority in the new community as are the epistles. The study of Paul thus provides a key to enter the intention of Gospels, which is here tested in relation to Mark. If Mark demonstrates a striking continuity with Paul in many of the strategies he employs, he also provides a much more convincing vindication of the moral criticism, which both he and Paul invite. Without Paul's letters we would read Mark's Gospel more naively – hardly recognizing its continual assertion of authority – but without Mark we might wonder whether the appraisal of authority to which this book is devoted can properly be described as Christian. The two earliest sets of Christian documents interpret each other. Paul provides the basis of the political analysis, Mark justifies the Christian identity of the moral appraisal. From this mutual interplay there emerges a Gospel of freedom and peace, which is as subversive and offensive to our world as to theirs. In both it articulates and sustains the hope of a future radically different from the past.

PART ONE

The Letters of Paul

I

I THESSALONIANS

The earliest surviving Christian document must be deeply disappointing to any scholar who is trying to reconstruct the historical Jesus. The epistle, while not devoid of reference to Jesus, provides little information. The doctrinal historian is perhaps more easily satisfied. The standard modern Roman Catholic commentary is able blandly to declare that the letters 'presuppose an initial doctrinal formation of considerable clarity and amplitude' (*The Jerome Biblical Commentary*, Geoffrey Chapman 1969, p. 228) and proceeds to refer to nine verses out of ninety. The emphasis of the epistle is not directed towards either history or doctrine: it is preoccupied with the assertion and exercise of the apostle's authority.

(a) The authority of the founding father

The letter opens on a note of collective leadership: 'From Paul, Silvanus, and Timothy'. The first person plural is continually used, but while Paul seems prepared to identify himself with his colleagues, and speaks in their name rather than his own, he is the author. Hence the rather uneasy transition: 'So we did propose to come to Thessalonica – I, Paul, more than once – but Satan thwarted us' (2.18). Significantly the last word is also his: 'I adjure you by the Lord to have this letter read to the whole brotherhood' (5.27). He is writing to a religious group that he has founded, and he repeatedly reminds them of their dependence (1.5, 6; 2.1, 7, 8, 9, 10, 11, 20; 3.5; 4.1; 5.25, 26). There is therefore little room for mutuality in the relationship between the writer and his readers: at best they are the witnesses to his success, living reminders of his influence (1.9; 2.10). In articulating his relationship to them, Paul resorts to images of nurse and father (2.7, 11), and offers these models of condescension as indications of his gentleness and individual concern.

He is not prepared to let the facts speak for themselves, but must write his own history in which the note of self-praise is continuous. In a revealing inversion he speaks of his readers as following 'the example set by us and by the Lord' (1.6). In a lengthy passage he reminds them of his effectiveness, his sufferings, his courage; his freedom from error, uncleanness and guile, his divine authority and disinterestedness; his indifference to public opinion and his tireless industry (2.1–12). The catalogue is fulsome and the work of his own hand. Moreover, his prestige cannot be affected by adversity; that only confirms his foresight: 'When we were with you we warned you that we were bound to suffer hardship; and so it has turned out, as you know' (3.4). This affliction is a divine appointment (3.3), and so it is in no way presumptuous to expect the Lord to look after his own: 'May our God and Father himself, and our Lord Jesus, bring us direct to you' (3.11).

(b) The prayer of thanksgiving: flattery and manipulation

Central to this letter, as to others from Paul's pen, is his use of the prayer of thanksgiving. It might be thought that in this he is only following his own precept: 'Give thanks whatever happens; for this is what God in Christ wills for you' (5.18). Yet the reality is not so simple. He strongly affirms: 'Our words have never been flattering words, as you have cause to know' (2.5), and yet in his hands that is just what the prayer of thanksgiving has become. He chooses to forget that in regaling them with the content of his prayers, while the language of prayer is retained, its audience and hence its function has been transformed. It is one thing to thank God for something: that is prayer addressed to God. It is quite another to tell somebody that you are thanking God for them: that is directed to an entirely human audience. Thus he is able to praise the Thessalonians, dwelling on 'how your faith has shown itself in action, your love in labour, and your hope of our Lord Jesus Christ in fortitude' (1.3). He assures them: 'You have become a model for all believers in Macedonia and in Achaia . . . and not in Macedonia and Achaia alone, but everywhere your faith in God has reached men's ears' (1.7, 8). Later in the letter he will remind them: 'You are all children of light, children of day. We do not belong to night or darkness' (5.5, 6). Moreover, his praise of himself and his flattery of his followers are mutually supportive, for their greatest achievement is precisely their recognition of himself. As he puts it with beguiling candour: 'This is why we thank God continually, because when we handed on God's message, you received it, not as the word of men, but as what it truly is, the very word of God at work in you who hold the faith' (2.13). Despite his professions to the contrary, Paul's own self-esteem is dependent upon their response. That is precisely the significance of such remarks as: 'It is you who are indeed our glory and our joy' (2.20). That is why their continuing loyalty to him is so important that he is driven to use extravagant language: 'It is the breath of life to us that you stand firm in the Lord' (3.8).

Flattery, however congenial, is rightly distrusted, as the initial stage of manipulation. Paul begins by praising his congregation and proceeds to accord them privileges. He speaks of them as chosen by God (1.4), and reminds them that God is calling them 'into his kingdom and glory' (2.12). He spells out the alternatives with relish: 'For God has not destined us to the terrors of judgment, but to the full attainment of salvation through our Lord Jesus Christ' (5.9). By the end of the letter the privilege of election has become the pledge of divine assistance: 'He who calls you is to be trusted; he will do it' (5.24). Paul makes no prior conditions; he offers the privileged status with reckless freedom. The price is disguised, for the conferring of privilege is also the imposition of obligation. They must 'live lives worthy of the God who calls you' (2.12). They must avoid fornication (4.3). They 'must keep sober' (5.8). Thus what looks like a free offer becomes a means of control. Paul dazzles his readers by the splendour of their status, and thus reconciles them to submitting to the authority of the man who has conferred it upon them.

The notion of imitation is even more useful, as it combines in its associations both status and obligation. It is good to be told that we have followed the example of the Lord (1.6), or that 'You have fared like the congregations in Judaea, God's people in Christ Jesus. You have been treated by your countrymen as they are treated by the Jews' (2.14). But the moral is plain: if you wish to retain the privilege, you must persevere in the behaviour that has established it. The praise of imitation is intended to rule out the possibility of defection.

(c) The use of divine authority: sexual prohibition and eschatological fantasy

It would be wrong to say that Paul confuses his own authority with God's. He can make the necessary distinctions, but in this letter the extent of the identity is striking and disturbing. His message is 'the word of the Lord' (1.8). Of himself he says: 'God has approved us as fit to be entrusted with the Gospel, and on those terms we speak. We do not curry favour with men; we seek only the favour of God' (2.4). Paul does not in fact live up to this horrid ideal of indifference to human response; but he is nevertheless attracted by the prestige which is achieved by refusing to listen to other people. The appeal from men to God is a resort to total privacy, where fragile convictions survive uncompromised by the doubts of others. The negative side of this closeness to God is the readiness with which he perceives the devil. Hindrance to his plans is attributed to Satan (2.18).

Defection is the work of the tempter (3.5). Paul, however, reserves his strongest assertions of divine authority for those parts of the letter where he meets challenges to his own authority: the prohibition of fornication, and uncertainty about the destiny of the faithful departed.

The vehemence of Paul's response to the sexual behaviour of the Gentile world is betrayed by the intensity with which he clings to the divine displeasure at such doings. Such a reaction articulates the familiar cultural imperialism which shuns with exaggerated hostility the practices of a society to which it is foreign: nineteenth-century missionaries on polygamy in Africa, or twentieth-century Muslim immigrants on the sexual mores of English comprehensive schools. However distanced Paul may be from his Jewish kin, he retains an instinctive repulsion at Gentile sexual licence. In quick succession he appeals to the authority of Jesus, the known will of God, the Gentiles' ignorance of God, the threat of divine vengeance, the promise of divine destiny, and ends: 'Anyone therefore who flouts these rules is flouting, not man, but God who bestows upon you his Holy Spirit' (4.8). It would seem that the reference to the Spirit in this context is meant to imply that they should have known better. The only considerations of a human character to which he appeals in this tirade are notions of sanctification and honour, and a reference to a brother's rights, which seem to imply proprietary rights of men over women. It does not augur well for the Christian contribution to sexual understanding.

He does not seem to be disturbed in the same way by uncertainties concerning the fate of the faithful departed, and outlines a solution to the problem: 'We believe that Jesus died and rose again; and so it will be for those who died as Christians; God will bring them to life with Jesus. For this we tell you as the Lord's word: we who are left alive until the Lord comes shall not forestall those who have died'. It is not entirely clear here (4.14, 15) what he means in using the phrase 'as the Lord's word'. He may be appealing to historical reminiscence or to immediate revelation. In either case, he would seem to be reinforcing a doctrine which might otherwise appear implausible.

(d) The gospel: privilege and alienation

The whole tone of the letter is assertive. As an example of Christian liberation and reconciliation it is not convincing: a small religious group bound up and manipulated by the self-esteem of the founder, gulled into submission by specious privileges, fertile only in sexual repression and eschatological fantasy. The church of the Thessalonians is perhaps still with us. The crucial misgivings must, however, surround the concept of the gospel on which the whole letter is centred. That phrase, with its associations of newness and freedom, is the theme of this study, and to its elucidation and assessment we must now turn. The positive associations of the word are with power, with the Holy Spirit and with joy (1.5, 6). It is seen as the most precious gift of God (2.2, 4), though there is one occasion, where Paul reveals a rather surprising sense of priorities. When commending his ministry he goes so far as to say: 'With such yearning love we chose to impart to you not only the gospel of God but our very selves, so dear had you become to us' (2.8). It is as if already in Christian history the religion has become a content professionally distant from those who purvey it. That apart, the sense of privilege in receiving the gospel is emphasized.

What are the associated beliefs which make the gospel so attractive? For Paul does not conceal that its immediate impact has a bitter-sweet quality. It may bring joy to the believer, but it comes surrounded by controversy and persecution, and will involve the believer in suffering and affliction (1.6; 2.2, 14; 3.3) In the short term virtue is by no means its own reward. For Paul the gospel is good news not primarily because it transforms the present, but because it assures the believer as to his ultimate destiny. The notion that history will end in judgment from which only the faithful will be saved is not an additional belief unconnected with and independent of the concept of the gospel; it is its necessary corollary in this context. The nature of the expected deliverance is made clear in such a phrase as 'Jesus our deliverer from the terrors of judgment to come' (1.10), or the prayer 'that you may stand before our God and Father holy and faultless when our Lord Jesus comes with all those who are his own' (3.13). Nor does Paul scruple to contrast the fragile privileges of the faithful with the fate which awaits the undefined others: 'While they are talking of peace and security, all at once calamity is upon them, sudden as the pangs that come upon a woman with child; and there will be no escape. But you, my friends, are not in the dark, that the day should overtake you like a thief' (5.3, 4). Hence the stress throughout the letter on waiting. (1.10; 3.13; 4.13–18; 5.1–10, 23). Despite the fundamentally passive nature of this stance, it presents opportunities to play on anxiety and hence to reinforce discipline and conformity. In this tense state of expectation and uncertainty the faithful are admonished to 'hearten one another, fortify one another – as indeed you do' (5.11). There is a nasty echo of the continuous propaganda which accompanies carefully nurtured anxiety in some modern totalitarian regimes: the reiterated party slogans to accompany the bread queues.

The cost in terms of alienation from others which the Christian privilege entails is heavy. It might be sweet to anticipate the future reserved for the faithful, but Paul counsels his brethren: 'You should not grieve like the rest of men, who have no hope' (4.13). In the same vein he shows himself utterly at variance with the whole Jewish and Gentile world outside the church. Of his own people he writes that they, 'killed the Lord Jesus and the prophets and drove us out, the Jews who are heedless of God's will and enemies of their fellow-men, hindering us from speaking to the Gentiles to lead them to salvation. All this time they have been making up the full measure of their guilt, and now retribution has overtaken them for good and all' (2.15, 16). But the apparently friendly reference to the Gentiles in the passage just quoted is entirely conditional on their submission to the gospel. They may follow the example of the Thessalonians themselves and turn 'from idols, to be servants of the living and true God' (1.9). Otherwise they are seen as given over to lust, sleep and drunkenness (4.5; 5.7). Given such a view of the entire and enormous non-Christian world, the occasional references to a love which is not confined to 'the brethren' ring hollow (3.12; 5.15). A more accurate indication of Paul's mind is given by his argument in favour of hard work, that it gives Christians independence from 'those outside your own number' (4.12).

(e) The delegation of authority
As if the burden of Pauline authority was not enough, his letter reveals a local organization with delegated authority, to which he demands conformity and submission. 'We beg you, brothers, to acknowledge those who are working so hard among you, and in the Lord's fellowship are your leaders and counsellors. Hold them in the highest possible esteem and affection for the work they do' (5.12, 13). This local leadership presumably supplied Paul with information, and the whole letter may be a response to their request for help. That would also explain the careful preservation of such a letter – not just a loving memento of the apostle, but a letter confirming the status of those in spiritual authority in Thessalonica. In such a context it is tempting to read even the little list of exhortatory proverbs with which the letter ends as one final attempt to remind the faithful of their inadequacy. Sweeping moral imperatives, like 'Be always joyful' (5.16), may occasionally inspire our imaginations, but more often depress the ordinary mortal.

Paul does not introduce himself attractively. It is only fair, however, to end by pointing to some glimmers of hope. In the midst of so much assertion and alienation, there is a surprising strand which looks towards a love that transcends all boundaries and an authority which is exercised in mutuality. Paul prays: 'May the Lord make your love mount and overflow towards one another and towards all, as our love does towards you' (3.12). He can envisage a sense of responsibility which is more mutual than anything he seems to practise: 'See to it that no one pays back wrong for wrong, but always aim at doing the best you can for each other and for all men' (5.15). And in the last resort, for all his aggressive and manipulative use of prayer, he does have the grace to ask his readers: 'Brothers, pray for us also' (5.25).

2

II THESSALONIANS

(a) Authority and authenticity

The second letter to the Thessalonians has many similarities to the first. There is the same uneasy tension between the collective leadership and the Pauline authorship (2.2). This has become more acute, as there seem to be forged letters in circulation, and this letter ends with stress on its genuineness: 'The greeting is in my own hand, signed with my name, PAUL; this authenticates all my letters; this is how I write' (3.17). The effective assertion of authority by means of letters made considerations of authenticity crucial. As in the first letter there is the same use of the prayer of thanksgiving to praise and cajole the readers (1.3–4; 2.13, 14); the same stress on their privilege of divine election and calling (1.5, 11; 2.13). Similarly the apostolic authority is conveyed not only directly in assertion and command, but by the implicit assumptions contained in the bestowal of grace and peace (1.2, 12; 3.16, 18). The very greetings imply that the writer has such goods at his disposal.

There is no mention in this letter of the local leaders: its concern is not for their authority, but for Paul's, which seems under attack in a way that the first letter did not envisage. He warns them against the danger of deceit: 'I beg you, do not suddenly lose your heads or alarm yourselves, whether at some oracular utterance, or pronouncement, or some letter purporting to come from us . . . Let no one deceive you in any way whatever' (2.2). He prays to 'be rescued from wrong-headed and wicked men' (3.2), and admits ruefully that 'it is not all who have faith'. Most revealing of all, he lays down procedures for dealing with the disobedient: 'If anyone disobeys our instructions given by letter, mark him well, and have no dealings with him until he is ashamed of himself. I do not mean treat him as an enemy, but give him friendly advice, as one of the family' (3.14, 15). The equivocations are obvious. How is one 'to have no dealings with somebody', and yet give 'him friendly advice'? The sweetness of the family image and the repudiation of enmity do not conceal the ultimate sanction should the shame-inducing tactics fail. Most of us would probably prefer not to be members of such a 'family'.

Faced by direct challenge, Paul lays particular stress on his role in founding the community, and there emerges a new emphasis on their faith. 'You did indeed,' he writes, 'believe the testimony we brought you' (1.10). In expounding his vision of the end, the only authority he cites is the memory of his own words when he was among them. 'You cannot but remember that I told you this while I was still with you' (2.5). He recalls their initial response as an encouragement to their continued obedience: 'From the beginning of time God chose you to find salvation in the Spirit that consecrates you, and in the truth that you believe. It was for this that he called you through the gospel we brought, so that you might possess for your own the splendour of our Lord Jesus Christ. Stand firm, then, brothers, and hold fast to the traditions which you have learned from us by word or by letter' (2.13–15). The example of their response informs his prayer for others (3.1). Paul subtly intertwines his faith and trust in God with their trust and obedience to him: 'The Lord is to be trusted, and he will fortify you and guard you from the evil one. We feel perfect confidence about you, in the Lord, that you are doing and will continue to do what we order. May the Lord direct your hearts towards God's love and the steadfastness of Christ!' (3.3–5). Paul then makes it plain that directing their hearts towards God's love means in practice doing what he tells them: 'These are our orders to you, brothers, in the name of our Lord Jesus Christ' (3.6). Once again the strongest argument he uses is the memory of his own life among them: 'You know yourselves how you ought to copy our example: we were no idlers among you; we did not accept board and lodging from anyone without paying for it; we toiled and drudged, we worked for a living night and day, rather than be a burden to any of you' (3.7, 8). In all this, two moves strongly emerge. The first is Paul's appeal to their initial faith against any second thoughts; the second is the extent to which he has identified himself as the object of their faith.

(b) The response to persecution

The crisis of Paul's authority in Thessalonica (1.4, 5) is the consequence of persecution. The violence of his response is seen in the compensation he offers: undisguised antagonism to a world from which he feels utterly distanced. Vengeance, precise retribution, the display of overwhelming power and the eternal ruin of their enemies are the future consolations which he offers to the persecuted (1.6, 8). This bloody scenario confirms, and indeed provides the substance of, their privilege: 'Then he will do justice upon those who refuse to acknowledge God and upon those who will not obey the gospel of our Lord Jesus. They will suffer the punishment of eternal ruin, cut off from the presence of the Lord and the splendour of his might, when on that Day he comes to be glorified among his own and adored among all believers' (1.8–10). It is devoid of any identity with or compassion for the world it condemns; nowhere can the cruel and unacceptable dimension of the gospel be more clearly seen. It does not sound like loving one's enemies.

(c) Eschatology and anxiety

It emerged in the first letter that 'waiting', a preoccupation with the future and a carefully cultivated anxiety about the timing and nature of the end, was an integral part of this version of the gospel. The second letter reveals the tensions which living with such a belief produced. The temptation to escape these by 'alleging that the Day of the Lord is already here' (2.2) is understandable, but Paul refuses to allow any such release (or possibility of being refuted). Instead he heightens their anxiety by a sense of worse to come. 'That day cannot come before the final rebellion against God, when wickedness will be revealed in human form, the man doomed to perdition. He is the Enemy. He rises in pride against every god, so called, every object of men's worship, and even takes his seat in the temple of God claiming to be a god himself' (2.3, 4). It is a singularly lurid fantasy about the future, which must immediately have provided the religious imagination with interesting possibilities of labelling particular people or events as 'The Man doomed to perdition', 'The Enemy', or 'The Lie'. So abhorrent is the vision that for a moment Paul even regards the idols of the heathen with some sympathy. It is not, however, a fantasy confined entirely to the future, for in his description of this anticipated monster Paul reveals his own contradictory understanding of those who reject him: 'Destroyed they shall be, because they did not open their minds to love of the truth, so as to find salvation. Therefore God puts them under a delusion, which works upon them to believe the lie, so that they may all be brought to judgment, all who do not believe the truth but make sinfulness their deliberate choice' (2.10–12). We see here how he regards those 'wrong-headed and wicked men' of whom he complains later in the letter (3.2); but there is an element of 'overkill' in his argument. For he accuses them both of deliberate dishonesty and divinely ordained blindness, and cites both as justifying their destruction. In this the rejected apostle has fused his irritation at men's obstinacy, his conviction of God's sovereignty and his hunger for divine vindication in a way which may be understandable, but is scarcely just, and sets a dangerous precedent for Christian attitudes to disbelief.

(d) *Exhortation to work*

The letter culminates in reinforcing an emphasis which was quite weak in the first letter, when he appealed to his readers 'to keep calm and look after your own business, and to work with your hands, as we ordered you' (4.12). He commended this partly for reasons of public relations, partly for their own self-interest. In the second letter, Paul's work ethic receives considerable elaboration. Clearly he derives some of his own prestige from a sense of gratuitous financial independence (cf. I Thess. 2.9). He earned his living 'not because we have not the right to maintenance, but to set you an example to imitate' (3.9). He then reminds them that 'even during our stay with you we laid down the rule: the man who will not work shall not eat' (3.10). No explanation is given for this, apart from an appeal to the name of the Lord Jesus Christ, but he does not indicate whether this is a matter of reminiscence or immediate revelation. It accords ill with the life-style of Jesus and the apostles in the Gospels, just as Paul's own working habits differed from those of other Christian leaders. Why is this emphasis on work so important to him? It has been customary to explain it in terms of his repudiation of an End that has already come, but there is nothing in the text which associates idleness with such beliefs. Instead the text sounds a different note: it links work with 'calmness', 'looking after your own business', obedience, quietness (I Thess. 4.11; II Thess. 3.11, 12). Perhaps Paul was worried by the prospect of public disorder, or he may have been aware of the way in which financial and religious security can foster each other. But it may be that he had discovered, what others have learned later, that if the faithful work hard and are kept tired, they will have less energy to challenge authority or to ask awkward questions. Paul's emphasis is today most clearly heard in the docile congregations of Mr Moon.

(e) *Retrospect*

The concern with authority is not something which has been imposed on these texts; it reflects their substance. They are the means by which Paul is asserting his control over the Christians of Thessalonica: they refer to a system of local discipline and the officers who enforce it. Quickly the authoritative letter became so important that forgery became attractive. This is shown by the growing stress on authenticity in a historical sense.

The exercise of authority in these letters is obvious, but it is an authority which invites criticism on almost every count: it fosters illusion, it contradicts itself, it demands alienation, and is stubbornly repressive. Already the gospel is understood as a privilege which reflects and re-inforces the alienation of a religious élite from others. As persecution and social antagonism increase, it can only take refuge in a growing stress on retribution. It is impossible to reconcile such a belief with any authentic love. The tension of waiting reinforces the anxiety of the believers and their hostility to the outside world, and the preoccupation with the future encourages fantasy. Paul is self-contradictory in his attitudes to the response both of believers and of unbelievers – proclaiming indifference, but manifesting passionate involvement. Already prayer is being used as a means of social control, and the earliest Christian community which we know seems based on a combination of vigorous sexual repression with a heavy emphasis on work. The church of Thessalonica is thus prophetic of some of the nastiest features of later Christian communities. Nor is this an accident; it is the direct consequence of the repressive and arbitrary authority on which the community is based.

3

GALATIANS

(a) The challenge to Pauline authority

Of all Paul's letters, none show his authority under greater threat than the letter to the Galatians; it therefore gives valuable insight into the nature of his ultimate sanctions. Here he has moved beyond a situation which can be resolved by his customary blandishments and a resolute exercise of authority. Astonishment and derision have replaced the flattery of the form of thanksgiving: 'I am astonished to find you turning so quickly away from him who called you by grace' (1.6). (Significantly the text is uncertain as to whether it is Paul or Christ who has been rejected by them.) Later in the epistle Paul resorts to straightforward abuse: 'You stupid Galatians! You must have been bewitched' (3.1). As so often in Paul's anger, he fails to notice that his charges are self-contradictory, and this reflects once more his deeply ambivalent attitude towards his audience. When angry with them, he refuses to admit his dependence upon them: 'Does my language sound as if I were canvassing for men's support? Whose support do I want but God's alone? Do you think I am currying favour with men? If I still sought men's favour, I should be no servant of Christ' (1.10). It is a curious way to open six chapters which plead so fervently for obedience and agreement. For Paul, dependence on God is a means of asserting his independence of men, which is why the prestige of persecution is so important for him. Thus he discredits his opponents – 'Their sole object is to escape persecution for the cross of Christ' (6.12) – while the persecution which he encounters is a sign of his authenticity: 'If I am still advocating circumcision, why is it I am still persecuted?' (5.11). For Paul, the acceptance of persecution, the ultimate sign of his alienation from his fellow-men, functions as a perverse proof of his dependence upon God.

A further measure of the threat under which Paul thought he was writing is his devotion of so much energy to the exposition and defence of his authority. As elsewhere, he resorts to his role as the founder of the community: 'You make me fear that all the pains I spent on you may prove

to be labour lost' (4.11). He takes care to remind them of their first
enthusiastic response: 'As you know, it was bodily illness that originally
led to my bringing you the Gospel, and you resisted any temptation to
show scorn or disgust at the state of my poor body; you welcomed me as if
I were an angel of God, as you might have welcomed Christ Jesus himself.
Have you forgotten how happy you thought yourselves in having me with
you? I can say this for you: you would have torn out your very eyes, and
given them to me, had that been possible!' (4.13–15). He then proceeds to
extract the full benefit from this emotional reminiscence: 'Have I now
made myself your enemy by being frank with you?' (4.16). He leaves them
in no doubt that their relation to him is one of utter dependence, illustrated
by his use of a maternal image: 'For my children you are, and I am in travail
with you over again until you take the shape of Christ' (4.19). All this
recalls similar passages in the letters to the Thessalonians.

(b) The basis of Paul's apostolate

There is, however, no precedent for the detailed defence of his own
authority which dominates the first two chapters of the letter. There is no
appearance of a collective leadership here; from the first sentence we are
left in no doubt that it is Paul who is writing, and he recalls his readers'
attention to this at the close: 'You see these big letters? I am now writing to
you in my own hand' (6.11). In the context of this letter, this is not simply a
reminder of autograph authenticity: the apostolic hand writes with a
divine authority. Paul is at great pains to deny any human dependence: he
is 'an apostle, not by human appointment or human commission, but by
commission from Jesus Christ and from God the Father who raised him
from the dead' (1.1). (The way in which Jesus Christ is contrasted with the
human is an interesting comment on the extent to which he has already
been accorded a divine status.) The association of Jesus Christ's commission with the description of God as 'the Father who raised him from the
dead', is an allusion to the basis of Paul's authority in his direct encounter
with the risen Christ, and Paul explicitly claims that God 'chose to reveal
his Son to me' (1.15). This relation between his own status and the truth of
the resurrection makes it possible to understand the degree to which Paul
identified in his own mind the authenticity of his authority with the truth
of the gospel, as is revealed in the claim: 'I must make it clear to you, my
friends, that the gospel you heard me preach is no human invention. I did
not take it over from any man; no man taught it me; I received it through a
revelation of Jesus Christ' (1.12). When later we try to disentangle Paul's
attitude towards the charismatic phenomena in the churches to which he
wrote, it should be remembered that he shared the same dependence on an

immediate, privately received and authenticated revelation. Like the charismatics, he stands in a tense relation to those whose authority is historic, and the content of whose message is a matter of mediated reminiscence rather than direct revelation.

The letter to the Galatians shows more clearly than the Book of Acts how strained and indeed bitter Paul's relation to the historic authorities in the early church had become. Having denied any human role in his conversion and commissioning, he claims that 'without consulting any human being, without going up to Jerusalem to see those who were apostles before me, I went off at once to Arabia, and afterwards returned to Damascus' (1.17). Apparently he waited three years before going to Jerusalem for a fortnight, and then his acquaintance with the apostles was limited to Peter and James the Lord's brother (1.18, 19). Commenting on his subsequent work in Syria and Cilicia, he stresses that he 'remained unknown by sight to Christ's congregations in Judaea' (1.22). When after fourteen years he next made his way to Jerusalem, he carefully rules out any suggestion that he was reporting to higher authority or had been summoned to give an account of himself. 'I went up,' he writes, 'because it had been revealed by God that I should do so' (2.2). When he speaks of the men 'of high reputation' in Jerusalem, he cannot resist adding, 'not that their importance matters to me: God does not recognize these personal distinctions' (2.6), which is perhaps surprising in view of the very special status he seems to have accorded Paul. According to Paul the consultation was brief and the recognition entire; they 'acknowledged that I had been entrusted with the Gospel for Gentiles as surely as Peter had been entrusted with the Gospel for Jews. For God whose action made Peter an apostle to the Jews, also made me an apostle to the Gentiles' (2.7, 8). If the recognition was so complete, why does Paul adopt such an ironic tone towards James, Peter and John, describing them as 'those reputed pillars of our society' (2.9)? His picture of Peter, in particular, is truculent and discourteous. He tells how at Antioch, 'I opposed him to his face, because he was clearly in the wrong' (2.11). He claims that under pressure from James, Peter behaved inconsistently in eating with Gentile Christians. He accuses the other Jewish Christians of 'the same lack of principle'. Presumably Paul found himself quite isolated when 'even Barnabas was carried away and played false like the rest'. Paul's obstinate response, his unswerving assumption that his own position is identical with the truth of the gospel, is entirely of a piece with his writing: 'When I saw that their conduct did not square with the truth of the Gospel, I said to Cephas, before the whole congregation, "If you, a Jew born and bred, live like a Gentile, and not like a Jew, how can you insist that Gentiles must live like

Jews?"' (2.14). It is also entirely in keeping with his standpoint that he shows no interest in how his outburst was received, and does not even bother to inform his readers of the outcome of the scene.

The same insistence on his own authority which makes Paul so defensive towards the historical apostolate at Jerusalem leads him to make the strongest claims for the historic tradition that he himself has founded. 'If anyone, if we ourselves or an angel from heaven, should preach a gospel at variance with the gospel we preached to you, he shall be held outcast. I now repeat what I have said before: if anyone preaches a gospel at variance with the gospel which you received, let him be outcast!' (1.8, 9). Here is the first recorded anathema in Christian history; it does not belong to the Hellenized and dogmatic church of the third century, but to one of the earliest documents of the first. Its purpose is to rule out any subsequent revision of Paul's original message. It is enough that the apostle has spoken, and that his hearers should be reminded of the message: 'I ask then: when God gives you the Spirit and works miracles among you, why is this? Is it because you keep the Law, or is it because you have faith in the gospel message?' (3.5). Paul is thus found to be demanding for himself and his own message a respect that he conspicuously fails to accord to the apostles at Jerusalem.

(c) The use of the authority of the Old Testament

One might have expected, when Paul proceeds to justify the content of his message, an appeal to the remembered teaching of Jesus in much the same way that he fortified his prohibition of fornication and his speculations on the fate of the faithful departed in the first letter to the Thessalonians (I Thess. 4). Perhaps because no such historic appeal was possible, Paul proceeds to justify his teaching quite differently: not by the authority of the remembered Jesus, but by his own interpretation of the Old Testament scriptures. The turning point comes when he concludes his exposition of justification by faith with the words, 'For by such deeds, Scripture says, no mortal man shall be justified' (2.16), and the rest of the letter is dominated by two lengthy expositions of Scripture: on the faith of Abraham, and on the meaning of Abraham's two children (3.6–14 and 4.21–5.1).

In Paul's hands scripture becomes a ventriloquist's dummy, by which he himself speaks, while attributing responsibility to God. For Paul, scripture has not only an identity, but a power of action. Scripture is represented by him as the subject of some very interesting verbs. It speaks. It declares. It foresees God's action (3.10, 8, 22). Such a highly personalized concept of scripture shows that it has become a synonym for God. Yet Paul's exegesis is so selective and idiosyncratic as to make him the master of any message he may attribute to the scriptures. His use of allegory is breath-taking in its freedom, of which this is probably the most famous example: 'The two women stand for two covenants. The one bearing children into slavery is the covenant that comes from Mount Sinai: that is Hagar. Sinai is a mountain in Arabia and it represents the Jerusalem of today, for she and her children are in slavery. But the heavenly Jerusalem is the free woman; she is our mother. For Scripture says, "Rejoice, O barren woman who never bore child; break into a shout of joy, you who never knew a mother's pangs; for the deserted wife shall have more children than she who lives with the husband"' (4.24–27). The conclusion is unavoidable that Paul dresses his convictions in Old Testament clothing to disguise a more immediate source of origin. It is a style of preaching which has never lacked imitators.

(d) Alienation and the Christian identity

As the letters to the Thessalonians revealed a view of the gospel which was intrinsically vindictive, so here the concept of salvation is the correlate to a suspicious and damnatory view of the world. He says that Jesus 'sacrificed himself for our sins, to rescue us out of this present age of wickedness' (1.4). It is precisely in this sense of alienation that he glories: 'God forbid that I should boast of anything but the cross of our Lord Jesus Christ, through which the world is crucified to me and I to the world' (6.14). It is not the case that Paul has a conviction of salvation and separately a disparaging attitude towards the people and institutions of the surrounding world so that one might retain the sense of being saved, while adopting a more liberal stance to the world. Paul's sense of salvation derives its savour and excitement from what it repudiates.

This social alienation was discerned in the letters to the Thessalonians, but the letter to the Galatians gives it a personal dimension which extends to Paul's perception of himself: as if his Christian identity is only achieved at the cost of his own personality. 'I have been crucified with Christ,' he writes; 'the life I now live is not my life, but the life which Christ lives in me' (2.20). It is customary in this context to speak reverentially of Paul's Christ-mysticism; but those who advocate such a confusion of identity should pause to consider how it appears to have functioned in the apostle's understanding of himself, and may conclude that the cost is too high. Certainly Paul's sense of identity with Christ is striking: 'In future let no one make trouble for me, for I bear the marks of Jesus branded on my body' (6.17). Here the baptismal identity is reinforced by the scars of persecution, but this manifest sanctity is paraded not to shoulder burdens, but to evade them. The appeal to 'the marks of Jesus branded on my body' has become a plea for immunity: 'Let no one make trouble for me.' It is the kind of self-pity which tends to afflict those who are consumed by a sense of their own importance. Paradoxically the scars become an argument for invulnerability.

Paul's sense of identity with Christ easily becomes an instrument of his own self-assertion, and makes it singularly difficult to detect self-deceit. 'United with you in the Lord, I am confident that you will not take the wrong view' (5.10). By identifying himself so relentlessly with Christ, he fails to appreciate how difficult he has made it for believers to oppose his authority. He displays also a disconcerting ambivalence towards personal responsibility in the shifting 'I, but not I, but Christ', and this is equally visible in the status he accords his readers. For just as Paul is confused as to his own responsibility, so he confuses their responsibility: 'Now that you do acknowledge God – or rather, now that he has acknowledged you' (4.9). Ambivalence as to whether God or a human being is the effective agent makes self-criticism almost impossible, and therefore limits the opportunities for honesty. Moreover their identity, like his own, is insecure. He may assure them that, 'There is no such thing as Jew and Greek , slave and freeman, male and female; for you are all one person in Christ Jesus' (3.28), but the model for this new identity rings false: 'You have all put on Christ as a garment' (3.27). (It is a curious contrast to Jesus's own teaching that the body is more important than clothes.) An identity which is assumed like a dress betrays an uneasy sense of super-ficiality. Significantly Paul cannot use the maternal imagery consistently: he speaks of being 'in travail with you over again' (4.19), but adds 'until you take the shape of Christ'. It is enough for the mother to labour to have a child, not to shape it. 'Shaping' belongs to the manipulative world of the potter, with formless clay in his hands. Both the dressing and the shaping imagery of Christian identity, assume a continuing and underlying hostility or indifference.

The corollary of Paul's close identity with Christ is the way in which it type-casts his opponents. They are to be outcast (1.8, 9). Their very success is a sign of witchcraft (3.1). They are accused of envy and the desire to enslave (4.17; 5.1). When Paul turns his attention directly towards his critics at the end of the letter his bitterness is unbridled: 'You were running well,' he assures the Galatians, 'who was it hindered you from following the truth? Whatever persuasion he used, it did not come from God who is calling you; "a little leaven," remember, "leavens all the dough" . . . The man who is unsettling your minds, whoever he may be, must bear God's judgment . . . As for these agitators, they had better go the whole way and make eunuchs of themselves!' (5.7, 8, 10, 12). The Christ-identity becomes very brittle when faced with criticism, and soon resorts to threat and obscene abuse. There is an ominous echo in the quotation of Scripture which condemns Hagar and Ishmael: 'Drive out the slave-woman and her son, for the son of the slave shall not share the inheritance with the free woman's son' (4.30).

(e) Privilege and manipulation: sonship and the spirit

In the letters to the Thessalonians proffered privilege was one of the crucial moves in Paul's exercise of authority. The very promise acts as a means of control. This letter contains themes with which the letters to the Thessalonians have already made us familiar; the stress on the grace of God's will in choosing and calling the Galatians is identical with the earlier letters (1.3, 4, 6; 5.8), though it is given a new twist here in mirroring the grace of God in his choice and calling of Paul: 'Then in his good pleasure God, who had set me apart from birth and called me through his grace, chose to reveal his Son to me and through me, in order that I might proclaim him among the Gentiles' (1.15, 16). Here is made plain the symbiotic relation between Paul's privileged authority and the believer's privileged status.

What is new in the letter to the Galatians is the development of the Christian privileges in terms of divine sonship and the reception of the Spirit, and the connection which is made with baptism. 'The power of the Holy Spirit' (1.5) is mentioned in contrast to mere words in I Thessalonians, but the reception of the Spirit is much more strongly appealed to in Galatians, and is explicitly linked to the working of miracles (3.2, 5), and to the freedom of Christians from their lower nature (3.5; 5.5, 16–18). The harvest of the Spirit is described in moral terms: 'Love, joy, peace, patience, kindness, goodness, fidelity, gentleness, and self-control' (5.22), so that once again Paul can appeal to the Spirit as a means of controlling the Galatians' behaviour: 'If the Spirit is the source of our life, let the Spirit also direct our course' (5.25). With the gift of the Spirit is entwined their status as sons of God: 'To prove that you are sons, God has sent into our hearts the Spirit of his Son, crying "Abba! Father!" You are therefore no longer a slave but a son, and if a son, then also by God's own act an heir' (4.6, 7). In exploring the origins of Christology, it should be remembered that the status of the early believers was a direct reflection of what they attributed to Jesus. In discovering his divinity, they were also discovering something about themselves. For Paul, baptism is the key to this new identity: 'Through faith you are all sons of God in union with Christ Jesus; baptized into union with him' (3.26, 27). In this letter the concept of sonship is particularly valuable to Paul: partly because of its relation to the concept of 'heir', with its associations of waiting and future reward, which as we have seen are fundamental to Paul's understanding of the gospel. More immediately useful is the dialectic it makes possible between the freedom of sons as opposed to the obedience of slaves. The crucial religious significance of this letter for the development of Christianity lies in its exposition of Christian freedom; among the orthodox this has inspired both Augustine and Luther. It has also been the source of the continuing antinomian criticisms of orthodoxy.

(f) The Law and the freedom of the Christian

I have already suggested that Christianity emerged as a criticism of and in conflict with repressive religious authority, and the basic question of this book is whether the freedom of the Christian is self-sustaining, or whether it simply prepares for a new tyranny. Paul's account of that freedom, its criticism of Law, and its exercise in love, is the earliest we possess. Because of its Gentile context, it may in some respects be idiosyncratic in terms of its Galilean origin; but in terms of its subsequent influence (and the Christian church has been an overwhelmingly Gentile institution) it is as significant as anything to be found in the gospels. Freedom is for Paul the mark of the church; he speaks of 'the liberty we enjoy in the fellowship of Christ Jesus' (2.4). 'Christ,' he says, 'bought us freedom from the curse of the Law by becoming for our sake an accursed thing' (3.13). The heart of this freedom lies in the repudiation of the Law; that indeed would almost seem to be the content of faith in Christ. In a brief passage which summarizes the doctrine he develops at length in the epistle to the Romans, he writes: 'We know that no man is ever justified by doing what the law demands, but only through faith in Christ Jesus; so we too have put our faith in Jesus Christ, in order that we might be justified through this faith, and not through deeds dictated by law; for by such deeds, Scripture says, no mortal man shall be justified' (2.16).

What is Paul repudiating when he speaks of having 'died to the Law' (2.19)? In the passage just quoted it appears to extend to the whole concept of obedient behaviour, and that impression is further strengthened by a passage in which he argues that 'those who rely on obedience to the law are under a curse' (3.10–12). He justifies this partly by claiming that nothing but total obedience is adequate: 'for Scripture says, "A curse is on all who do not persevere in doing everything that is written in the Book of the Law"'. But his other argument seems to envisage that faith and obedience are simply incompatible religious stances: 'It is evident that no one is ever justified before God in terms of law; because we read, "he shall gain life who is justified through faith". Now law is not at all a matter of having faith: we read, "he who does this shall gain life by what he does".'

Such passages are the basis of a straightforward antinomian reading of Paul, but there are other passages which suggest that his repudiation of the Law is more limited and specific. For instance, his contrast between the spiritual and the material (3.3) might indicate a distinction between the moral and ritual aspects of the Law, and it is certainly its ritual observances which receive his fiercest condemnation, particularly the practice of circumcision. He speaks of those who urge it on Gentiles as 'sham-Christians' (2.4). He solemnly warns them: 'I, Paul, say to you that if you receive circumcision Christ will do you no good at all . . . If we are in union with Christ Jesus circumcision makes no difference at all, nor does the want of it; the only thing that counts is faith active in love' (5.2, 6). But his criticism is not confined to circumcision; he rejects the whole concept of a sacred calendar: 'You keep special days and months and seasons and years. You make me fear that all the pains I spent on you may prove to be labour lost' (4.10, 11). (Paul is very distant from the Lord's Day Observance Society or the institution of Lent and Saints' Days.) Faced by this lack of clarity we have to ask: is Paul's repudiation of circumcision and the sacred calendar only part of a much more radical repudiation of legal obedience, or is he defending his own radical position on circumcision and the calendar by employing an exaggerated rhetoric which, while polemically useful, misrepresents his real position?

The Christian Paul's attitude to the Law might easily be dismissed as simply ambivalent; but he is more consistent than such criticism allows. He derogates the Law in comparison with the promise to Abraham, so that he is prepared to relativize it and give it a purely temporary significance: 'Then what of the Law? It was added to make wrongdoing a legal offence. It was a temporary measure pending the arrival of the "issue" to whom the promise was made' (3.19). Or again: 'Before this faith came, we were close prisoners in the custody of law, pending the revelation of faith. Thus the law was a kind of tutor in charge of us until Christ should come, when we should be justified through faith; and now that faith has come, the tutor's charge is at an end' (3.23–25). In developing this educational view of the Law, the concept of 'sonship' is most helpful, as it enables Paul both to affirm the Law in its historical context and yet deny its permanent value. In this way he can criticize and transcend his previous position without being simply negative towards it.

He has another approach to criticizing the Law, which has the most astonishing implications. At first sight there is nothing very curious about his description of it as 'promulgated through angels' (3.19), for while not in Scripture, this view does reflect a widespread contemporary Jewish belief, but apparently he identifies these angels with 'the elemental spirits of the universe' (4.3), so that he can speak of the period dominated by the Law thus: 'During our minority we were slaves to the elemental spirits of the universe' (4.3). This enables him to make the amazing equation, for any Jew, that the Jews' observance of the Law is exactly parallel to the Gentiles' service of the gods. Nothing is more eloquent of the extent to which Paul has dissociated himself from his Jewish past than this passage where he intertwines the Jewish Law and pagan polytheism: 'Formerly, when you did not acknowledge God, you were the slaves of beings which in their nature are no gods. But now that you do acknowledge God – or rather, now that he has acknowledged you – how can you turn back to the mean and beggarly spirits of the elements? Why do you propose to enter their service all over again? You keep special days and months and seasons and years. You make me fear that all the pains I spent on you may prove to be labour lost' (4.8–11). If this equation of the Law with polytheism is a correct reading of Paul's meaning, it strongly suggests that his repudiation of the Law must be understood, not simply in a ritual sense, but as having the widest possible extent. This equivalence of Law and polytheism may explain the rather surprising attitude to polytheism noted in II Thessalonians 2.4, where the eschatological Enemy is seen not as the instrument of heathen demons, but as the opponent both of God and the gods, who seem to form a common front in this respect: 'He rises in his pride against every god, so called, every object of men's worship, and even takes his seat in the temple of God claiming to be God himself.' This equivalence may also have facilitated the process by which Christians made themselves the heirs and beneficiaries of the philosophical criticisms of polytheism.

This equation of Law and polytheism helps to explain the positive role which Paul ascribes to the Law, not in bestowing righteousness, but in making Jews and Gentiles equal as sinners, and so potentially equal as saints. 'Scripture has declared the whole world to be prisoners in subjection to sin, so that faith in Jesus Christ may be the ground on which the promised blessing is given, and given to those who have such faith' (3.22). Much has been said about the evidence of deep alienation in Paul's thought; this stress on man's solidarity in sin points to a contrary aspect of his thought, which is the more impressive coming from a man who still found it natural to speak with an easy parallelism of 'Gentiles and sinners' (2.15).

The most unexpected development of Paul's thought in this letter is, however, the final passage in which Law is in some sense rehabilitated; for the last references to the Law in this letter are straightforward and positive: 'The whole law can be summed up in a single commandment: "Love your neighbour as yourself"' (5.14). Who would have guessed after the violent polemic of the earlier chapters that Paul would end by speaking of fulfilling 'the Law of Christ' (6.2)? Has he in his own words started 'building up again a system which I have pulled down' (2.18)? This final passage is obviously crucial for assessing the kind of Christian freedom which Paul has in mind. Does all the ringing language of liberty only prepare for a new tyranny? On the one hand he speaks here not primarily of obedience, but of mutual service in love (5.13). On the other hand, the behaviour he envisages is strongly reinforced by prudential considerations: 'If you go on fighting one another, tooth and nail, all you can expect is mutual destruction' (5.15), or, in a more threatening vein: 'I warn you, as I warned you before, that those who behave in such ways will never inherit the kingdom of God' (5.21). Any thought that behaviour may disqualify, but cannot entitle to the promised reward, is ruled out by the simple moralism of the following passage: 'Make no mistake about this: God is not to be fooled; a man reaps what he sows. If he sows seed in the field of his lower nature, he will reap from it a harvest of corruption, but if he sows in the field of the Spirit, the Spirit will bring him a harvest of eternal life' (6.7, 8). The Law may have been repudiated, but a system of behaviour reinforced by rewards and punishments is clearly in good health.

(g) The Spirit and the lower nature

Equally, the contrast between the Spirit and the material which had earlier been used to discredit the Law is now used to provide a positive, if dangerous guide to conduct. 'If you are guided by the Spirit you will not fulfil the desires of your lower nature. That nature sets its desires against the Spirit, while the Spirit fights against it. They are in conflict with one another so that what you will to do you cannot do. But if you are led by the Spirit, you are not under Law' (5.16–18). Thus the Spirit may bring freedom from the Law, but it still supplies its own imperative, not least in what it prohibits: 'Anyone can see the kind of behaviour that belongs to the lower nature: fornication, impurity, and indecency; idolatry and sorcery; quarrels, a contentious temper, envy, fits of rage, selfish ambitions, dissensions, party intrigues and jealousies; drinking bouts, orgies, and the like' (5.19–20). A certain suspicion is called for whenever the allegedly self-evident is asserted with such force. Subsequent Christian experience would suggest that this conflict-laden view of man's moral life is as burdensome as anything in traditional Judaism, engendering either a smug self-righteousness or a guilty sense of inadequacy. Neither here nor elsewhere does Paul give any satisfactory account of the relation between the Spirit and man's lower nature: the conflict is unremitting, and the only solution he envisages is one of successful suppression. Moreover, there is emphasis on the divided self: 'That (lower) nature sets its desires against the Spirit, while the Spirit fights against it. They are in conflict with one another, so that what you will to do you cannot do' (5.17), and it is this which makes Paul so prone to confuse his own with the divine identity. The chaos that the individual will is powerless to control can only be ordered by the divine Lord. In all this there is nothing inconsistent with what we have already observed of the worst features of Paul's exercise of authority.

(h) Self-sustaining freedom

As Paul develops his understanding of the Law of Christ, a new note is struck which suggests that he could at least envisage a self-sustaining freedom very different from anything that he himself practised. 'If a man should do something wrong, my brothers, on a sudden impulse, you who are endowed with the Spirit must set him right again very gently. Look to yourself, each one of you: you may be tempted too. Help one another to carry these heavy loads, and in this way you will fulfil the law of Christ. For if a man imagines himself to be somebody, when he is nothing, he is deluding himself. Each man should examine his own conduct for himself; then he can measure his achievement by comparing himself with himself and not with anyone else. For everyone has his own proper burden to bear' (6.1–5). At first it may seem that there are overtones of the public criticism practised by the Chinese as a means of the most thorough-going social control. That however, would be unfair; it fails to note the sensitive individualism which complements and tempers the social discipline. Here Paul has succeeded in outlining a pattern of mutual spiritual cooperation which is marked by forbearance to others and a careful and critical attention to oneself. It is even tempting to suggest an element of irony in the phrase 'you who are endowed with the Spirit', but that is probably to betray a modern rather than a Pauline sensibility. There is a surprising preference for a model of development rather than an appeal to absolute standards. Here at last is the possibility of replacing the pursuit of conformity by a moral stance that is more exploratory and tolerant: this freedom represents a real alternative to legal observance. That there is much in the letter which is inconsistent with it does not diminish its importance. The freedom which Paul here envisages may discredit much else that he writes, but the continuing vitality of his writing derives from the fact that it hints at its own criticism. Equally, this analysis of his letters is not subjecting him to an entirely alien scrutiny; it is rather an attempt to subject the writer to the canons of his own criticism.

(i) A financial footnote

Before we leave this fascinating document, a brief look at its financial implications is necessary. Already the support of the Christian authorities has become a financial burden on the faithful, which they require admonishment to shoulder: 'When anyone is under instruction in the faith, he should give his teacher a share of all good things he has' (6.6): an exchange of material for spiritual goods, which provides an interesting sidelight on the apostle's exaltation of the spiritual over the material in the doctrinal content of the letter. It is also to be noted that Paul's relation to the Jerusalem apostles has a financial aspect (it almost sounds as if he has purchased the Gentile franchise): 'Recognizing, then, the favour thus bestowed upon me, those reputed pillars of our society, James, Cephas and John, accepted Barnabas and myself as partners, and shook hands upon it, agreeing that we should go to the Gentiles while they went to the Jews. All they asked was that we should keep their poor in mind, which was the very thing I made it my business to do' (2.9, 10). Perhaps Paul wished to discredit them by emphasizing that their only conditions were financial, but already a religious stance which condemns preoccupation with money is being transformed by its social commitments, and has acquired an interest in the financial possibilities of the faithful.

4

PHILIPPIANS

Much scholarly attention has been given to the unity of this letter, and the suggestion that it is a compilation of several Pauline writings has attracted considerable support; but that would only be relevant to this study if the common Pauline authorship was denied, which it has not been. Moreover, even if its composite parts were by different hands, the document's historic life and impact is as a unity, in which any internal tensions stand unresolved. This literary unity, even if historically fictitious, is further enhanced by the fact that despite the dual greeting from Paul and Timothy, the letter is written throughout in the first person singular, and conveys Paul's particular concerns and predicament. It envisages a community under some corresponding delegated authority of 'bishops and deacons' (1.1).

(a) Authority and persecution

Both the writer and his audience share a similar situation of persecution and internal conflict, which informs the content of Paul's opening prayer. In this context the thankful affirmation, 'Of one thing I am certain: the One who started the good work in you will bring it to completion by the Day of Christ Jesus' (1.6), also functions as a challenge to persevere both against external threats and internal revision. This last is reinforced elsewhere in the letter by a stress on the example of Paul, their founder, and the tradition he has given them: 'Agree together, my friends, to follow my example. You have us for a model; watch those whose way of life conforms to it' (3.17). Or again: 'The lessons I taught you, the tradition I have passed on, all that you heard me say or saw me do, put into practice; and the God of peace will be with you' (4.9). Similarly, when Paul's prayer for them culminates in the hope that they may receive 'the gift of true discrimination' (1.9), behind the language of piety lurks the implication that this is something which at present they lack. It thus prepares for Paul's strident attack on his Christian opponents in ch. 3.

This letter is particularly important for understanding the role of persecution in one of the earliest Christian communities of which we have knowledge. The very persecution which posed a threat to religious authority, ultimately provided its greatest vindication. The cult of the martyrs was one of the most distinctive features of the early Christian centuries, and its replacement after the Christianization of the Empire proved a most testing adjustment. It is therefore a phenomenon of which the Christian origins deserve the most careful attention.

There is an inherent tension in a religious position which promises its adherents peace and joy, and yet promptly involves them in conflict and suffering. It must have been a contradiction of which believers were quickly made aware, and as they were the victims of the tension, their questioning must often have been insistent. Paul's arguments here illustrate the kind of justifications which were offered to such doubts. One line of defence was to point to the good consequences of persecution, which Paul takes care to spell out: 'Friends, I want you to understand that the work of the Gospel has been helped on, rather than hindered, by this business of mine. My imprisonment in Christ's cause has become common knowledge to all at headquarters here, and indeed among the public at large; and it has given confidence to most of our fellow-Christians to speak the word of God fearlessly and with extraordinary courage' (1.12–14). (Once again the apostle, who has no interest in any human response, has a surprising eye for public relations.) The advantage of this kind of argument in sustaining both the morale of the faithful and the prestige of their leaders is its suggestion that persecution must ultimately be ineffectual and self-defeating.

There were, however, two much stronger factors which made it possible for the Christian authorities to avoid being discredited by persecution. One is common to all persecuted groups – the prestige of courage, which conferred a special status on those who were proved brave in adversity. This is the quality which Paul is claiming for himself when he parades his indifference to outward circumstances: 'I have learned to find resources in myself whatever my circumstances. I know what it is to be brought low, and I know what it is to have plenty. I have been very thoroughly initiated into the human lot with all its ups and downs – fullness and hunger, plenty and want. I have strength for anything through him who gives me power' (4.11–14). The other factor was peculiar to the new Christian community: the dialectic of the crucifixion and resurrection of Jesus quickly suggested an understanding of persecution as the gateway to heaven. Paul gives this unambiguous expression: 'All I care for is to know Christ, to experience the power of his resurrection, and to share his sufferings, in growing conformity with his death, if only I may finally arrive at the resurrection from the dead' (3.10–11). In this way experiences of suffering which might have discredited the claims of the new religion and have seemed to the new believers a poor reward for their faith were transformed (at least in rhetoric) into enviable privilege.

Thus Paul is conferring a favour when he invites the Philippians to identify themselves with his imprisonment: 'When I lie in prison or appear in the dock to vouch for the truth of the Gospel, you all share in the privilege that is mine' (1.7). The same prestige lies behind the status which he asks for Epaphroditus: 'You should honour men like him; in Christ's cause he came near to death, risking his life to render me the service you could not give' (2.30). This prepares for the more daring claim that it is a privilege for the Philippians to identify with Paul's suffering not simply in the relative security of prayer and support, but in actually suffering persecution themselves: 'You have been granted the privilege not only of believing in Christ but also of suffering for him. You and I are engaged in the same contest; you saw me in it once, and, as you hear, I am in it still' (1.29, 30). That such a privilege was not unanimously acclaimed by his readers is suggested by the repeated exhortations that reinforce it: 'Rejoice, you no less than I, and let us share our joy' (2.18). 'I wish you joy in the Lord' (3.1). 'My friends, beloved friends whom I long for, my joy, my crown, stand thus firm in the Lord, my beloved.' (4.1). 'I will say it again: all joy be yours' (4.4). 'The Lord is near; have no anxiety, but in everything make your requests known to God in prayer and petition with thanksgiving. Then the peace of God, which is beyond our utmost understanding, will keep guard over your hearts and your thoughts, in Christ Jesus' (4.6, 7). A peace which is beyond understanding has the merit of not encouraging awkward questions.

Paul's attitude to his own fate is eloquent of the tensions involved in this courting of persecution. With one voice he looks forward to his release as an unequivocal good: 'Rejoice I will, knowing well that the issue of it all will be my deliverance, because you are praying for me and the Spirit of Jesus Christ is given me for support' (1.19). He then anticipates his own courage, but having envisaged the possibility of death, magnanimously declines it, because he is too precious and important for the Philippians to spare: 'For, as I passionately hope, I shall have no cause to be ashamed, but shall speak so boldly that now as always the greatness of Christ will shine out clearly in my person, whether through my life or through my death. For to me life is Christ, and death gain; but what if my living on in the body may serve some good purpose? Which then am I to choose? I cannot tell. I am torn two ways: what I should like is to depart and be with Christ; that is better by far; but for your sake there is greater need for me to stay on in the body. This indeed I know for certain: I shall stay, and stand by you all to help you forward and to add joy to your faith, so that when I am with you again, your pride in me may be unbounded in Christ Jesus' (1.20–26). Elsewhere in the letter, however, he returns to the thought of sacrificing his life, which even in anticipation confers status on himself. He embraces such a future with positive joy, which is doubtless intended to encourage his readers to take the same attitude in their trials: 'If my life-blood is to crown that sacrifice which is the offering up of your faith, I am glad of it, and I share my gladness with you all' (2.17). Despite its contradictions, such a belief has great practical strength, as either outcome can only reinforce it. If delivered from death, that is a sign of God's mercy and protection; if suffering is to be borne, that also is a mark of God's single favour, promising, as it does, resurrection. It is also a recipe for invincible obstinacy, and makes it almost impossible to learn from experience.

The concomitant of the cult of persecution is a suspicion and distance from others, which in this letter goes to alarming lengths. Animosity towards persecutors may not be edifying, but it is understandable when he consoles his readers that their enemies' 'doom is sealed' (1.28). It is less easy to sympathize with the virulence of his attacks on his Christian opponents: 'Some indeed, proclaim Christ in a jealous and quarrelsome spirit; others proclaim him in true goodwill, and these are moved by love for me; they know that it is to defend the Gospel that I am where I am. But the others, moved by personal rivalry, present Christ from mixed motives, meaning to stir up fresh trouble for me as I lie in prison. What does it matter? One way or another, in pretence or sincerity, Christ is set forth, and for that I rejoice' (1.15–18). His readiness to impugn his critics' motives, his suggestion that they are conniving at his persecution, and the self-righteous identification of those who proclaim Christ 'in true good-will' with those who 'are moved by love for me' is entirely consistent with the vindictive abuse of the same critics in ch. 3. His warnings are repetitive and striking: 'Beware of those dogs and their malpractices. Beware of those who insist on mutilation – "circumcision" I will not call it' (3.2). He clearly recognizes no common ground with his Christian critics, and dismisses them in a way which would be the despair of the modern ecumenical movement: 'There are many whose way of life makes them enemies of the cross of Christ. They are heading for destruction, appetite is their god, and they glory in their shame. Their minds are set on earthly things. We, by contrast, are citizens of heaven' (3.18–20). They are part of that 'warped and crooked generation', which in Paul's mind comprise the 'dark world' (2.15). Already the suspicion is not confined to external enemies, but is corrupting the Christian community itself, and the way in which Paul refers to his companions in persecution is breathtaking in the isolation it reveals: 'There is no one else here who sees things as I do, and takes a genuine interest in your concerns; they are all bent on their own ends' (2.20, 21). This complaint is calculated to evoke a similar suspicion among the Philippians. He is enlisting them on his side. It seems very distant from Paul's own advice: 'All that is true, all that is noble, all that is just and pure, all that is lovable and gracious, whatever is excellent and admirable – fill all your thoughts with these things' (4.8). Paul had discovered for himself the limitations of mood-control, however determined the 'positive thinking'.

(b) The Law in retrospect

As in Galatians, a large part of this letter expounds Paul's attitude to the Law. The continuing attraction for him of his Jewish past is unmistakable: 'If anyone thinks to base his claims on externals, I could make a stronger case for myself: circumcised on my eighth day, Israelite by race, of the tribe of Benjamin, a Hebrew born and bred; in my attitude to the Law, a Pharisee; in pious zeal, a persecutor of the church; in legal rectitude, faultless' (3.4–6). It is prophetic of the attitude of some of the Church Fathers to the pagan literature in which they had been educated; the breach was so painful that it could only be achieved by violent and exaggerated language: 'But all such assets I have written off because of Christ. I would say more: I count everything sheer loss, because all is far outweighed by the gain of knowing Christ Jesus my Lord, for whose sake I did in fact lose everything. I count it so much garbage, for the sake of gaining Christ and finding myself incorporate in him, with no righteousness of my own, no legal rectitude, but the righteousness which comes from faith in Christ, given by God in response to faith' (3.7–9). Paul's language here is a reminder to those who have never had to make a sharp and painful decision in their lives that even after the decision has been made it often continues to hurt.

In view of the terrifying history of antisemitism in the church, it is understandable that some have seen its origins in the rhetoric of Paul's repudiation of the Law. There are certainly traces of antisemitism elsewhere in the New Testament, and it may well be that some of Paul's language has subsequently fed that prejudice; but that would not be a fair assessment of his admittedly conflicting and ambivalent attitude. He is after all criticizing his own identity, not somebody else's; it was costly and painful precisely because that Jewish identity was so precious to him, and remained so after his conversion. As in Galatians, he describes the relation of the new Christian identity to the Law in terms of the opposition of the spiritual and heavenly to the external and earthly. Paul did not handle this tension satisfactorily in Galatians, nor does he in this letter, but we can see more clearly here why the model was so attractive to Paul: two passages will show how neatly it enables him to fuse together diverse strands in his thought: 'We are the circumcised, we whose worship is spiritual, whose pride is in Christ Jesus, and who put no confidence in anything external' (3.3). 'Their minds are set on earthly things. We, by contrast, are citizens of heaven, and from heaven we expect our deliverer to come' (3.19, 20). Here we can see how this model enables Paul to bring together the gift of the Spirit to Christians, their repudiation of religious externals, their present liberation from their lower nature, and their eschatological hopes and fantasies. More positively, it enables Paul to rehabilitate Jewish concepts in a 'spiritual' sense, and just as in Galatians he ends by rehabilitating the Law, so here he rehabilitates circumcision by giving it a new 'spiritual' meaning.

(c) Unity and conformity

As in Galatians, we are faced by the question: has Paul repudiated the Jewish Law simply to replace it by a new law, which is the instrument of his own will? In answering that question, the stress in this epistle on unity needs careful examination. Nothing raises more problems for spiritual authority than quarrels between the faithful, so that when Paul pleads for the reconciliation of those two quarrelsome women, Euodia and Syntyche, he is not simply trying to resolve a situation which is tiresome to the Philippians; he is almost certainly attempting to end a conflict which is embarrassing to him; as they both 'shared my struggles in the cause of the Gospel' (4.3). A concern for unity can function in two very different ways: it may foster a concern for mutual attention and forbearance, or it may mask a concern for obedient conformity. In sifting Paul's teaching on unity, it is therefore useful to ask, are the Philippians being urged to listen to each other, or to listen to Paul? It is, for instance, to obey Paul's teaching about meeting persecution that he urges them to stand firm: 'One in spirit, one in mind, contending as one man for the Gospel faith' (1.27). Elsewhere unity and obedience are clearly equated: 'Agree together, my friends, to follow my example' (3.17). Most striking is the way in which the condescension of Christ 'assuming the nature of a slave' (2.7) is used not to temper the exercise of Paul's authority, but to reinforce it: 'So you too, my friends, must be obedient, as always; even more, now that I am away, than when I was with you' (2.12). This is not, however, the only understanding of unity provided here by Paul: he can envisage a much more mutual concept: 'If then our common life in Christ yields anything to stir the heart, any loving consolation, any sharing of the spirit, any warmth of affection or compassion, fill up my cup of happiness by thinking and feeling alike, with the same love for one another, the same turn of mind, and a common care for unity. There must be no room for rivalry and personal vanity among you, but you must humbly reckon others better than yourselves. Look to each other's interest and not merely to your own' (2.1–3).

Paul cannot, therefore, be simply represented as exchanging one tyranny for another. If he is often tempted to fill the vacuum created by repudiation of the Law with a vigorous assertion of his own authority, this is continually questioned by the freedom to which he himself has appealed. His self-assertion is obvious, but it is qualified by a modesty which is not simply verbal, but reflects a new notion of spiritual learning. It is not as if the progress from polytheism and from the Law to Christ has brought the process of learning to an end; the apostle himself still has much to learn: 'It is not to be thought that I have already achieved all this. I have not yet reached perfection, but I press on, hoping to take hold of that for which Christ once took hold of me. My friends, I do not reckon myself to have got hold of it yet. All I can say is this: forgetting what is behind me, and reaching out for that which lies ahead, I press towards the goal to win the prize which is God's call to the life above, in Christ Jesus' (3.12–14). It is also important to note that Paul extends to the Philippians the same educational tolerance that he claims for himself: the Philippians are told that they 'must work out (their) own salvation with fear and trembling' (2.12). Indeed, this process of learning is ascribed to the working of God himself: 'For it is God who works in you, inspiring both the will and the deed, for his own chosen purpose' (2.13). Paul here concedes to the faithful a degree of autonomy that he does not always find it possible to respect; but he can at least envisage disagreements, not only among the Philippians, but between the Philippians and himself, being resolved by the slow teaching of God: 'Let us then keep to this way of thinking, those of us who are mature. If there is any point on which you think differently, this also God will make plain to you. Only let our conduct be consistent with the level we have already reached' (3.15, 16). As in Galatians, there is a strong emphasis on what is appropriate to a particular person; in respecting different 'levels' of spiritual achievement Paul has made the most radical criticism of absolute standards and imperatives.

(d) A financial footnote

Paul is exceptionally forthcoming in this letter about the nature of his financial relation to the Philippians. With a coyness that has become a

mark of clerical attitudes towards money, he prefers to speak euphemistically of their 'care' for him blossoming afresh (4.10), or their 'kindness' in
sharing the burden of his troubles (4.14). He is at pains not to compromise
his spiritual authority by admitting actual financial dependence: 'Not that
I am alluding to want, for I have learned to find resources in myself
whatever my circumstances' (4.11). Eventually, however, he braces
himself and recognizes the financial aspect of their relationship: 'As you
know yourselves, Philippians, in the early days of my mission, when I set
out from Macedonia, you alone of all our congregations were my partners
in payments and receipts; for even at Thessalonica you contributed to my
needs, not once but twice over . . . However, here I give you my receipt for
everything – for more than everything; I am paid in full, now that I have
received from Epaphroditus what you sent' (4.15, 16, 18). This throws a
rather unexpected light on Paul's vaunted financial independence while
among the Thessalonians, and portrays the apostle in a way which must
have been much more acceptable to those Christian leaders who made no
secret that they depended upon their followers for financial support.
Typically Paul is quick to deny any self-interest: 'Do not think I set my
heart upon the gift' (4.17). Instead, with some audacity, he concentrates
the minds of his readers, not on the benefit they have conferred on him, but
on the benefit they have conferred on themselves! 'All I care for is the profit
accruing to you . . . My God will supply all your wants out of the
magnificence of his riches in Christ Jesus' (4.17, 19). The passage
concludes with words which leave the impression that an offering has been
made to God rather than to Paul: 'It is a fragrant offering, an acceptable
sacrifice, pleasing to God' (4.18). This is a different aspect of the close
identity Paul felt with his Lord.

5

I CORINTHIANS

(a) The divisiveness of Paul's unique authority

This letter, which contains the most famous of all Paul's writings, the lyrical passage on love in ch. 13, is in other respects an exercise of magisterial authority. Its keynote is struck in the second verse – the Lordship of Christ. In the name of that Lord Paul demands unity and obedience. He is to be seen subduing critics, subjecting the faithful to his unsolicited censure, and giving firm rulings to their most intimate queries. It is a style that the officials of the Vatican can rightly claim as their own. It is perhaps a sign of Paul's confidence in the exercise of his authority that only a few verses of the letter are devoted to prayer. He briefly thanks God for the spiritual achievement of the Corinthians, 'because in you the evidence for the truth of Christ has found confirmation' (1.6), and declares his confidence that God will maintain their loyalty – sentiments which both confirm the Corinthians in their position of obedience and rule out of court the possibility of their defection. Here he needs neither to flatter nor cajole, and so he proceeds to command.

Some of the contradictions of a demand for unity have already been examined in the letter to the Philippians. It is one of the paradoxes of social experience that calls for unity are often most vigorously made by those whose activity is peculiarly divisive. Thus a government which has acted on behalf of sectional interests will need to appeal to national unity to disarm criticism. Paul's position is not dissimilar. He gives a vivid picture of the divisions among the Corinthians: 'Each of you is saying, "I am Paul's man", or "I am for Apollos'"; "I follow Cephas", or "I am Christ's". Surely Christ has not been divided among you!' (1.12). Yet Paul himself seems directly responsible for much of the trouble: he cannot, for instance, resist distinguishing himself from all the rest of God's workers in the Corinthian vineyard. Having commented on the divisions which have arisen from loyalty to the various ministers of baptism, Paul proceeds to congratulate himself: 'Thank God, I never baptized one of you – except

Crispus and Gaius. So no one can say you were baptized in my name. – Yes, I did baptize the household of Stephanas; I cannot think of anyone else. Christ did not send me to baptize, but to proclaim the Gospel; and to do it without relying on the language of worldly wisdom, so that the fact of Christ on his cross might have its full weight' (1.14–17). Even in his exhortation to unity, Paul draws attention to his own special position.

(b) The unique wisdom and spirit of the gospel

The distinctiveness of Paul's position leads naturally to a consideration of the complementary distinctiveness of the gospel: its unique wisdom and spirit. The subsequent influence of this passage has been immense, as it is the first attempt in Christian writing to define the relationship between religious authority and secular reason. It informs both the agonized attempts of the Church Fathers to express a coherent attitude to the heritage of classical literature and the more recent dilemmas of church leaders in relation to science. It is a striking and early instance of the way in which the religious insistence on transcendence, which makes possible the freedom of the oppressed, at the same time establishes a new authority which is beyond criticism.

There is a disturbing reiteration of that fundamental alienation which underlies Paul's understanding of the gospel and informs his commitment to it. His position gains its excitement and significance from the contrast with 'those on their way to ruin' (1.18), the ignorance of 'the powers that rule the world' (2.8). He relishes the distinction: 'This is the Spirit that we have received from God, and not the spirit of the world' (2.12). There is, however, an element of real freedom and liberation in Paul's transcendence of the wisdom and power of this passing age. Generations of the poor and uneducated have thrilled to his celebration of deliverance from the structures of power and culture which oppress them. 'Scripture says, "I will destroy the wisdom of the wise, and bring to nothing the cleverness of the clever." Where is your wise man now, your man of learning, or your subtle debater – limited all of them, to this passing age? God has made the wisdom of this world look foolish. As God in his wisdom ordained, the world failed to find him by its wisdom, and he chose to save those who have faith by the folly of the Gospel' (1.19–21). In a world where the inarticulate are usually condemned to be manipulated by those who express themselves easily, and where education has from its very beginnings been associated with economic privilege and political power, Paul voices a widespread yearning and resentment. Anyone who has ever been made to feel stupid in argument can share his scorn of the 'subtle debater', and feel something of the same delight at his divine discomfiture.

Similarly, Paul gives the disadvantaged a new self-respect when he makes their very deprivation a pledge of God's favour: 'Divine folly is wiser than the wisdom of man, and divine weakness stronger than man's strength. My brothers, think what sort of people you are, whom God has called. Few of you are men of wisdom, by any human standard; few are powerful or highly born. Yet, to shame the wise, God has chosen what the world counts folly, and to shame what is strong, God has chosen what the world counts weakness. He has chosen things low and contemptible, mere nothings, to overthrow the existing order' (1.25–27). God shares the resentment of the oppressed towards those who exploit them, and asserts himself by overturning such structures.

The sense of deliverance and the new self-respect are real: they are the source of the continuing power of Paul's writing; but the price is heavy. For the apostle moves directly from the proclamation of freedom to the evasion of criticism. Neither Jew nor Gentile need be listened to. 'Jews call for miracles, Greeks look for wisdom; but we proclaim Christ – yes, Christ nailed to the cross; and though this is a stumbling-block to Jews and folly to Greeks, yet to those who have heard his call, Jews and Greeks alike, he is the power of God and the wisdom of God' (1.22–24). The progression of thought is fascinating: the reader scarcely notices the intrusion of the words 'we proclaim'. Paul directs attention away from himself towards the bleeding figure of Christ and, thus fortified, does not establish his claims on his own experience, but appeals to the vanity of the Corinthian readers who can complacently identify themselves as 'those who have heard' God's call. Attention is carefully directed towards the message; only on reflection are the implications about the status of the messenger perceived. The privilege of his readers is entirely dependent on the invulnerability of the writer to criticism. Thus the promise of self-respect does not lead to autonomy, but only to a more devastating dependance. In social relationships, however unequal, dominance is qualified by the paradoxical dependance of the master on the services of the slave. The sovereignty of God is qualified by no such dependance: 'There is no place for human pride in the presence of God. You are in Christ Jesus by God's act, for God has made him our wisdom; he is our righteousness; in him we are consecrated and set free. And so (in the words of Scripture), "If a man must boast, let him boast of the Lord"' (1.29–31). Because their sense of privilege, of consecration and freedom, is entirely dependent on God's initiative, expressed through that of his apostle, the new believers have no possibility of properly asserting their independence of the apostle. They may safely be encouraged to boast of the Lord, because in practice that is indistinguishable from obedience to the man of his choice, and so quite naturally Paul turns to a self-conscious description and defence of his own style.

He begins with apparent humility, by disclaiming all eloquence or wisdom. 'I declared the attested truth of God without display of fine words or wisdom' (2.1). 'I came before you weak, nervous, and shaking with fear. The word I spoke, the gospel I proclaimed, did not sway you with subtle arguments' (2.3, 4). The effect is disarming, but it only prepares for the most sweeping assertion of spiritual and divine power: 'It carried conviction by spiritual power, so that your faith might be built not upon human wisdom but upon the power of God' (2.5). The self-assertion is devious and unrelenting, and the very disclaimers which at first disguise it are soon qualified, indeed revoked. 'And yet I do speak words of wisdom to those who are ripe for it' (2.6). Thus ready agreement with Paul becomes itself a sign of privilege. The recipient can congratulate himself on his 'ripeness', in happy contrast to 'this passing age', and 'its governing powers, which are declining to their end' (2.6). With great subtlety Paul intertwines his own exaltation above criticism with the freedom of his readers. 'I speak God's hidden wisdom, his secret purpose framed from the very beginning to bring us to our full glory' (2.7). The reader submits to the arrogance of Paul's claim because he has the satisfaction of being identified with it. Paul may speak the secret, but the reader shares it. The concentration on 'Christ nailed to the cross' (2.2) merely serves to discredit the existing rival structures of power which live in ignorance of that secret: 'The powers that rule the world have never known it; if they had, they would not have crucified the Lord of glory' (2.8). Similarly, the gift of the Spirit, which is the believer's privilege, serves to place Paul beyond attack. He boldly associates the reader with the highest spiritual claims: 'But, in the words of Scripture, "Things beyond our seeing, things beyond our hearing, things beyond our imagining, all prepared by God for those who love him", these it is that God has revealed to us through the Spirit. For the Spirit explores everything, even the depths of God's own nature' (2.9, 10). Excited by these grand assertions, the reader scarcely notices the way in which Paul's use of the first person plural is silently transformed. When he writes, 'This is the Spirit that we have received from God, and not the spirit of the world, so that we may know all that God of his own grace has given us' (2.12), it seems that the first person plural is inclusive and involves the reader. The end of the sentence, however, makes it clear that there has been an unacknowledged transition to a 'we' which refers solely to Paul and buttresses his prerogative: 'Because we are interpreting spiritual truths to those who have the Spirit, we speak of these gifts of God in words found for us not by human wisdom but by the Spirit' (2.13). Moreover, the concept of the gift of the Spirit provides an easy way of disposing of criticism: the gift has not been given. 'A man who is unspiritual refuses what belongs to the Spirit of God; it is folly to him; he cannot grasp it, because it needs to be judged in the light of the Spirit' (2.14). Finally, the notion of inspiration conceals the human author, thus facilitating claims of the most astonishing arrogance: 'A man gifted with Spirit can judge the worth of everything, but is not himself subject to judgment by his fellow-men. For (in the words of Scripture) "who knows the mind of the Lord? Who can advise him?"' (2.15, 16). The reader may well assent to that generalized and abstract claim, which Paul then exploits boldly: 'We, however, possess the mind of Christ.'

(c) The demand for unity

It is not surprising after such extravagant language that in the exhortation to unity which follows, the common mind is built around attention and obedience to the apostle rather than the mutual and social model of unity which Paul glimpses in the letter to the Philippians. The notion of spiritual learning, related to the individual's history rather than some absolute standard, here takes on a rather different colour. There is the same recognition of different levels and achievements, but they do not establish mutual tolerance: rather, they emphasize the apostle's dominance: 'For my part, my brothers, I could not speak to you as I should speak to people who have the Spirit. I had to deal with you on the merely natural plane, as infants in Christ. And so I gave you milk to drink, instead of solid food, for which you were not yet ready' (3.1). Nor is this unequal relationship something which has been outgrown, as Paul immediately makes clear: 'Indeed, you are still not ready for it, for you are still on the merely natural plane' (3.2). The very fact of conflict in their community is then cited as a sign of their immaturity and thus serves to enhance the status of Paul. The disclaimer of any distinction between God's agents which follows appears modest, but functions as a means of putting the Corinthians in their place, which is entirely passive. Apollos and Paul may only be gardeners, entirely dependent upon God who makes the seed grow; but the distinction between them and the Corinthians is striking: 'We are God's fellow-workers; and you are God's garden' (3.9). Paul then proceeds to explore the possibilities of another model: the builder and the building. Significantly he suffers from some uncertainty as to whether he or Jesus laid the foundation: 'I am like a skilled master-builder who by God's grace laid the foundation, and someone else is putting up the building. Let each take care how he builds. There can be no other foundation beyond that which is already laid; I mean Jesus Christ himself' (3.10–11). The implication would seem to be that the real initiative lies in Paul's hands! Paul uses the building analogy to express his concern with authenticity and to provide a vivid image of judgment: 'If anyone builds on that foundation with gold, silver and fine stone, or with wood, hay and straw, the work that each man does will at last be brought to light; the day of judgment will expose it. For that day dawns in fire, and the fire will test the worth of each man's work. If a man's building stands, he will be rewarded; if it burns, he will have to bear the loss; and yet he will escape with his life, as one might from a fire' (3.12–15). It is not entirely clear whether these words are addressed to Paul's fellow labourers or the Christian faithful, but the latter could not fail to understand their own lives in the same threatening context. While similar imagery is used in the Gospels to stress the sufficiency of the foundation, here it is the quality of the building which is Paul's preoccupation. He does not want his work to be jeopardized. Thus the Corinthians' consciousness of their status as God's temple, 'where the Spirit of God dwells', is used to alert them to the dangers of interference: 'Anyone who destroyed God's temple will himself be destroyed by God, because the temple of God is holy; and that temple you are' (3.16, 17). This conclusion is the spiritual equivalent of a 'trespassers will be prosecuted' notice.

The unity which Paul demands is based on obedience and makes criticism impossible. Internal debate and discrimination are ruled out of order by appeals to Scripture: 'The wisdom of this world is folly in God's sight. Scripture says, "He traps the wise in their own cunning", and again, "The Lord knows that the arguments of the wise are futile"' (3.19–20). The Corinthians are therefore encouraged to share God's detachment from argument. Paul lures the Corinthians with the most flattering account of their position: 'Everything belongs to you – Paul, Apollos, and Cephas, the world, life, and death, the present and the future, all of them belong to you' (3.21–23). The prospect before them is immense, but it is entirely dependent on their recognition of their master: 'Yet you belong to Christ, and Christ to God.' Paul here reveals the stark subordinationism of his understanding of Jesus' relation to God. Nor is this simply to be dismissed as doctrinal 'immaturity'. It is not that Paul has not yet developed 'a full christology'; his whole exercise of authority and his understanding of obedience demand the subordination of the Son to the Father. His christology legitimizes his rule. If even Jesus is obedient to his Father, it is a small thing for the Corinthians to be obedient to Paul; they have no grounds for expecting anything else.

(d) Paul's demand for obedience

Paul completes his call for unity with a subtle demand for obedience. He begins by proclaiming his own subordination to Christ: 'We must be regarded as Christ's subordinates and as stewards of the secrets of God' (4.1); but while his readers are reminded of their subordination to make them responsible to Paul, his subordination to Christ rules out responsibility to any one else: 'For my part, if I am called to account by you or by any human court of judgment, it does not matter to me in the least' (4.3). In the same way, the eschatological element which so often heightens anxiety, in the case of the apostle makes his authority unassailable: 'My judge is the Lord. So pass no premature judgment; wait until the Lord comes. For he will bring to light what darkness hides, and discloses men's inward motives; then will be the time for each to receive from God such praise as he deserves' (4.5). Although the apostle makes any criticism from other people irrelevant, he does admit an openness to God's verdict on himself: 'I have nothing on my conscience; but that does not mean I stand acquitted' (4.4). Too much, however, should not be made of such verbal modesty; in the absence of the possibility of social criticism it is entirely hypothetical. It is also a comment which may discomfort Paul rather less than his readers. If even the great apostle could not be entirely certain of his state, they had all the more cause to worry about their own condition.

Paul perceives that for his authority to be effective over the Corinthians he must make no secret of his solidarity with Apollos. He strengthens the importance of 'keeping within the rules' (4.6), by pointing to their pride 'as you patronize one and flout the other' (4.6). Any chance of the Corinthians gaining some autonomy through the divisions of their religious leaders is checked by reminding them of their irreversible dependence: 'Who makes you, my friend, so important? What do you possess that was not given you? If then you really received it all as a gift, why take the credit to yourself?' (4.7). There follows a long passage designed to undermine their confidence, by the ironic contrast of their own complacent achievement with the prestige of the apostle's affliction. The irony is savage: 'All of you, no doubt, have everything you could desire. You have come into your fortune already. You have come into your kingdom – and left us out. How I wish you had indeed won your kingdom; then you might share it with us!' (4.8). He then deliberately discredits his readers by playing on their guilt at their own safety and comfort, all the time contrasting it with the authenticity of his own sufferings: 'We are fools for Christ's sake, while you are such sensible Christians. We are weak; you are powerful. We are in disgrace; you are honoured' (4.10). There follows a catalogue of Paul's hardships, at the end of which he has the audacity to claim: 'I am not writing thus to shame you, but to bring you to reason' (4.14). Even Paul detects that here he may have gone too far, and so he tries to qualify the severity of his impact without in any way relinquishing the extent of his claims. He calls the Corinthians to follow his example, using a paternal image of such force that it threatens to render Christ practically redundant: 'You may have ten thousand tutors in Christ, but you have only one father. For in Christ Jesus you are my offspring, and mine alone, through the preaching of the Gospel' (4.15). Perhaps Paul has never heard or has temporarily forgotten the dominical injunction to call no man 'father'. Curiously he here ascribes to Christ a passive maternal role, which leaves the masculine initiative with the apostle. It is equally striking that Paul can then go on to accuse his critics of 'self-importance' (4.19).

The passage ends with an almost eschatological threat which illustrates how the expectation of the second coming intertwines with and makes more plausible the exercise of the apostle's distant authority, which may be strengthened by the surprise of his presence at any time. We can hear how the words of Paul echo those of the ascended Christ: 'There are certain persons who are filled with self-importance because they think I am not coming to Corinth. I shall come very soon, if the Lord will; and then I shall take the measure of these self-important people, not by what they say, but by what power is in them. The kingdom of God is not a matter of talk, but of power. Choose, then: am I to come to you with a rod in my hand, or in love and a gentle spirit?' (4.19–21). In this fascinating passage the miracle-working power of the apostle combines with the power of the eschatological judge. For all his talk of weakness, he is still prepared to invoke avenging power as the ultimate deterrent. It may be that the decline in the expectation of the second coming is related to the way in which church authority was exercised. Here the distant exercise of authority, enforced by occasional and uncertain visits, directly mirrors the eschatological fantasies of the early Christians. Belief is thus made plausible by present experience, and authority gains something of its terror by identifying its style with that of the returning Christ. As Christian authority became rooted more firmly in local institutions, with permanent representatives who no longer looked to far-away apostles, the belief became less plausible to the faithful, as it also ceased to be so useful to their rulers.

(e) The limitations of Christian freedom

(i) The discrediting of rival authority

Paul's approach to the Corinthians is quite uncompromising. Having established the basis of his own authority, he does not immediately proceed to reply to their queries. Instead he takes the initiative by defining the limitations of the Christian freedom which he has preached, and so disarms any local criticism of his leadership which may have arisen. On the one hand the severest sexual prohibitions are used by him to discredit his Corinthian critics, while the emphasis on legal isolation eliminates any possibility of outside interference with the autonomy of Christian discipline.

The opening verses of ch. 5 show how Paul uses strong sexual prohibitions to enhance his own prestige and to attack his opponents. He appeals strongly to the Corinthians' sense of shame: 'I actually hear reports of sexual immorality among you, immorality such as even pagans do not tolerate' (5.1). The appeals to the pagan world from which they have alienated themselves prepares for the social sanction of exclusion: 'A man who has done such a deed should have been rooted out of your company' (5.2). Once again Paul assumes something of the identity of the ascended Christ to enforce his remote judgment: 'For my part, though I am absent in body, I am present in spirit, and my judgment upon the man who did this thing is already given, as if I were indeed present' (5.3–5). He then sketches in imagination the outcome he desires: 'You all being assembled in the name of our Lord Jesus, and I with you in spirit, with the power of our Lord Jesus over us, this man is to be consigned to Satan for the destruction of the body, so that his spirit may be saved on the Day of the Lord.' The dichotomy in Paul's mind between the body and the spirit gives a charitable veneer to exclusive and vindictive behaviour: a chilling anticipation of the mediaeval inquisition, with Satan conveniently filling the function of the secular arm. In both instances cruelty is made possible by a refusal to recognize the dependence of the spirit on the body and a consequent indifference to the body, which serves to enhance the value of the spirit.

The following verses indicate the narrowly exclusive community which is the essential corollary to the exercise of Paul's kind of authority. He does not plead for obedience and by accident slip into exclusive patterns of thought: as alienation provides the incentive, so exclusion provides the sanction for his style of leadership. The anxiety of mutual suspicion within the community is deliberately fostered: 'Your self-satisfaction ill becomes you. Have you never heard the saying, "A little leaven leavens all the dough"?' (5.6). To preserve the fragile sense of newness and a fresh beginning he orders a purge: 'The old leaven of corruption is working among you. Purge it out, and then you will be bread of a new baking' (5.7). Once again the bestowal of a privileged identity is used to direct behaviour. Paul then rehabilitates paschal imagery, reinterpreting the ritual in a spiritual sense: 'As Christians you are unleavened Passover bread; for indeed our Passover has begun; the sacrifice is offered – Christ himself. So we who observe the festival must not use the old leaven, the leaven of corruption and wickedness, but only the unleavened bread which is sincerity and truth' (5.7, 8). As the affirmation of Jesus' divinity is related to the deification of the believers, so here the desire to direct the conduct of the faithful leads to an emphasis on the sinlessness of Christ. Again, while the imagery of Passover may have been moralized, it also gains exclusive and authoritarian associations. The new community articulates alienation from the world, and would lose its point if it became confused with it. Nevertheless, the position demands that there continue to be a pagan world as a suitable contrasting background. 'In my letter I wrote that you must have nothing to do with loose livers. I was not, of course, referring to pagans who lead loose lives or are grabbers and swindlers or idolaters. To avoid them you would have to get out of the world altogether. I now write that you must have nothing to do with any so-called Christian who leads a loose life, or is grasping, or idolatrous, a slanderer, a drunkard or a swindler' (5.9–11). Pagan deviation can be tolerated because that poses no threat to the community's identity; indeed, it contributes to it. Christian deviation, however, has to be treated in the harshest terms. Thus the Jew who is liberated to eat with Gentiles demands that his followers refuse to eat with his opposing co-religionists.

(ii) Legal isolation

This incidental reference to pagans prompts Paul to give an account of his own jurisdiction which emphasizes the autonomy and isolation of the new Christian community. He readily disclaims any jurisdiction over outsiders, contenting himself with threatening them with divine retribution: 'What business of mine is it to judge outsiders? God is their judge' (5.12, 13). This disclaimer is a sign not so much of modesty as of the alienation revealed in the rhetorical questions which follow: 'How can you entrust jurisdiction to outsiders, men who count for nothing in our community?' (6.4). 'Must brother go to law with brother – and before unbelievers?' (6.6). But Paul has raised a dangerous issue, for the reader might well ask what right Paul has to judge him. Perhaps with the pagan he is simply accountable to God. Paul answers this by stressing the purity of the new community, and its divinely bestowed sovereignty: 'You are judges within the fellowship. Root out the evil-doer from your community. If one of your number has a dispute with another, has he the face to take it to pagan law-courts instead of to the community of God's people? It is God's people who are to judge the world; surely you know that. And if the world is to come before you for judgment, are you incompetent to deal with these trifling cases? Are you not aware that we are to judge angels? How much more, mere matters of business!' (5.13–6.3). Paul here is very distant from those passages in the Gospels which repudiate power and separate Jesus from involvement in secular conflicts. Instead he embraces such responsibilities with an enthusiasm worthy of the church of Constantine. There is, moreover, a fascinating shift from a communal justification of sovereignty in terms of 'God's people' to a highly individual concept of its exercise: 'Can it be that there is not a single wise man among you able to give a decision in a brother-Christian's cause?' (6.5). A surprising reversion to the wisdom Paul has so vigorously denounced in the opening chapters of this letter!

Paul's ambivalence towards the search for equity has influenced the whole development of Christian attitudes towards social justice. Because his concern centres on the unity and purity of the community, and because he envisages this in terms of conformity rather than justice, he readily repudiates any insistence on equity: 'You already fall below your standard in going to law with one another at all. Why not rather suffer injury? Why not rather let yourself be robbed?' (6.7). Here the repudiation of a concern for earthly justice which is found in the Gospels no longer directs men's attention to their heavenly goal but to a more immediate ecclesiastical tribunal. Thus Paul inculcates an attitude of passive resignation to injustice on the part of the oppressed, while himself vigorously castigating evil-doers: 'Surely you know that the unjust will never come into possession of the kingdom of God. Make no mistake: no fornicator or idolater, none who are guilty either of adultery or of homosexual perversion, no thieves or grabbers or drunkards or slanderers or swindlers, will possess the kingdom of God' (6.9, 10). This bewildering confusion of social evils and personal weaknesses demonstrates the extent to which Paul's notion of righteousness remains, for all his theology of justification, fundamentally one of purity. As the castigator of personal vice, he emphasizes his freedom from it, and establishes his superiority. His condemnation of those social ills, such as theft and slander, illustrates the tension which will haunt much of subsequent Christian social teaching. By counselling patience to the victims, he is in danger of appearing in collusion with the oppressors. This collusion is then disguised by a stern chiding of the evil-doer which serves to distance the church leader from the oppressor, and at the same time enhances ecclesiastical prestige in the eyes of the afflicted. In that way the church appears to preserve its moral integrity without having to imitate the suffering of its Lord.

The sanction on which Paul ultimately relies to enforce his authority is that of the heavenly reward: 'possessing the kingdom of God'. Present advantages are to be sacrificed for a promised future benefit, for his gospel is fundamentally concerned with privileges hereafter. But he does strengthen this sanction by arguing from the privilege of baptism to its obligations: he outlines their former course of wicked behaviour, and then firmly distances them from it: 'Such were some of you. But you have been through the purifying waters; you have been dedicated to God and justified through the name of the Lord Jesus and the Spirit of our God' (6.11). Once again the flattering description conceals the implicit control.

(iii) Sexual prohibition

Once the sovereignty and purity of the new community has been affirmed, Paul concludes his demand for sexual repression by carefully distinguishing the freedom of the gospel from any sexual liberation. His position is the more uncomfortable because he wishes to acknowledge the reality of freedom, while resisting its sexual implications. Apparently the Corinthians had responded to Paul's message of freedom with disconcerting enthusiasm. ' "I am free to do anything", you say' (6.12). Paul dare not directly contradict that understanding of the gospel; instead he acknowledges the freedom which the Corinthians had seized upon in his message, but then proceeds to subvert it. He does this partly on grounds of individual prudence: 'Not everything is for my good' (6.12), and partly by appealing to the individual's desire to retain sexual autonomy: 'I for one will not let anything make free with me.' The second appeal reflects Paul's deep distrust of man's sexuality which is made plain later in the letter. The first argument fails to recognize that if the freedom which he and the Corinthians both claim is real, then this may restrict Paul's right to tell them what is for their own good. That, however, is an implication which the apostle refuses to admit.

Instead he puts forward a series of arguments to support his own commitment to sexual restraint. First he faces the view which sees human sexuality as a natural appetite which must be satisfied, on the analogy of hunger. He acknowledges the naturalism of hunger for food, 'Food is for the belly and the belly for food', but places this in a disparaging perspective by adding 'and one day God will put an end to both' (6.13). This establishes a temporary view of the body and its needs, and successfully conveys both Paul's own distaste for the body and God's disapproval of it. He then denies that there is any analogy between physical and sexual hunger. 'It is not true that the body is for lust; it is for the Lord – and the Lord for the body' (6.13). It is interesting that in this strong statement of Jesus' proprietary rights over the bodies of believers, he is referred to by that title which most emphasizes his authority – Lord. Paul develops the inversion of this proprietary relationship, 'The Lord is for the body', by promising the believer identity with the risen Christ. 'God not only raised our Lord from the dead; he will also raise us by his power. Do you not know that your bodies are limbs and organs of Christ?' (6.14, 15). It is an exhilarating vision, but it is immediately used by Paul to control the believer's behaviour: 'Shall I then take from Christ his bodily parts and make them over to a harlot?' (6.15). The passionate implication that Christ has nothing to do with prostitutes is not entirely easy to reconcile with the picture of Jesus in the Gospels. Paul shares with the Jesus of the Gospels a stress on the Old Testament exaggeration, 'the pair shall become one flesh', with its implication that sexual intimacy establishes physical identity. He adds to this his own sense of spiritual identity with Christ. It must be a mark of the insecurity of Paul's position that in this passage he adds argument to argument with little concern for consistency or development. So having explored the resources of sacramental mysticism, he then resorts to a much more private and prudential argument: 'Every other sin that a man can commit is outside the body; but the fornicator sins against his own body' (6.18). The implication of this point is a strong identity between self and body which contrasts with Paul's more customary distrust and disaparagement of the physical. In the next verse he uses another version of the familiar argument from privilege to obligation: 'Do you not know that your body is a shrine of the indwelling Holy Spirit, and the Spirit is God's gift to you?' (6.19). It sounds a prestigious description of the body, but not only is the flattery being used to indicate appropriate behaviour, it also reflects a displacement of identity and an underlying alienation from the body, which is made plain in the next sentence: 'You do not belong to yourselves; you were bought at a price' (6.20). Once again there is a disturbing dependence on the social analogy of slavery which provides an exact model combining a sense of self-alienation and the encouragement to obedience: a revealing paradox of the gospel of freedom.

(f) Apostolic rulings

(i) Sexual behaviour

The rest of the epistle gives a series of apostolic rulings on the limits of the freedom of the new community. Here the apostle is not so much taking the initiative as replying to their questions and uncertainties. That in itself is a tribute to his success in undermining the autonomy of the new Corinthian community. Their requests for guidance are a sign of their continuing dependence, and this is encouraged by the magisterial nature of Paul's response, from which any note of mutuality or consultation is absent. The first topic to which he turns his mind is that of the new sexual morality.

He begins on an abrupt and striking note: 'It is a good thing for a man to have nothing to do with women' (7.1). Some readings of the text have tried to distance the apostle from such a view, by adding the preface, 'You say', but that is probably a sign of the church's acute embarrassment at such teaching in the face of gnostic dualism. While there is no sign of any tendency to exaggerated asceticism in the Corinthian community, there is every evidence for this in Paul's writings. This chapter is therefore most plausibly read as the apostle's agonized attempt to adjust himself to the sexuality of others which he has renounced in himself, rather than as a judicious attempt to mitigate the dangers of sexual abstinence by the disciplined release of marriage. The implications of this prefacing sentence are too important and too embarrassing to be quickly glossed over to avoid ecclesiastical discomfort. Most innocently, Paul implies that the choice and initiative lie entirely with the man. Woman is simply a passive commodity, which like certain kinds of food should be avoided: indeed food is the next subject to which Paul turns in the following chapter. More seriously, it expresses a deep alienation from women, and reflects his distrust of the body which has already been noticed. It is difficult to ignore the homosexual implications of such an attitude. Paul consciously condemns homosexuality in this letter (6.9) and in the letter to the Romans (1.27), and his language is vehement. If this verse does faithfully convey his attitude towards women, then his position seems to be a combination of unperceived homosexual preference and repudiation of the body and its attendant sexuality. That would account both for the vehemence of his sexual prohibitions and the exaltation of celibacy. Be that as it may, the maxim, 'It is a good thing for a man to have nothing to do with women', is a difficult basis for sexual morality. It ensures that shame is a precondition of any expression of sexuality. It elevates the prestige of celibacy, and appeals to the immature fear of sexuality. Moreover such a notion of the 'good', strikingly at variance with the biological and social reality of man, inevitably condemns most human beings to lives of inconsistency, and in Paul's own teaching this notion of the 'good' is incoherent. He can give no consistent account of his own advocacy of celibacy and the virtues of married life. It is a far cry from the figure in the Gospels who, while not married, is certainly not isolated from women nor apparently averse to their company.

The inconsistency becomes plain when Paul gives his understanding of marriage. It is a prudential concession to avoid worse evils: 'because there is so much immorality, let each man have his own wife and each woman her own husband' (7.2). Its basis is one of exclusive possession, in which the sexual act is seen as one of mutual obligation: 'The husband must give the wife what is due to her, and the wife equally must give the husband his due . . . Do not deny yourselves to one another' (7.3, 5). Yet what at first appears as mutual exchange betrays a more oppressive dimension: 'The wife cannot claim her body as her own; it is her husband's. Equally, the husband cannot claim his body as his own; it is his wife's' (7.4). At first sight this seems a ringing declaration of sexual reciprocity and equality, but it reflects once again the capacity to confuse identity which lies at the heart of Paul's belief, and represses the truth that our bodies are our own. Moreover, by stressing the element of mutual obligation, he ignores the importance of emotional consent. Sexual activity thus becomes obligatory; only devotion to prayer justifies 'a temporary abstinence' (7.5); an exception which defines sexuality as contrary to and in competition with prayer. That there is something vindictive in the way in which Paul stresses obligation to the exclusion of delight in his teaching on marriage is suggested by the self-conscious caveat which he introduces at this point: 'All this I say by way of concession, not command. I should like you all to be as I am myself; but everyone has the gift God has granted him, one this gift and another that' (7.6, 7). The concession sounds magnanimous, but it smugly reminds Paul's readers of the apostle's superiority. His complacency is such that he fails to discern the implication of the conflict between what he would like and what God has given. If God had wanted more Pauls he would have created them; as this particular gift is in short supply, it would seem that one was enough. The sublime egoism of 'I should like you all to be as I am myself' prevents Paul from suspecting that perhaps he should be more like other people.

He then proceeds to give terse advice to those contemplating marriage and to those contemplating divorce. 'To the unmarried and to widows I say this: it is a good thing if they stay as I am myself; but if they cannot control themselves, they should marry. Better be married than burn with vain desire' (7.8, 9). Such liberality is illusory. Paul's own self-love is quite uncriticized, and asserted in such a way that any other policy is debased as a lack of self-control. Thus the freedom which Paul gives to his disciples to marry has to be bought at the cost of humiliation. That there might be other descriptions of their respective situations does not apparently occur to Paul. The cynical motto, 'better be married than burn with vain desire', might from a married man be a compassionate admission of human realism; on celibate lips it is condescending. 'To the married I give this ruling, which is not mine but the Lord's: a wife must not separate herself from her husband; if she does she must either remain unmarried or be reconciled to her husband; and the husband must not divorce his wife' (7.10, 11). Divorce is here ruled out on Jesus' specific authority, but in this context it adds a further vindictive twist to the obligations which Paul delights to impose on a condition which he himself has avoided. Moreover, it is not clear whose authority is invoked to prohibit second marriage after separation, for Jesus' teaching on divorce would seem to assume it as the consequence of divorce.

There then follows a lengthy section which defines the limitations of the new Christian freedom and which Paul frankly recognizes as his own: 'I say this, as my own word, not as the Lord's' (7.12). Once again there is a stress on possession as being the most appropriate model for marriage. 'For the heathen husband now belongs to God through his Christian wife, and the heathen wife through her Christian husband. Otherwise your children would not belong to God, whereas in fact they do' (7.14). To understand this stress on proprietary rights, it must be remembered that Paul belongs to a slave-owning society. It is no accident that in a passage on marriage he can easily include a digression on slavery: 'Were you a slave when you were called? Do not let that trouble you; but if a chance of liberty should come, take it. For the man who as a slave received the call of Christ is the Lord's freedman, and, equally, the free man who received the call is a slave in the service of Christ' (7.21–23). The appropriate time to examine Paul's attitude towards slavery will come when we examine the letter to Philemon. Here it will suffice to point out how deeply this social experience has informed his religious imagination. This theme has already appeared in this letter: 'For though everything belongs to you – Paul, Apollos, and Cephas, the world, life, and death, the present and the future, all of them belong to you – yet you belong to Christ, and Christ to God' (3.22, 23). On the one hand it makes models of ownership much more acceptable to him in interpreting personal relationships than they are to us. On the other hand it makes more intelligible the confusion of identity to which he so often resorts: it is the alienated consciousness of one human being owned by another.

In the first part of this passage Paul considers the position of a Christian married to an unbeliever, which puts a charitable stress on the attitude of the unbelieving partner. The unbelieving partner's attitude must be paramount in deciding whether such marriages are to continue, and this accommodation is only slightly tainted by the religious aggression with which the section concludes: 'Think of it: as a wife you may be your husband's salvation; as a husband you may be your wife's salvation' (7.16). The bestowal of salvation is difficult to distinguish from agreement with Paul. The apostle then draws the general conclusion from this that Christian freedom is indifferent to circumstances, and so should not be used as an excuse to change them, be they marriage, the status of Jew or

Gentile, of master or slave. It is an argument of extreme practical conservatism which has marked the church's stance through most of its history until modern times. Significantly, Paul himself abandons the language of freedom and deliverance: 'What matters is to keep God's commandments' (7.19). It is a surprising *volte face* from the author who has castigated the Law. It strengthens the impression that Paul found it easier to proclaim freedom than to live with its implications.

After this excursus, Paul returns to the subject of celibacy. He again recognizes that the teaching is his own, rather than Jesus', but he stresses his divine mandate: 'I give my judgment as one who by God's mercy is fit to be trusted' (7.25). He bases his advocacy of celibacy on a combination of anxiety about the end of the world and paternalist prudence. The anxiety is underlined: 'A time of stress like the present' (7.26); 'The time we live in will not last long' (7.29); 'The whole frame of this world is passing away' (7.31). In such circumstances the single life is only prudent, and Paul stresses his concern to save his readers from themselves: 'It is best for man to be as he is' (7.26); 'Those who marry will have pain and grief in this bodily life, and my aim is to spare you' (7.28); 'I want you to be free from anxious care' (7.32). The detachment which he counsels might be described as a morality of alienation: 'Married men should be as if they had no wives; mourners should be as if they had nothing to grieve them, the joyful as if they did not rejoice; buyers must not count on keeping what they buy, nor those who use the world's wealth on using it to the full' (7.30, 31). Christian history has shown how easily this can become a recipe for irresponsibility and a rationale for moral inconsistency. At first Paul is at pains to absolve the married from blame: 'If, however, you do marry, there is nothing wrong in it; and if a virgin marries, she has done nothing wrong' (7.28). Ultimately he cannot, however, resist a negative view of marriage, which is difficult to reconcile with his more conciliatory teaching and probably more truthfully expresses his mind, providing as it does a rationale for his own position: 'The unmarried man cares for the Lord's business; his aim is to please the Lord. But the married man cares for worldly things; his aim is to please his wife; and he has a divided mind. The unmarried or celibate woman cares for the Lord's business; her aim is to be dedicated to him in body as in spirit; but the married woman cares for worldly things; her aim is to please her husband' (7.32–34). This aggressive view of marriage as distraction from God makes Paul aware that he may have gone too far, and so he adds a mitigating gloss: 'In saying this I have no wish to keep you on a tight rein. I am thinking simply of your own good, of what is seemly, and of your freedom to wait upon the Lord without distraction'

(7.35): a strange combination of paternalist prudence, respect for social convention, and eschatological concentration.

Paul then gives a special ruling on a man's conduct towards his fiancée or ward (the Greek is ambiguous). The crucial equivocation in his whole position re-emerges in his final advice: 'He who marries his partner does well, and he who does not will do better' (7.38). The contrast between 'well' and 'better' does not relate to different educational levels reflecting individual circumstances; it indicates different levels of absolute achievement. The attitude towards marriage is grudging: 'There is nothing wrong in it; let them marry' (7.36). The attitude towards celibacy is of uncritical enthusiasm. In such circumstances the logic of Paul's position and the unacknowledged implication of his teaching is to disparage marriage. Paul concludes this section with a little advice to widows. Their freedom to marry is restricted to the Christian community: here we have an early instance of the adoption by the new Christian community of one of the most disruptive and legalistic of Jewish attitudes. It reveals the same alienation and antagonism towards the external community which has already been observed in Paul's understanding of the gospel. Even here Paul cannot resist a final affirmation of his own position: 'But she is better off as she is; that is my opinion, and I believe that I too have the Spirit' (7.40). Thus the prestige of celibacy and the possession of the Spirit are mutually supportive. Paul here does not resort to the example of Jesus, but to his own charismatic identity.

(ii) Observance of the food laws

If the passage on sexual morality shows the apostle at his least attractive, little influenced by the gospel of freedom which he preached, his treatment of the food laws and the limits of Christian freedom presents him in a more reassuring light. It is only sad that he should be most impressive in the area of least concern to his modern readers. In relation to the food laws Paul carefully states the dilemma of the freedom he proclaimed and indicates a possible solution: '"We are free to do anything," you say. Yes, but is everything good for us? "We are free to do anything," but does everything help the building of the community? Each of you must regard, not his own interests, but the other man's' (10.23, 24). This suggests a solution to the limitations of freedom based in mutual respect rather than in the exercise of domineering authority, and while Paul is not perhaps entirely successful in the way he develops the idea, he does achieve considerable consistency. He prefaces his teaching by contrasting knowledge and love: 'Of course we all "have knowledge", as you say. This "knowledge" breeds conceit; it is love that builds' (8.1). If Paul uses this distinction to disarm his critics, there is also a genuine concern to protect the unenlightened. As Paul forcefully expresses it later in the passage: 'This "knowledge" of yours is utter disaster to the weak, the brother for whom Christ died' (8.11). By stressing love with its demand for mutual attention, Paul recognizes the destructive and divisive impact which is often made by those who 'know' that they are right.

Paul then considers how the superstition of others should be treated. As the false gods to whom food has allegedly been consecrated have no real existence, it might be assumed that Christians are free to eat it. But not everybody knows that the false gods do not exist, and they feel shame in eating such food: 'There are some who have been so accustomed to idolatry that even now they eat this food with a sense of its heathen consecration, and their conscience, being weak, is polluted by the eating' (8.7). Paul emphasizes that food is religiously neutral: 'Certainly food will not bring us into God's presence; if we do not eat, we are none the worse, and if we eat, we are none the better' (8.8). The limitations on Christian freedom come not from any intrinsic quality in such food, but from responsibility to the sensitivity of others: 'Be careful that this liberty of yours does not become a pitfall for the weak' (8.9). Paul then reinforces his point, or perhaps diminishes it, by considerations of public relations: 'If a weak character sees you sitting down to a meal in a heathen temple – you, who "have knowledge" – will not his conscience be emboldened to eat food consecrated to the heathen deity?' (8.10). By referring to the belief that Christ died for all men, Paul is able to identify offence to the brethren with offence to Christ: 'In thus sinning against your brothers and wounding their conscience, you sin against Christ' (8.12). It is not entirely clear in this passage in what 'wounding the conscience' consists. The disapproving way in which Paul has just referred to 'emboldening the conscience to eat food consecrated to the heathen diety' might seem to justify an interpretation of wounding as misleading the conscience of the weak. But the context gives greater probability to the interpretation of the phrase as 'giving offence'. While such a view is very different from the individualist self-righteousness which has often marked subsequent Christianity, it can easily be distorted into an argument for conformity. 'Don't weaken other people's faith' has a tendency to become 'don't rock the boat', a sentiment delivered by those whose position makes them apprehensive for the security of their own authority and status. Paul concludes in his customary manner by directing the attention of his readers towards himself: 'If food be the downfall of my brother, I will never eat meat any more, for I will not be the cause of my brother's downfall' (8.13). This prepares for a long digression on the example of Paul's restraint and charity in the use of his freedom: an example which explicitly reinforces his message and implicitly reinforces his status.

Indeed it is precisely by reminding the reader of his status that Paul begins: 'Am I not a free man? Am I not an apostle? Did I not see Jesus our Lord? Are not you my own handiwork, in the Lord? If others do not accept me as an apostle, you at least are bound to do so, for you are yourselves the very seal of my apostolate, in the Lord' (9.1, 2). Paul here proclaims his freedom in order to emphasize the gratuitous nature of his restraint. In the same way he emphasizes his status as an apostle, because that stresses both his example and his charitable condescension. He legitimizes his authority in two ways. First, he appeals to his vision of the risen Christ: as will be suggested later, the connection between the authority of the apostle and the witness to the resurrection leads Paul to place a peculiar emphasis on the resurrection. Secondly, he repeats the argument from his role as founding father of the community of Corinthian Christians: their very Christian identity is dependent on the authenticity of his authority.

Thus fortified, Paul draws their attention to his own ascetic restraint in celibacy and self-support. The prestige of such behaviour comes primarily from its gratuitous nature: 'Have I no right to eat and drink? Have I no right to take a Christian wife about with me . . .? Are Barnabas and I alone bound to work for our living?' (9.4, 5, 6). He uses various common-sense analogies, which all underline the astonishing generosity of his attitude: 'Did you ever hear of a man serving in the army at his own expense? or planting a vineyard without eating the fruit of it? or tending a flock without using its milk?' (9.7, 8). Surprisingly he does not scruple to use the Law to strengthen his case: 'In the Law of Moses we read, "You shall not muzzle a threshing ox." Do you suppose God's concern is with oxen? Or is the reference clearly to ourselves? Of course it refers to us, in the sense that the ploughman should plough and the thresher thresh in the hope of getting some of the produce' (9.9, 10). Both the analogies he uses and the law that he cites reveal Paul's ambivalence towards his apostolic activity: service in the army, labour on the land – the overtones of necessity and compulsion are strong. He then repeats a point he made to the Galatians, where the alleged primacy of the spiritual over the material is used to sanction the exploitation of the producers by the non-productive: 'If we have sown a spiritual crop for you, is it too much to expect from you a material harvest?' (9.11). Paul then prepares for an appeal to the teaching of Jesus, by pointing to its supposed anticipation in the Law: 'You know (do you not?) that those who perform the temple service eat the temple offerings, and those who wait upon the altar claim their share of the sacrifice. In the same way the Lord gave instructions that those who preach the Gospel should earn their living by the Gospel' (9.13, 14). Although the end of the letter to the Galatians sees some rehabilitation of the Law, in terms of 'the Law of Christ', it is astonishing to see Paul apparently legitimizing a contentious part of Jesus' teaching by reference to its continuity with the Mosaic Law.

The whole elaboration of arguments to justify the payment of the Christian leaders is only a foil to Paul's own disinterestedness: 'But I have never taken advantage of any such right, nor do I intend to claim it in this letter. I had rather die! No one shall make my boast an empty boast' (9.15). The vehemence of the disclaimer sits uneasily with the admission of financial dependence in the letter to the Philippians, but it is not so much its questionable honesty as its distancing self-righteousness which is most worrying. In the letter to the Galatians Paul contrasts his own asceticism with the relative domesticity and comfort of the other Christian leaders; here there is a disparaging contrast between his own celibacy and 'the rest of the apostles and the Lord's brothers, and Cephas' (9.5), but more striking is the cavalier attitude towards Jesus' own teaching. (Paul is apparently quite happy to upstage not only the other apostles, but Jesus himself.) Paul then expresses the other side of his ambivalence towards his position: having talked of his role in terms of military service and agricultural labour, he now admits much more positive attitudes: 'Even if I preach the Gospel, I can claim no credit for it; I cannot help myself; it would be misery to me not to preach . . . Then what is my pay? The satisfaction of preaching the Gospel without expense to anyone; in other words, of waiving the rights which my preaching gives me' (9.16, 18). Like many others who exercise power, Paul distracts the attention of those whose freedom he has subverted by speaking of his own burdens, and by a mixture of self-pity and self-righteousness he seeks the gratitude of those he oppresses: the one satisfaction which he will not admit to is the satisfaction of wielding power. Verse 17 is obscure: if translated, 'If I do it willingly I am earning my pay; if I did it unwillingly I should still have a trust laid upon me', it stresses the compulsion in Paul's position and strengthens the element of self-pity. The translation, 'If I did it of my own choice, I should be earning my pay; but since I do it apart from my own choice, I am simply discharging a trust', emphasizes the gratuitous nature of Paul's activity, and seems designed to answer the suspicion that Paul is self-supporting because he is self-appointed.

Once Paul has established the prestige of his position, he describes the example of sensitivity and adaptability in his own observance of the Law. He cannot resist drawing attention to the tactics by which he gains first an audience and ultimately some converts: 'I am a free man and own no master; but I have made myself every man's servant, to win over as many as possible . . . I have become everything in turn to men of every sort, so that in one way or another I may save some' (9.19, 22). Here Paul is daring to confess to the Corinthians the very means by which he established his own authority over them. It is not entirely clear whether Paul simply observed the Law when he was among Jews, but not when he was among Gentiles, or whether he does not demand observance of the Law from Gentiles, but in either case the technique of manipulation is the same. The language of salvation acts as an effective disguise. Its emphasis on the benefit which Paul is conferring distracts attention from the obedience which he is demanding and for which he seeks consent. Something of this is expressed in the celebration of self-discipline and purposiveness in which he both reminds the Corinthians of their duty and points to himself as an exemplar. Paul has apparently no squeamishness about using the aggressive values of the stadium to make his point; he thus baptizes both the desire to win and the commitment to training. The only distinction he admits is between 'the fading wreath' of the athlete (9.25) and the never-fading wreath of the Christian. The fact that he is not embarrassed by the competitiveness and divisiveness of such imagery again betrays the alienation implicit in his understanding of the gospel. By a final twist he turns the narcissistic physical training of the athlete into a vehicle for his own distrust and repudiation of the body: 'I bruise my own body and make it know its master, for fear that after preaching to others I should find myself rejected' (9.27). Once again the fragility of the apostle's status is a reminder to the disciples that they can take nothing for granted. Even the anxiety of the stadium finds a Christian parallel.

Paul now turns away from himself and uses the Jewish scriptures to express the continuing need for limits to the Christians' use of their freedom. Thus according to Paul the gospel which seemed to give men freedom from the Law ends by resorting to the Law to sanction its prohibitions. The repressive and threatening use of Old Testament precedent is stark: having reminded them that all their ancestors had shared in the freedom of the Exodus, he continues: 'Yet, most of them were not accepted by God, for the desert was strewn with their corpses. These events happened as symbols to warn us not to set our desires on evil things, as they did. Do not be idolaters, like some of them; as Scripture has it, "the people sat down to feast and rose up to revel". Let us not commit fornication, as some of them did – and twenty-three thousand died in one day. Let us not put the power of the Lord to the test, as some of them did – and were destroyed by serpents. Do not grumble against God, as some of them did – and were destroyed by the Destroyer. All these things that happened to them were symbolic, and were recorded for our benefit as a warning' (10.5–11). It is difficult to share Paul's enthusiasm for the vindictiveness of the divine hand, but such menacing language was well calculated to arouse the anxiety of the faithful. He deliberately draws an analogy between the Christian participants in the sacraments and the ancient Israelites who perished in the wilderness: 'They all ate the same supernatural food, and all drank the same supernatural drink' (10.3, 4). There is no word here of any discontinuity between Law and Gospel. The same anxiety is apparently only more appropriate: 'For upon us the fulfilment of the ages has come. If you feel sure that you are standing firm, beware! You may fall' (10.12). Lest such words should foster any subversive self-reliance, Paul immediately counters them by reminding the Corinthians that their confidence is not based on any experience of theirs, for 'so far you have faced no trial beyond what man can bear'. Their strength rests solely on the faithfulness and mercy of God: 'God keeps faith, and he will not allow you to be tested above your powers, but when the test comes he will at the same time provide a way out, by enabling you to sustain it' (10.13).

This lengthy preamble on Paul's example and the precedent of the Jewish scriptures prepares for his actual rulings on the food laws. First, he makes it clear that the Christian identity is incompatible with participation in pagan polytheism. Paul surprisingly argues from the Corinthians' experience of participation in the eucharist that bread and wine, i.e. food, can convey a particular religious identity. We become what we eat, or in Paul's words, 'Because there is one loaf, we, many as we are, are one body; for it is one loaf of which we all partake' (10.17). The same participation is conferred by sharing in the Jewish sacrifices: 'Are not those who partake in the sacrificial meal sharers in the altar?' (10.18). Now it might be thought that if the gods of polytheism do not exist, no harm can be done by sharing in their worship: indeed the Corinthians may have used such an argument to justify their practice. Paul rules this out by identifying, on the basis of Scripture, idols with demons. The gods of the heathen may not exist, but demons in Paul's mind certainly do, and their existence justifies a firm line in relation to food sacrificed to them: 'I will not have you become partners with demons. You cannot drink the cup of the Lord and the cup of demons. You cannot partake of the Lord's table and the table of demons' (10.20, 21). Thus the dualism of Paul's theology is given practical expression in divisive social behaviour. The teaching is consummated by an appeal to Jesus as Lord: 'Can we defy the Lord? Are we stronger than he?' (10.22). The use of a biblical quotation takes the passage from the second person plural to the first person plural. This gives an impression of modesty, but behind the inclusive 'we' there lies an imperative 'you'. Once again, in asserting his own authority, Paul stresses the Lordship of Jesus.

Much in Paul's response to the food question has been self-regarding, authoritarian and manipulative, but this should not conceal either the radical nature of his teaching or the sophisticated way in which he permits the conscience of others to limit the freedom of the Christian. His abrogation of the food laws gives complete freedom to eat any secular food: 'You may eat anything sold in the meat-market without raising questions of conscience; for the earth is the Lord's and everything in it' (10.25, 26). The repudiation of the Jewish food laws is total, and the respect for the physical world one which might well have mitigated Paul's distrust of matter and the body. Because we take the principle which it enunciates so much for granted, it is easy to underestimate the boldness of such a stance for a first-century Jew, and to forget its social implications. The startling freedom and courage of his attitude serves to create new possibilities of human relationship, for Paul puts no barrier to Christians eating with pagans. It is not the Christian's task aggressively to raise issues of principle: 'If an unbeliever invites you to a meal and you care to go, eat whatever is put before you, without raising questions of conscience' (10.27). Again the absence of any sense of taboo gives the Christian a novel freedom. Only if tested by a question or statement which draws attention to the controversial nature of the food does the Christian have to refuse it. As earlier, Paul's thought is not entirely clear: 'But if somebody says to you, "This food has been offered in sacrifice", then, out of consideration for him, and for conscience' sake, do not eat it – not your conscience, I mean, but the other man's' (10.28, 29). At first it seems that Paul's concern is with what the modern evangelical might in similar circumstances term 'witnessing' – not losing the opportunity to instruct the conscience of the unbeliever; in that case the emphasis on consideration to the other person's conscience is only another form of condescension. But the whole tenor of the passage suggests a quite different and much more interesting reading.

What seems to worry Paul is not that the other person might remain unenlightened, but that he might be shocked. Thus he concludes the passage: 'Give no offence to Jews, or Greeks, or to the church of God' (10.32). The moral sensitivity of other people would seem here to be a constraint on the Christian's freedom. Paul is trying to avoid a situation where freedom is aggressively asserted without regard to the response of other people. Paul uses an imaginary dialogue to illustrate his thought: ' "What?" you say, "is my freedom to be called in question by another man's conscience? If I partake with thankfulness, why am I blamed for eating food over which I have said grace?" Well, whether you eat or drink, or whatever you are doing, do all for the honour of God' (10.29–31). This honour of God is immediately translated as not giving offence to others. The prayer of thanksgiving does not simply justify aggressive behaviour. honouring God is thus intimately linked to loving others and listening to them, a feature not always prominent in Christian practice. The respect for the other person is far removed from the dogmatism which has so often marked Christian attitudes; it is only sad that once again Paul has to underline the tactical expediency of his charity and to reinforce his authority by his own recognition of Christ's. 'For my part I always try to meet everyone half-way, regarding not my own good but the good of the many, so that they may be saved. Follow my example as I follow Christ's' (10.33). The mediation of the apostle only emphasizes the subordination implicit in the infant hierarchy: the disciple, the apostle, Jesus, God. Hierarchy with a strong emphasis on non-reciprocal relations which demand obedience is not some invention of the Constantinian church; it is present in this early part of the New Testament.

(iii) The public deportment of women

Paul's directions for the conduct of Christian meetings deal with the place of women and the expression of unity. It is not clear whether Paul is replying to queries or making his own unprompted criticism, but the latter sounds more likely. It may be that complaints from dissidents in the Christian community at Corinth had reached his ears having by-passed local leaders, for no mention is made of them, nor is there any suggestion that Paul is trying to strengthen their hand. The praise of their careful regard for Paul's authority and teaching with which the passage begins is an oblique rebuke, concerning their practice in the matters on which he then writes. 'I commend you for always keeping me in mind, and maintaining the tradition I handed on to you. But I wish you to understand . . .' (11.2). As so often, Paul's encouraging words only serve to underline an implicit censure, for that is the force of the 'but'.

Paul's preoccupation with the covering of women's heads during Christian meetings should not be hastily dismissed, for it is very important in understanding him. This is because he links the issue of the covering of women's heads with the heart of his theology: 'While every man has Christ for his Head, woman's head is man, as Christ's head is God' (11.3). Paul's subordinationist christology legitimates a hierarchy which compensates men for their submission to Christ by sanctioning their dominance over women. Paul correctly realizes that anything which infringes that hierarchy is not simply re-ordering the relations between men and women;

it is undermining the whole notion of hierarchy on which his theology is based, and in which his own apostolate is grounded. In Paul's mind this is combined with very strong feelings about the significance of hair, which now as then plays a major role in projecting the person's visual image, and is therefore a most important means of non-verbal communication. Paul's attitudes are conflicting. On the one hand he is inclined to attribute to the hair of men and of women a quite different significance. Following a line of thought found in the Old Testament which equates man's hair with glory, he sees in this something of the divine image: 'A man has no need to cover his head, because man is the image of God, and the mirror of his glory, whereas woman reflects the glory of man' (11.7). It sounds as if Paul would have preferred women to be without hair to make this distinction plain. However, as biology is refractory and women do have hair, lest it be thought that they have a glory of their own which is not beholden to men, Paul understands the hair of women, not primarily as glory, but as covering. Yet when he comes to denounce long hair in men, he speaks of 'flowing locks' being a 'woman's glory' (11.14). The difficulty he has in formulating a coherent attitude suggests that we are here dealing with deeply ingrained, if conflicting, social prejudices.

The nearest we have to a key to Paul's attitude is to be found in the following chapter: 'To our unseemly parts is given a more than ordinary seemliness, whereas our seemly parts need no adorning' (12.23). For Paul, women's hair seems to have pubic associations; its function is to cover shame. The very feeling of disgrace a shaven woman might feel is (11.5, 6) used as an argument to reinforce this. Why does a woman feel ashamed if her hair is cut off unless it is hiding something? Moreover Genesis 6, which tells how the sons of the gods lusted after the daughters of men and produced an offspring of giants, is a cautionary tale which reinforces this attitude (11.10). Paul, however, does not seem to be entirely easy with his own explanations. On the one hand he appeals to the Genesis account of the creation of woman as justifying male dominance (11.8, 9), but he then proceeds to qualify it by reminding men of present biological facts (11.12). Presumably this inversion of Paradise is the result of the Fall. Moreover, while he starts from a divine hierarchy which justifies male dominance, he cautiously qualifies it by referring to Christian mutuality: 'In Christ's fellowship woman is as essential to man as man to woman' (11.11). It may be that what was really worrying Paul was not simply that women did not have their heads decently covered, but that they were also taking a vocal part in worship. In this passage Paul introduces the notion that women might pray in public (11.4, 5), in literary parallelism with appropriate male behaviour, and he does not repudiate such behaviour directly but lets

it pass without comment. In the light of the subsequent strict prohibition on such activities (14.34, 35), that may only represent a description of the situation in the Corinthian church, not an acceptance of it.
Instead, the criticism of bare-headed women may serve to discredit those
whom he will proceed to silence. Another reason why Paul responds so
strongly to the social deviancy of women with uncovered heads in
public is that he is facing the consequences of his own teaching. Once
again, Paul shows a deep ambivalence towards the freedom which he
generously proclaims, but of which he is frightened in others. The
Corinthian women seem to have made the mistake of taking him at his
word.

In practice, the elements of liberty and mutuality in Paul's preaching are
here undermined by an appeal to social conformity and a curious use of
natural law. Paul appeals directly to the prejudices of his readers to
discredit deviant behaviour: 'Judge, for yourselves; is it fitting for a
woman to pray to God bare-headed?' (11.13). Paul forgets that such an
appeal to his fellow Jews would never have given him the freedom to eat
with Gentiles. The appeal to natural law, as so often with such appeals,
either proves nothing or it proves too much: 'Does not Nature herself
teach you that while flowing locks disgrace a man, they are a woman's
glory? For her locks were given for covering' (11.14, 15). Here Paul seems
to be exploiting a Gentile attitude to long hair in men: there also seems to
be an implication that the woman's hair is to be reserved for her husband
alone. The argument seems to be that nature endowed women with long
hair for a covering, and that this needs to be reinforced with a veil; but
either it does cover, in which case no further reinforcement is necessary, or
it is not such covering. Paul is probably not entirely unaware of the
weakness of his position, and so he ends further debate by a complacent
description of Christian practice: 'If you insist on arguing, let me tell you,
there is no such custom among us, or in any of the congregations of God's
people' (11.16). It would seem that the amount of practical diversity that
the Pauline church could tolerate was small.

(iv) The conduct of Christian meetings

Having dealt with the deportment of women at Christian meetings, Paul
then turns to the way in which such meetings should be a visible expression
of unity. He begins by asserting his authority in sweeping condemnation of
their actual practice: 'In giving you these injunctions I must mention a
practice which I cannot commend: your meetings tend to do more harm
than good' (11.17). Paul seems to be taking up a complaint which one of
the Corinthians has brought to him: 'To begin with, I am told that when

you meet as a congregation you fall into sharply divided groups; and I believe there is some truth in it' (11.18). Paul does not indicate that the source of his information is the local leadership, and it may be that he is siding with a local critic. He charges the Corinthian Christians with divisiveness (11.18), gluttony (11.20) and insensitivity to the poor (11.21, 22) in their meetings. In a curious aside he implies that the home is the place for gluttony and drunkenness – 'Have you no homes of your own to eat and drink in?' (11.22). By contrast, the meeting should express a purity and solidarity which can only be preserved by vigilance. The same desire to create a separate, homogeneous and distinct community demands constant internal suspicion, which Paul himself encourages: 'Dissensions are necessary if only to show which of your members are sound' (11.19).

Paul then proceeds to invoke the historical tradition of the Lord's supper. He asserts that this has come to him unmediated 'from the Lord himself' (11.23). It is not immediately clear why Paul rehearses the tradition. In itself it says nothing about the precise charges of division, disorder and neglect of the poor with which he taxes his readers. All, however, becomes plain in the sequel, which introduces the concept of unworthy participation and thus prepares for the verdict of divine retribution. 'It follows that anyone who eats the bread or drinks the cup of the Lord unworthily will be guilty of desecrating the body and blood of the Lord' (11.27). The individual is exhorted to self-criticism (11.28, 30): 'A man must test himself', but Paul does not neglect to inform such criticism by pointing to the sanction of divine punishment: 'For he who eats and drinks eats and drinks judgment on himself if he does not discern the Body. That is why many of you are feeble and sick, and a number have died' (11.29, 30). Illness in their community is therefore a sign of divine judgment, which Paul uses to sanction his own condemnation of their conduct. He quickly overrules any murmuring at the severity of such measures by interpreting them as a sign of God's mercy. 'When, however, we do fall under the Lord's judgment, he is disciplining us, to save us from being condemned with the rest of the world' (11.32). Thus the reminder of the far worse fate which awaits the rest of mankind reconciles the Corinthians to their own sufferings. Once again their alienation from others serves only to increase their bondage to the authority which bestows on them their privileged status. Paul summarizes his teaching: mutual attention is to reign at the meal, urgent hunger is to be satisfied at home (11.33, 34). 'The other matters I will arrange when I come.' The coming of the apostle, awaited and decisive, mirrors the hopes of the second coming of Christ.

(v) The discipline of the Spirit

It has been argued that in this letter Paul is attempting to fix limits to the subversive gospel of freedom which he preached. His Corinthian followers seem to have responded with a joy that could easily get out of hand and challenge the God-given authority of the apostle himself. So throughout the letter Paul endeavours to discipline the freedom he has proclaimed, and in so doing to reassert his continuing control. Sexual license, the flouting of the food laws, disorderly meetings, all give him opportunities to order and set right, but in themselves they do not directly challenge his position. The outpouring of the Spirit is, however, a threat to his authority which is both embarrassing and fundamental. Because his own authority is charismatic rather than traditional, based on immediate revelation rather than historical knowledge of Jesus, he cannot afford to disown the charismatic phenomenon entirely. If, however, he fails to discipline it, his own authority over the Corinthian community is at an end, and the local charismatic leaders will gain an autonomy separate from Paul in much the same way that he achieved independence from the Jerusalem leaders. The political problem was, therefore, extremely delicate: how to restrict their autonomy without underminding his own. Paul's solution to this dilemma shows the apostle at his most brilliant and adroit.

He begins by making it plain to his readers that about the gifts of the Spirit they are ignorant, while he can speak on a basis of knowledge and experience (12.1). If they are so minded to challenge that assumption, he quickly reminds them of their recent condition: 'You know how, in the days when you were still pagan, you were swept off to those dumb heathen gods, however you happened to be led' (12.2). Naturally those who have so lately been contaminated by demonic idol worship must be forewarned against recurrences. Regression to their previous state can easily occur. 'For this reason I must impress on you that no one who says "A curse on Jesus!" can be speaking under the influence of the Spirit of God' (12.3). (Perhaps it was not Jesus, but Paul, who was being thus repudiated.) Such a reminder serves to enhance the apostle's superiority by pointing to their precarious condition and suggesting that their ecstasy, unlike Paul's, might easily become the vehicle of hostile powers. The only sure test which authenticates the Holy Spirit is the acknowledgment of Jesus' authority (12.3), for the man who says 'Jesus is Lord' must recognize the authority of his apostle. 'Jesus is Lord' in this context is not primarily a piece of evidence for the development of christology: it has a quite clear reference to Paul's own status, as he was at pains to establish in the first four chapters of the letter.

Paul then proceeds to use the analogy of the body to reconcile the unity of the Spirit with the diversity of gifts. He introduces the analogy to encourage mutual respect and cooperation: 'All these gifts are the work of one and the same Spirit, distributing them separately to each individual at will' (12.11). In this way Paul reconciles the rival sources of prestige and power in the early church – wisdom, miraculous power, effective oratory, healing, prophecy, the discernment of spirits and ecstasy. The appropriateness of the body analogy is grounded by Paul in baptism: 'For Christ is like a single body with its many limbs and organs, which many as they are, together make up one body. For indeed we were all brought into one body by baptism, in the one Spirit' (12.12, 13). Here the Spirit seems to be conceived as the consciousness or personality of Christ which unifies the body, but it also displaces the believer's identity. For in Paul's thought, as in others who have resorted to corporate social models, the individual consciousness is suppressed. The individual's special social contribution is recognized, but at the cost of surrendering his self-awareness. In Paul's words: 'The eye cannot say to the hand, "I do not need you"; nor the head to the feet, "I do not need you"' (12.21). Precisely: they cannot 'say' – they have no self-consciousness – so the use of the privileged analogy of the body of Christ deprives its members of identity, and this is a heavy price to pay for the eloquent exposition of mutual dependence with which it is associated. Furthermore, although the analogy is grounded in sacramental imagery, it is developed by a vigorous appeal to natural theology which makes criticism of the Christian organization impious: 'If the body were all eye, how could it hear? If the body were all ear, how could it smell? But, in fact, God appointed each limb and organ to its own place in the body, as he chose' (12.17, 18). The language of divine appointment and choice of the body in creation is thus subtly applied to the organization of the church, which is thereby sanctified. The same legitimation is taking place when Paul says that 'God has combined the various parts of the body, giving special honour to the humbler parts, so that there might be no sense of division in the body' (12.24, 25). Once the analogy of the body has been justified on the basis of baptism, Paul can use it as a blueprint for the new community which has behind it the divine intention of the creator. Against such an author it is difficult to argue.

Throughout Paul's initial exposition of the body of Christ, the stress is on the mutual dependence of the varied members, but towards the end, mutuality is quietly replaced by hierarchy. 'You are Christ's body, and each of you a limb or organ of it' (12.27). The privilege is striking, but as so often it prepares for control. The divine appointment, which earlier had sanctioned mutuality (12.18, 24), is now represented as the origin of the hierarchy in the new society. 'Within our community God has appointed, in the first place apostles, in the second place prophets, thirdly teachers;

then miracle-workers, then those who have gifts of healing, or ability to help others or power to guide them, or the gift of ecstatic utterance of various kinds' (12.28). The grading is careful, and the voice of ecstasy comes last, as Paul's own status comes first. Moreover, the emphasis on diversity of gifts, which at first stressed the value of each person's contribution, is now used to disarm critics by reminding them of their place: 'Are all apostles? all prophets? all teachers? Do all work miracles? Have all gifts of healing? Do all speak in tongues of ecstasy? Can all interpret them? (12.29, 30). Eventually he deserts the analogy of the body completely – the gifts cease to be mutually dependent, and are now graded and a proper object of effort: 'The higher gifts are those you should aim at. And now I will show you the best way of all' (12.31). Thus the introduction to the famous passage on love makes it clear that it is designed as a description of the highest gift, which crowns and sanctifies the social and religious hierarchy by which Paul seeks to place and discipline the charismatic challenge.

Paul's polemical art is here at its highest, and he achieves his most powerful effects by the skilful device of the shifting subject. He begins by speaking with powerful immediacy in his own person. He conditionally ascribes to himself every competing gift, and then modestly disparages each one by pointing to its total dependence on love: 'I may speak in tongues of men or of angels, but if I am without love, I am a sounding gong or a clanging cymbal. I may have the gift of prophecy, and know every hidden truth; I may have faith strong enough to move mountains; but if I have no love, I am nothing. I may dole out all I possess or even give my body to be burnt, but if I have no love, I am none the better' (13.1–3). Paul thus succeeds in disarming all his critics by himself relativizing every source of prestige. Only later does one notice that the one gift which has not been so treated is that to which he lays claim – the apostolate.

The subject now changes. Paul no longer speaks directly in the first person, but describes personified love. He dare not say, 'I am patient, I am kind and envy no one. I am never boastful, conceited, or rude.' Instead, he makes love the subject of this idealized description, and in the name of love, rather than in his own name, disposes of his gnostic and charismatic critics: 'Love will never come to an end. Are there prophets? their work will be over. Are there tongues of ecstasy? they will cease. Is there knowledge? it will vanish away: for our knowledge and our prophecy alike are partial, and the partial vanishes when wholeness comes' (13.8, 9). The mantle of personified love enables Paul to say everything he needs to say to his critics without either exposing himself or taking direct responsibility. The moment this has been done, he reverts to speaking in his own person, as he places love as the goal of man's maturity: 'When I was a child, my speech, my outlook, and my thoughts were all childish. When I grew up, I had finished with childish things' (13.10, 11). This very different view of childhood from that found in the Gospels (cf. 14.20) is difficult to contradict because of its confessional first person singular. But the implication is clear, that Paul's gnostic and charismatic critics are immature and childish. In Paul's view, knowledge cannot in this life transcend its own limitations, of which the distance between reflection and encounter is a symbol (13.12). The believer is deftly reminded of the non-reciprocal nature of divine knowledge before the primacy of love is roundly declared. Faith and hope are suddenly introduced with little preparation. Unlike knowledge and prophecy, they last for ever, but the reference to them here only serves to emphasize the pre-eminence of love.

Having crowned his hierarchy, Paul proceeds to expound its lower levels. Paul does not deny ecstatic utterance, but he emphasizes its privacy (14.2, 4, 5). By contrast prophecy, is social, it builds up the community (14.3, 4, 5). Paul reinforces this by a personal illustration: 'Suppose, my friends, that when I come to you I use ecstatic language: what good shall I do you, unless what I say contains something by way of revelation or enlightenment or prophecy or instruction?' (14.6). This subordination of ecstatic utterance to prophecy is then followed by further criticism of its lack of structure and meaning. Ecstasy is compared unfavourably to the order and clarity of music (14.7, 8); Paul insists on the importance of communication and meaning: 'If your ecstatic utterance yields no precise meaning, how can anyone tell what you are saying?' (14.9). He even flirts with the accusation of nonsense: 'If I do not know the meaning of the sound the speaker makes, his words will be gibberish to me, and mine to him' (14.11). Once again ecstasy is subordinated to social edification (14.12), an emphasis which the primacy of love has sanctioned.

For all the disparagement of wisdom earlier in the letter, Paul here places a surprising stress on the importance of rationality. The ecstatic is not so much silenced as instructed to pray differently. 'The man who falls into ecstatic utterance should pray for the ability to interpret' (14.13). Understanding and intelligence are commended (14.14, 15, 16). Paul makes his own criticism palatable by asserting his own ecstatic pre-eminence: 'Thank God, I am more gifted in ecstatic utterance than any of you' (14.18). As Paul here rehabilitates intelligence, he once again reveals his ambivalence towards public relations. On the basis of Old Testament scripture, he argues that ecstatic utterance is a sign of offence to unbelievers, while prophecy builds up believers and is therefore superior (14.21, 22). Yet it is precisely to the response of the uninstructed and the unbelievers that he then appeals to discredit ecstasy and vindicate prophecy (14.23, 25). The hierarchical ordering of gifts is summarized by the careful ordering of the meetings for worship. The variety is acknowledged, but 'all of these must aim at one thing: to build up the church' (14.26). Ecstatic utterance is limited to two or three, who must speak one at a time, and only if there is an interpreter present (14.27, 28). Prophets must also wait their turn before speaking to contribute their revelation (14.30). The strong emphasis on order (14.33) leads naturally to the silencing of women. Conformity to Christian practice and observance of the Law alike (14.34) demand their public silence. Curiosity can be satisfied by their husbands at home. 'It is a shocking thing that a woman should address the congregation' (14.35). Such flagrant disorder is only to be expected among a community which tolerates women appearing in public uncovered (cf. 9.5), but it is a duty of the apostle to bring them back to a proper sense of shame. We arrive at last at the bottom of the Pauline hierarchy: silent and obedient women.

Paul's response to charismatic competition has now run its full course. He first gained the consent and sympathy of his readers by acknowledging the variety and mutual dependence of the Spirit's gifts. Developing their sense of being the body of Christ, he derived divine sanction first for reciprocity between the members, then for an order and hierarchy among them. Love is placed at the summit, in a way which disparages gnostic and charismatic claims and makes it possible to assess other gifts by their usefulness in building up the community. Ecstasy is thus subordinated to prophecy, and women, who are usually most prone to ecstatic utterance, are silenced in the name of decency and order. Paul can now safely recall the Corinthians to the sovereignty of his own authority. With sarcasm he reminds them of their dependence on himself, and puts them in their place by recalling that they are only a small part of a greater whole: 'Did the word of God originate with you? Or are you the only people to whom it came?' (14.36). Any claims to inspiration can only be valid if they acknowledge Paul's authority, which is identical with God's and can rely on God for sanction: 'If anyone claims to be inspired or a prophet, let him recognize that what I write has the Lord's authority. If he does not acknowledge this, God does not acknowledge him' (14.37, 38). On such a basis the apostle can afford to be magnanimous: prophecy can be commended, ecstasy tolerated: 'but let all be done decently and in order' (14.40). For so long as Paul's authority to regulate them is not in question, neither prophecy nor ecstasy are a threat. The danger has been dealt with.

(g) The apostle of the resurrection

The last major theme with which Paul concerns himself in this letter is the resurrection of the dead. This is the only detailed witness to the resurrection of Jesus which comes directly from the pen of someone who claimed himself to have experienced it. The passage has therefore received considerable historical investigation, but attention has concentrated on Paul's affirmations rather than his audience's reservations. For if this chapter is remarkable for the first hand testimony it provides for the resurrection of Jesus, it is also fascinating evidence for an early Christian community which did not accept that claim. Paul is not facing hypothetical or academic objections; he is facing actual Christians who repudiate resurrection: 'How can some of you say that there is no resurrection of the dead?' (15.12), he asks. 'If the dead are not raised to life at all, what do they mean by being baptized on their behalf?' (15.29). 'But you may ask, how are the dead raised? In what kind of body?' (15.35). There is no suggestion that Paul is here addressing cultured scoffers outside the Christian community, as Acts represents him doing at Athens. The criticism is coming from the faithful themselves, from those who have been baptized, and the implication of this is very destructive of those accounts of the earliest Christian churches which see them as resurrection creations. Here is a very early community in which certainly some elements felt able to repudiate resurrection while expecting to retain a Christian identity. That can only mean, *pace* Paul and his modern followers, that it was at least possible in the early Gentile church to be a Christian without being committed to resurrection. At least for some Christians, other convictions and beliefs must have been the key to their religious identity.

I am primarily concerned with the importance of the resurrection in validating Paul's authority as an apostle. The passage cannot be properly understood apart from that concern. It is not mere historical reminiscence, although it contains reminiscence. It is the triumphant and conclusive exposition by Paul of his status, but it would be cowardly and evasive to give no assessment of the historical claim that Paul is making. The passage provides very strong evidence for the sincerity of Paul's conviction that Jesus rose from the dead. The desperate urgency of the assertions remains curiously compelling. It is not the work of a deliberate deceiver, but that does not rule out the probability of delusion; it merely defines it. If Paul was not consciously lying, it is most probable that he was himself deluded. The expectations aroused by the claims he had heard among those he had persecuted combined with his own secret insecurities to produce the powerful experience which changed his life. The precise steps cannot now be reconstructed, but the resulting anxiety expressed in aggressive assertiveness is apparent in all his writing, and particularly in this chapter, as he approaches its source. At the origin of his claim to authority there is illusion. Whatever true insights he may have gained from his own change of heart, embracing the values and the community which he had previously repressed, it is in the highest degree unlikely that he actually met the risen Christ on the road to Damascus. That he had a convulsive experience which he interpreted in the light of claims he had already heard is quite probable. That Christ was raised to life anywhere other than in Paul's imagination is unlikely. I would suggest that it is this basic illusion which constantly lures him to undermine the very freedom which he preached. Only the obedience and conformity of others can allay his own misgivings; their recognition of his claims is what ultimately makes them credible to him.

He begins by rehearsing his role as the founding father who has established an authoritative tradition: 'And now, my brothers, I must remind you of the gospel that I have preached to you; the gospel which you received, on which you have taken your stand, and which is now bringing you salvation. Do you still hold fast the Gospel as I preached it to you? If not, your conversion was in vain' (15.1, 2). Once again Paul uses their initial recognition of his claims to deter them from reconsideration. Unlike the letter to the Galatians, Paul here recognizes that he himself stands in a historic tradition: 'First and foremost, I handed on to you the facts which had been imparted to me' (15.3), and goes on to speak of Christ's death 'for our sins', its accordance with Scripture, his burial, and his various resurrection appearances, in which that to Cephas heads the list. But this recognition of a historic tradition on which Paul is dependent is then almost reversed by his appeal to his own experience, which is final, extraordinary, and the foundation of his successful apostolate: 'In the end he appeared even to me. It was like an abnormal birth; I had persecuted the church of God and am therefore inferior to all other apostles – indeed not fit to be called an apostle. However, by God's grace I am what I am, nor has his grace been given to me in vain; on the contrary, in my labours I have outdone them all – not I, indeed, but the grace of God working with me. But what matter, I or they? This is what we all proclaim, and this is what you believed?' (15.8–11). The humility towards the other apostles is only momentarily assumed; it is the foil to his assertion of God's particular favour; a claim which he makes acceptable by ascribing to the agency of God. Ultimately, however, apostolic solidarity triumphs, and Paul fortifies himself by identifying himself totally with his colleagues.

Only now does he directly face the objections in the Corinthian community. He stakes his own honesty and the truth of his gospel on the resurrection of Christ. 'If Christ was not raised, then our gospel is null and void, and so is your faith; and we turn out to be lying witnesses for God, because we bore witness that he raised Christ to life, whereas, if the dead are not raised, he did not raise him' (15.14, 15). This rhetoric begs the question, which is Paul's reliability. He takes care, however, to implicate his readers in his difficulties – not only his apostolate but 'their faith' is at risk: 'If Christ was not raised, your faith has nothing in it and you are still in your old state of sin' (15.17). Their desire for moral regeneration and possibly their experience of it are now used to ensure their consent. Moreover, there is a note of menace in the words 'your old state of sin'. That is not simply an uncomplimentary moral description; it reminds Paul's readers of the vengeance of God. He reinforces this by the gambler's refusal to admit past stupidity: 'It follows also that those who have died within Christ's fellowship are utterly lost. If it is for this life only that Christ has given us hope, we of all men are most to be pitied' (15.18, 19). Paul correctly calculates that most of us prefer not to admit a loss. Instead, he invites us to double the stake. The apostle knows his readers; he does not at this stage attempt to argue with them.

Instead, he expounds the resurrection of Christ in a way which intertwines themes of sovereignty and subordination. The sovereignty of Christ is presented in cosmic terms: 'As in Adam all men die, so in Christ will all be brought to life' (15.22). The 'all' sounds universalist, but is soon qualified by the stress in the next verse on 'those who belong to Christ', which in its turn prepares us for the 'enemies' of v. 25. The resurrected Christ will at the end abolish all competing authority, 'every kind of domination, authority and power' (15.24). The new sovereignty is absolute, but it does not subvert hierarchy; it exemplifies it. The resurrection itself brings to life 'each in his own proper place: Christ the firstfruits and afterwards, at his coming, those who belong to Christ' (15.23). The sovereignty of the Son reaches its culmination in subordination to God: 'When all things are thus subject to him, then the Son himself will be made subordinate to God who made all things subject to him, and thus God will be all in all' (15.28). The Corinthians' example of subordination to duly ordered authority is no less powerful for being implicit.

After a brief *ad hominem* argument from baptism for the dead (perhaps the best New Testament precedent for the principles of infant baptism), Paul distinguishes himself from his critics. He establishes his own prestige by parading his courage and flirting with death: 'And we ourselves – why do we face these dangers hour by hour? Every day I die: I swear it by my pride in you, my brothers – for in Christ Jesus our Lord I am proud of you. If, as the saying is, I "fought wild beasts" at Ephesus, what have I gained by it? If the dead are never raised to life, "let us eat and drink, for tomorrow we die"' (15.30–32). Having identified himself with the martyrs, he impugns the morals of his critics: 'Make no mistake: "Bad company is the ruin of a good character." Come back to a sober and upright life and leave your sinful ways. There are some who know nothing of God; to your shame I say it' (15.33, 34). In a few deft words he both encourages internal suspicion in the pursuit of purity and succeeds in equating criticism of himself with immorality.

Paul may abuse the questioner (15.35, contrast Matthew 5.22), but his account of the resurrection body is unconvincing. He appeals to the analogy of germination, but the seed is not dead in the sense that the body is, and there is no natural analogy for the reversal of biological death. He resorts to the variety of physical bodies (15.39–41) to justify talk of a spiritual body, as opposed to an animal body, without recognizing any contradictions in the notion of a spiritual body (15.44). Instead he conveys the excitement of transformation by a series of rhetorical paradoxes: 'So it is with the resurrection of the dead. What is sown in the earth as a perishable thing is raised imperishable. Sown in humiliation, it is raised in glory; sown in weakness, it is raised in power; sown as an animal body, it is raised as a spiritual body' (15.42–44). Only the association of harvest serves to make these stark contrasts plausible; but the use of harvest language itself is nowhere justified. Similarly, he appeals to Old Testament Scripture to validate the Adam anthropology: 'If there is such a thing as an animal body, there is also a spiritual body. It is in this sense that Scripture says, "The first man, Adam, became an animate being," whereas the last Adam became a life-giving Spirit' (15.45). But the scriptural reference does not establish the point at issue. It provides backing for Paul's account of the first man, but his account of the last Adam has no scriptural warrant. It is simply a matter of his assertion. It is as if the outcome of the resurrection of Jesus is not an ascended human body, but Jesus' transformation into the Holy Spirit. Presumably Paul can use Genesis 2.7 as a basis for giving priority to the animal body before the Spirit, but there is no notion in Genesis of a spiritual body. More plausibly, he uses the Genesis 2 account of man's creation as the key to man's historic development, so that the breathing into man's nostrils the breath of life is less an account of man's actual condition, compromised by the Fall (Genesis 3.19), more a prophecy of the incarnation and its consequences. 'The first man was made "of the dust of the earth": the second man is from heaven. The man made of dust is the pattern of all men of dust, and the heavenly man is the pattern of all the heavenly. As we have worn the likeness of the man made of dust, so we shall wear the likeness of the heavenly man' (15.47–49). The 'we' of that last sentence is not all-embracing; it is a specific promise to Christians.

Paul can simply assert it without justification, because it echoes the language and imagery of baptism. He is, so to speak, expounding the significance of the baptismal robe which they have all worn. The deeper ambiguities of an identity which is acquired by dressing up, he has no need to face.

He does, however, attempt to relate the old body to the new by the proclamation of a new creation. He distrusts the physical body too much to envisage any continuity between the two states: 'Flesh and blood can never possess the kingdom of God, and the perishable cannot possess immortality' (15.50). Instead, he asserts as a prophetic mystery the transformation of the earthly body and the reversal of death. 'Listen! I will unfold a mystery: we shall not all die, but we shall all be changed in a flash, in the twinkling of an eye, at the last trumpet-call. For the trumpet will sound, and the dead will rise immortal, and we shall be changed' (15.51–52). The basis of this revelation is far from clear. Paul does not refer to the authority of Jesus to authenticate it. Instead, it seems to be an ecstatic revelation that has come to him, and which he understands as suggesting the fulfilment of an Old Testament text: 'And when our mortality has been clothed with immortality, then the saying of Scripture will come true: "Death is swallowed up; victory is won!" "O Death, where is your victory? O Death, where is your sting?"' (15.54, 55). He does, however, indicate why such a belief is plausible to him, holding that death is the punishment of sin, and sin is the outcome of the Law: 'The sting of death is sin, and sin gains its power from the Law; but, God be praised, he gives us the victory through our Lord Jesus Christ' (15.56, 57). Through Christ's death we are freed from the Law, and therefore from sin, and so from death. This is the heart of the Christian privilege. This hope of a new creation confirms effort, persistence and work; it does not make them redundant: 'Therefore, my beloved brothers, stand firm and immovable, and work for the Lord always, work without limit, since you know that in the Lord your labour cannot be lost' (15.58). Precisely because the Christian is privileged to hope, he can labour confidently. Paul here returns to an emphasis on work which we have already examined in II Thessalonians, and once again manipulates privilege to exert control.

(h) Postscript

After all the bold assertions of authority, there comes a brief financial postscript, in which Paul makes arrangements for a collection in aid of the Jerusalem community to which he also refers in Galatians 2.10 as the one requirement of his Gentile apostolate on which the Jerusalem leaders insisted. The instructions are revealing: 'Every Sunday each of you is to put aside and keep by him a sum in proportion to his gains, so that there may be no collecting when I come' (16.2). Apparently there is as yet no common treasurer in the new community. Each person saves up his own contribution, and the weekly offering is envisaged as being related to income rather than to property. The rich of the Corinthian church are not so much encouraged to divest themselves of their wealth as to bear the appropriate charge. As in the letter to the Philippians, Paul exhibits a certain coyness towards money. He wants to raise money, as this letter makes clear, but he does not want to be associated with it. He prefers, therefore, the fund-raising to be done before his arrival.

The postscript also shows signs of an emerging élite in the new community, which the apostle himself encourages: 'I have a request to make of you, my brothers. You know that the Stephanas family were the first converts in Achaia, and have laid themselves out to serve God's people. I wish you to give their due position to such persons, and indeed to everyone who labours hard at our common task' (16.15, 16). There is little sign here of the criticism of public religious status which is a marked feature of much of the teaching ascribed to Jesus in the Gospels. Instead, social deference in a carefully ordered community seems to be the ideal which Paul is attempting to realize.

Not inappropriately, the letter ends with a series of brief sentences which combine exclusiveness, menace and blessing: 'If anyone does not love the Lord, let him be outcast. *Marana tha* – Come, O Lord! The grace of the Lord Jesus Christ be with you. My love to you all in Christ Jesus. Amen' (16.22–24). The threat of anathema is followed immediately by an appeal to divine retribution. The vindication to which Paul looks forward at the coming of the Lord is a very particular one: it will be the peculiar privilege of the community which he has established.

6

$6 6 3 9 7$

II CORINTHIANS

Studying the exercise of authority in Paul's letters and the accompanying attitudes to the surrounding world, has the advantage that texts which might otherwise seem of little interest take on an unexpected significance. For instance, the doctrinal content of this letter is slight. Much has been made of its reference to other letters, and the possibility that it is a compilation of Pauline writings. Considerable ingenuity has been directed towards reconstructing the nature of the opposition which Paul faced, but the letter itself does not at first seem theologically significant. It is, however, misleading to bracket a concern with authority as if it were theologically incidental. It does not arise as a private *ad hoc* concern of the apostle in a difficult situation, like a parson handling the personalities of a fractious church council. The way in which authority is used is a central religious concern, and the structure of argument which makes authority plausible is of crucial importance. As with Philippians, it is not necessary to take a view about the unity of this letter. That would only be significant if the aim was to reconstruct its social background. Whatever its origins, the text presents itself as a unity, and makes no attempt to reconcile or order any contradictions it possesses. It is that unified text which has made the historic impact, and with which we are primarily concerned.

(a) The praise of God and self-dramatization

The prayer of thanksgiving has been given a new twist in this letter. It is no longer used to flatter and control the readers; instead, it is directed towards the praise of God, which incidentally projects a highly dramatized image of the apostle. In a series of passages in the first part of the epistle, largely written in the first person plural, Paul begins by praising God and ends by sketching an account of his own activity which is full of self-congratulation (1.2–11; 2.12–17; 4.1–5.10; 6.3–10). 'Praise be to the God and Father of our Lord Jesus Christ, the all-merciful Father, the God whose consolation never fails us' (1.3). 'Thanks be to God, who continually leads us about, captives in Christ's triumphal procession, and everywhere uses us to reveal and spread abroad the fragrance of the knowledge of himself!' (2.14). 'Seeing then that we have been entrusted with this commission, which we owe entirely to God's mercy, we never lose heart' (4.1). Quickly the praise of God turns to a claim of unfailing consolation; this may be referred to a power external to the apostle, but it is a power to whom he claims a unique relationship. The thanks of God is transformed into an assertion of divine guidance. The humble ascription of his commission to God's mercy is used to justify an invincible confidence. The praise of God is thus first used to silence self-doubt.

Crucial to Paul's understanding, both of God and of himself, is the pattern which is based on the suffering and resurrection of Jesus: 'As Christ's cup of suffering overflows, and we suffer with him, so also through Christ our consolation overflows' (1.5). 'Wherever we go we carry death with us in our body, the death that Jesus died, that in this body also life may reveal itself, the life that Jesus lives' (4.10). Most strikingly in a famous series of paradoxes: 'Honour and dishonour, praise and blame, are alike our lot: we are the imposters who speak the truth, the unknown men whom all men know; dying we still live on; disciplined by suffering, we are not done to death; in our sorrows we have always cause for joy; poor ourselves, we bring wealth to many; penniless, we own the world' (6.8–10). The boldness of the contrasts both secures the reader's attention and gives to the life it illuminates a dramatic excitement with which it is difficult not to identify. Moreover, it is a religious belief of immense practical strength. Adverse experience becomes the precise grounds for expecting the contrary. 'Our hope for you is firmly grounded; for we know that if you have part in the suffering, you have part also in the divine consolation' (1.7). As in Philippians, Paul deliberately involves his readers in his experience, as he also identifies himself with the experience of Christ: if God comforts Paul, that is to enable him to comfort them (1.4). 'If distress be our lot, it is the price we pay for your consolation, for your salvation; if our lot be consolation, it is to help us to bring you comfort, and strength to face with fortitude the same sufferings we now endure' (1.6). Paul apparently attributes to his sufferings a vicarious merit, or more prosaically uses such language to describe the risks and afflictions attendant on his preaching the gospel which has brought them salvation. Equally, whenever his followers see Paul rescued by God, they gain a new confidence in God's power and willingness to rescue them. Paul is therefore concerned to leave them in no doubt about the reality of his dangers, and hence the divine initiative in his escape. 'We should like you to know, dear friends, how serious was the trouble that came upon us in the province of Asia. The burden of it was far too heavy for us to bear, so heavy that we even despaired of life. Indeed, we felt in our hearts that we had received a death-sentence. This was meant to teach us not to place reliance on ourselves, but on God who raises the dead. From such mortal peril God delivered us; and he will deliver us again, he on whom our hope is fixed' (1.8–10). In condemning his own self-reliance, which is rebuked by God, Paul successfully conveys a message which undermines the autonomy of his readers. Here belief in the death and resurrection of Jesus and present experiences of alternating disappointment and success mutually sustain each other. The beliefs about Jesus gain a resonance and reinforcement from immediate experience, while the life of the apostle (and by implication of his readers) gains boldness and confidence from the beliefs. They are encouraged to identify with Paul's plight, which has come about because of his concern for them and can be resolved by their prayer: 'Yes, (God) will continue to deliver us, if you will co-operate by praying for us' (1.10). The Corinthians gain in self-esteem from associating themselves with such prestigious affliction. Paul gains an audience which will appreciate the divine intervention on his behalf: 'With so many people praying for our deliverance, there will be many to give thanks on our behalf for the gracious favour God has shown towards us' (1.11). It is an effective way of obtaining the sympathy of his readers before he turns to more contentious matters: his failure to visit them and tensions over discipline.

A little later in the letter, he speaks of his anxiety and frustration in Troas while waiting for Titus (2.12–13), which eventually resulted in his journey to Macedonia. This is then hailed as God's guidance, and leads him to speak of himself: 'We are indeed the incense offered by Christ to God, both for those who are on the way to salvation, and for those who are on the way to perdition: to the latter it is a deadly fume that kills, to the former a vital fragrance that brings life' (2.15–16). Thus the humility of speaking of himself as a captive 'in Christ's triumphal procession' has only served to introduce the most arrogant and divisive claim. Paul delights in the double-edged nature of his mission; the sense of deliberate destruction is as strong as the sense of salvation. He can therefore congratulate himself, whichever way he is received: welcome and hostility both strengthen his image of himself, while those who have been prudent enough to receive him can congratulate themselves on the danger they have avoided. But for the grace of God Paul might have proved to them a deadly fume that kills. 'Who is equal to such a calling?' Paul asks. Words which seem an outburst of modesty are also designed to elicit awe and astonishment. Nor is Paul embarrassed to point to a certain logic in the

divine choice: 'At least we do not go hawking the word of God about, as so
many do; when we declare the word we do it in sincerity, as from God and
in God's sight, as members of Christ' (2.17). The same divisiveness which
informs Paul's sense of mission here marks him off from possible
competitors. There is a strong implication that his financial disinterestedness guarantees his sincerity in a way which reflects adversely on those
who live by their teaching.

The most elaborate example of the way in which Paul uses the dialectic
of suffering and resurrection to dramatize his life and sanction the
transition from humility to assertiveness is yet to come (4.1–5.10). On the
one hand he speaks of his commission being owed 'entirely to God's
mercy'; on the other hand he reminds his readers of his merits: 'We have
renounced the deeds that men hide for very shame; we neither practise
cunning nor distort the word of God; only by declaring the truth openly do
we recommend ourselves' (4.2). Paul then concludes his explanation of
why his message is received so differently, before taking up the theme of
humiliation as the gateway to exaltation. He first points to the discrepancy
between himself and his claims, which instead of justifying caution is itself
celebrated as proof of total dependence upon God. 'We are no better than
pots of earthenware to contain this treasure, and this proves that such
transcendent power does not come from us, but is God's alone. Hard-
pressed on every side, we are never hemmed in; bewildered, we are never at
our wits' end; hunted, we are never abandoned to our fate; struck down,
we are not left to die' (4.7–9). Paul flaunts the precariousness of his
position as proof of God's blessing because he can identify it so easily with
a vulnerable Jesus eventually vindicated by God: 'Wherever we go we
carry death with us in our body, the death that Jesus died, that in this body
also life may reveal itself, the life that Jesus lives. For continually, while still
alive, we are being surrendered into the hands of death, for Jesus' sake, so
that the life of Jesus also may be revealed in this mortal body of ours'
(4.10–11). Immediately the Corinthians are reminded that it is for their
benefit that Paul is running such risks: 'Thus death is at work in us, and life
in you' (4.12). The resurrection and vindication of Jesus is the pledge of
Paul's vindication and the Corinthians' also, so that the origin of his
authority is also the source of their hope: 'Scripture says, "I believed, and
therefore I spoke out", and we too, in the same spirit of faith, believe and
therefore speak out; for we know that he who raised the Lord Jesus to life
will with Jesus raise us too, and bring us to his presence, and you with us'
(4.13, 14). The use of scriptural reference is not merely one of incidental
allusion. We see here the way in which a quite tangential text was used by
the early church to indicate that Jesus' resurrection was indeed 'according

to the Scriptures'. Paul directs his readers towards the benefit and the privilege which is theirs: 'Indeed, it is for your sake that all things are ordered, so that, as the abounding grace of God is shared by more and more, the greater may be the chorus of thanksgiving that ascends to the glory of God' (4.15). The reader is assured both of particular divine attention and of membership of a growing throng: both of these consolations culminate in the glory of God.

Paul proceeds to anticipate his own death in the light of his identification with the crucified and risen Jesus. He can see this validated even in the immediate experience of physical decay contrasted with growing spiritual maturity: 'Though our outward humanity is in decay, yet day by day we are inwardly renewed' (4.16). The contrast between the visible and the invisible which this analogy sanctions is then transferred to the much broader context of this world and an alleged world to come. 'Our troubles are slight and short-lived; and their outcome an eternal glory which outweighs them far. Meanwhile our eyes are fixed, not on the things that are seen, but on the things that are unseen; for what is seen passes away; what is unseen is eternal. For we know that if the earthly frame that houses us today should be demolished, we possess a building which God has provided – a house not made by human hands, eternal, and in heaven' (4.17–5.1). Here the early Christian indifference to the significance of the temple, the earthly building, devalued by reference to a transcendent, heavenly temple, identified with the ascended body of Jesus, is used to suggest the individual's indifference to his own body. So Paul can go on to say: 'We know that so long as we are at home in the body we are exiles from the Lord' (5.6). In the intervening verses Paul expresses with some clarity his sense of alienation from his own body. He refuses to identify himself with his body, and distances himself from it by using analogies of housing and clothing. This earthly body makes us vulnerable: 'We groan indeed, we who are enclosed within this earthly frame; we are oppressed because we do not want to have the old body stripped off' (5.4). Affection for the body we inhabit is not, however, condemned by Paul; he respects 'our desire to have the new body put on over it, so that our mortal part may be absorbed into life immortal' (5.4), and declares that 'God himself has shaped us for this very end; and as a pledge of it he has given us the Spirit' (5.5). The identity is conceived apart from the body, so that the heavenly body is imagined as an extra coat added to the nakedness of the flesh. Alienation from the body would seem therefore to render its resurrection credible.

The pattern of cross and resurrection sanctions a passionate repudiation of what can be seen, for the sake of a future and invisible vindication expressed by Paul's phrase to be 'with the Lord' (5.8). Repeatedly he stresses his confidence (4.16; 5.6, 8), and rightly, for every contrary experience only alienates him further from this world and makes him long more vehemently for the next. He can recount with pride his 'steadfast endurance: in distress, hardships, and dire straits; flogged, imprisoned, mobbed; overworked, sleepless, starving' (6.4, 5). Everyone of these afflictions identifies him more deeply with the sufferings of Jesus, and acts therefore as a pledge of his ultimate reward. If, however, such confidence gives boldness to the apostle, he takes care that it does not degenerate into complacency among his readers. Resurrection, life with the Lord, has a two-edged character: 'We therefore make it our ambition, wherever we are, here or there, to be acceptable to him. For we must all have our lives laid open before the tribunal of Christ, where each must receive what is due to him for his conduct in the body, good or bad' (5.9, 10). Strong in the catalogue of his afflictions, Paul's life lies open to inspection: 'With this fear of the Lord before our eyes we address our appeal to men. To God our lives lie open, as I hope they also lie open to you in your heart of hearts' (5.11). The transition from confidence to anxiety is abrupt, but in a way it is deceptive. Paul speaks of having the fear of the Lord before his own eyes, but the implied menace is directed towards his readers.

(b) The relation of the apostle to his audience
Previous letters have already displayed the ambivalence of Paul's attitude towards his audience, which also features in this letter. He praises his own godly sincerity and openness in his dealings with the Corinthians (1.12, 13). He assures them that his original plan to visit them was a sign of his confidence in them (1.15), and then proceeds to justify his change of plan as evidence of his concern for them. His determination to retain their goodwill is eloquently demonstrated in the following passage: 'I appeal to God to witness what I am going to say; I stake my life upon it: it was out of consideration for you that I did not after all come to Corinth. Do not think we are dictating the terms of your faith; your hold on the faith is secure enough. We are working with you for your own happiness. So I made up my mind that my next visit to you must not be another painful one. If I cause pain to you, who is left to cheer me up, except you, whom I have offended? This is precisely the point I made in my letter: I did not want, I said, to come and be made miserable by the very people who ought to have made me happy; and I had sufficient confidence in you all to know that for me to be happy is for all of you to be happy' (1.23–2.4). Paul's manipulation of his audience and his concern to establish his good standing among them is obvious. He invokes God in his cause (contrast

Matt. 5. 33–37), and refers indirectly to his risk of martyrdom, to compel them to regard his absence as a sign of his love. He soothes any suspicion of spiritual dictatorship on his part by flattering their grasp of the faith. His work and their happiness are boldly identified. He admits that he took the decision to delay his visit, but then diverts responsibility by introducing a notion of painfulness, which can refer either to himself or to his readers. On the one hand he speaks ruefully of himself paining them, of having offended them. On the other hand he appeals to their pity and sense of shame: 'I did not want . . . to come and be made miserable by the very people who ought to have made me happy' (2.3). Having earlier asserted their happiness as his own objective, he ends by assuming that his happiness is theirs.

It is a mark of the distrust which Paul feels has arisen between himself and the Corinthians that he only appeals to his authority as the founder of their community with some caution: 'Are we beginning all over again to produce our credentials? Do we, like some people, need letters of introduction to you, or from you? No, you are all the letter we need, a letter written on our heart; any man can see it for what it is and read it for himself' (3.1, 2). If Paul refuses to produce his credentials again and regards that as unnecessary, he nevertheless reminds them of their own significance as evidence of his mission and authority. The use of the existence of a community as his own authentication is by no means new, but the element of doubt and uncertainty in the relationship has no precedent, and it is accompanied by a stress on his openness and an appeal to a broad public: 'There is nothing in our letters to you but what you can read for yourselves, and understand too' (1.13). 'We neither practise cunning nor distort the word of God; only by declaring the truth openly do we recommend ourselves, and then it is to the common conscience of our fellow men and in the sight of God' (4.2). 'Men of Corinth, we have spoken very frankly to you; we have opened our heart wide to you all. On our part there is no constraint' (6.11). He can no longer rely on their total understanding: 'Partial as your present knowledge of us is, you will I hope come to understand fully that you have as much reason to be proud of us, as we of you, on the Day of our Lord Jesus' (1.14). Flattery and indirect menace cannot conceal the loss of confidence that has taken place. 'To God our lives lie open, as I hope they also lie open to you in your heart of hearts. This is not another attempt to recommend ourselves to you: we are rather giving you a chance to show yourselves proud of us; then you will have something to say to those whose pride is all in outward show and not in inward worth' (5.11, 12). Paul may boldly try to turn the tables upon them, but he is clearly still looking forward to a reconciliation which has not yet taken place. He is uneasily aware that his audience is not with him, and must be treated with great care: 'Any constraint there may be is in yourselves. In fair exchange then (may a father speak so to his children?) open wide your hearts to us' (6.12, 13).

(c) Tension between local and apostolic discipline

The heart of this distrust seems to derive from a conflict concerning discipline between the apostle and the Corinthian community. The exercise of authority at a distance by means of letter made it easy for the apostle to lose touch with his audience. Paul repeatedly refers to a previous letter and appears to be trying to undo the damage of an earlier intervention which had proved ill-judged. He stresses the personal cost to himself of writing such a letter, and asks them to see it as evidence of his love rather than his hostility: 'That letter I sent you came out of great distress and anxiety; how many tears I shed as I wrote it! But I never meant to cause you pain; I wanted you rather to know the love, the more than ordinary love, that I have for you' (2.4). He hastens to assure them that it is not his prestige that is at stake; he was not therefore acting to defend himself, but to protect or compensate them: 'Any injury that has been done, has not been done to me; to some extent, not to labour the point, it has been done to you all' (2.5). He then refers to a penalty which had been imposed by the Corinthians themselves, presumably with some reluctance. He welcomes and ratifies their sentence, but having gained his point is now eager to appear magnanimous and generous: 'The penalty on which the general meeting has agreed has met the offence well enough. Something very different is called for now: you must forgive the offender and put heart into him; the man's sorrow must not be made so severe as to overwhelm him. I urge you therefore to assure him of your love for him by a formal act' (2.6–8). Perhaps Paul is only urging them to do something which he suspects they may have done already: he is obviously concerned to diminish the importance of the whole incident. He retreats from the substance of the issue so that it is never made clear what misdemeanour has caused the trouble. Instead he encourages them not to examine the merits of the case, but to congratulate themselves on their obedience to himself: 'I wrote, I may say, to see how you stood the test, whether you fully accepted my authority' (2.9). Then follow words which indicate that although Paul may have secured their obedience, it was reluctant and accompanied by remonstration: 'But anyone who has your forgiveness has mine too' (2.10). This strongly implies that in fact the initiative for forgiveness has come from the Corinthians rather than Paul, and that he is associating himself retrospectively with decisions which he may not originally have welcomed. These tactics of compromise eventually allow him to restate his own position undiminished: 'And when I speak of forgiving (so far as there is anything for me to forgive), I mean that as the representative of Christ I have forgiven him for your sake' (2.10). This recognizes that the initiative for forgiveness has come from the Corinthians, carefully excludes any suggestion of offended *amour-propre* on Paul's part, and yet preserves the plenitude of his Christ-given authority. Further recrimination is discouraged by a timely reminder of the real nature of opposition: 'For Satan must not be allowed to get the better of us; we know his wiles all too well' (2.11).

Paul cannot, however, leave the matter alone, but returns to it in the same defensive and uncertain tone later in the letter. 'Do make a place for us in your hearts! We have wronged no one, ruined no one, taken advantage of no one. I do not want to blame you. Why, as I have told you before, the place you have in our heart is such that, come death, come life, we meet it together. I am perfectly frank with you. I have great pride in you. In all our many troubles my cup is full of consolation, and overflows with joy' (7.2–4). He appeals to their affection, and as he proclaims his innocence, it is difficult not to sense a contrast with someone who has injured them in all the ways he specifies. With ostentatious forebearance he declines to blame them. He effusively praises them while asserting his sincerity, and by identifying them with his consolation artfully sets the scene for receiving Titus' good news from them. Once again he applies to his own history the pattern of death and resurrection by divine intervention which has been previously examined. 'Even when we reached Macedonia there was still no relief for this poor body of ours; instead, there was trouble at every turn, quarrels all round us, forebodings in our heart. But God, who brings comfort to the downcast, has comforted us by the arrival of Titus, and not merely by his arrival, but by his being so greatly comforted about you' (7.5–7). Paul then proceeds to share with his readers his gratification at their penitence and support: 'He has told us how you long for me, how sorry you are, and how eager to take my side; and that has made me happier still' (7.7).

He can now return to the vexed question of his previous letter with new confidence and a sense of victory. By having shared with his readers his doubts and anxieties, he encourages them to identify themselves with his justification: 'Even if I did wound you by the letter I sent, I do not now regret it. I may have been sorry for it when I saw that the letter had caused you pain, even if only for a time; but now I am happy, not that your feelings were wounded but that the wound led to a change of heart. You bore the smart as God would have you bear it, and so you are no losers by what we did' (7.8, 9). Paul cannot conceal a sense of relief at a dangerous gamble that has come off. He compensates his readers for their precarious submission by praising them for their divinely inspired behaviour: 'For the wound which is borne in God's way brings a change of heart too salutary to regret; but the hurt which is borne in the world's way brings death. You bore your hurt in God's way, and see what the results have been' (7.10–11). As they congratulate themselves on the prudence of the path they have chosen, as opposed to that of the 'world', they have also absorbed a lesson for the future, which will sustain a ready obedience. Paul will only see the good in the outcome of this venture, and is determined to present the consequences as both desirable and foreseen: 'It made you take the matter seriously and vindicate yourselves. How angered you were, how apprehensive! How your longing for me awoke, yes, and your devotion and your eagerness to see justice done! At every point you have cleared yourselves of blame in this trouble. And so, although I did send you that letter, it was not the offender or his victim that most concerned me. My aim in writing was to help to make plain to you, in the sight of God, how truly you are devoted to us. That is why we have been so encouraged' (7.11–13). He now feels able to praise their moral indignation, which only serves to emphasize the strength of their devotion to him. He reminds them of their anger, which belongs safely to the past. He confuses their enthusiasm for justice with their attachment to himself. He disguises his uneasiness about his own course of action by assuring his readers that they are blameless. The whole incident is portrayed as a test to bring home to them the depth of their devotion to Paul. Titus' report has entirely confirmed Paul's assessment of the Corinthian situation: 'Anything I may have said to him to show my pride in you has been justified. Every word we ever addressed to you bore the mark of truth; and the same holds of the proud boast we made in the presence of Titus: that also has proved true' (7.14). Paul's reputation among his colleagues, which might have been put at risk by the Corinthians, has now been established. The nature of Paul's confidence in the Corinthians is plainly indicated by his account of Titus' response to them: 'His heart warms all the more to you as he recalls how ready you all were to do what he asked, meeting him as you did in fear and trembling' (7.15). The representative of God's apostle has been met with appropriate deference; Paul's honour has been vindicated.

(d) The separateness of the new community

It is not clear that the letter gives any indication of the *cause celebre* which had threatened to divide the apostle from the Corinthians. If the letter to which Paul continually refers is to be identified at least in part with

I Corinthians, then the most obvious explanation is that we have here the end of the incident of the man who married his stepmother (I Cor. 5ff.), but that passage itself refers to other letters of Paul (I Cor. 5.9), and his language there hardly seems strong enough to account for his subsequent unease over it. The offence does not seem to have anything to do with the major preoccupations of II Corinthians: the collection for the Jerusalem poor, or the sham-apostles whom Paul opposes later in the letter. His forgiveness would not probably be forthcoming for anyone connected with the latter, and his reference to 'the offender and the victim' (7.12) suggests a sexual rather than a financial misdemeanour. The only passage, which may be related to the offence in question is that which apparently forbids Christians to marry outside their own community. It is difficult to see its relevance in its context unless it does refer to the offence which occasioned Paul's letter of rebuke. It comes between an earnest request for the Corinthians' goodwill and Paul's final apologia for his letter. If it does not refer to marriage at all, as some commentators suggest, then it is an attempt to discredit his critics by associating them with unbelief and thus isolating them. Another possibility is to interpret this passage as having some connection with the letter mentioned in I Corinthians 5 which has already been referred to: 'In my letter I wrote that you must have nothing to do with loose livers' (5.9). He then makes it plain that he was not referring to pagans, but to so-called Christians leading immoral lives. There is an emphasis on uncleanness and the avoidance of impurity in the second letter which might at first sight support the identification, but Paul's pagan charges seem too strong for even him to apply to unworthy Christians: 'What has righteousness to do with wickedness? Can light consort with darkness? Can Christ agree with Belial, or a believer join hands with an unbeliever? Can there be a compact between the temple of God and the idols of the heathen? And the temple of the living God is what we are' (6.14–16). It is ironic that the scourge of the Law can quote the Scriptures to justify one of the most divisive of Jewish practices: 'God's own words are: "I will live and move about among them; I will be their God, and they shall be my people". And therefore, "come away and leave them, separate yourselves, says the Lord; touch nothing unclean. Then I will accept you", says the Lord, the Ruler of all being; "I will be a father to you, and you shall by my sons and daughters." Such are the promises that have been made to us, dear friends. Let us therefore cleanse ourselves from all that can defile flesh or spirit, and in the fear of God complete our consecration (6.16–7.1).

Although Paul's prohibition of marriage outside the Christian community will seem unacceptably sectarian and divisive to many modern

Christians, it is entirely consistent with his teaching on marriage in I Corinthians. The command to maintain marriages already contracted with pagan partners is only sanctioning marriages which have already taken place (I Cor. 7.12–16). Exactly the same attitude towards marriage outside the community, which is found here, is also found in his advice on the second marriage of widows (I Cor. 7.39). There is therefore no inconsistency between Paul's teaching here and elsewhere, and it is a devastating reflection on the kind of community he has created. Its identity and his authority can only be preserved by deliberate separation and exclusion, expressed in strict endogamy. This is the price of their privilege of being God's temple, and having the Ruler of all being as their Father.

(e) The understanding of dissent: the veil

A tightly defined and controlled community is always threatened by those who repudiate it. Such repudiation challenges its fragile identity and undermines sectarian authority. If the example of rebellion is not to prove infectious, then it has to be understood in a way which inhibits imitation. Paul readily attributes opposition to Satan (2.11), and later quotes the Genesis story of the serpent as a cautionary and explanatory tale, 'But as the serpent in his cunning seduced Eve, I am afraid that your thoughts may be corrupted and you may lose your single-hearted devotion to Christ' (11.3), but his most elaborate treatment of this difficulty is an ingenious development of the notion of a 'veil' that hides the truth. It is a fascinating passage, which on the one hand disclaims any esoteric teaching, and then rehabilitates the notion to discredit dissent.

Paul begins by praising the Corinthians, describing them as a spiritual letter: 'As for you, it is plain that you are a letter that has come from Christ, given to us to deliver: a letter written not with ink but with the Spirit of the living God, written not on stone tablets but on the pages of the human heart' (3.3). Having compared them to their advantage to the written letter, Paul proceeds to validate his status in precisely the same terms: 'There is no question of our being qualified in ourselves: we cannot claim anything as our own. The qualification we have comes from God; it is he who has qualified us to dispense his new covenant – a covenant expressed not in a written document, but in a spiritual bond; for the written law condemns to death, but the Spirit gives life' (3.5, 6). The Corinthians cannot challenge such a claim without jeopardizing their own privileged status, and the contrast between life and death reminds them of what is at stake. Paul then argues that since the death-dispensing written law was inaugurated with such splendour that it 'made the face of Moses so bright that the Israelites could not gaze steadily at him . . . must not even greater splendour rest upon the divine dispensation of the Spirit?' (3.7, 8). In that way Paul underlines the privilege which he and the Corinthians share. He then seizes upon a detail in the story of the giving of the Law, and uses it to contrast his own open behaviour and to explain the unresponsiveness first of the Jews and more immediately of his own enemies: 'With such a hope as this we speak out boldly; it is not for us to do as Moses did: he put a veil over his face to keep the Israelites from gazing on that fading splendour until it was gone' (3.12, 13). Here Paul is repudiating any claim to esoteric teaching, and subsequently he develops the point by stressing the community of the Spirit: 'And because for us there is no veil over the face, we all reflect as in a mirror the splendour of the Lord; thus we are transfigured into his likeness, from splendour to splendour; such is the influence of the Lord who is Spirit' (3.18). The element of reserve and hierarchy which Paul discerned in the veil over Moses' face has been abolished in the new fellowship of the Spirit.

Not so elsewhere. The veil that the Christians have brushed aside still obscures the minds of the Jews: 'But in any case their minds had been made insensitive, for that same veil is there to this very day when the lesson is read from the old covenant; and it is never lifted, because only in Christ is the old covenant abrogated. But to this very day, every time the Law of Moses is read, a veil lies over the minds of the hearers' (3.14, 15). Paul here uses an idea derived from the Old Testament scriptures to discredit those who based their position on those scriptures, while at the same time he contrives to present Moses as a witness, not to the written law, but to the Spirit: 'However, as Scripture says of Moses, "whenever he turns to the Lord the veil is removed". Now the Lord of whom this passage speaks is the Spirit; and where the Spirit of the Lord is, there is liberty' (3.16, 17). The same imagery which Paul has used to explain the unbelief of the Jews he then extends to all those who reject his gospel: 'If indeed our gospel be found veiled, the only people who find it so are those on the way to perdition. Their unbelieving minds are so blinded by the god of this passing age, that the gospel of the glory of Christ, who is the very image of God, cannot dawn upon them and bring them light' (4.3, 4). The derivation of the veil from scripture conceals the fact that Paul's description of his enemies as 'blinded by the god of this passing age' is entirely his own. Nevertheless it provides for the faithful an explanation of the dissent of others which confirms their own very different response.

(f) The uses of a confused identity

Even Paul himself can sense the dangers in his position: 'It is not ourselves that we proclaim; we proclaim Christ Jesus as Lord, and ourselves as your servants, for Jesus' sake' (4.5). Yet although he has perceived and disclaimed the danger, he continues to involve himself with the revelation he proclaims in the most intimate way: 'For the same God who said, "Out of darkness let light shine", has caused his light to shine within us, to give the light of revelation – the revelation of the glory of God in the face of Jesus Christ' (4.6). It is not, therefore, surprising that Paul easily uses the divine authority to sanction or justify his own decisions. When he is defending his change of plan in not visiting the Corinthians he evades the charge of equivocation by identifying himself with the positive and direct response of Christ: 'Do I, when I frame my plans, frame them as a worldly man might, so that it should rest with me to say "yes" and "yes", or "no" and "no"? As God is true, the language in which we address you is not an ambiguous blend of Yes and No. The Son of God, Christ Jesus, proclaimed among you by us (by Silvanus, and Timothy, I mean, as well as myself), was never a blend of Yes and No. With him it was, and is, Yes. He is the Yes pronounced upon God's promises, every one' (1.17–20). It is a rare moment, when Paul unpacks the second person plural that he so often uses, to include his colleagues. The affirmation is so powerful and compelling that the reader easily forgets that Paul has deflected the charge rather than answered it. He ends not by defending his own consistency, but by pointing to the common dependence of apostle and reader on God, a dependence which makes further criticism inappropriate: 'That is why, when we give glory to God, it is through Christ Jesus that we say "Amen". And if you and we belong to Christ, guaranteed as his and anointed, it is all God's doing; it is God also who has set his seal upon us, and as a pledge of what is to come has given the Spirit to dwell in our hearts' (1.20–22). This strong assertion of the divine initiative forecloses the debate.

Identification with the life and purposes of Christ and the proclamation of divine initiative are fused together in Paul's understanding of his own function. It is a recipe which both compels attention and seeks consent. 'It may be we are beside ourselves, but it is for God; if we are in our right mind, it is for you' (5.13). Paul's behaviour, if strange, is sanctioned by his devotion to God, while if it is intelligible it is sanctioned by their approval. Paul then describes the radical displacement of the personality that lies at the heart of his religion. 'For the love of Christ leaves us no choice, when once we have reached the conclusion that one man died for all and therefore all mankind has died. His purpose in dying for all was that men, while still in life, should cease to live for themselves, and should live for him who for their sake died and was raised to life' (5.14, 15). His convictions are presented as an objective constraint which replaces the self-directed life with a life oriented towards Christ. Its consequence is presented as a view of other men which subordinates all ordinary human distinctions to the new Christian identity. The rejection of 'worldly standards' is balanced by a passionate affirmation of the newness, the discontinuity of the Christian (5.16, 17). The death of Christ is mirrored in the life of the believer by this radical change of perspective, so radical indeed that Paul must say: 'From first to last this has been the work of God' (5.18). In all that follows the reconciliation of man to God through Christ is balanced and expressed by the God-given mission of the apostle: '(God) has reconciled us men to himself through Christ, and he has enlisted us in this service of reconciliation. What I mean is, that God was in Christ reconciling the world to himself, no longer holding men's misdeeds against them, and that he has entrusted us with the message of reconciliation. We come therefore as Christ's ambassadors. It is as if God were appealing to you through us: in Christ's name, we implore you, be reconciled to God! . . . Sharing in God's work, we urge this appeal upon you' (5.18–21). Paul thus begins by ascribing initiative to God, and ends by removing responsibility from himself to God. The exchange of identity is crucial: the believer is urged to respond to the gracious condescension of Christ by surrendering his identity to God: 'Christ was innocent of sin, and yet for our sake God made him one with the sinfulness of men, so that in him we might be made one with the goodness of God himself . . . You have received the grace of God; do not let it go for nothing' (5.21–6.1). The positions of apostle and believer are, however, very different. The apostle gains his divine identity by submitting to a Christ who is largely the creation of his own projections. The believer can only achieve a divine identity by surrendering to Christ's apostle, who is no projection, but has a will and a determination of his own. It is a difference which the apostle does not encourage us to perceive.

(g) The apostle as fund-raiser

Most of Paul's letters contain a minor financial sub-plot. In this letter the apostle devotes considerable attention to fund-raising, which is a major preoccupation. Paul insists that the money is not for his own use, but for the poor of Jerusalem; he indicates elsewhere that his good standing with the Jerusalem apostles is not unconnected with this financial support, and he is not unaware in this passage of the public relations benefit to be derived from such activities. He shows great care to protect himself against any suggestion of using funds improperly. Titus, who is being sent to organize the collection among the Corinthians, is someone they already know, and Paul goes out of his way to establish his *bona fide* status: 'If there is any question about Titus, he is my partner and my associate in dealings with you' (8.23). Furthermore, Titus does not come alone, but with two other representatives; the objective is clearly that they should be a check on one another's honesty: 'With (Titus) we are sending one of our company whose reputation is high among our congregations everywhere for his services to the Gospel. Moreover they have duly appointed him to travel with us and help in this beneficent work, by which we do honour to the Lord himself and show our eagerness to serve. We want to guard against any criticism of our handling of this generous gift; for our aims are entirely honourable, not only in the Lord's eyes, but also in the eyes of men. With these men we are sending another of our company whose enthusiasm we have had many opportunities of testing, and who is now all the more earnest because of the great confidence he has in you . . . they are delegates of our congregations' (8.18–22). Paul has carefully respected Jewish laws of evidence and taken every precaution to protect himself from misunderstanding or subsequent charges of misappropriation.

He quite shamelessly plays off one congregation against another to encourage their generosity. Thus to the Corinthians he expatiates on the generosity of the Christians in Macedonia: 'We must tell you, friends, about the grace of generosity which God has imparted to our congregations in Macedonia. The troubles they have been through have tried them hard, yet in all this they have been so exuberantly happy that from the depths of their poverty they have shown themselves lavishly open-handed. Going to the limit of their resources, as I can testify, and even beyond the limit, they begged us most insistently, and on their own initiative to be allowed to share in this generous service to their fellow-Christians. And their giving surpassed our expectations' (8.1–5). In this account he emphasizes the spontaneity and poverty of the Macedonians to shame the Corinthians: 'You are so rich in everything – in faith, speech and knowledge, and zeal of every kind, as well as in the loving regard you have for us – surely you should show yourselves equally lavish in this generous service! This is not meant as an order; by telling you how keen others are I am putting your love to the test' (8.7 8,). Very wisely he does not risk his authority by staking it on their financial response; instead he relies on his considerable powers of manipulation.

For if Paul uses the example of the Macedonians to shame the Corinthians into generosity, he has first used the example of the Corinthians to inspire the Macedonians. He may speak demurely of the Macedonians acting on their own initiative (8.4), but his reference to his own expectations (8.5) suggests that the intiative was not entirely unsolicited, and so he eventually reveals: 'About the provision of aid for God's people, it is superfluous for me to write to you. I know how eager you are to help; I speak of it with pride to the Macedonians: I tell them that Achaia had everything ready last year; and most of them have been fired by your zeal' (9.1–2). Indeed one of the purposes of sending Titus and his two colleagues on ahead of Paul is to make sure that Paul's picture of the Corinthians' generosity is not shown to be false: 'My purpose in sending these friends is to ensure that what we have said about you in this matter should not prove to be an empty boast. By that I mean, I want you to be prepared, as I told them you were; for if I bring with me men from Macedonia and they find you are not prepared, what a disgrace it will be to us, let alone to you, after all the confidence we have shown! I have accordingly thought it necessary to ask these friends to go on ahead to Corinth, to see that your promised bounty is in order before I come; it will then be awaiting me as a bounty indeed, and not as an extortion' (9.3–5). The deviousness may all be in a good cause, but the impression of manipulation is inescapable, and Paul's respect for truth is not impressive.

The inducements to generosity which Paul employs shed considerable light both on his relation to his followers and on their expectations of their religion. He can obviously play on the traditional competitiveness of Greek communities, and can portray giving as a sign of their commitment both to God and to himself. He praises the Macedonians because 'they gave their very selves, offering them in the first instance to the Lord, but also, under God, to us' (8.5). He encourages the Corinthians to give by referring to 'the loving regard you have for us' (8.7), and describes his fund-raising 'as putting your love to the test' (8.8). Generosity is sanctioned and fostered by reference to the example both of God and of Jesus. 'For you know how generous our Lord Jesus Christ has been: he was rich, yet for your sake he became poor, so that through his poverty you might become rich' (8.9). Already in Christian history Jesus is associated with the condescension of the rich rather than with any revolutionary violence by the poor. The looked-for generosity of the Corinthians is put into perspective by reference to the generosity of God: 'Thanks be to God for his gift beyond words!' (9.15).

Paul is careful not to compromise his authority by insisting on a particular level of contribution. 'Give according to your means' (8.11), he insists. On this delicate matter he respects the autonomy of the believer: 'Each person should give as he has decided for himself; there should be no reluctance, no sense of compulsion' (9.7). He praises the Macedonians that 'from the depths of their poverty they have shown themselves lavishly open-handed – going to the limit of their resources, as I can testify, and even beyond that' (8.2, 3). Nevertheless he reassures the Corinthians that God 'does not ask for what (a man) has not. There is no question of relieving others at the cost of hardship to yourselves' (8.13). Paul disarms criticism by being unspecific in his demands, and his stress on the generous attitude as primary, rather than any particular level of response, makes it difficult for his readers to oppose him (8.2, 4, 9, 12; 9.7, 9, 12). It also puts no limit to their giving – that is left to their means, their self-esteem and their anxiety. Paul does not hesitate to present giving as a form of insurance which gains mutual and divine benefits: 'What I ask you to do is in your own interests' (8.10). 'Remember: sparse sowing, sparse reaping; sow bountifully, and you will reap bountifully' (9.6). From men they can expect the present benefit of their prayers: 'As they join in prayer on your behalf, their hearts will go out to you because of the richness of the grace which God has imparted to you' (9.14), and also an element of insurance against reversals of fortune in the future: 'At the moment your surplus meets their need, but one day your need may be met by their surplus' (8.14). But generosity also establishes claims to divine bounty: 'God loves a cheerful giver. And it is in God's power to provide you richly with every good gift; thus you will have ample means in yourselves to meet each and every situation, with enough and to spare for every good cause' (9.7, 8). Or again: 'He who provides seed for sowing and bread for food will provide the seed for you to sow; he will multiply it and swell the harvest of your benevolence, and you will always be rich enough to be generous' (9.10, 11). He supports his appeal partly by the use of Old Testament texts (8.15; 9.9) and partly by a notion of 'equality' (8.14) which is not often heard in the New Testament.

Unlike some of the teaching ascribed to Jesus in the Synoptic Gospels, there is no stress in Paul on secrecy in giving; quite the reverse. The desire for a divine and human audience are not seen as incompatible, but complementary: 'Our aims are entirely honourable, not only in the Lord's eyes, but also in the eyes of men' (8.21). He tells the Corinthians to give his representatives 'clear expression of your love and justify our pride in you; justify it to them, and through them to the congregations' (8.24). Ultimately Paul succeeds in identifying generous giving with a public expression of the Corinthians' obedience and faith: 'Through the proof which this affords, many will give honour to God when they see how humbly you obey him and how faithfully you confess the gospel of Christ; and will thank him for your liberal contribution to their need and to the general good' (9.12, 13). This stress on raising money, which is at the same time quite uncritical of wealth, has no parallel in the New Testament. Because Paul is so concerned to deny any personal financial gain from the collection he fails to perceive the egotism of his own behaviour. In pursuit of a goal to which his own prestige is committed he deliberately exploits individual and communal self-esteem.

(h) Paul's determination to use his authority

An abrupt change of tone is apparent in the last four chapters of the letter. Since a concern for finance often brings a Pauline letter to an end, it is natural to suspect that we have here two letters, and that the first ended with the financial appeal which has just been considered. As the letter has been preserved, however, it gives no hint of discontinuity, and conveys the rather disagreeable impression that the author has exchanged an obsequious for a bullying tone towards his readers. The hesitancy and uncertainty which marked the earlier chapters of the letter have disappeared. They are replaced by a vigorous assertion of Paul's claims: 'If I am somewhat over-boastful about our authority – an authority given by the Lord to build you up, not pull you down – I shall make my boast good' (10.8). He is emphatic about his divine appointment: 'Not the man who recommends himself, but the man whom the Lord recommends – he and he alone is to be accepted' (10.18). Earlier in the letter he has used his position as founding father with some timidity about their response. Here he seems to be addressing not primarily the Corinthians, but spiritual interlopers who are trespassing in his sphere of influence, and his assurance is correspondingly greater; 'With us there shall be no attempt to boast beyond our proper sphere; and our sphere is determined by the limit God laid down for us, which permitted us to come as far as Corinth. We are not overstretching our commission, as we should be if it did not extend to you, for we were the first to reach Corinth in preaching the gospel of Christ. And we do not boast of work done where others have laboured, work beyond our proper sphere. Our hope is that, as your faith grows, we may attain a position among you greater than ever before, but still within the limits of our sphere' (10.13–15). The apostle, however, is careful not to limit himself to Corinth or compromise his all-embracing commission: 'Then we can carry the Gospel to lands that lie beyond you, never priding ourselves on work already done in another man's sphere' (10.16). A parson defending his parish boundaries could not speak in a more peremptory manner. It is also a reminder of how universal claims are driven to become imperialist the moment they are challenged.

Paul is particularly concerned to rebut the suggestion that his bark is worse than his bite: that his letters are severe, but his personal presence unimpressive (10.1, 9, 10). It throws an interesting light on the possible distance between the man and the writer if much of the assertion and self-importance of the letters is compensation for a man whose personal impact was unremarkable. Paul, however, will have none of this. Despite his admissions in I Corinthians 2.2, here it is not his weakness but his strength that he wishes to emphasize. 'Weak men we may be, but it is not as such that we fight our battles. The weapons we wield are not merely human, but divinely potent to demolish strongholds; we demolish sophistries and all that rears its proud head against the knowledge of God; we compel every human thought to surrender in obedience to Christ; and we are prepared to punish all rebellion when once you have put yourselves in our hands' (10.3–6). Paul wishes to combine miraculous power and destructive argument; it is a parade of strength which makes consistent use of military imagery: a battle, weapons, strongholds rebellion, are the nouns – demolish, compel, surrender and punish are the verbs. The apostle's mood is militant, and the tone menacing. It has as its background the militarism both of the Roman empire and of much eschatological hope: 'When I come, my actions will show the same man as my letters showed in my absence' (10.11).

(i) The discrediting of opposition

Paul is afraid that the loyalty of the Corinthians has been lost. He intertwines divine and marital imagery to convey both the nature of their obligation and the depravity of their faithlessness: 'I am jealous for you, with a divine jealousy; for I betrothed you to Christ, thinking to present you as a chaste virgin to her true and only husband. But as the serpent in his cunning seduced Eve, I am afraid that your thoughts may be corrupted and you may lose your single-hearted devotion to Christ' (11.2, 3). Paul adopts a tone of hypothesis and anxiety which enables him to avoid blaming the Corinthians while directing his animosity towards their corrupters. He sarcastically refers to them as 'those superlative apostles', and accuses them of introducing another Jesus, another Spirit, another gospel, and pours scorn on the Corinthians for tolerating them. 'You manage to put up with that well enough' (11.4). Paul admits that he lacks eloquence, but contrasts his own openness with the esoteric claims of his competitors: 'At all times we have made known to you the full truth' (11.6). His abuse of the rival Christian authorities who have dared to set themselves up as his equals gives a vivid insight into the tensions among the early Christian leadership: 'I shall go on doing as I am doing now, to cut the ground from under those who would seize any chance to put their vaunted apostleship on the same level as ours. Such men are sham-apostles, crooked in all their practices, masquerading as apostles of Christ. There is nothing surprising about that; Satan himself masquerades as an angel of light. It is therefore a simple thing for his agents to masquerade as agents of good. But they will meet the end their deeds deserve' (11.12–15). Here on Paul's lips the same charges occur which in the Synoptic Gospels are brought against Jesus himself. Perhaps this is an echo of the way in which the Jerusalem apostles had at one time regarded the renegade and equivocal Paul. The elevation of his own authority is such that he can tolerate no independent source of power in the communities which he has founded. Paul accuses his opponents of being sham-apostles, but, as soon becomes apparent, his own claims cannot very easily be substantiated. For the moment he contents himself with making general charges of dishonesty, encouraging suspicion of Satanic influence, and issuing dark threats.

As in Galatians he established his *bona fides* in relation to the Jerusalem apostles by stressing his financial disinterestedness and at the same time making unflattering comparisons with them, so here he uses the same tactics to discredit his opponents in Corinth: 'Was this my offence, that I made no charge for preaching the gospel of God, lowering myself to help in raising you? It is true that I took toll of other congregations, accepting support from them to serve you. Then, while I was with you, if I ran short I sponged on no one; anything I needed was fully met by our friends who came from Macedonia; I made it a rule, as I always shall, never to be a burden to you. As surely as the truth of Christ is in me, I will preserve my pride in this matter throughout Achaia, and nothing shall stop me' (11.7–10). He repeats the point in 12.13. In a revealing admission he asserts: 'It is you I want, not your money' (12.14). That is almost certainly a correct account of his motivation. It is power over individuals rather than the acquisition of wealth which is important to Paul; though the sceptic might argue that if he gains control of the person, he will also have access to the pocket. It seems, however, that Paul here is not simply flaunting his independence to discredit his opponents – he himself has been charged with malpractice: 'Granted that I did not prove a burden to you, still I was unscrupulous enough, you say, to use a trick to catch you. Who, of the men I have sent to you, was used by me to defraud you? I begged Titus to visit you, and I sent our friend with him. Did Titus defraud you? Have we not both been guided by the same Spirit, and followed the same course?' (12.16–18). This gives the impression that Paul is deliberately misunderstanding the charges against him in such a way that he can give a satisfactory answer. He stresses the honesty of Titus and his own financial independence, but he does not address himself to the suggestion of trickery. Both in his playing off the generosity of one congregation against another and in his claim to financial disinterestedness while being supported by congregations elsewhere, Paul does not seem to have behaved entirely straightforwardly. He chooses to treat it as an accusation of swindling, which he can rebut. He seems much more open to a charge of misrepresentation.

(j) Paul's defence of his apostolate

We are so used to Paul's accounts of his own apostolate that we easily overlook certain curious features of his story. He will boldly denounce his opponents as 'sham-apostles', but when he comes to defend himself there is one obvious omission. He has no historical connection with Jesus. His apostleship comes neither from Jesus' public ministry nor from the authorization of the Twelve. He therefore has to give an account of his legitimacy which will conceal this defect. He succeeds by reverting to the pattern of suffering and resurrection with which he has strongly identified himself earlier in the letter. In I Corinthians he based his claims on his witness to the resurrection. Here he proceeds very differently; the resurrection claims are presented in another way and are not given the same weight. He refers, for instance, to 'visions and revelations granted by the Lord' (12.1), and whets the reader's curiosity by briefly describing some of them (12.2–5). He insists on his truthfulness, but depreciates the importance of such claims: 'If I should choose to boast, it would not be the boast of a fool, for I should be speaking the truth. But I refrain, because I should not like anyone to form an estimate of me which goes beyond the evidence of his own eyes and ears' (12.6). Despite the disclaimer, he has made sure that the assertion is not forgotten, even if he refuses to hang too much on it. Similarly, he appeals to the 'signs, marvels, and miracles' (12.12) which accompanied his work in Corinth, but he gives priority to his 'constant fortitude' (12.12).

In this account 'the marks of a true apostle' are neither resurrection appearances nor any relation to the historic Jesus or the Twelve. The apostle demonstrates his authenticity by his affliction or, as Paul describes it, his 'weakness' (11.21, 29, 30; 12.5, 9, 10). He catalogues at length his sufferings in the service of Christ. He sees the same significance in his own bouts of illness: 'I was given a sharp physical pain which came as Satan's messenger to bruise me; this was to save me from being unduly elated. Three times I begged the Lord to rid me of it, but his answer was: "My grace is all you need; power comes to its full strength in weakness"' (12.7–9). He concludes his vindication of his apostolate on the same note: 'I shall therefore prefer to find my joy and my pride in the very things that are my weakness; and then the power of Christ will come and rest upon me. Hence I am well content, for Christ's sake, with weakness, contempt, persecution, hardship, and frustration; for when I am weak, then I am strong' (12.9–10). It needs to be noted that this stress on weakness is the reverse of hopeless or despairing. It is the visible pledge of future vindication: weakness is praised because it is the path to strength. Paul produces these credentials because he knows they are unassailable. Others may have lived with Jesus, or be recognized by the Twelve. Others might claim visions or experience of the Risen Christ. Paul knows that no one can match his sufferings in the cause.

The defence of his apostolate by reference to his sufferings has two interesting implications. The first is for the unity of the letter, because the strong emphasis in the earlier part of the letter on identification with the suffering and resurrection of Christ prepares for the vindication of the apostle with which the letter ends. This is not to say that the pattern is not found elsewhere in Paul's thought, particularly when he deals with persecution, but there is a strong continuity on this issue throughout II Corinthians. The second is more disturbing. Since identification with the sufferings of Christ seems to have been one of the ways in which Paul established his own apostolic authenticity, it may be that his distinctive perspective of death and resurrection is itself related to his own position. It is customary to see this as the core of primitive Christianity, attested in baptism and the earliest preaching. At the least it has to be recognized that Paul has very strong reasons of his own for emphasizing this pattern. His charismatic contemporaries or the Jerusalem apostles might have given a quite different perspective. It is often remarked that Paul is highly selective in his references to Jesus' life, and this is usually explained by reference to the occasional and polemical nature of his writing. It may be that the selection he made did not represent so much an early Christian consensus about what was most important in the new religion as a Pauline perception of these elements in the new religion which were most compatible with his own claims and might be exploited for his own advantage.

(k) Paul's third coming: the threat of judgment

All Paul's talk of his weakness has only been preparation for the most aggressive assertion of power. He does not scruple to identify his own exercise of discipline among the Corinthians with the vindication of Christ: 'When I come this time, I will show no leniency. Then you will have the proof you seek of the Christ who speaks through me, the Christ who, far from being weak with you, makes his power felt among you. True, he died on the cross in weakness, but he lives by the power of God; and we who share his weakness shall by the power of God live with him in your service' (13.2–4). The language of service should not conceal the exercise of power. Christ is today vindicated by the discipline of the refractory Corinthians, as he was in the past by being raised from the dead. Both are witnesses to the power of God. Paul now feels sufficiently confident to deny any apologetic aim: he does not look for the approval of a human, but of a divine audience. His purpose is not to gain the good opinion of the Corinthians, but to improve them (12.19, 20). He first anticipates his disappointment in them at his forthcoming visit: 'I fear I may find quarrelling and jealousy, angry tempers and personal rivalries, backbiting and gossip, arrogance and general disorder' (12.20). Every evidence of dissatisfaction with Paul is thus interpreted as sinful. This prepares him to make the familiar justification of those about to use repressive power that it is done more in sorrow than in anger: 'I am afraid, that when I come again, my God may humiliate me in your presence, that I may have tears to shed over many of those who have sinned in the past and have not repented of their unclean lives, their fornication and sensuality' (12.21). He proceeds to give ample warning of his intention to use his power as their judge: 'This will be my third visit to you; and all facts must be established by the evidence of two or three witnesses. To those who have sinned in the past, and to everyone else, I repeat the warning I gave before; I gave it in person on my second visit, and I give it now in absence. It is that when I come this time, I will show no leniency' (13.1–2). It is not clear whether the reference to the two or three witnesses is a reference to the repetition of his visits, which establishes his view of what is going on, or is a reminder of the nature of judicial procedure. In either case the menace is unmistakable.

He then delivers a final appeal to his readers to exercise self-discipline rather than have to be disciplined by himself: 'Examine yourselves: are you living the life of faith? Put yourselves to the test' (13.5). Paul would much prefer his rule to be interiorized. This is not so much a gain for the autonomy of the Corinthians as the culmination of his own successful assertion of power. 'Surely you recognize that Jesus Christ is among you?' (13.5). That is a reminder which recalls both the gift of the Spirit which enables them to live a spiritual life, and also the power of the apostolic discipline should they succumb to temptation. Paul goes on to refer to a process of testing which involves both himself and his readers, though in very different ways. They are being challenged to re-examine the moral tenor of their lives; Paul is being challenged to exercise his jurisdiction. Paul refuses to acknowledge any reciprocity in their relationship: he is responsible for their behaviour, but he is not answerable to them: 'Our prayer to God is that you may do no wrong; we are not concerned to be vindicated ourselves; we want you to do what is right, even if we should seem to be discredited. For we have no power to act against the truth, but only for it. We are well content to be weak at any time if only you are strong. Indeed, my whole prayer is that all may be put right with you'

(13.7–9). The tenor of such a prayer is an insistent accusation, but Paul is primarily concerned not to condemn but to procure a change of heart. He knows that his authority will be weakened if he has actually to use it. Unlike Jonah, he does not want to see their condemnation but their repentance, even if it seems to evade his threats. Paul has a clear understanding of the limits of his power. The threat of exclusion and loss of privilege are far more effective if they can persuade the Corinthians to obey him; the use of such authority is a recognition of failure: 'My purpose in writing this letter before I come, is to spare myself, when I come, any sharp exercise of authority – authority which the Lord gave me for building up and not for pulling down' (13.10). Paul's dilemma is that his use of authority to improve is dependent on the effectiveness of his threat to destroy. For all his talk of weakness and identification with the cross, it is by no means clear that he stands with the crucified. There is a horrid suspicion that he ultimately stands with those who were prepared to crucify in order to defend and preserve their position. In this the Christian Paul is not perhaps so different from the persecuting Saul.

7

COLOSSIANS

(a) Paul's relation to the Colossian church

All the Pauline letters which have been examined so far have been written to Christian communities founded by the writer. There is in all of them a stress on his apostolic status and his role as the founding father. By contrast, Paul recognizes that the Colossian church was founded by the teaching of Epaphras (1.7). In the final greetings Paul refers to him as 'Epaphras, servant of Christ, who is one of yourselves' (4.12). He thus takes care to recognize Epaphras' relation to the Colossians, knowing that it strengthens his own claim on their attention. The variant readings of the text make it unclear whether Paul directly subordinates Epaphras to himself by describing him as 'a trusted worker for Christ on our behalf' (1.7) or is simply referring to Epaphras' commitment to the Colossians, but Paul makes it plain to his readers that Epaphras is the source of his information about them (1.8). Having thus established his credentials, he subsequently asserts his sovereignty over the Colossians in ways which repudiate any dependence on local knowledge or presence. 'I want you to know how strenuous are my exertions for you and the Laodiceans and all who have never set eyes on me' (2.1). Just because they have never met him, they are not to think they are free from his attention. Likewise, absence does not imply forgetfulness: 'For though absent in body, I am with you in spirit' (2.5). The impression of immediacy is heightened by the detailed instruction to an individual: 'This special word to Archippus: "Attend to the duty entrusted to you in the Lord's service, and discharge it to the full"' (4.17). Such direct and slightly menacing words must have served to convey to many others of those present at the letter's first reading the precise and effective style of Paul's supervision. Such distinction was perhaps embarrassing to the recipient.

(b) Paul as the suffering servant

Paul eschews in this letter a whole range of arguments based on his role as founding father, and he does not place much explicit weight on his apostolate. True, he sharply distinguishes himself as 'apostle of Christ Jesus commissioned by the will of God' from 'our colleague Timothy' in the opening words (1.1), but it is as suffering servant rather than as apostle that he projects himself here. It is therefore much more in keeping with those passages in II Corinthians which establish his authenticity on the basis of his suffering. In drawing attention to his affliction, he asserts the benefit which he conveys. 'It is now my happiness to suffer for you. This is my way of helping the complete, in my poor human flesh, the full tale of Christ's afflictions still to be endured, for the sake of his body which is the church' (1.24). 'We instruct everyone in all the ways of wisdom, so as to present each one of you as a mature member of Christ's body. To this end I am toiling strenuously with all the energy and power of Christ at work in me' (1.28, 29). It is an astonishingly self-conscious variety of vicarious suffering, and it is a mark of the significance which Paul ascribes to his trials that he can envisage them completing the unfinished work of Christ. It is a quite different attitude towards Christ's death from the 'once, only once for all' theme found in the letter to the Hebrews. For despite his language of suffering and service Paul is advancing the most extravagant claims. The note of divine appointment is explicit: 'I became its servant by virtue of the task assigned to me by God for your benefit' (1.25). The humble language of service is transformed by the cosmic dimensions of its scope. 'This is the gospel which has been proclaimed in the whole creation under heaven; and I, Paul, have become its minister' (1.23). He has a universal task 'to make known how rich and glorious it is among all nations' (1.27). It is therefore only appropriate that 'we admonish everyone without distinction' (1.28). To Paul has been entrusted the fullness of God's message (1.26). He can therefore admonish his readers 'to come to the full wealth of conviction which understanding brings' (2.2). If he does not immediately proceed to exert control over his readers, such a passage is nonetheless effective in establishing his dominance.

(c) The use of prayer

Although the problem of writing to a church which he has not himself founded renders unusable some of Paul's most familiar means of establishing his authority, he is not thereby prevented from resorting to prayer. Once again he uses the form of thanksgiving to convey oblique praise: 'We have heard of the faith you hold in Christ Jesus, and the love you bear towards all God's people' (1.4). Such behaviour springs from 'the hope of which you learned when the message of the true Gospel first came to you' (1.5). Their initial discernment and response is recognized as the

basis of their privilege and thus confirmed. Any sense of isolation or
eccentricity is removed by reassuring them that they belong to a universal
phenomenon. 'In the same way (the message of the true gospel) is coming
to men the whole world over; everywhere it is growing and bearing fruit as
it does among you' (1.6). From the flattery of thanksgiving Paul then turns
to the implicit control of intercession, making his readers aware of possible
inadequacy. He asks that they may receive from God 'all wisdom and
spiritual understanding for full insight into his will' (1.9) and that they
may 'grow in the knowledge of God' (1.10). Thus they are prepared to be
receptive to the very precise lessons that the apostle has in store for them
later in the letter. Similarly, prayer is used to attack any complacency
about the quality of their life. Paul reminds them of their responsibility to
God: may 'your manner of life ... be worthy of the Lord and entirely
pleasing to him. We pray that you may bear fruit in active goodness of
every kind' (1.10). The same priorities are reflected in the final section of
the letter in the greeting to Epaphras: 'He prays hard for you all the time,
that you may stand fast, ripe in conviction, and wholly devoted to doing
God's will' (4.12). The possibility of persecution is anticipated in a way
which quietly draws attention to Paul's own position, explicitly stated in
the final verse: 'Remember I am in prison' (4.18). Here it suffices to make
his readers aware of their untested state: 'May he strengthen you, in his
glorious might, with ample power to meet whatever comes with fortitude,
patience and joy' (1.11). The prayer ends with the request that God may
enable the readers to appreciate their privilege: so they may 'give thanks to
the Father who has made you fit to share the heritage of God's people in the
realm of light' (1.22). In his closing instructions Paul returns to the theme
of prayer. It stimulates attention and thankfulness (4.2). He encourages
the readers to identify themselves with his task, while reminding them of
its cost: 'Include a prayer for us, that God may give us an opening for
preaching, to tell the secret of Christ ... Pray that I may make the secret
plain, as it is my duty to do' (4.3, 4). To that secret we must now turn.

(d) The gospel as secret

In II Corinthians the use of the notion of 'veil' has been closely examined.
This notion of hiddenness which is so ambivalently handled is developed
in that letter to discredit dissent, and is worked out in predominantly
Jewish categories. Here Paul used a word with different and Hellenistic
associations – 'secret'. He uses it, moreover, not to disarm critics, but to
convey privilege. Talk of the secret establishes a community between
writer and reader, who alike share in privileged knowledge which is itself a
pledge of special status. On the one hand Paul stresses the excitement of

the disclosure: 'The secret hidden for long ages and through many generations, but now disclosed to God's people, to whom it was his will to make it known' (1.26, 27). The secret is not something elusive: it can be grasped (2.2) and it is to be proclaimed (1.28) and made plain (4.4). But just as Paul first repudiates the esoteric when speaking of the 'veil' and then proceeds to reinstate it, the element of hiddenness about the secret remains, carefully wrapped in the future. The moment he has given explicit statement to the secret, he qualifies it by a future reference: 'The secret is this: Christ in you, the hope of a glory to come' (1.27). Hidden knowledge may have been revealed, but only enigmatically. It is like a series of Chinese boxes. Revelation only prefaces further concealment: 'That secret is Christ himself; in him lie hidden all God's treasures of wisdom and knowledge' (2.2, 3). The reward remains 'stored up for you in heaven' (1.5), or, as Paul puts it most explicitly: 'Now your life lies hidden with Christ in God. When Christ, who is our life, is manifested, then you too will be manifested with him in glory' (3.3, 4). Once again Paul stresses the future benefit which alone will justify the sense of privilege he attributes to the new believers. Heaven conceals the origin of the secret which gives it its excitement, and conceals its future which makes it irrefutable.

The possibilities of manipulation and deceit in such a position are obvious; but in a world where the financial status of people was very much more dependent upon the accidents of inheritance than in our society, the contrast between present penury and future prospects would have been familiar and plausible. The presence in the New Testament of the concepts of heir and inheritance is not surprising: they reflect the anxieties and jealousies of social ambitions which were widespread. Part of the attraction of the Pauline gospel is the promise that you too can be an heir. It gives a new self-esteem to those without prospects in their society, and reconciles them to immediate deprivations. It encourages a use of the imagination to transcend present limitations, but at the cost of action and initiative. The heir cannot do anything; he can only wait and hope. In one respect, however, the Christian heir is more fortunate than his secular counterpart. The latter is always conscious of and made guilty by the dependence of his good fortune on the death of another. He may look towards his inheritance, but must refrain from anticipating the death which will release it. By contrast the Christian can look towards the end of all things with enthusiasm and relish. He benefits, not from the death of a fellow-creature, but from the righteous and obliterating judgment of God.

(e) The use of christology

The most distinctive characteristic of the letter to the Colossians is the sweeping exposition of the significance and status of Christ which marks the first two chapters. It is customary to remark on the grandeur and extravagance of the claims, and to contrast such language with that found in Paul's other letters. As so often with doctrinal passages, very little attention has been given to the way in which the doctrinal claims function within the letter as a whole. Here the christological emphasis is the direct outcome of Paul's relation to this particular community, and the doctrine cannot be properly understood apart from the use to which it is put in the letter. Because Paul did not establish the Colossian church, he cannot appeal to his founding authority, and the significance of his apostolic authority would appear remote to the experience of such readers. He does not therefore spend time establishing his own apostolic claims; instead, the place in the structure of this letter, which in previous letters has been spent elaborating and defending his apostolic claims, is here devoted not to himself but to his Lord. Paul begins with a ringing declaration of freedom and release: 'God rescued us from the domain of darkness and brought us away into the kingdom of his dear Son, in whom our release is secured and our sins forgiven' (1.13, 14). Such claims about God and Jesus are repeatedly grounded in the experience of the Colossians themselves. Paul does not need to convince, he can appeal to their own experience: 'Through (Christ) God chose to reconcile the whole universe to himself, making peace through the shedding of his blood upon the cross – to reconcile all things, whether on earth or in heaven, through him alone. Formerly you were yourselves estranged from God; you were his enemies in heart and mind, and your deeds were evil. But now by Christ's death in his body of flesh and blood God has reconciled you to himself' (1.20–22). Because Paul can refer to his readers' experience of moral renewal and release from their past, he does not have to explain its relation to Christ's sufferings and death; he can simply assert it (cf. also 2.13). Where later in the letter he does give some account of the process, it is entirely consonant with his understanding of the matter in his other letters. God 'has forgiven us all our sins; he has cancelled the bond which pledged us to the decrees of the Law. It stood against us, but he has set it aside, nailing it to the cross. On that cross he discarded the cosmic powers and authorities like a garment; he made a public spectacle of them and led them as captives in his triumphal procession' (2.13–15). This passage cannot be understood apart from Paul's teaching in Galatians (see p. 50). There is the same emphasis on the cross discrediting the Law, the same equation of its angelic mediation with the demonic world.

Paul thus begins his christology by making claims of salvation which are plausible in terms of the experience of his readers, but he then proceeds to intertwine the unique status of Christ with the special privileges of the believers: 'He is the image of the invisible God; his is the primacy over all created things. In him everything in heaven and on earth was created, not only things visible but also the invisible order of thrones, sovereignties, authorities and powers; the whole universe has been created through him and for him. He is, moreover, the head of the body, the church. He is its origin, the first to return from the dead, to be in all things alone supreme. For in him the complete being of God, by God's own choice, came to dwell' (1.15–19). The authority claimed is breathtaking, but we misinterpret the force of the passage if we isolate the claims made about Christ from those who are making them. The reader thrills to such a description precisely because he can identify himself with Christ. Paul repeatedly emphasizes this identity: 'The secret is this: Christ in you' (1.27). 'Since Jesus was delivered to you as Christ and Lord, live your lives in union with him. Be rooted in him; be built in him' (2.6, 7). 'Did you not die with Christ?' (2.20). 'Were you not raised to life with Christ?' (3.1). Thus the exaltation of Christ serves also to exalt the believer. He also reflects the invisible God. He also shares in the sovereignty of the cosmos. He shares in Christ's pre-existence. He is no longer a latecomer into an alien world. As a member of the body which has such a head, he shares in the fullness of God's being and is himself the object of God's choice.

If the doctrinal passage in ch. 1 stood alone, such an interpretation might seem fanciful, but its elaboration in the letter makes it plain that this is precisely the use to which Paul puts the doctrine. Paul expounds the privileged status of the believer on the basis of the unique status of Christ: 'For it is in Christ that the complete being of the Godhead dwells embodied, and in him you have been brought to completion. Every power and authority in the universe is subject to him as Head. In him also you were circumcised, not in a physical sense, but by being divested of the lower nature; this is Christ's way of circumcision' (2.9–11). In the other letters we have studied, Paul has argued from the privileged status of his readers to his own privileged status as apostle, and has then proceeded to use the privilege he has extended to control those who have been thus benefited. Here he identifies the believer with Christ, and then proceeds to use that privileged identity in order to control. He speaks of God willing to 'present you before himself as dedicated men, without blemish and innocent in his sight. Only you must continue in your faith, firm on your foundations, never to be dislodged from the hope offered in the gospel which you heard' (1.22, 23). At first it is the perseverance and conformity of the believer that he wishes to secure. Slowly this reveals a more polemical intent. The emphasis on Christ serves to discredit other voices:

'That secret is Christ himself; in him lie hidden all God's treasures of wisdom and knowledge. I tell you this to save you from being talked into error by specious arguments' (2.2–4). Finally, the bid for control becomes unmistakable: 'Be consolidated in the faith you were taught; let your hearts overflow with thankfulness. Be on your guard; do not let your minds be captured by hollow and delusive speculations, based on man-made teaching and centred on the elemental spirits of the universe and not on Christ' (2.7, 8).

The precise polemical intent of the whole christological exposition is only revealed towards the end of the second chapter, where Paul vigorously repudiates Jewish forms of visibility and external ritual. His emphasis on the hidden, secret nature of the gospel is here given practical expression. Esoteric doctrine and inward 'spiritual' discipline go hand in hand. 'Allow no one therefore to take you to task about what you eat or drink, or over the observance of festival, new moon, or sabbath. These are no more than a shadow of what was to come; the solid reality is Christ's' (2.16–17).

Later in the letter Paul reveals how isolated he has become within the church: 'Aristarchus ... Mark ... and Jesus Justus. Of the Jewish Christians, these are the only ones who work with me for the kingdom of God, and they have been a great comfort to me' (4.10, 11). Paul's position is thus precarious, and he gives no quarter to his opponents. Rivals are ruthlessly discredited. 'Such people, bursting with the futile conceit of worldly minds, lose hold upon the Head' (2.19). Having identified Christ with the fullness of Godhead, Paul emphasizes the purely human origin of his critics: 'People who go in for self-mortification and angel-worship, and try to enter into some vision of their own' (2.18). To listen to them is 'to follow merely human injunctions and teaching' (2.22). What is dismissed as angel-worship is most probably the Jewish Law, mediated by angels and already equated by Paul with 'the elemental spirits of the universe' (2.20). Thus the Jewish ritual prescriptions are repudiated: 'Why let people dictate to you: "Do not handle this, do not taste that, do not touch the other" – all of them things that must perish as soon as they are used?' (2.21, 22). Developing the hierarchy implicit in his use of the analogy of the body in I Cor. 12, he insists upon the dependence of the whole body upon the head: 'It is from the head that the whole body, with all its joints and ligaments, receives its supplies, and thus knit together grows according to God's design' (2.19). As in I Corinthians, the divine ordering of the body is used to sanction conformity and obedience.

(f) Baptismal asceticism: alienation and oppression

Despite the gnostic overtones of much of the language in this letter, it is

Jewish criticism which Paul is primarily concerned to overcome. Hence there is an emphasis on baptismal asceticism as the answer to Jewish claims of legitimacy based on circumcision: 'In (Christ) also you were circumcised, not in a physical sense, but by being divested of the lower nature; this is Christ's way of circumcision. For in baptism you were buried with him, in baptism also you were raised to life with him through your faith in the active power of God who raised him from the dead. And although you were dead because of your sins and because you were morally uncircumcised, he has made you alive with Christ' (2.11–13). It is by the prestige of asceticism that Paul seeks to triumph over Jewish criticism: 'True, it has an air of wisdom, with its forced piety, its self-mortification, and its severity to the body; but it is of no use at all in combating sensuality' (2.23). Paul here assumes that his readers and his critics alike share his repudiation of the earthly and corporeal. They do not differ in their religious aims, but in the effectiveness of their remedies. The transcendent Christ, concealed in the heavens, enables the Christian effectively to direct his attention from the earth. As so often assertion and command are intertwined: 'Were you not raised to life with Christ? Then aspire to the realm above, where Christ is, seated at the right hand of God, and let your thoughts dwell on that higher realm, not on this earthly life' (3.1, 2). As in Galatians and Philippians, the new life is expressed by a radical contrast between the earthly and the heavenly, articulated in the experience of the readers in their own baptism. The language of putting 'to death those parts of you which belong to the earth' (3.5), of having 'discarded the old nature with its deeds and . . . put on the new nature' (3.10), the command to 'put on the garments that suit God's chosen people, his own, his beloved' (3.12), is all reminiscent of baptism.

On the one hand baptism bound together prohibition and repudiation. The list is revealing: 'Fornication, indecency, lust, foul cravings, and the ruthless greed which is nothing less than idolatry' (3.5). 'Anger, passion, malice, cursing, filthy talk' (3.8). As so often with Pauline moral teaching it is a curious mixture: social disruptiveness is associated with sexual shame and loss of self-possession. Resentment at man's physical constitution and emotional volatility is artfully combined with social criticism: greed and malice. In the prohibitions it is sexual morality which predominates. In the positive aspirations, social harmony and conformity provide the keynote: 'Compassion, kindness, humility, gentleness, patience. Be forebearing with one another, and forgiving, where any of you has cause for complaint: you must forgive as the Lord forgave you. To crown all, there must be love, to bind all together and complete the whole. Let Christ's peace be arbiter in your hearts; to this peace you were called as members of a single body' (3.12–15). At first sight the mutuality and reciprocity of the ideal appear impressive, as does the reconciliation implied in the transcendence of all previous identities: 'There is no question here of Greek and Jew, circumcised and uncircumcised, barbarian, Scythian, slave and freeman; but Christ is all, and is in all' (3.11).

The price of this new identity is, however, considerable, if largely concealed. The universal note which is struck, and which suggests that Christ transcends all human barriers, is misleading. True enough, he relativizes all previous distinctions, but that is only to involve his followers in a much more radical alienation. Behind the language of prohibition there is the sanction of divine vengeance: 'Because of these, God's dreadful judgment is impending; and in the life you once lived these are the ways you yourselves followed' (3.6, 7). The readers are left in no doubt of their own precarious condition. If they are to escape, they must clearly differentiate themselves from the objects of God's wrath. Their attitude to outsiders is to be self-conscious and manipulative: 'Behave wisely towards those outside your own number; use the present opportunity to the full. Let your conversation be always gracious, and never insipid; study how best to talk with each person you meet' (4.5, 6). Those outside are simply perceived as possible converts. They are respected only as potential insiders. It is the logical outcome of the esoteric emphasis of the secret.

Secondly, the pursuit of social harmony within the new community, while speaking the language of mutuality and reciprocity, refuses to acknowledge present injustice and the actual disequilibrium of power. It only weakly tries to mitigate the injustice of structures which it refuses fundamentally to challenge. 'Wives be subject to your husbands; that is your Christian duty. Husbands, love your wives and do not be harsh with them' (3.18, 19). The dominance of the man over the woman is legitimized as a religious duty; the husband is advised how to use his power prudently and effectively. The presence of commands which involve both wife and husband gives the illusion of balance, but their substance is very different. Similarly, 'Children, obey your parents in everything, for that is pleasing to God and is the Christian way. Fathers, do not exasperate your children, for fear they grow disheartened' (3.20, 21). Parental authority is given the strongest legitimation; parental responsibilities are given a purely prudential justification. This is most spectacularly the case in Paul's treatment of slavery: 'Slaves, give entire obedience to your earthly masters, not merely with an outward show of service, to curry favour with men, but with single-mindedness, out of reverence for the Lord. Whatever you are doing, put your whole heart into it, as if you were doing it for the Lord and not for men, knowing that there is a Master who will give you your heritage as a reward for your service. Christ is the Master whose slaves you must be. Dishonesty will be requited, and he has no favourites. Masters, be just and fair to your slaves, knowing that you too have a Master in heaven' (3.22 – 4.1). The disparity in emphasis is as obvious as the difference in length. The institution itself is unchallenged, and exploitation of the slave facilitated. Far from finding freedom in his new religion, he has acquired a more exacting and all-seeing Master. All the grand christological claims of release and reconciliation end in practice by reconciling slaves to their lot and conniving at their exploitation.

8

PHILEMON

The gospel of freedom and social conflict

Something has already been said of Paul's attitude to slavery in the
concluding words on the letter to the Colossians. The present letter, to the
owner of a runaway slave, gives a fascinating example of Paul exerting his
authority in a particular instance. Paul's attitude to the institution of
slavery cannot be properly understood apart from its implicit challenge to
his own position. His predicament, which can be most clearly seen in this
letter, is that once he becomes involved in a situation of real social conflict
it is difficult for him to preserve his credibility in the eyes of both parties to
the dispute. The runaway slave puts him in a position which tests the
Christian claims to bring freedom and reconciliation. The Christian
identity of the slave-owner forces Paul to define his attitudes towards
property and its infringement. The conflict of interest between the
runaway slave and the dispossessed owner threatens to embarrass the
vaunted harmony of the new community. It provides valuable insight into
the nature of the constraints on Paul's power, and his response to those
limitations.

Paul has obligations and authority over both parties to the dispute, and
the letter shows how he endeavours to maintain his credibility in the eyes
of each of them. Paul has converted the runaway Onesimus, and now
stands towards him in the relation of a father to a son (10). It is in virtue of
that authority that Paul now sends him back to his master (12). The
initiative comes from Paul, and in virtue of this he is able to make claims on
Philemon, which the runaway slave could not have made for himself. Paul
stresses Onesimus' importance to him: 'I am sending a part of myself. I
should have liked to keep him with me' (12, 13). Paul speaks of him as 'a
dear brother, very dear indeed to me' (16). Onesimus therefore shares
something of Paul's privileged status, and Paul dares to suggest to his
master a personal justification for his flight: 'Perhaps this is why you
lost him for a time, that you might have him back for good, no longer as a
slave, but as more than a slave – as a dear brother' (15, 16). Such a

mitigation of the slave's offence entirely overlooks the slave's desire for freedom, and confirms him in his condition. Paul would seem to have reconciled Onesimus to his bondage by promising him a welcome and a pardon. Accordingly he asks: 'Welcome him as you would welcome me. And if he has done you any wrong or is in your debt, put that down to my account. Here is my signature, PAUL; I undertake to repay' (17–19). In thus offering to make restitution, Paul clears himself of any failure to respect law and property. In that respect the letter lays to rest the suspicion of subversive behaviour on his part. He may be the runaway's advocate, he is not his abettor.

Paul's primary concern in this letter is to establish his credibility in Philemon's eyes. The runaway Onesimus has already yielded to him, first in conversion and now in returning to his master, a remarkable obedience, given the danger of exemplary punishment to which a runaway slave was liable. Philemon's response is still a matter of anxiety (20). To this end Paul constantly reminds him of his status as 'a prisoner of Christ Jesus' (1, 10, 23). He envisages Onesimus looking after him in prison on his master's behalf: 'To look after me as you would wish, here in prison for the Gospel (13). Paul reminds Philemon of his apostolic authority, 'ambassador as I am of Christ' (10), and of his role in saving Philemon, 'you owe your very self to me' (19), but he prefers not to put his authority to the test. Instead, he self-consciously appeals to the claims of affection: 'Although in Christ I might make bold to point out your duty, yet, because of that same love, I would rather appeal to you' (8). In his opening salutation and prayer of thanksgiving Paul flatters Philemon, conveying both his own esteem for him and Philemon's reputation for loving both God and his fellow Christians (4–7). He addresses him in terms which identify him with Paul's own work and status: 'Philemon our dear friend and fellow-worker' (1). Modestly Paul asks to be considered as a 'partner in the faith' (17). Apostle speaks to the slave owner as an equal: 'We are both in Christ' (20). It is a persuasive example of condescension designed to elicit from Philemon a similar perception of Onesimus, so that he may see him as 'much dearer to you, both as man and as Christian' (16).

Faced by the starkest form of social oppression in the ancient world, the apostle of freedom has taken care to avoid any possible recrimination. The writer who elsewhere speaks so eloquently of the offence of the cross takes care that it is not confused with the freedom of slaves. He has seen that the slave returns to his bondage, and has pandered to the wealth and power of the owner to mitigate any further injustice to the victim. Doubtless both the slave and the owner thanked him for his good offices.

9

ROMANS

Literary pretension and an appearance of sustained argument distinguish this letter from the rest of Paul's work. The last chapter will be treated as a separate letter, reflecting a quite different relation between the writer and his readers, which provides an informative contrast with the major work. By comparison with Paul's other letters, Romans 1–15 seems reflective rather than polemical in tone, and has sometimes been described, not as a letter but as a treatise; that, however, is to mistake its purpose. Paul's other letters are all written to communities with which he has a long established position. Most of them he has himself founded, and in the exception of Colossians he is able to identify himself with their founder. In those letters he is defending a position of authority which has already been recognized: the vehemence with which he does this reflects both the level of his investment and his confidence of success. When writing to the Romans he necessarily writes more circumspectly. It is a matter of some embarrassment to the self-proclaimed apostle to the Gentiles that the most significant church in the Gentile world is not of his founding. He is not attempting here to defend an established position; instead we have an attempt to establish his authority in a community where he must appear a latecomer with implausible pretensions. He is therefore attempting to create an audience which will be responsive to his claims; he cannot assume that it already exists. In such circumstances he cannot afford to alienate his readers by any premature exercise of his apostolate. Instead he projects himself obliquely, playing on the internal tensions of the new community, and asserting his sovereignty in the name of the sovereignty of God. His practical teaching is designed to gain the confidence of both parties in a matter of sensitive dispute. Because Paul's approach in this letter is often indirect, it serves as a convenient transition to the study of Mark's Gospel. We can begin to see here the way in which aggressive and divisive claims can be given a doctrinal disguise which renders critical assessment of such authority almost impossible. The implicit claims are the most effective. It is no accident that this has been the most influential of all Paul's writings. Its apparent objectivity has disarmed criticism.

(a) The apostle of the gospel

Paul does not make an issue of his apostolic status. It has not yet been attacked by this community, so he does not need self-consciously to defend it. Instead he asserts his authority with great economy, by the claims he makes not for himself, but for the gospel. It is the gospel which is first honoured and defined. Its continuity with the Old Testament Scriptures is asserted (1.2), so that the prestige of the prophetic writings is transferred to the gospel which they heralded. The tensions which the relation between gospel and Scripture create will preoccupy Paul through much of this letter. The content of the gospel is Jesus Christ. Attention is focused upon him in a way which immediately states in a new form the same dichotomy: 'On the human level he was born of David's stock, but on the level of the spirit – the Holy Spirit – he was declared Son of God by a mighty act in that he rose from the dead' (1.3, 4). The Jesus of historic reminiscence and scriptural fulfilment is disparaged in a way which is at first surprising. Only on reflection does one realize that Jesus' authority had been proclaimed in a way which mirrors that of his apostle: it is charismatic and attested by resurrection.

Paul's description of himself appears modest. He proclaims himself the 'slave of Christ Jesus'. If he is an apostle it is 'by God's call'. He makes a pun of his previous Pharisaism – 'set apart for the service of the Gospel'. Yet each of these descriptions, which rigorously suppresses his own identity, enables him to assume a divine authority. The language of grace with which he clothes his apostolate (1.5) only dramatizes his elevation; it does not qualify it. 'Faith and obedience' are revealingly linked together as its goal. Unable to argue from his role in founding the Roman church, he gives a universal dimension to his authority, and thus succeeds in including them as an apparent afterthought: 'Through him I received the privilege of a commission in his name to lead to faith and obedience men in all nations, yourselves among them, you who have heard the call and belong to Jesus Christ' (1.5, 6). Thus he uses their allegiance to Christ Jesus to gain attention for his apostolate.

(b) Paul's relation to the Romans

The moment that Paul has asserted his authority over the Roman community he retreats into flattery. He greets them as those 'whom God loves and has called to be his dedicated people' (1.7). In his prayer of thanksgiving he assures them of their celebrity: 'All over the world they are telling the story of your faith' (1.8). Paul then associates himself with their achievement by assuring them of the continuous place they have in his prayers (1.9). He emphasizes his determination to visit Rome (1.10, 13). His failure to do so is not to be interpreted as any indifference or neglect, and he makes the same point at the close of the letter (15.22); he is anxious to prevent misunderstanding on that score. When he proceeds to explain his intention to visit them, his account fluctuates in a way which betrays unease. At first he speaks as one who is conferring a benefit: 'I want to bring you some spiritual gift to make you strong' (1.12). But as soon as he has made that patronizing claim he feels the need to qualify it, to make it more palatable: 'or rather, I want to be among you to be myself encouraged by your faith as well as you by mine' (1.12). It may seem unfair to interpret his recognition of mutuality as purely tactical, but the disarming language only prepares for a more sweeping example of personal aggression, for he continues: 'But I should like you to know, my brothers, that I have often planned to come, though so far without success, in the hope of achieving something among you, as I have in other parts of the world' (1.13). He then returns to his universal mission: 'I am under obligation to Greek and non-Greek, to learned and simple; hence my eagerness to declare the Gospel to you in Rome as well as to others' (1.14, 15). The language of obligations conceals Paul's own responsibility for his intentions, and renders them difficult to oppose.

At the end of the letter Paul again gives us some direct insight into his relation to his readers. He begins by generously recognizing their independence, their maturity, and their capacity to sustain each other: 'My friends, I have no doubt in my own mind that you yourselves are quite full of goodness and equipped with knowledge of every kind, well able to give advice to one another' (15.14). But once again this seems to be purely tactical. His real interest is declared in what follows, which entirely subverts the concessions he has just made: 'Nevertheless I have written to refresh your memory, and written somewhat boldly at times, in virtue of the gift I have from God' (15.15). Unlike some of his modern commentators, Paul is aware of the aggressive and polemical nature of much of this letter. In his own words he has 'written somewhat boldly at times', and he then proceeds to justify such behaviour in terms of his God-given authority: 'His grace has made me a minister of Christ Jesus to the Gentiles; my priestly service is the preaching of the gospel of God, and it falls to me to offer the Gentiles to him as an acceptable sacrifice, consecrated by the Holy Spirit' (15.16). The Greek is not clear whether Paul is making the Gentiles the purely passive object of his sacrifice, or whether it should read: 'so that the worship which the Gentiles offer may be an acceptable sacrifice.' Even if the latter reading is followed, Paul is still asserting that the possibility of their acceptable worship depends on the consecration of 'the Holy Spirit', which it is his privilege to dispense.

Paul then allows himself to speak very candidly of the way in which his own self-esteem and his service of God are in collusion with each other. 'In the fellowship of Christ Jesus I have ground for pride in the service of God' (15.17). He will cheerfully surrender his own identity to Christ, content simply to speak of himself as 'Christ's instrument' (15.18), but this enables him to appropriate imperialist language. He speaks of 'bringing the Gentiles to Christ's allegiance', as a tribe might be subdued to the Emperor. His authenticity is supported 'by the force of miraculous signs, and by the power of the Holy Spirit' (15.19). The extent to which this 'service' has become the vehicle of Paul's own self-aggrandizement is revealed in his refusal to acknowledge dependence on the work of other Christian leaders: 'It is my ambition to bring the Gospel to places where the very name of Christ has not been heard, for I do not want to build on another man's foundation' (15.20). It is disturbing to discover how much of Paul's missionary excitement and zeal reflects an alienation from even his co-religionists. He seems unhappy with any relation to other people that does not reflect his own supremacy.

The final passage of the letter shows Paul attempting to reconcile the conflicting claims on his time and attention in a way which will be acceptable to his Roman readers and provides a most striking commentary on the doctrinal arguments which dominate the letter. It is surprising that the apostle to the Gentiles is at present bound for Jerusalem. Paul must have been aware of the discrepancy, and he explains it in some detail: 'For Macedonia and Achaia have resolved to raise a common fund for the benefit of the poor among God's people at Jerusalem. They have resolved to do so, and indeed they are under an obligation to them. For if the Jewish Christians shared their spiritual treasures with the Gentiles, the Gentiles have a clear duty to contribute to their material needs' (15.26, 27). There are several striking anomalies in this account. In the first place, both the initiative and the obligation are ascribed by Paul to others than himself; yet his previous letters make it plain that the initiative came from him, and that the obligation was one that he had accepted when the Jerusalem leadership recognized his apostolate. What is really fascinating, however, is the relationship between Jewish and Gentile Christians which the collection seems to have implied in his mind. The conferring of material goods to recognize a spiritual benefit is often cited by Paul to justify the support of the Christian leaders. Here the same argument is used to vindicate the financial support of the Jewish Christians in Jerusalem. They have conferred a spiritual benefit on the Gentiles.

When therefore in this letter Paul is speculating on the primacy of the Jews and the nature of the benefit conferred upon the Gentiles, he is not simply exploring an abstract theological issue; he is vindicating very precise financial arrangements to which he has devoted considerable time and energy. The financial exploitation of the Gentile church by the Jewish Christians could itself be seen as a fulfilment of prophecy. Isaiah speaks of the time when 'You shall enjoy the wealth of other nations and be furnished with their riches' (61.6). This may have made Paul's Gentile mission acceptable to the church at Jerusalem, but it would also serve to underline the divisions within the new community. By his collection Paul may well have been identifying himself with Jewish claims to primacy which many Gentiles deeply resented. Moreover Paul himself seems far from confident of the success of his enterprise: 'I implore you by our Lord Jesus Christ and by the love that the Spirit inspires, be my allies in the fight; pray to God for me that I may be saved from unbelievers in Judaea and that my errand to Jerusalem may find acceptance with God's people' (15.30, 31). Paul is anxious whether the relation between Jew and Gentile which the collection expresses will after all prove acceptable to the church at Jerusalem. It would appear that he is treading a difficult path between Jewish imperialism and Gentile self-confidence. The relation that the collection is designed to exemplify is an attempt to reconcile these conflicting attitudes, and Romans is a reflection on its implications and an attempt to secure further Gentile support for that policy. The extent to which Paul had staked his own reputation on the acceptability to both parties of his way forward is indicated by his closing words. He asks that by God's 'will I may come to you in a happy frame of mind and enjoy a time of rest with you' (15.32). This should not be simply dismissed as egoism; it is a sign of the extent to which Paul felt himself to be vulnerable to the outcome of his undertaking.

(c) The condemnation of the Gentiles

'If the Jewish Christians shared their spiritual treasures with the Gentiles, the Gentiles have a clear duty to contribute to their material needs' (15.27). That argument implies certain definite features of the relation between Jews and Christians within the church. First, the spiritual treasures are conceived as belonging to the Jews, so that any act of sharing on their part is an act of magnanimity which creates an obligation among those who are so favoured. Secondly, although the Gentiles are conceived as having access to those treasures, it is solely through the generosity of the Jewish Christians. Their admission to such treasures does not abrogate the privileges of the Jewish Christians; rather, it indicates their basis. Such a relation between Jew and Gentile provides a precise explanation of Paul's repeated words throughout the letter: 'the Jew first, but the Greek also', which makes its initial appearance in 1.16. Paul defends this understanding of the relation between Jew and Gentile by first establishing his own superiority to both, subjecting them equally to the judgment of God. Having discredited both parties in a way which enables him to transcend the judgment he has meted out he is then free to reorder their relationship as he thinks fit. Neither Jew nor Gentile are in any position to remonstrate.

Because Paul's first move is the absolute repudiation and condemnation of the Gentile and Jewish world, he introduces his detailed exposition of the gospel as something which creates offence but which is nevertheless to be grasped boldly. 'For I am not ashamed of the Gospel' (1.16). Paul is able to identify himself so enthusiastically with the gospel because it exactly serves his own aggressive and self-exalting purpose. The words in which he outlines its significance cannot be understood as abstract doctrinal statements apart from their function in the argument, which is to sanction Paul's own prestige and position: '(The Gospel) is the saving power of God for everyone who has faith – the Jew first, but the Greek also – because here is revealed God's way of righting wrong, a way that starts from faith and ends in faith; as Scripture says, "he shall gain life who is justified through faith"' (1.16, 17). The claim to power is direct and unmistakable. It derives its force from the horrifying picture of condemnation and wrath in the following chapters. The power may be attributed to God, but Paul's unique relation to the gospel gives him privileged access to it. The description of that power as 'saving' makes it appear beneficent, but it is only possible to acquire the benefit by acquiescing in the expression of vindictive alienation which is its context. Moreover it is carefully circumscribed: 'to everyone who has faith'. The stress on the inclusion of Jew and Greek only serves to underline that both are in the wrong, and therefore in desperate need of the revelation of 'God's way of righting wrong'. Scripture provides a justification for rewarding 'faith' with 'life'. Paul is thus able to derive a scriptural rationale for his structure of privilege and control. The justification is, however, purely verbal. As the letter makes plain, faith in Paul's hands has acquired a new and very specific meaning, which cannot be divorced from obedience and conformity to God's apostle.

The passage on the condemnation of the Gentiles which follows is one of the most violent and hate-filled in Scripture. Paul uses the message of God's judgment to express his own antagonism and repudiation of the Gentile world. At the same time he elevates himself by proclaiming a condemnation from which he is exempt. Amid the fury of the invective one scarcely notices that the speaker emerges unscathed. In a curious and unconscious transposition of roles the apostle speaks in the manner once reserved to Satan, as the energetic public prosecutor. He needs therefore to emphasize the Gentiles' knowledge of God in order to underline their culpability: 'All that may be known of God by men lies plain before their eyes; indeed God himself has disclosed it to them. His invisible attributes, that is to say his everlasting power and deity, have been visible, ever since the world began, to the eye of reason, in the things he has made. There is therefore no possible defence for their conduct; knowing God, they have refused to honour him as God, or to render him thanks' (1.19–21). Because Paul is only concerned to attribute guilt, he does not need to argue the curious transition from the visible creation to the invisible attributes of God; conveniently he needs only to assert it. This primal *lèse-majesté* brings in its train a pattern of immediate retribution: first the folly of idolatry (1.22–25), which in turn is punished by the shame of homosexuality (1.24–27). Thus fired, Paul ends with a diatribe which revels in the alleged social disintegration of the Gentile world.

The breakdown of society is not presented as a threat; it is offered as a description of the present: 'For we see divine retribution revealed from heaven and falling upon all the godless wickedness of men' (1.18). He expects his attributions of folly, shame and wickedness to express the response of his readers. In adopting this deeply negative attitude towards surrounding society both writer and reader are distancing themselves from the world which they observe and condemn. Both achieve the illusion of transcendence, but the values to which Paul is appealing are supplied by the Gentile and Jewish cultures he repudiates. Paul not only describes idolatry, for instance, as a crime, duly punished by sexual perversion; he also sees it as itself a punishment. Because men have deliberately stifled the truth (1.18), 'All their thinking has ended in futility, and their misguided minds are plunged in darkness. They boast of their wisdom, but they have made fools of themselves, exchanging the splendour of immortal God for an image shaped like mortal man, even for images like birds, beasts, and creeping things' (1.21–23). From Jewish tradition Paul derives the notion of idolatry as a crime deserving divine punishment; but he is also making his own criticisms of pagan polytheism by the Greek philosophers. Without that unacknowledged debt, idols might be perceived as sin, but not as absurdity. Similarly his account of homosexuality, conveniently attributed to women rather than to men in the first instance: Judaism might account it a sin, only Gentile attitudes would make it plausible as a punishment. Surprisingly, divine responsibility for the condition is unhesitatingly asserted: 'God has given them up to the vileness of their own desires, and the consequent degradation of their bodies' (1.24); 'God has given them up to shameful passions' (1.26). It is the same word which in the gospels signifies the betrayal by Judas. This is not to say that Paul has repudiated Jewish notions of sin in this respect, but that he has added to them Gentile notions of shame. It is a punishment because it affects a person's public standing.

The picture of social disintegration which follows from the repudiation of Paul's God probably articulates every existing social and personal anxiety of the time. Whisperers and scandal-mongers jostle with murder and treachery. Neglect of parents, social disorder, arrogance and boasting are all muddled together. It is the exact mix of the tabloid newspaper: it represents no coherent critique of society; instead, it mirrors the antagonisms and insecurity of the confused individual. It gains its force, not from the consistency of its analysis, but from the faithfulness with which it reflects confusion. Moreover Paul is concerned that the punishment fits the crime. On his account the refusal to acknowledge God is irrational and in its turn leaves men totally at the mercy of 'their own depraved reason' (1.28). Thus mistaken error, far from being a mitigation of the offence, becomes a sign of the irredeemable culpability of the offender. In heaping abuse on the sinner Paul has little regard for consistency: 'They know well enough the just decree of God, that those who behave like this deserve to die, and yet they do it; not only so, they actually applaud such practices' (1.32). The moment one punctures the flow of Paul's rhetoric and asks how he knows that this is so, the incoherence in his position becomes apparent. Paul may be convinced that those who behave in such a way deserve death, and his readers may agree with his judgment; but he is determined that the sinner be self-condemned, that he be aware of his offence. Yet the inconsistencies on which he seizes between awareness, behaviour and speech would naturally suggest a quite different conclusion. Paul will not face the possibility that when they 'actually applaud such practices' they mean what they say. The speech and behaviour of the world he is condemning is entirely consistent; it is only forced into contradiction by Paul's attribution of an awareness of God which neither their action nor their speech justifies.

Paul can now evade the possibility of any human judgment. In a brilliant use of guilt and the awareness of contradiction, he seeks to transcend the restraint of his audience and establish his own unfettered freedom: 'You therefore have no defence – you who sit in judgment, whoever you may be – for in judging your fellow-men you condemn yourself, since you, the judge, are equally guilty. It is admitted that God's judgment is rightly passed upon all who commit such crimes as these; and do you imagine –

you who pass judgment on the guilty while committing the same crimes yourself – do you imagine that you, any more than they, will escape the judgment of God?' (2.1–3). The prosecution is conducted with such force that the reader does not notice that the same arguments must undermine the position of the writer. It is Paul 'who sits in judgment'. It is Paul who is determined to acknowledge 'that God's judgment is rightly passed upon all who commit such crimes as these'. Yet the second person singular skilfully seeks to protect him from the dangerous implications of his own argument. Instead the reader is encouraged to exclude the writer from the general condemnation, because it is by identifying himself with the writer that the reader is offered a way of escape. For Paul takes care to indicate the only way to safety: 'Do you think lightly of his wealth of kindness, of tolerance, and of patience, without recognizing that God's kindness is meant to lead you to a change of heart?' (2.4). By 'a change of heart' Paul is referring to absolute and continuing surrender to himself. Only by totally adopting Paul's point of view can the reader hope to share in his immunity to judgment. The choice and the sanction are clearly indicated: 'To those who pursue glory, honour, and immortality by steady persistence in well-doing, (God) will give eternal life; but for those who are governed by selfish ambition, who refuse obedience to the truth and take the wrong for their guide, there will be the fury of retribution' (2.7, 8). One might have imagined that the pursuit of 'glory', 'honour' and 'immortality' was an entirely 'selfish ambition'. Paul is, however, quite prepared to approve such motives: selfishness is baptized, provided it undeviatingly ('persist-ently') submits to his authority. The crucial issue is to 'refuse obedience to the truth and take the wrong for their guide'. As Paul has identified himself with truth and right, the inference is clear. The sanction to which he ultimately appeals is the vindictive use of divine power. The attention and obedience which men give to Paul is the issue on which their ultimate fate entirely depends. Beside that division any distinction between Jew and Gentile pales into insignificance.

Paul now begins to turn his attention from Gentile to Jew. The universal scope and absolute impartiality of the divine judgment with which Paul associates himself demand that 'God has no favourites' (2.11). In order to discredit Jewish privilege, Paul will momentarily elevate the Gentiles by entertaining the possibility that they have access to the Law 'by the light of nature' (2.14). Their conscience and awareness of virtue which make them culpable do give them at least a possibility of realizing righteousness. His closing words to them carefully leave the anxiety concerning judgment unresolved: 'Their conscience is called as witness, and their own thoughts argue the case on either side, against them or even for them, on the day when God judges the secrets of human hearts through Christ Jesus. So my gospel declares' (2.15, 16). His gospel needs to leave the inscrutable judgment of God undeclared at this point. The anxiety of his Gentile readers can only be maintained by an element of continuing suspense. To challenge the complacency of his Jewish readers he must leave open the possibility, however remote, that the Gentiles may be vindicated by God. Divine silence is not a consistent mark of Paul's gospel, quite the reverse, but here it is necessary for the structure of his argument.

(d) The condemnation of the Jews

Paul's condemnation of the Jews is complicated by his conflicting objectives. His first priority is to discredit the Jews in a way which establishes his superiority. This is much the dominant strand in his argument at this stage of the letter. He begins by attacking their identification with their God through the very law on which they base their self-esteem. Paul portrays their religious identity with cruel perception: 'You rely upon the law and are proud of your God; you know his will; instructed by the law, you know right from wrong; you are confident that you are the one to guide the blind, to enlighten the benighted, to train the stupid, and to teach the immature, because in the law you see the very shape of knowledge and truth' (2.17–20). Through a series of questions, he implies but does not establish the case that 'while you take pride in the law, you dishonour God by breaking it' (2.23). Paul relies on the guilty conscience of the Jewish reader to substantiate his charge. Instead of relying on argument or evidence, he clinches his case by a text, quoted out of context, from the very Scriptures to which the Jews appeal: 'For, as Scripture says, "Because of you the name of God is dishonoured among the Gentiles"' (2.24). He discredits circumcision in much the same way: 'If you break the law, then your circumcision is as if it had never been' (2.25). Here again Paul is prepared to envisage elevating Greek moralism in order to question Jewish self-esteem: 'If an uncircumcised man keeps the precepts of the law, will he not count as circumcised? He may be uncircumcised in his natural state, but by fulfilling the law he will pass judgment on you who break it' (2.26, 27). It is difficult to avoid the impression that this is a purely tactical concession to the Gentiles, which is inconsistent with his earlier position.

This determination to discredit Jewish identity repeatedly drives him to insist on points which (he is conscious) contradict his own argument. His prosecuting brief is clear: 'For we have already drawn up the accusation that Jews and Greeks alike are all under the power of sin' (3.9). He must therefore assert the justice of divine retribution on the Jews, because only in that way can their self-confidence be destroyed: 'Another question: if our injustice serves to bring out God's justice, what are we to say? Is it unjust of God (I speak of him in human terms) to bring retribution upon us?' (3.5). Here Paul is aware that his own account of divine providence, whereby the disbelief of the Jews makes possible the extension of God's promise to the Gentiles, threatens to excuse the Jews of sin. The same argument which vindicates the wisdom and benevolence of their God can be extended to vindicate them. This implication subverts Paul's whole position, and he attempts to disparage it by reminding his readers of the temerity of finite, sinful human beings questioning the justice of God. Paul sees the acuteness of the danger, but he can only answer it by counter-assertion rather than by argument: 'Certainly not!' he declares. 'If God were unjust, how could he judge the world?' (3.6). The repudiation is bold, but the argument which is supposed to support it is weak. A Jew, already committed by religious education and conviction to a belief in God's judgment, might not be able to detect and repudiate the inconsistency; but the logic of Paul's argument suggests precisely that 'God does not judge the world,' because on Paul's own showing he is unjust. Clearly Paul himself is not satisfied that he has dealt satisfactorily with the problem, because he immediately restates it in only a slightly modified form: 'Again, if the truth of God brings him all the greater honour because of my falsehood, why should I any longer be condemned as a sinner? Why not indeed "do evil that good may come", as some libellously report me as saying? To condemn such men as these is surely no injustice' (3.7, 8). Once again the repudiation is vigorous. Paul speaks of being libellously reported. There can be no doubt of his desire to disclaim the description; the problem lies in whether he can fairly escape the charge. He strongly claims to have been misrepresented and misunderstood, but he provides no argument to show how he evades the unacceptable implications of his position.

Paul concludes his condemnation of the Jews by again turning their own scriptures against them. He quotes a long catena of passages which use damnatory language, and his justification for assuming that such passages must be applied to the Jews is derived from their own proprietary attitude towards the law: 'Now all the words of the law are addressed, as we know, to those who are within the pale of the law' (3.19). It is a masterly performance, but Paul is not unaware of its dangers. For instance, although in order to establish his own superiority to Jew and Gentile alike he has to insist on their equal condemnation, his concern for the residual privilege of the Jewish Christians over their Gentile co-religionists (expressed in the rationale of the collection) demands that some basis for that privilege is retained. This introduces a note of contradiction into his argument which he cannot afford to suppress. He asks: 'Then what advantage has the Jew? What is the value of circumcision?' The logic of his argument would suggest that there is none, but Paul will not accept that conclusion. Instead he makes the strongest claims for the privilege, describing it as, 'Great, in every way. In the first place, the Jews were entrusted with the oracles of God' (3.2). It is, however, a defence which delivers considerably less than it promises. 'In the first place' leads one to expect a catalogue of reasons. Conspicuously Paul only mentions one: the trust of prophecy. Moreover he gives no explanation of how that trust gives the Jew an advantage; for his exposition of the trust turns not on the benefit derived by the Jews, but on the reliability of God which is uncompromised by their faithlessness. A similar difficulty is found in his assertion of the benefit of circumcision: 'Circumcision has value, provided you keep the law' (2.25). Paul, however, gives no indication of what that value is. Verbally he maintains its prestige, but the logic of his argument is to subordinate it totally to obedience to the law.

Another fundamental source of contradiction in this passage comes from Paul's desire to continue to legitimate his position in Jewish categories. Thus he appeals to the Jewish Scriptures to condemn the Jews (2.24; 3.10–18). He is dependent on Jewish convictions about divine judgment (3.6). Like most of the early Christians, he places great stress on the Christian fulfilment of Jewish prophecy (3.2–4). Fundamentally he wishes to see himself (by implication immune from condemnation) as the epitome of the Jewish identity: 'The true Jew is not he who is such in externals, neither is the true circumcision the external mark in the flesh. The true Jew is he who is such inwardly, and the true circumcision is of the heart, directed not by written precepts but by the Spirit; such a man receives his commendation not from men but from God' (2.28, 29). We have here Paul's own image of himself: a person who has repudiated religious externals for the sake of a change of heart, whose identity is determined not by conformity to the letter but by the gift of the Spirit, and who is vindicated not by men but by God. He is thus seeking to establish the legitimacy of his own position in Jewish categories, so that he may successfully discredit other Jews. It is in this picture of himself that Paul most nearly approaches a justification of his role as God's prosecutor. The true Jew is the instrument rather than the victim of divine judgment.

(e) The transcendence of the gospel

The heart of this study is to appraise the claims of the Christian gospel to bring freedom and reconciliation, and the passage in which Paul asserts its transcendence and victory over all other claims is crucial to this task. The opening chapters of the letter have disposed of all competing religious traditions: 'So that no one may have anything to say in self-defence, but the whole world may be exposed to the judgment of God. For (again from Scripture) "no human being can be justified in the sight of God" for having kept the Law: Law brings only the consciousness of sin' (3.19, 20). Only by such a universal condemnation can the unique and universal significance of Paul's mission be maintained. It is from this context that Paul derives the novelty and urgency of his message: 'But now, quite independently of law, God's justice has been brought to light' (3.21). The 'now' which claims our attention derives its uniqueness from the previous context with which the 'but' contrasts it. The imagery of bringing to light harks back to the related associations of 'the secret' and 'the veil', which we have already examined in Paul's writing. All serve to dramatize Paul's image of himself, and at the same time flatter the reader by the importance they attribute to the reading. Paul reinforces this later in the passage by again stressing the privilege of the present moment: 'In his forbearance (God) had overlooked the sins of the past – to demonstrate his justice now in the present, showing that he is himself just and also justifies any man who puts his faith in Jesus' (3.26).

When Paul expounds the justice of God, he is also stating the formal basis of his own authority; for in providing a rationale for God's sovereignty, he articulates his understanding of the power which authorizes and vindicates his own position. He insists on its legitimacy in Jewish categories: 'The Law and the prophets both bear witness to it' (3.22). All other claims and distinctions are obliterated by the absolute sovereignty of God: 'All without distinction' (3.22) is his slogan. The faith which he proclaims abrogates even the division of Jew and Gentile: 'Do you suppose God is the God of the Jews alone? Is he not the God of Gentiles also? Certainly, of Gentiles also, if it be true that God is one. And he will therefore justify both the circumcised in virtue of their faith, and the uncircumcised through their faith' (3.29, 30). Here the imperialism of Jewish monotheism and the universalism of Greek philosophical theology converge to insist on the unity of God, and apparently the insistence on the divine unity functions as a means of reconciling divergent humanity. The impression of reconciliation, is, however, misleading.

'Faith in Christ' is emphasized again and again in this passage (3.22, 25, 26, 27, 28, 30, 31). It is difficult to read it without echoes of the Lutheran doctrine of justification by faith or the brilliant paradoxes of the young Barth sounding in Protestant ears. It is the genius of their expositions of this text that they have succeeded in totally losing sight of the author. Instead they concentrate the reader's mind on the great doctrinal concepts in the passage: 'faith', 'Christ', 'justification', 'grace', 'expiation'. It is a text of immense richness; but we quite misunderstand the nature of the 'faith' of which Paul speaks if we fail to notice its relationship to himself. Once 'faith in Christ' has been abstracted from 'obedience to his apostle', the real nature of the argument has been obscured. Faith here is not the peculiar psychological release of the guilt-laden Luther, nor the insecure balancing act by which the young Barth defies the pull of his own scepticism; it has already been defined by reference to the God-given authority of the apostle, who identifies himself totally with the Christ to whom he calls us. Throughout this passage the practical meaning of faith in Christ is surrender to Paul.

It is because faith has this very particular reference that it cannot promote the reconciliation which it promises. There is much in Paul's language which sounds universalist and inclusive: 'For all alike have sinned, and are deprived of the divine splendour, and all are justified by God's free grace alone' (3.23, 24). But the 'all' is deceptive. It is inclusive in relation to sin, but has a much more selective sense in relation to the justified. Its real sense there is: 'all who are justified are justified by God's free grace'; this is made plain in v. 27 where Paul speaks of God justifying 'any man who puts his faith in Jesus'. In practice 'putting faith in Jesus' cannot be distinguished from submitting to the unique assertions of his apostle about him. Paul gives a very good example of such assertion in this passage: 'For God designed (Jesus Christ) to be the means of expiating sin by his sacrificial death, effective through faith' (3.25). The believer has to submit to a series of apparently arbitrary claims, the basis of which lies solely in the authoritative word of the apostle. The divine appointment of Jesus, the expiation of sin and the sacrificial death are all asserted by the apostle, but no rationale is provided for any of the claims. If he is alluding to widely held Christian beliefs, which reader and writer share, he makes no reference to any such tradition. Instead, the apostle speaks with bold independence: the selection takes place in the response or lack of it in the believer.

If it is impossible to take Paul's proclamation of reconciliation at face value, similar doubts have to be expressed about the freedom he promises. He speaks here of God's 'act of liberation in the person of Christ Jesus' (3.24). Christ is thus identified with freedom in the most definite way, but the liberation which he announces can only be appreciated if one assents to the preceding condemnation. Without that it has no force. It comes, therefore, as little surprise that Paul's notion of freedom is inimical to human self-esteem, yet entirely compatible with a strengthening of law and social control. Paul adopts the most hostile attitude to any kind of self-confidence: 'What room is left for human pride? It is excluded. And on what principle? The keeping of the law would not exclude it, but faith does. For our argument is that a man is justified by faith quite apart from success in keeping the law' (3.27, 28). Any understanding of freedom rooted in individual autonomy is ruthlessly discarded. Paul perceptively realizes that obedience to objective law might enable the individual to build up some self-respect and independence. By elevating faith in the way that he does, the believer is compelled to substitute for objective written law with its traditional restraints the untrammelled authority of the divine apostle. The sovereign freedom of God celebrated throughout this passage is represented by the arbitrary will of his human representative, and is an effective remedy against any sinful and subversive self-reliance. Paul demonstrates in this passage his genius for destroying the autonomy of others, and insisting on their dependence on himself. He is also quite correct in claiming that his message of freedom will do nothing to abrogate the social control which the law represented: 'Does this mean that we are using faith to undermine law? By no means: we are placing law itself on a firmer footing' (3.31). A Protestant reading of the text which interiorizes faith by identifying it with some particular attitude of trust will inevitably be perplexed at this point. The advantage of interpreting 'faith' as 'surrender to the apostle' in contrast to 'obedience to law' is that it makes Paul's thought at this point entirely coherent. Obedience has in no way been subverted by the freedom he bestows; instead, a more abject and absolute obedience is now required. The social control which the law vainly sought to impose has been given in Paul's grim words 'a firmer footing'.

(f) Faith as the key to the true Jewish identity and privilege

The whole logic of Paul's argument in the opening chapters of this letter is incompatible with any continuing Jewish identity or privilege. All have been made equal before God as sinners. Paul, however, is concerned to present not a consistent argument, but an effective and vigorous proclamation of the apostolic gospel. Critical though he may be towards his Jewish religious inheritance, he still wishes to legitimate his new position in terms which are derived, however tendentiously, from his previous one. So then, when he asks, 'What, then, are we to say about Abraham, our ancestor in the natural line?' (4.1), he does not reply negatively or with silence, but by an ingenious exposition of Abraham's faith. It is a brilliant and innovative use of Scripture. In the first place it provides a scriptural justification for Paul's language: 'For what does Scripture say? "Abraham put his faith in God, and that faith was counted to him as righteousness"'

(4.3). Paul assumes throughout that the faith which Scripture ascribes to Abraham and the faith which he demands of Christians are identical. This is the more convincing because it is never argued through. The reader is given no opportunity or encouragement to dissent. Moreover, by directing the reader's attention towards Abraham's faith, he conceals the radical difference between the faith of Abraham and the faith of the reader. Abraham's surrender in faith to God is unmediated; his dependence on God is direct. The faith which Paul commends here is significantly different. The Christian surrenders himself in theory to Christ, but in practice to his apostle. Thus the legitimation of his position that Paul derives from Abraham is really only verbal. It provides a sanction for language which he then uses in a quite different way; nevertheless the sanction is in many ways made plausible by the analogies he succeeds in drawing between the faith of Abraham and the faith of a Christian.

In both instances faith and its reward are entirely gratuitous. Paul expounds this with care: 'Now if a man does a piece of work, his wages are not "counted" as a favour; they are paid as debt. But if without any work to his credit he simply puts his faith in him who acquits the guilty, then his faith is indeed "counted as righteousness"' (4.4, 5). He is then able to reinforce his point by reference to a 'Davidic' psalm. Later in the passage he returns to the same point: 'The promise was made on the ground of faith, in order that it might be a matter of sheer grace' (4.16). In Protestant interpretation the emphasis on grace has been presented as a liberation from the anxieties which obedience to law necessarily creates. It certainly conveys to the believer a notion of his privileged status which is dramatic: based on the sheer decision and favour of God. The cost, however, is considerable. Whatever the anxieties and difficulties of legal obedience, it did hold out the possibility of some independence in man's dealings with God. The whole notion of a covenant or contract between two parties established some mutuality between them and recognized their separate integrity. It is precisely this covenant religion which Paul is concerned to abrogate. He may continue to use the language in much the same way that the terms of unconditional surrender may ape the language of a negotiated settlement; the reality is starkly different. It is customary at this point to speak loftily of the sovereignty of God, to which this gratuitous faith is the appropriate response. That, however, is to be deceived by the rhetoric of the apostle, so that one forgets the crucial difference already alluded to. The same abrogation of covenant with its mutuality and respect for the separate parties leaves Paul's readers defenceless before his assertion of authority. Their privilege is entirely dependent on their acquiescence and submission.

In Paul's hands Abraham's faith is able to provide an alternative to the Jewish law as the basis first of the Jew's privilege and so ultimately of the Christian's. 'We say, "Abraham's faith was counted as righteousness"; in what circumstances was it so counted? Was he circumcised at the time, or not? He was not yet circumcised, but uncircumcised; and he later received the symbolic rite of circumcision as the hall-mark of the righteousness which faith had given him when he was still uncircumcised' (4.9–11). Here Paul argues that the temporal priority of Abraham's faith to the practice of circumcision gives to the observance of the law a purely secondary role which merely expresses the prior reality of faith. Thus Abraham's faith and the promise and privilege with which it is associated are used by Paul deliberately to discredit legal observance: 'For if those who hold by the law, and they alone, are heirs, then faith is empty and the promise goes for nothing, because law can bring only retribution; but where there is no law there can be no breach of law' (4.14, 15). Paul here begins by using Abraham's faith to undermine law and ends by elevating faith precisely because it evades the punishment which is integral to law. Moreover the same argument enables Paul to give an account of Abraham which includes the believing Gentiles as well as the believing Jews: 'Consequently, he is the father of all who have faith when uncircumcised, so that righteousness is "counted" to them; and at the same time he is the father of such of the circumcised as do not rely upon their circumcision alone, but also walk in the footprints of the faith which our father Abraham had while he was yet uncircumcised' (4.11–12). Paul sees in this the fulfilment of the scriptural promise to Abraham: 'For he is the father of us all, as Scripture says: "I have appointed you to be father of many nations"' (4.17). In this way Abraham gives legitimacy to the mixed communities which have been established as a result of Paul's preaching. These are not to be regarded as some kind of adulteration of Jewish identity, but as a fulfilment of the divine promise which reveals the true nature of that identity.

Finally, Paul uses this promise of multi-racial paternity to Abraham to justify his emphasis on that feature of Abraham's life which most easily anticipates the pattern of death and resurrection, central to Paul's gospel. At first the claim is made as a general description of the nature of God: 'This promise, then, was valid before God, the God in whom he put his faith, the God who makes the dead live and summons things that are not yet in existence as if they already were' (4.17). This prepares for Paul's presentation of the birth of Isaac as a transition from death to life: 'When hope seemed hopeless, his faith was such that he became "father of many nations", in agreement with the words which had been spoken to him: "Thus shall your descendants be". Without any weakening of faith he contemplated his own body, as good as dead (for he was about a hundred years old), and the deadness of Sarah's womb, and never doubted God's promise in unbelief, but, strong in faith, gave honour to God, in the firm conviction of his power to do what he had promised. And that is why Abraham's faith was "counted to him as righteousness"' (4.19–22). It is difficult not to be reminded here of the Baptist's preaching as recorded in Luke: 'Do not begin saying to yourselves, "We have Abraham for our father". I tell you that God can make children for Abraham out of these stones here' (Luke 3.8). In Paul's mind it is as if God originally provided Abraham with children by such a miraculous intervention, and in the church continues to do so. This identification of the content of Abraham's faith with that of the Christian skilfully distracts the reader's attention from Paul's role in the latter. Moreover it enables him to introduce his exposition of the Christian's crucified and risen identity which occupies the next four chapters, as a fitting commentary on Abraham's faith: 'Those words were written, not for Abraham's sake alone, but for our sake too: it is to be "counted" in the same way to us who have faith in the God who raised Jesus our Lord from the dead; for he was given up to death for our misdeeds, and raised to life to justify us' (4.23–25). The reader, like Abraham, is encouraged to give ready agreement to 'the words which had been spoken to him' (4.18). Paul's excitement is so contagious that it seems almost churlish to point out that in the case of Abraham the speaker is God, while in our case it is Paul.

(g) Reconciliation with God: astonishment and certainty

Paul prepares the reader to embrace a crucified identity by first dwelling on the wonder and astonishment of his privilege. He assures 'us' that 'we have been justified through faith' (5.1). He assumes that we are 'at peace with God through our Lord Jesus Christ' (5.1). He permits us some present confidence in our position: 'We have been allowed to enter the sphere of God's grace, where we now stand' (5.2). He invites us to 'exult in the hope of the divine splendour that is to be ours' (5.2). For once Paul does not simply play on anxieties about the future, but permits some release from such tension in the certainty of present experience: 'Such a hope is no mockery, because God's love has flooded our inmost heart through the Holy Spirit he has given us' (5.5). Such complacency, however, is only allowed in order to reconcile the reader to present sufferings. These are not merely to be accepted, but positively to be 'exulted' in (5.3). Once again, suffering, instead of discrediting the claims of the new religion serves to enhance them: 'Because we know that suffering trains us to endure, and endurance brings proof that we have stood the test, and this proof is the ground of hope' (5.4). It is an argument which, once accepted by the reader, makes further criticism impossible. The only path to certainty is unwavering perseverance.

Paul then develops the believer's startling privilege in terms of his reconciliation with God brought about by the death of Christ. He returns to his emphasis on the sinfulness of man to underline the gratuitousness of God's love. Then having first asserted the amazing paradox of divine love, he uses the astonishment of the reader to make plausible its certainty and effectiveness. In verse after verse he points to the astonishing, unmerited, paradoxical character of the divine love revealed in Christ's death. We were 'powerless' (5.6), 'wicked' (5.6), 'sinners' (5.8, 12–14), 'God's enemies' (5.10). God's love is thus portrayed as utterly creative, indeed arbitrary. Paul rules out any notion of merit and hence of rationale. The relation between God and man is non-reciprocal, and defies explanation. His love is simply asserted or proclaimed, and is expected to gain its credibility from its very unlikeliness. In the same way the effects of Christ's death are asserted, but are nowhere explained. We are told that 'Christ died for the wicked' (5.6), or 'died for us' (5.8). Paul asserts that 'we have now been justified by Christ's sacrificial death' (5.9), or that 'we were reconciled to (God) through the death of his Son' (5.10). The benefit is stressed but is nowhere analysed, and at least in part the emphasis on the divine grace renders any such explanation redundant. The reader is not encouraged to question but to confirm Paul's message, by exulting in the same exclamation of relief and surprise (5.11).

Paul expounds the universality of sin stemming from the sin of one man (5.12–14), and the fact of human death both illustrates and provides evidence for this. A new point is introduced here. In the earlier chapters sin is to be punished by divine retribution and final vengeance. Here sin is already punished by death itself, and its universality only makes more plausible the common culpability of mankind. Paul is emphatic about the causal connection between sin and death: 'It was through one man that sin entered the world, and through sin death, and thus death pervaded the whole human race, inasmuch as all men have sinned' (5.12). 'The wrongdoing of that one man brought death upon so many' (5.15). Or again: 'Sin established its reign by way of death' (5.21). On the one hand death itself is seen as a sign of guilt, so that its reversal in the case of Jesus is proof of his vindication. On the other hand it enables the moralist to place the responsibility for death and its attendant fears on the behaviour of the deviant. It is a biological fiction which has proved to have immense imaginative power. Having thus introduced a new element of anxiety into the argument, Paul returns to the gratuitous and disproportionate nature

Romans

157

of God's love: 'God's act of grace is out of all proportion to Adam's wrongdoing' (5.15). He highlights the surprise and generosity of the divine love by making the following contrast: 'The judicial action, following upon the one offence, issued in a verdict of condemnation, but the act of grace, following upon so many misdeeds, issued in a verdict of acquittal' (5.16). Against such a background of sin the verdict is intended to be astonishing. Even the Law is now seen simply as a means of underlining the generosity of God: 'Law intruded into this process to multiply law-breaking. But where sin was thus multiplied, grace immeasurably exceeded it' (5.20).

Paul's insistence on God's unmerited action, arousing as it does in the reader amazement and gratitude, silences any doubts about the certainty and effectiveness of that action. Thus the inexplicable death of Christ for the wicked becomes for Paul 'God's own proof of his love towards us' (5.8). But it can only function as such a proof if the claim implied in the words 'for the wicked' can be substantiated. Otherwise it is much easier to see Christ's death in terms of the parable of the wicked husbandmen. (There the death of the son at the hands of evil men does not establish peace between man and God, but more intelligibly provokes God's wrath and retribution.) Compared with the paradoxes of the past centred in that allegedly reconciling death, the future is a matter of certain anticipation: 'Since we have now been justified by Christ's sacrificial death, we shall all the more certainly be saved through him from final retribution. For if, when we were God's enemies, we were reconciled to him through the death of his Son, how much more, now that we are reconciled, shall we be saved through his life!' (5.9,10). Similarly the comparison with Adam only serves to heighten Paul's certainty: 'For if by the wrongdoing of that one man death established its reign, through a single sinner, much more shall those who receive in far greater measure God's grace, and his gift of righteousness, live and reign through one man, Jesus Christ' (5.17). The passage culminates in a frenzy of striking assertion: 'The issue of one just act is acquittal and life for all men' (5.18), 'Through the obedience of the one man the many will be made righteous' (5.19). 'So God's grace might establish its reign in righteousness, and issue in eternal life through Jesus Christ our Lord' (5.21). In each case it appears as if the assertion is justified by the preceding state of sin and death which it has reversed. The style is one of argument: 'It follows, then, that . . . so' (5.18). 'For as through . . . so through (5.19). 'As . . . so' (5.21). This impression is, however, quite misleading. As in the rather similar reasoning in I Corinthians 15 (see p. 98), his thought gains its power not from any logical development, but from the excitement of a series of bold contrasts vigorously stated.

The believer is thus dependent for his sense of reconciliation with God on nothing other than the robust assurance of the preacher that such is the case. Moreover, what is at stake is not merely (!) the reversal of death. The privilege of reconciliation gains its distinction from the universality of sin and condemnation, and its urgency from the prospect of 'final retribution' (5.9). For all the impassioned language of reconciliation to God, it is a reconciliation which is partial, and leaves most human beings outside its scope. Far from furthering the reconciliation of men, it gives to human alienation a divine sanction and an ultimate significance.

(h) The exploitation of the crucified identity

The suggestion that the primary contribution of the law was to multiply sin, underlining the gratuitous nature of God's love, has antinomian implications which Paul hurriedly denies (6.1). Instead he draws out the implications of the Christian's identification with the crucified Christ to exalt the prestige of asceticism and facilitates the most far-reaching social control. Centuries of exposure to the imagery of crucifixion tend to disguise from us the violence and brutality of the language. In verse after verse Paul speaks of death and destruction to articulate a savage discontinuity in the lives of reader and writer alike. This is not the language of harmonious and integrated development, but of fragile and exaggerated repudiation. 'We died to sin' (6.2), Paul states, but curiously sin remains sufficiently alive to necessitate further remonstrance: 'How can we live in it any longer?' (6.2). Using inclusive language, which unites the experience of reader and writer, Paul speaks of being 'baptized into union with Christ's death' (6.3), so that 'by baptism we were buried with him, and lay dead' (6.4). 'We have become incorporate with him in a death like his' (6.5). Sharing this cruel experience is itself a pledge that 'as Christ was raised from the dead in the splendour of the Father, so also we might set our feet upon the new path of life' (6.4, see also vv. 5 and 8). That is the future reward, but the price is immediate and painful: 'We know that the man we once were has been crucified with Christ, for the destruction of the sinful self' (6.6). The violence which was perpetrated on Christ is now to be directed by the believer against his own deviant nature, and thus interiorized and affirmed. Not surprisingly, the rationale for this is unclear: Paul refers to the legal adage: 'A dead man is no longer answerable for his sin' (6.7). That expresses his thought, but it does not justify it; for it is not really consistent with his own view of the relation of sin and death whereby death itself is seen as the culmination and punishment of sin. Therefore to use a legal maximum drawn from disputes between men is not relevant in a context where men are in dispute with God. Again the crucial phrase in which the significance of Christ's death in relation to sin is stated is enigmatic: 'For in dying as he died, he died to sin, once for all' (6.10). This presumably goes beyond the force of the legal maxim just examined, if for no other reason than that the maxim depends for its cogency on the person being a sinner. It is unclear whether Paul intends here a reference to Jesus' final obedience in death, by which sin in the form of temptation is conclusively repudiated, or whether it alludes to the effect of Christ's death in discrediting the law and thus depriving sin of its opportunity. Furthermore the subsequent parallel, 'in living as he lives, he lives to God' (6.10), suggests that neither of these explanations is entirely adequate. For in the parallel God has an active initiative in Christ's life which seems to call for sin to play a similar role in Christ's death. If that is the case, then 'dying to sin' refers at least in part to the sinfulness of others in bringing about Christ's death. Whichever interpretation or combination of interpretations is preferred, none of them provides a satisfactory analogy for the plight of the Christian, for on Paul's terms the sinlessness of Christ breaks the analogy at its most vital point. Paul repeatedly speaks as if 'Christ dying to sin' and the believer dying to sin are the same, when they are so fundamentally different that any resemblance is tendentious. Because it is so uncertain, Paul has to compensate by vigorous exhortation.

The transition takes place in v. 11. The inclusive 'we' there gives place to the controlling and accusing 'you'. Imperative language replaces description, and reveals its intention. 'So sin must no longer reign in your mortal body, exacting obedience to the body's desires. You must no longer put its several parts at sin's disposal, as implements for wrongdoing. No: put yourselves at the disposal of God, as dead men raised to life; yield your bodies to him as implements for doing right' (6.12, 13). The identity of the reader is dissociated from his body; the latter is mortal, and obedience to its desires is equated with sin and wrongdoing. This appeals to our desire to transcend both our mortality and our physical compulsions, and Paul has always found readers prepared to divorce themselves from their bodily identity in the way he recommends. For that vulnerable and embarrassing identity Paul urges us to substitute the resurrected identity equated with 'life' and 'doing right'. The hostility and repudiation of human autonomy which this conception conceals is remarkable: 'put yourselves at the disposal of God, as dead men raised to life'. Harking back to the origins of slavery where the lives of the conquered were spared at the price of their freedom, Paul envisages the new life in terms of a surrender to God in which the individual's rights and identity are abandoned.

For all Paul's language of freedom and emancipation, it would seem that the most men can hope for is to exchange one master for another. This is articulated in terms of a personalized dualism in which Christ breaks the dominion of sin and death (6.9). The effect of these personifications is to distance the reader from responsibility for sin and involvement in death. Both are seen as alien impositions : the element of our complicity is thus ignored, and with our complicity our freedom. We may prefer to speak of sin as something which overcomes us, but in fact both in behaviour and in conception sin is our construction. Similarly, while human beings often die unwillingly and experience death as restraint, we sometimes go out to meet death in tiredness or despair, so that death is not something which is invariably imposed upon us. Once the reality of human freedom has been disguised by such dominating personifications, it is hard to regain it. The distancing of the self from experience in order to repudiate freedom and responsibility gives rise to an essentially passive conception of the self. Paul makes this plain when he describes any antinomian understanding of his teaching in such a way that rules it out: 'Because we are not under law but under grace' (6.15). The subordination of man to external power remains: in either case we are 'under' something. Paul spells out this change of master with brutal clarity: 'You know well enough that if you put yourselves at the disposal of a master, to obey him, you are slaves of the master whom you obey; and this is true whether you serve sin, with death as its result; or obedience, with righteousness as its result' (6.16). The interpretation of Pauline faith as obedient surrender is here made plain, and any respect for human autonomy is ruled out. Moreover this abject condition is immediately made the subject of praise and thanks to God in a way which inhibits criticism: 'But God be thanked, you, who once were slaves of sin, have yielded whole-hearted obedience to the pattern of teaching to which you were made subject' (6.17).

The mention of 'teaching' reminds us of the implicit reference to the teacher, Paul, whose authority is directly served by the language of continuing slavery that he propagates. He prefers, however, not to speak of himself but to direct the attention of his readers to the radical contrast in their condition, and the privileges which now are theirs. The readers, 'emancipated from sin, have become slaves of righteousness' (6.18). So certain is Paul of his mastery that he dares to abuse his readers directly, telling them that he is using 'words that suit your human weakness' (6.19). Slaves must get used to being talked down to. The previous life and identity of the reader are disparaged as 'the service of impurity and lawlessness, making for moral anarchy' (6.19). It is a source of shame and incurs death (6.21). By contrast, 'bound to the service of God, your gains are such as make for holiness, and the end is eternal life' (6.22). Yet even such privilege is used to undermine the complacency and autonomy of the believer. Sin may pay a wage (6.23), so that the slave gets what he deserves, 'but God gives freely'. Before him the believer has no rights; there is no mutuality of obligation or exchange: simply an act of gratuitous generosity, which can only be received with passive gratitude. Once a slave, always a slave, would seem to be Paul's rather unhelpful contribution to the quest for human freedom.

In much the same way that at the beginning of the letter Paul first condemned the Gentiles and then condemned the Jews, having expounded the crucified identity in ways which subdue the immoral Gentile, he now turns it against the law-observing Jew. As with his understanding of the significance of the crucifixion, Paul relies on legal arguments: here on the maxim that death cancels previous obligations, so that for instance death makes possible the remarriage of a widow. Arguing from the reality of the Christian's death in baptism, he contends that the Christian is now 'discharged from the law' (7.6), and taking up the imagery of the church as the bride of Christ assures the reader that 'you have found another husband in him who rose from the dead, so that we may bear fruit for God' (7.4). Paul reverts to his familiar contrast between the flesh and the spirit (7.5, 6). On the one hand sinful passions, evoked by the law, worked in our bodies and produced death, but now the old way of the written code has been replaced by the new way of the Spirit (7.5, 6). The transition is plain, but the moment that Paul has made it, he becomes aware that he has said too much; and so before expounding the new way of the Spirit, he first reaffirms the prestige of the law.

(i) The prestige of the law reaffirmed

The autobiographical passage which now occurs has given great trouble to commentators. Partly, this is because it seems to clash in its personal tone with the supposedly abstract and detached nature of the letter; partly, it is because of controversy as to whether Paul's experience of law belongs to his Pharisaic or Christian periods. Paul's use of the first person singular is relatively rare in his letters. Here it seems to indicate a temporary change of audience. His attention is briefly distracted from his readers and has turned in upon himself. Before he can continue to address them, he must first allay his own anxieties. For the transition to autobiography is provoked by the implications of his own words. Both the general logic of his argument and the particular contrast between 'the way of the spirit' and the 'written code' (7.6) prompts the horrid suspicion that the law is itself to be equated with sin. Taken at its face value, the freedom which Paul proclaims can only have antinomian implications. His dilemma is that however much he may repudiate the law in general or criticize it in

detail, he is compelled in some sense to reaffirm it. This paradox has
already been noticed in Galatians (see p. 51) and Philippians (see p. 59),
but it is faced here in is starkest form. 'Is the Law identical with sin? Of
course not' (7.7); but the way in which Paul then describes the law betrays
why such a suspicion is so subversive. 'The law is in itself holy and the
commandment is holy and just and good' (7.12). Those adjectives of
absolute and transcendent value are a reminder that the prestige of the law
remains identical in Paul's mind with the honour of God. Unlike Marcion
and some of the second-century Gnostics, Paul is not prepared to place the
Gods of the Old Testament and New Testament in conflict, for he continues to derive much of the legitimation of his new position from the
very tradition from which he has dissociated himself.

   For all his celebration of the Spirit, his glorying in persecution and the
assertion of his apostolate given by the risen Christ, Paul dare not admit
the radical implications of his own religious message. Instead, whatever
the logical inconsistency or personal humiliation, he is determined that the
prestige of his own religious tradition shall not be totally discredited. It is a
stance which has many parallels in sacred and secular history. Mediaeval
heretics resorting to the poor Christ or nineteenth-century liberals
appealing to the historical Jesus were both opposing actual religious
institutions by citing an authority derived from those institutions.
Similarly, in monarchical societies it is repeatedly the king's advisers rather
than the king himself who is opposed (a polite fiction in which both subject
and monarch have an obvious interest). Dissident Marxists or disaffected
Labour MPs want to identify the party with themselves, even when
repudiating the reality of that party. In all this there is something of
cowardice, fear of launching into the unknown; and something of
intellectual dishonesty, a refusal to acknowledge the dangerous and
destructive implications of the position which has been adopted. But there
is also something of prudence. The mediaeval peasant in revolt might hope
that royal power would itself remedy abuses. The dissident Christians
hoped to use the religious prestige created by the institutions they opposed
to further their own ideals. The modern political party represents
attractions of organization and finance which discourage hasty repudiation. In this letter the residual but definite privileges which Paul still claims
for the Jews are some explanation of his reluctance to disown the law
entirely.

   In Galatians and Philippians Paul used analogies drawn from education
and learning to give the Law a real, if temporary, value. Here he has come
to the agonizing perception that his notions of sin and law are in some way
correlates: 'Except through law I should never have become acquainted

with sin' (7.7). Such a contrary lesson he cannot attribute to the divine schoolmaster, for the dualism of his moral vision gains its excitement and hence its plausibility from the unreconciled conflict between good and evil. Without that antagonism the believer is relieved of anxiety, and any solution loses its urgency and attractiveness. The suggestion that law and sin are in collusion must therefore be forcefully repudiated, so Paul tries to maintain the contradiction by resorting to personifications which conceal responsibility. He speaks of 'the commandment' and 'sin'. The commandment speaks (7.7) and comes (7.9). Logically it must be a roundabout way of referring to God, but Paul needs to dissociate God from his commandment because he will turn to God to reconcile the conflict which the commandment has created. The personification of sin enables Paul to suggest that sin relates to commandment as criminal agent to opportunity: 'Through that commandment sin found its opportunity, and produced in me all kinds of wrong desires. In the absence of law, sin is a dead thing . . . when the commandment came, sin sprang to life and I died . . . sin found its opportunity in the commandment, seduced me, and through the commandment killed me' (7.8, 9,11). In this way he hopes to preserve the conflict of good and evil in such a way that the goodness of the commandment is not compromised by its association with sin: 'Are we to say then that this good thing was the death of me? By no means. It was sin that killed me, and thereby sin exposed its true character: it used a good thing to bring about my death, and so, through the commandment, sin became more sinful than ever' (7.13). In itself, however, this fails to absolve God of all responsibility for sin, for some responsibility attaches to those who create opportunities, as well as to those who take advantage of them.

As so often, Paul seems to have sensed the weakness of his argument here, and so instead of developing it, he uses the personification of sin for a different purpose – to project a humiliated image of himself as the slave of sin. He has already prepared for this by a piece of romantic reminiscence: 'There was a time when, in the absence of law, I was fully alive; but when the commandment came, sin sprang to life and I died' (7.9). Here Paul claims to remember an idealized time of innocence, before the intrusion of law. In so far as this idealized childhood has any reality, it can only refer to Paul's Pharisaic experience; but to endeavour to reconstruct Paul's biography here is to misunderstand the passage. Paul needs to assert a primal innocence in order to make plausible his view of himself as the slave of sin, a role full of pathos, which nevertheless effectively distances him from what he wishes to repudiate. By humiliating himself, Paul is able to affirm the spiritual integrity and prestige of the Law: 'We know that the law is spiritual; but I am not' (7.14). The notion of a self in bondage to sin enables him to identify himself at the deepest level with that law: 'If what I do is against my will, it means that I agree with the law and hold it to be admirable' (7.16). 'The good which I want to do, I fail to do' (7.19). 'In my inmost self I delight in the law of God' (7.22). By presenting himself as a slave to an alien force, he can admit his own contradictory behaviour without compromising his commitment to that law: 'I am unspiritual, the purchased slave of sin. I do not even acknowledge my own action as mine, for what I do is not what I want to do, but what I detest' (7.14, 15). Paul portrays his self-alienation in terms which effectively deny his own responsibility for his actions: 'As things are, it is no longer I who perform the action, but sin that lodges in me. For I know that nothing good lodges in me – in my unspiritual nature, I mean – for though the will to do good is there, the deed is not . . . What I do is the wrong which is against my will; and if what I do is against my will, clearly it is no longer I who am the agent, but sin that has its lodging in me' (7.17–21). The personification of sin in this autobiographical passage is not simply a literary device. It is a fiction which Paul is compelled to construct in order to safeguard his identity and his ideals. Without it he would have to admit that he rather than 'sin' is opposed to law, and might have been compelled to modify his ideal in the light of his experience. Slavery to personified sin enables him to discount his own experience, and relieves him of any necessity to reassess his commitment to the law. Its prestige is thus preserved undiminished.

The price of this refusal to learn is a strident dualism, which has already been observed in Paul's inability to relate the flesh to the spirit except in terms of conflict. 'I perceive that there is in my bodily members a different law, fighting against the law that my reason approves and making me a prisoner under the law that is in my members, the law of sin' (7.23). At last the dualism of his perception has produced its logical outcome, a vision no longer of one law, but of two, locked in hopeless conflict. Reason and Paul's true identity are committed to the law of God, his body and his self in bondage are under the power of the law of sin. The picture, for all its anguish, is a flattering one, both to Paul and to his readers; for Paul's identity remains uncompromised. He may in self-pity refer to himself as a 'miserable creature' in a 'body doomed to death', but he can call out for deliverance. It is the same self making that cry who answers his own question with the words: 'Who is there to rescue me? . . . God alone, through Jesus Christ our Lord! Thanks be to God!' (7.24, 25). Most readers of Paul have been innocent. They have seen his confession of himself as the slave of sin simply as humiliation; but it is precisely that device that enables him to preserve his own self-esteem, which cannot be separated from the prestige of the God to whose law he is committed. The radical identification of law and sin threatened to drive Paul to self-criticism, but the threat is short lived, and by the end of the chapter Paul feels confident to expound the promise which is the substance of the Christian's privilege.

(j) The privilege of the Spirit and the promise of resurrection

The following passage immediately brings the reader into the excitement and exhilaration of the gospel Paul proclaimed, and if one wishes to understand its attraction, then it repays the most careful study. Generations of Christians have responded to the passionate promises it contains, with its haunting vision of human freedom and cosmic splendour. At its outset condemnation is left behind (8.1), and at its end comes the magisterial proclamation: 'It is God who pronounces acquittal; then who can condemn?' (8.33). The same God who acquits, bestows life (8.11). Slavery and the life of fear (8.14) have been replaced by the confidence of sons. This is no mere private or individual hope; it is given a cosmic significance: 'The universe itself is to be freed from the shackles of mortality and enter upon the liberty and splendour of the children of God' (8.21). It ends on a note of assured victory: 'What can separate us from the love of Christ? Can affliction or hardship? Can persecution, hunger, nakedness, peril, or the sword? "We are being done to death for thy sake all day long," as Scripture says; "we have been treated like sheep for slaughter" – and yet, in spite of all, overwhelming victory is ours through him who loved us. For I am convinced that there is nothing in death or life, in the realm of spirits or superhuman powers, in the world as it shall be, in the forces of the universe, in heights or depths – nothing in all creation that can separate us from the love of God in Christ Jesus our Lord' (8.35–39).

In those words Paul transcends every conceivable constraint, and gives an impressive example of the freedom that he proclaimed; yet he thinks in terms of victory rather than reconciliation, and any reading of this passage which ignores elements of alienation and hostility is sentimentally selective. From the outset the promises are the preserve of those 'who are united with Christ Jesus'. The vision of all-embracing harmony is strictly reserved: the Spirit 'co-operates for good with those who love God and are called according to his purpose' (8.28). The divine origin of the Christian privilege and distinction is proclaimed in terms which, while they flatter Paul's co-religionists, are the reverse of universal: 'For God knew his own before ever they were, and also ordained that they should be shaped to the likeness of his Son, that he might be the eldest among a large family of brothers; and it is these, so fore-ordained, whom he has also called. And those whom he called he has justified, and to those whom he justified he has also given his splendour' (8.29–30). The rehearsal of the divine initiative is repeated and emphatic, and ends with the revealing assumption that 'God is on our side' (8.31), which is hardly surprising in view of what has preceded it, but not particularly edifying. Paul expects his readers to share his antagonisms. On the one hand he encourages them to distance themselves from other people: 'Those who live on the level of our lower nature have their outlook formed by it, and that spells death . . . Those who live on such a level cannot possibly please God. But that is not how you live' (8.5–9). This social alienation is intertwined with the repudiation of the body: 'The outlook of the lower nature is enmity with God; it is not subject to the law of God; indeed it cannot be' (8.7). Consistently the embarrassed translators of the New English Bible have substituted the pale abstraction of 'the lower nature' for Paul's much more concrete expression 'the flesh'. This obscures the extent to which social alienation and bodily repression accompany each other in the apostle's thought.

Both the alienation and the repression are legitimated by the gift of the Spirit. It is the Spirit which distinguishes the Christian from other people: 'If a man does not possess the Spirit of Christ, he is no Christian' (8.9). It is the Spirit which makes possible the effective repression of the body: 'By the Spirit you put to death all the base pursuits of the body' (8.13). The Spirit is thus socially divisive and psychologically repressive. It cannot, however, be removed from the passage without destroying the whole basis of Paul's religious message. For the account which Paul gives of the Spirit in this passage indicates the central role which it played in the experience of the churches with which he was associated. Non-charismatic Christians are naturally reluctant to acknowledge this, but Paul for all his concern in I Corinthians to control the phenomenon is most careful not to repudiate it: yet even charismatic Christians, who have been more than willing to acknowledge the role of the Spirit in the Pauline churches, have failed to see the way in which the experience of the Spirit made plausible to the early believers the resurrection of Jesus. For generations the impact of the credal divisions has been to separate the resurrection of Jesus from the Holy Spirit, so that it has been natural to articulate the belief in terms of historical reminiscence of empty tombs and resurrection meetings. Paul's language in this chapter is a vivid reminder that for the early Christians such reminiscences were made plausible by their own experience of Jesus speaking among them. Jesus' Spirit speaking in their midst was a sign both of Jesus' continuing life, and also of their inclusion in that life. Paul's language leaves us in no doubt that he is not simply referring to an abstraction or to personified moral qualities. The Spirit to which he refers is recognized, like the wind, by the sound it makes: it cries (8.15), it groans (8.23), it pleads (8.27). So that when Paul weaves together the presence of the Spirit and the assurance of life (8.9–11), he is giving his readers a very definite basis for their hope.

The corollary of this position is that the validity of much of Paul's gospel is dependent on the authenticity of the charismatic phenomena to which he appealed in the experience of his hearers. Once it has been granted that charismatic phenomena have a social rather than a supernatural origin (and the presence of such manifestations in other religious and indeed in secular contexts makes that conclusion unavoidable), much of Paul's gospel crumbles. The divisive and repressive aspects of the Spirit in Paul's thought may make this seem but a slight loss, but with the Spirit must also disappear the most widespread basis for belief both in the resurrection of Jesus and in our own life after death. The excitement of the privilege which Paul offered his followers was the participation in Jesus's Spirit: that assured them of both Jesus' life and their own life beyond death. Once that Spirit has been explained in social terms the privilege he proffered has proved specious and the promise illusory.

(k) The quest for legitimacy: the dependence of the new on the old

In the following three chapters Paul endeavours to defend the legitimacy of his position, despite its essential inconsistency. For he will not repudiate the continuing reality of Jewish privilege. If he had been prepared to grant a temporary or functional Jewish privilege, leading up to and preparing for the new Christian dispensation, he could have been consistent. The educational account of the law in Galatians and Philippians suggests such a treatment, but it is not the path he takes here. Paul presents the problem in personal terms of sorrowful affection and natural fellow-feeling: 'In my heart there is great grief and unceasing sorrow. For I could even pray to be outcast from Christ myself for the sake of my brothers, my natural kinsfolk' (9.2, 3). This is not simply a concern for the ultimate fate of his kinsmen, like that of the rich man in the parable (Luke 16.19–31). Paul is far from the humility of Dives, who merely pleads that his five brothers 'may not come to this place of torment'. Paul may be grieved and sorrowful because of his fellow Jews, but he can still rehearse their unique privileges with pride: 'They are Israelites: they were made God's sons; theirs is the splendour of the divine presence, theirs the covenants, the law, the temple worship, and the promises. Theirs are the patriarchs, and from them, in natural descent, sprang the Messiah. May God, supreme above all, be blessed for ever! Amen' (9.4, 5). The thanks to God is a reminder both that Paul does not regard their privileges as passing, and that he conceives the honour of God himself as demanding their vindication: 'It is impossible that the word of God should be proved false' (9.6). The position which Paul adopts here is fundamental both to his conception of religious legitimacy and to the ecclesiastical relation between Jew and Gentile that he is advocating. Thus on the theoretical level he will attempt to vindicate the Gentile mission in Jewish terms, and to rationalize in Jewish terms both the rejection of Christ by the Jews and his welcome by the Gentiles. Finally in the letter the ecclesiastical reality of Jewish privilege is given the most concrete expression in the exaction of Gentile tribute.

The premise of Paul's argument throughout this passage is the inerrancy of Scripture, identified without equivocation as the word of God. Thus he defends the Gentile mission by describing the Gentiles as part of the true Israel. This far from obvious conclusion is achieved by two moves. First he argues for a selective understanding of Israelite descent which qualifies the notion of natural descent by combining it with God's promise. 'Not all descendants of Israel are truly Israel, nor, because they are Abraham's, offspring are they all his true children' (9.7). Thus the price of including some Gentiles within Israel is the repudiation of many actual Israelites. This is then defended on scriptural grounds, as being implied by the descent from Isaac the child of promise. 'In the words of Scripture, "Through the line of Isaac your descendants shall be traced". That is to say, it is not those born in the course of nature who are children of God; it is the children born through God's promise who are reckoned as Abraham's descendants' (9.7, 8). Once again social attitudes of alienation are expressed in the unresolved conflict of flesh and spirit.

The second point which Paul makes on the basis of Scripture to justify the inclusion of the Gentiles as part of the true Israel is the mystery of divine election. The assertion is made in the starkest possible form: 'Rebekah's children had one and the same father, our ancestor Isaac; and yet, in order that God's selective purpose might stand, based not upon men's deeds but upon the call of God, she was told, even before they were born, when they had as yet done nothing, good or ill, "The elder shall be servant to the younger"; and that accords with the text of Scripture, "Jacob I loved and Esau I hated"' (9.10–13). Thus stated, Paul's claim allows neither qualification nor argument. To the questions which such a claim naturally provokes, 'Is God to be charged with injustice?' (9.14) or, 'Why does God blame a man? For who can resist his will?' (9.19), Paul replies with a celebration of the arbitrary nature of God's choice and the sovereignty of his power. In dismissing any notion of 'man's will or effort' (9.16), he rules out of order any rational consideration of God's choice. He revels in the disparity of power between God and man, and on the basis of that disparity silences criticism: 'Who are you, sir, to answer God back? Can the pot speak to the potter and say, "Why did you make me like this?"? Surely the potter can do what he likes with the clay' (9.20, 21). The exaltation of Paul's God demands the demeaning of man. Human initiative and consciousness are projected on to God and then denied to man, who is reduced to the formless, passive and silent clay. Such a view of God and man is only tolerable to writer and reader because of the consciousness of privilege which it serves. Conveying the horrid implications of his position by a tentative question, Paul asks: 'What if God, desiring to exhibit his retribution at work and to make his power known, tolerated very patiently those vessels which were objects of retribution due for destruction, and did so in order to make known the full wealth of his splendour upon vessels which were objects of mercy, and which from the first had been prepared for this splendour?' (9.22, 23). Paul can only articulate such a vision with complacency because he is in no doubt that he and his readers belong to that last category: 'Such vessels are we, whom (God) has called from among the Gentiles as well as Jews' (9.24). It is a classic example of the way in which the religious privilege and the divisive social attitudes complement each other, and demand a God whose cruelty betrays the savage temper of his worshippers.

Having contrived to give the Gentiles a Jewish identity, Paul now endeavours to explain the error of the Jews, which he justifies as the fulfilment of Old Testament prophecy (9.27–29; 10.19–21). Thus the authority of the Jewish texts is again turned against them; the prophecies of divine retribution, with the exception of only a remnant, are used by Paul to rationalize an embarrassment he clearly perceived: 'Gentiles, who made no effort after righteousness, nevertheless achieved it, a righteousness based on faith; whereas Israel made great efforts after a law of righteousness, but never attained to it' (9.30, 31). This prompts Paul to repeat his teaching on the conflict of law and faith which he expounded earlier in the letter. There is the same insistence on the transcendence of old boundaries: 'There is no distinction between Jew and Greek, because the same Lord is Lord of all, and is rich enough for the need of all who invoke him' (10.12). But this apparent universalism again only introduces a more radical cleavage between those who have faith and those who have not, and Paul makes yet more plain the personal and particular significance of 'the word of faith which we proclaim'. Its terms are simple: 'If on your lips is the confession, "Jesus is Lord", and in your heart the faith that God raised him from the dead, then you will find salvation' (10.9). Historians of dogma may concentrate on the combination of the authority of Jesus and belief in his resurrection, but that only mirrors the way in which the recognition of Paul's authority is bound up with his testimony to the resurrection. Paul underlines this point by introducing a rhapsody on the theme, not of the message, but the messenger: 'How could they invoke one in whom they had no faith? And how could they have faith in one they had never heard of? And how hear without someone to spread the news? And how could anyone spread the news without a commission to do so? And that is what Scripture reaffirms: "How welcome are the feet of the messengers of good news!"' (10.14, 15). Here excitement, privilege and authority all culminate in the praise of the apostle.

By vindicating the Gentile mission in Jewish terms, and explaining the Jewish rejection of Christ as the fulfilment of Jewish Scriptures, Paul prepares for the vigorous reassertion of the continuing Jewish privilege: 'I ask then, has God rejected his people? I cannot believe it! I am an Israelite myself, of the stock of Abraham, of the tribe of Benjamin. No! God has not rejected the people which he acknowledged of old as his own' (11.1–12). The repudiation of the possibility of God's ultimate rejection of Israel is revealingly interjected by words of Paul's own Jewish self-esteem. The reliability of God and the identity of Paul are alike at stake in the ultimate vindication of Israel. He thus chooses to interpret the presence of Jewish Christians like himself as a remnant which will ensure the continuation of Israel. Having rehearsed God's promise to Elijah, he proclaims: 'In just the same way at the present time a "remnant" has come into being, selected by the grace of God' (11.5). He then proceeds to argue that as Jewish failure allowed the admission of the Gentiles, so the Gentiles' response will drive the Jews first to envy, and eventually to obedience: 'Because (Israel) offended, salvation has come to the Gentiles, to stir Israel to emulation. But if their offence means the enrichment of the world, and if their falling-off means the enrichment of the Gentiles, how much more their coming to full strength' (11.11, 12). He then gives concrete expression to this rhapsody: 'If their rejection has meant the reconciliation of the world, what will their acceptance mean? Nothing less than life from the dead!' (11.15). For Paul it is not the preaching of the gospel throughout the world, but the conversion of the Jews, which will usher in the resurrection.

This enables Paul to rule out any Gentile complacency (11.25). The response of the Gentiles in no way changes the relation between Jew and Gentile. Jewish privilege and superiority remain undiminished by their temporary failure to respond. Paul brutally puts his Gentile readers in their place: 'If some of the branches have been lopped off, and you, a wild olive, have been grafted in among them, and have come to share the same root and sap as the olive, do not make yourself superior to the branches. If you do so, remember that it is not you who sustain the root: the root sustains you' (11.17, 18). The assertion of continuing dominance is clear: 'God's choice stands, and they are his friends for the sake of the patriarchs. For the gracious gifts of God and his calling are irrevocable' (11.28, 29). But the disequilibrium can only be maintained at the price of inconsistency and incoherence. The analogy of grafting is itself horticultural nonsense, nor can Paul give any intelligible account of the divine plan of history. 'Just as formerly you were disobedient to God, but now have received mercy in the time of their disobedience, so now, when you receive mercy, they have proved disobedient, but only in order that they too may receive mercy. For in making all mankind prisoners to disobedience, God's purpose was to show mercy to all mankind' (11.30–32). Once again care has to be taken not to accept Paul's universalism at its face meaning. He nowhere envisages the salvation of all men; what he does envisage is the selection of all those who are saved simply by God's grace and mercy. It is this that the defection of Israel, albeit temporary, underlines. The ground of God's choice is not open to rational enquiry, nor can the nature of his friendship for Israel be given any coherent expression, granted the admission of at least some Gentiles. Paul is, however, able to escape the inherent contradictions in the power relationship he fosters by celebrating the divine incoherence, which rules out embarrassing human questions and legitimates relationships which are non-reciprocal: 'O depth of wealth, wisdom, and knowledge in God! How unsearchable his judgments, how untraceable his ways! Who knows the mind of the Lord? Who has been his counsellor? Who has ever made a gift to him, to receive a gift in return? Source, Guide,and Goal of all that is – to him be the glory for ever! Amen' (11.33–36). The doxology thus precisely sanctifies the tribute which Gentile must pay to Jew.

(l) The spiritual sacrifice of social conformity

Now that Paul has established his framework of privilege and authority, he puts it to use by addressing the most urgent problem of the mixed communities in the infant church: how to maintain social cohesion. He begins by offering a radical reinterpretation of sacrifice which reflects both Jewish and Gentile elements in the new community: 'My brothers, I implore you by God's mercy to offer your very selves to him: a living sacrifice, dedicated and fit for his acceptance, the worship offered by mind and heart' (12.1). Here Paul is the heir of Jewish prophetic criticism of sacrifice and pagan philosophical questioning. Paul, however, cuts at the heart of the whole sacrificial system of the ancient world. Having no investment in either the holy places or the priestly families, he does not simply offer a 'spiritual' interpretation and legitimation of existing practice; he offers an alternative which eventually displaced the entire sacrificial establishment of the Mediterranean world. The person becomes the victim, not by literally dying, but by committing a kind of psychological suicide. The person dedicates himself by total obedience to God, who has made his will authoritatively known. Paul correctly perceives the revolutionary consequences of his teaching: 'Adapt yourselves no longer to the pattern of this present world' (12.2). The language may be eschatological, but it faithfully reflects the social consequences of his teaching. The worshipper's participation, however, is fundamentally passive: 'Let your minds be remade and your whole nature thus transformed' (12.2). Only a person who has submitted to such a process of re-education is sufficiently enlightened to 'discern the will of God, and to know what is good, acceptable and perfect'. The individual's moral sense has itself first to be changed before it is capable of proper judgment. The motive for this change is eschatological anxiety, since the reader knows that this present world, however immediately impressive, is doomed. 'In all this, remember how critical the moment is. It is time for you to wake out of sleep, for deliverance is nearer to us now than it was when first we believed. It is far on in the night; day is near' (13.11). Expectations of the end elsewhere in the New Testament may be the authentic voice of the oppressed and displaced, protesting against the structures of power from which they suffer by imagining their downfall. Here, however, a more sophisticated phenomenon is at work. Existing millenarian beliefs are being manipulated to control behaviour. 'Let us therefore throw off the deeds of darkness and put on our armour as soldiers of the light. Let us behave with decency as befits the day: no revelling or drunkeness, no debauchery or vice, no quarrels or jealousies! Let Christ Jesus himself be the armour that you wear; give no more thought to satisfying the bodily appetites' (13.12–14). The military imagery evokes conflict and discipline but the enemy is internal, not external. The antagonism intrinsic to millenarian fantasy is directed towards the divided self to ensure social harmony and sexual-control. The juxtaposition of these two social goals is at first surprising; but both demand a curbing of the individual's self-love, and both indicate the kind of society in which the apostle might shine. The social harmony facilitates his rule; the sexual restraint confers instant prestige upon the celibate.

The main emphasis of these chapters is, however, the achievement of social harmony. This is what provokes Paul to appeal to his own God-given authority (12.3). Conceit (12.3), arrogance (12.3), social competition (12.10) and snobbery (12.16) are all condemned. Mutual affection

(12.10), hospitality and mutual help (12.13) and ready sympathy (12.15) are all inculcated. Once again the analogy of the body is used (12.4, 5), this time as a model of reciprocity to bridle unruly individualism, but this is balanced by a stress on the full use of God's various gifts (12.6–8). The description of people's differing abilities as gifts is itself a contribution to social harmony. The individual is encouraged to dissociate himself from his particular abilities and to see himself as accountable for their use, not to his own whims, but to God understood in social terms. The personal pursuit of vengeance is rigorously prohibited (12.17–21). In a society where the feud was never far below the surface and connected with powerful notions of kinship and honour, this both freed the Christian from dangerous obligations and decisively separated him from inherited social groupings. The immediate gain in social peace should not, however, be mistaken for reconciliation. Social antagonisms themselves are contained rather than repudiated. Their immediate expression is bought off by the promise of more effective divine intervention: 'My dear friends, do not seek revenge, but leave a place for divine retribution; for there is a text which reads, "Justice is mine, says the Lord, I will repay." But there is another text: "If your enemy is hungry, feed him; if he is thirsty, give him a drink; by doing this you will heap live coals on his head"' (12.19, 20). Behaviour may be checked, but the expectations remain the same.

This should be borne in mind when reading the surprising eulogy of secular power. When Paul writes, 'there is no authority but by act of God, and the existing authorities are instituted by him' (13.1), it is in line with his maxim, 'Call down blessings on your persecutors – blessings, not curses' (12.14). Even so, the tone is astonishingly optimistic. When one reads such sentences as, 'For government, a terror to crime, has no terrors for good behaviour' (13.3), or, 'The authorities are in God's service and to these duties they devote their energies' (13.6), it is easy to forget that the Jesus who is Paul's Lord was put to death by those authorities acting in their judicial capacity. Moreover Paul himself in I Corinthians 6 tends to speak in a rather different voice; in a sense, however, the ineffectiveness of Pilate's proceedings against Christ is a clue to why Paul can afford to take such a positive view of secular authority. Its worst threats have proved empty. Nevertheless in this letter, as in that to Philemon, Paul is anxious to dissociate himself from any suspicion of conniving at civil disorder. By refusing to be trapped into a cycle of antagonism to secular authority, Paul prepared the way for the eventual triumph of Christendom. The Book of Acts shows Paul's appeal to Rome against Jewish opposition, and here there is the same awareness that civil power might profitably be used to protect the new community: 'It is not for nothing that they hold the power of the sword, for they are God's agents of punishment, for retribution on the offender' (13.4). The same God who could delight in creating 'vessels which were objects of retribution due for destruction' might quite plausibly not be squeamish about using Nero or Caligula. It should be noted, however, that while God is given responsibility for authority, the individual is not. To the believer authority is seen as something purely external, a force like the weather, which has to be lived with and accepted. Effectively in Paul's thought the responsible citizen has given place to the obedient subject. Autonomy in civil life might have dangerous religious implications. In such a context Paul's emphasis that love is the fulfilment of the law takes on a rather unlooked-for complexion (13.7–10). This is usually expounded in contrast to detailed Jewish regulation and ceremonial law, but that does not seem to be Paul's point here: 'Discharge your obligations to all men; pay tax and toll, reverence and respect, to those to whom they are due. Leave no claim outstanding against you, except that of mutual love' (13.7, 8). Such love is a recipe for the ideal subject in a ruler's eye. Law with its detailed regulations and frequent reciprocity is a far cry from the total obedience which love demands.

To read these two chapters is almost to discern the social programme of the Christian church for the next five centuries. They certainly outline the social impact of Christianity in a prophetic manner. In their opposition to the sacrificial cult, their praise of obedience to divinely authorized rulers, their distrust of divisive aristocratic culture, and their pursuit of social conformity, these chapters anticipate the end of the ancient world. By AD 500 only the abolition of the feud remained to be achieved. It is a mark of their influence that while Western readers will see here the origin of mediaeval Christendom, the same thinking also determined the relation of the Eastern churches to victorious Islam.

(m) Freedom and mutual respect: the food laws

In this letter Paul is establishing his position in a community of independent foundation which is of mixed Jewish and Gentile origins. He plays on the tensions between the two communities, commending himself in different ways to both sides, and suggests a particular account of the relationship between them with which he associates himself. In the first part of the letter he began by condemning both Jew and Gentile in a way which left his own position unscathed. He then rehabilitated both Jew and Gentile as Christians, in such a way that some kind of Jewish superiority or privilege was still recognized: a relation which finds its financial expression in the arrangements for the collection which end the letter. The unease of the relation between Jew and Gentile accounts for his stress on social harmony in the two previous chapters, and the letter culminates in definite proposals to deal with that tension. Conflict apparently centred on the observance of food taboos and holy days. Paul's solution ingeniously endeavours to be acceptable to both parties, while attempting to secure respect for the scruples of Jewish Christians. In doing this he gives his most sustained treatment of the nature of Christian freedom and the restraints of mutual respect. It is perhaps his most impressive work.

Throughout the passage there is a continuing advocacy of those qualities which will ensure social cohesion. Mutual acceptance is not conditional on settling 'doubtful points' (14.1). Habits of censoriousness, which the early Christian stress on purity easily created, and the giving of offence or scandal, are repeatedly rejected: 'Let us therefore cease judging one another, but rather make this simple judgment: that no obstacle or stumbling-block be placed in a brother's way' (14.13). 'If your brother is outraged by what you eat, then your conduct is no longer guided by love . . . What for you is a good thing must not become an occasion for slanderous talk' (14.15, 16). The building up of the community is given overriding priority: 'Each of us must consider his neighbour and think what is for his good and will build up the common life' (15.2, see also 14.19). It is a powerful description of a community in which mutual respect is the key to achieving reconciliation. Peace is something which has to be created by both parties in cooperation; it is not to be imposed by external human authority. Paul does not here exert his authority over his Roman readers: instead he reminds them first of their equality before God: 'The man who eats must not hold in contempt the man who does not, and he who does not eat must not pass judgment on the one who does; for God has accepted him. Who are you to pass judgment on someone else's servant? Whether he stands or falls is his own Master's business; and stand he will, because his Master has power to enable him to stand' (14.3, 4). The themes of accountability to God and the believer's slavery to Christ which so easily undermine human autonomy are here used to encourage mutual respect and individual integrity. 'For no one of us lives, and equally no one of us dies, for himself alone. If we live, we live for the Lord; and if we die, we die for the Lord. Whether therefore we live or die, we belong to the Lord. This is why Christ died and came to life again, to establish his lordship over dead and living. You, sir, why do you pass judgment on your brother? And you, sir, why do you hold your brother in contempt? We shall all stand before God's tribunal. For Scripture says, "As I live, says the Lord, to me every knee shall bow and every tongue acknowledge God." So, you see, each of us will have to answer for himself' (14.7–12). The sovereignty of God and the Lordship of Christ in this passage free the believer from social criticism, and from any human hierarchy.

Paul is not, however, simply enunciating grand abstract principles or rehearsing platitudes of community life; he is advocating a particular solution to a definite problem. His approach to those who have interpreted the freedom of the gospel as liberating them from food taboos and respect for the sacred calendar is flattering and approving. Repeatedly he refers to them, by implication and explicitly, as 'strong in faith' (14.1, 2; 15.1). He gives them emphatic support by identifying himself with their position: 'Those of us who have a robust conscience must accept as our own burden the tender scruples of weaker men, and not consider ourselves' (15.1). He eagerly concedes their argument and makes it his own: 'I am absolutely convinced, as a Christian, that nothing is impure in itself' (14.4). He gives convincing expression to their own heady experience of personal liberation: 'If you have a clear conviction, apply it to yourself in the sight of God. Happy is the man who can make his decision with a clear conscience!' (14.22). By contrast his description of the scrupulous is grudging and patronizing. They are repeatedly described as 'weak in faith', which given Paul's stress on that quality earlier in the letter is a devastating criticism. Nevertheless Paul's defence of the individual's moral judgment is surprisingly generous. Talking of the observance of holy days he remarks: 'On such a point everyone should have reached conviction in his own mind' (14.5). Moreover he develops it in a way which respects a point of view he himself strongly opposed, by making the most astonishing concession: 'If a man considers a particular thing impure, then to him it is impure' (14.14). He is thus able to understand and defend the point of view of the scrupulous: 'A man who has doubts is guilty if he eats, because his action does not arise from his conviction, and anything which does not arise from conviction is sin' (14.23). Thus although the strong win the argument, it is the weak who get their way, a conclusion which Paul neatly summarizes: 'Everything is pure in itself, but anything is bad for the man who by his eating causes another to fall. It is a fine thing to abstain from eating meat or drinking wine, or doing anything which causes your brother's downfall' (14.24).

The solution which Paul has proposed is then given the strongest of Christian sanctions, the example of Christ. This is developed in three ways. First Paul presents Christ as a model of self-denial: 'For Christ too did not consider himself, but might have said, in the words of Scripture, "The reproaches of those who reproached thee fell upon me"' (15.3). – It is fascinating that once again Paul seems to realize that his scriptural citation does not entirely meet the case, and so he reinforces a weak point by a rhapsody on the value of Scripture: 'For all the ancient Scriptures were written for our instruction, in order that through the encouragement they give us we may maintain our hope with fortitude' (15.4) – Jesus is then cited as an example of agreement in the prayer that they 'may agree with one another after the manner of Christ Jesus' (15.5). Here the claim is made, but is given no definite substance. It is assumed to be self-evident, a curious assumption, given the involvement of Jesus in so many stories of controversy. Thirdly, Jesus is cited as the model of mutual acceptance and generosity: 'In a word, accept one another as Christ accepted us, to the glory of God' (15.7). This is expounded by a summary of Paul's view of divine history elaborated earlier in the letter: 'I mean that Christ became a servant of the Jewish people to maintain the truth of God by making good his promises to the patriarchs, and at the same time to give the Gentiles cause to glorify God for his mercy' (15.8, 9). Scriptural citations then follow to strengthen Paul's point. Again the appeal is to Pauline theory, rather than to any reminiscence of the actual Jesus. It would seem therefore that this is an early example of the persistent Christian habit of projecting on to Jesus those qualities which it is felt appropriate that he should sanction.

Romans culminates in a profound and concrete exposition of the Christian gospel's claim to bring freedom and reconciliation. The practical outcome which respects the scruples of the Jewish Christians is of a piece with Paul's whole position in this letter. Just as the Gentiles are admitted to the church, but at the price of recognizing a continuing Jewish superiority, so they are allowed the theoretical victory in return for practical conformity to Jewish prejudice. For the weakness of Paul's position is that by describing the two positions as 'strong' and 'weak', he has robbed them of equality; thus the weak are allowed to take offence at the behaviour of the strong, but the strong are not permitted to be scandalized by the scruples of the weak. Thus repeatedly this passage has been used by conservative establishments to reduce subversive voices to conformity, in the name of Christian charity and forbearance. Paul cannot entirely evade responsibility for such use of his thought; it is exploiting a concession to prejudice which he himself has made. It would, however, be quite unfair to him to confuse the conservative and conformist interpretation of this passage with Paul's intention, for two reasons. First, it contains one of the most radical expressions of Christian freedom in the New Testament: 'Everything is pure in itself' (14.20). Of course, there is much in Paul's thought which is inconsistent with that attitude; for instance his sexual teaching is quite unaffected by it, and in this the church followed him until quite modern times. In making such a statement Paul is not simply creating an ideology which justifies his own position; such an insight is not a rationalization but a programme. Its implications are subversive of much of his thought and teaching. To this day the Christian church has only slowly begun to think out the implications of such an insight. Its value is not that it describes the values of Paul or the Christian community, but that it provides their criticism; it points to a direction, a way of learning. Secondly, it has to be recognized that for all his Jewish identity Paul is here qualifying his own position, and not someone else's. The self-discipline is genuine. The degree of understanding he accords to Jewish-Christian scruple can be measured if we compare his attitude towards the food laws and the calendar in Galatians (see p. 49). By contrast Romans is the work of a man who has made painful concessions at the cost of his own deepest convictions. It is not the case that Paul is calling for mutual respect simply to manipulate parties to a dispute in which he is uninvolved. He is himself practising that respect in this letter, and he does so with an exemplary sensitivity and restraint. It is a fitting climax to his greatest work.

(n) Romans 16

The last chapter of Romans must be treated as a separate letter to a different community, for it is addressed to a church which Paul himself has founded. It is therefore markedly different in tone from the letter to the Romans. To the Romans he is conciliatory and eirenic: he has as yet to establish his position among them. In this letter he is defending his position as founding father, and adopts a much more aggressive stance.

(i) Status in the new community

The list of greetings gives some insight into the patterns of status which were developing within the new Christian community. It would, of course, have been a matter of immediate distinction to receive Paul's personal attention in this way. Those who are greeted by him in a letter to the community are thus distinguished from those whom he only greets in general terms. Women are prominent among them (16.1, 3, (7?), 12), which suggests that one of the attractions of the churches that Paul founded was the recognition it gave them. The letters to the Corinthians show that this should not be confused with any modern notions of sexual equality; nevertheless the Pauline churches gave women the opportunity to distinguish themselves, and this distinction was recognized. The basis of the new elite is very varied. There is an emphasis on reciprocal service and esteem. Paul says of Phoebe: 'Stand by her in any business in which she may need your help, for she has herself been a good friend to many, including myself' (16.2). Of Prisca and Aquila he notes: 'They risked their necks to save my life, and not I alone but all the gentile congregations are grateful to them' (16.4). Here their service is compounded by the prestige of courage in dangerous times, and such prestige acquired in persecution also marks out Andronicus and Junias and possibly Apelles. Historical precedence in the faith is carefully marked. Epaenetus is described as 'the first convert to Christ in Asia' (16.5), and of Andronicus and Junias Paul says: 'they were Christians before I was' (16.7). Hard work in the service of the church is repeatedly recognized (16.6, 12).

Hospitality of which the new communities stood in great need, confers prestige (16.3, 23). Their lack of accommodation immediately made the new communities dependent on those of their number who could afford to provide such a facility, and secular distinction obtrudes in the description of Erastus: 'treasurer of this city' (16.23). The reference to Andronicus and Junias (or Junia) as 'apostles' is confused. If they are indeed apostles, it is surprising that Paul does not take more notice of them, and the fact that they do not head his list perhaps suggests that he only means to describe them as well regarded by the apostles. We see here the social reality of Paul's teaching on a variety of gifts. The new communities were not simply societies of passive acquiescence, where congregations sat and listened; they also provided many different opportunities for their members to gain recognition and status.

(ii) The kiss of peace: Paul's defence of his teaching

Paul introduces his major concern in this letter by extending to his readers the liturgical kiss of peace, and reminding them of their connections with 'all Christ's congregations' (16.16). Paradoxically this reminder of harmony serves to introduce and sanction a violent attack on his opponents: 'I implore you, my friends, keep your eye on those who stir up quarrels and lead others astray, contrary to the teaching you received. Avoid them, for such people are servants not of Christ our Lord but of their own appetites, and they seduce the minds of innocent people with smooth and specious words' (16.17, 18). Paul thus discredits his critics by implying that they are selfish and carnal, while carefully not attacking his readers. They are 'innocent': in so describing them, he makes it easier for them to dissociate themselves from his opponents. As elsewhere in his letters Paul resorts to flattery and prayer to gain his ends: 'The fame of your obedience has spread everywhere. This makes me happy about you; yet I should wish you to be experts in goodness but simpletons in evil; and the God of peace will soon crush Satan beneath your feet' (16.19, 20). Thus the language of peace in no way inhibits Paul from violent

The Letters of Paul

antagonism towards his opponents, whom he readily identifies with Satan. Once again the dualism of his beliefs is easily given social expression. The God of peace has disconcerting resemblances to the self-styled Ministry of Defence.

(iii) Doxology and control

Paul's closing words combine in his distinctive manner the praise of God and firm direction to his readers. The importance of their perseverence and its object is indicated by describing God as the one 'who has power to make your standing sure, according to the Gospel I brought you and the proclamation of Jesus Christ' (16.25). They are reminded of their privileged access to 'that divine secret kept in silence for long ages' (16.26). The extension of such a privilege to Gentiles is the more amazing, but Paul gives it the strongest justification: 'Through prophetic scriptures by eternal God's command made known to all nations' (16.26). The goal of God whom he praises so extravagantly is very close to home – their 'faith and obedience'. The glory of God is to be manifested in their attention and deference to his apostle.

IO

THE SIGNIFICANCE OF
THE PAULINE LETTERS

(a) The recognition of authority – the appropriateness of a method
Whatever may be the case with other documents in the New Testament,
the Pauline letters lend themselves readily to the kind of approach which
was outlined in the Introduction. This is not to deny that the historian of
Christian doctrine can find any material in these letters, but it is to insist
that Paul's doctrine cannot be properly understood if it is abstracted from
what might be called the political motives of his writing. Repeatedly these
have been shown to concern Paul's own relation to his readers. The
assertion of authority has proved complex but unrelenting. The apostle
has both to gain his reader's attention and obscure his dependence on his
audience. Often he explicitly defends his own position, as divinely
appointed apostle, with a commission direct from the risen Christ, and
endowed with the Spirit, which gives immediate authentication of his
claims. He clings to a legitimacy based on Scripture, and succeeds in
rehabilitating his Jewish identity, albeit in a spiritual sense. Through his
reassessment of the Law the prestige of a morality and the social structure
it sanctioned are reinterpreted, in the hope of discrediting its social
expression while retaining the old sanctions for new purposes. The rule of
Christ is given concrete and practical expression in the many rulings of his
human representative.

Besides the direct assertion of authority and the unmistakable exercise
of power, the letters have been shown to contain a great deal of material
which serves the same ends, but indirectly. The Pauline prayers, for
instance, are not simply an early chapter in the history of Christian
spirituality: in their context they have a blatantly manipulative function.
The eschatological phantasies of the early believers are consistently
exploited to inculcate an anxiety which only membership of the apostle's
privileged community can allay. A rationale of persecution is put forward
which makes Paul's position unassailable and provides him with fertile

means of projecting his image. Accounts are given of hostility and dissent, which enable them to be easily discounted. Repeatedly in writing to communities which he has founded, the privileges he accords to his readers compel them to assent to his own privileged position. His approach involves the pervasive inculcation of bitterly divisive attitudes which he needs to provide both the sanctions which protect his authority and the privileges which make it palatable. This implicit social antagonism finds its cosmic expression in demonic dualism, and its psychological equivalent in the unresolved conflict of flesh and spirit.

(b) The appraisal of authority – the interpretation of Paul

There is little difficulty in discerning Paul's concern with his authority and his strategies for establishing it. The problem lies in their appraisal. This is not simply a Christian embarrassment at the self-assertive style of so much of his argument, although that embarrassment must be acute. This is the more so because I have argued that the brittle, arbitrary and divisive nature of much of Paul's leadership is intimately connected with self-delusion about the resurrection, and a mistaken value attributed to charismatic phenomena. If the intention of this study was the defence of the articles of the creed, its implications would be devastating, but the real difficulty in this study lies in the interpretation of the deeply contradictory nature of the material. There may have been an appearance of unfairness to Paul, a determination to place his teaching in the most self-regarding perspective; though I would argue that that is the undeniable drift of many of the texts. I have myself been saddened and surprised by the weight of such material. It does not represent an occasional lapse; it is deeply embedded in the structure of his thought. If that was the whole of Paul, the verdict would be plain. The difficulty lies in the existence of some material that is radically different. Particularly in his teaching concerning the food laws Paul articulates an astonishing freedom from convention and taboo, and at the same time develops notions of mutual respect which are entirely convincing manifestations of a gospel of liberation and reconciliation. Moreover he can on occasion expound a theory of gradual learning in religion which is in sharp contrast to much of his shrill certainty.

It is not enough simply to applaud the one and dissociate oneself from the other, for both are expressions of the same religious phenomenon. Some account must be given of the relation between these two very different aspects of Paul's thought. At this stage it may be as well to dispose of one argument which is sometimes appealed to in the apostle's defence. It is tempting to plead in mitigation the particular circumstances of the early church. Only effective discipline and a strong sense of group identity, it is argued, could ensure the survival of these new and fragile communities in a pagan world. The precarious religious background and the uneducated composition of the early church necessitated the strong leadership which Paul provided. To judge him by the liberal standards of a more assured Christian community is on this argument inappropriate and anachronistic. There are two major objections to such a defence. First it ignores the surprising fact that the liberal standards by which Paul's style of authority is challenged are not the product of a later age, but are derived from different strands of his own thought. He stands condemned not by twentieth-century liberalism but by expectations he himself has aroused. Secondly, once untoward circumstances are allowed as an excuse for postponing the exercise of freedom and the achievement of reconciliation, the Christian gospel is at an end. The gospel is not an ideal programme which awaits a perfect world for its implementation. It proclaims the good news that in this world, with all its difficulties and constraints, freedom and peace are possible. No considerations of expediency can qualify that claim without immediately destroying it.

Paul uses the rhetoric of deliverance and reconciliation; at the same time he often acts in ways which domineer and divide. That is why the secular parallels referred to in the Introduction (see p. 5) are so disturbing. Secular gospels promising a new beginning and appealing to aspirations to freedom and fraternity have repeatedly graced the transition from one tyranny to another. Moreover the comparison with the secular gospels is revealing on two other counts. First, as Paul's claims are given real plausibility by the radical replacement of the food laws, so the secular gospels have usually been able to point to some dramatic achievement or concrete goal: the abolition of slavery, the destruction of a feudal aristocracy, drastic changes in land-ownership. Secondly, although with hindsight the leaders of such movements may appear to use rhetoric cynically, in order to manipulate others while pursuing their own ends, they are seldom entirely conscious of what they are doing. Indeed their effectiveness depends upon a degree of self-deception which gives force to their conviction. It is a mistake to portray Paul as a deliberate deceiver, as one might perhaps regard Mr Moon; but a lack of self-awareness is no very adequate defence. We may feel that the person who is self-deceived is in some sense a victim and deserves a pity we might not extend to the deliberate deceiver, but from neither would we look for truth.

The crucial issue must therefore be whether Paul simply uses language of freedom and reconciliation to clothe aggressive self-assertion, or whether he submits himself, albeit partially, to the discipline of the gospel he proclaims. In two important respects I believe this to be the case. The 'spiritualizing' of the Jewish Law, with the radical changes in ritual and taboo and corresponding changes in social relations, represents for Paul a most costly re-ordering of his own identity. Its pain is indicated by his difficulty in achieving entire consistency. This initial transformation is not the end of the story. What is remarkable is the extent to which Paul remains ready to modify his position. That is the importance of Romans 14. The demands of reconciliation and freedom are adjusted in such a way that it is Paul's own convictions which are compromised out of respect for the integrity of others. Moreover, he allows the notion of learning to qualify his own absolute claims, and admits the possibility of transcending his present position. This represents an openness to criticism that the secular gospels have conspicuously lacked. Here indeed may be the precise difference between a religious and a secular gospel. The latter, in the absence of God, is driven to take itself with utter seriousness, and cannot escape elevating particular objectives into absolute goals. The transcendence of God allows his worshippers a certain playful freedom towards their most cherished projects and achievements. The transcendence of God is a reminder that there is always more to be learnt, and that awareness inevitably qualifies the complacency of our knowledge.

I would suggest that Paul's writing does not simply represent the anxious pursuit of power to allay uncertainty about his alleged experience of the risen Christ. For although the texts contain much anxiety, aggression and illusion, they also portray a man learning to exercise freedom and love. If that gospel is only partially applied, it is because we see in his writings the actual process of learning. They do not provide us with some abstract perfection. Instead we see the leaven at work. A transformation has begun, but it is incomplete. To endeavour to appropriate a difficult message inevitably involves frequent inconsistency and failure. The measure of Paul's honesty is that he has not suppressed the radical demands of freedom and reconciliation which, far from simply sanctioning his leadership, frequently provide the basis for criticizing it. We cannot imitate Paul by repeating his conclusions or by insisting on the perpetuation of his limitations of vision and sympathy. Paul can only create the belief that Freedom and reconciliation are possible and compatible, but the exercise of freedom and the achievement of reconciliation still remain the task of his readers. For each generation and every individual they are goals which have to be realized in the face of newly perceived constraints and fresh antagonisms. We can only learn from Paul if we submit his writing to the criticism which he himself invites. To elevate his texts by ascribing to them an infallible authority is to condemn the church to repeat indefinitely his mistakes.

(c) The transition to Mark's Gospel

This study is concerned to recognize the working of authority within the texts, not as an end in itself but in order to appraise the way in which authority is used and the cost of its effectiveness. This is primarily an exercise of moral rather than historical judgment – thus Paul has not been assessed by any reference to the historical Jesus, though some blatant contradictions of Gospel material have been pointed out. The criterion, however, to which we have subjected Paul's writing has not been one of historical authenticity: instead we have judged him by the expectations which his own exposition of the gospel has aroused. In this study there will be little attempt to associate particular strands of tradition with the historical Jesus, though instances of obviously anachronistic projection will be noted. Instead, having identified the exercise of authority in the text, we will subject it to the same kind of questioning to which we have subjected Paul. Does it sustain freedom and encourage autonomy? Does it necessitate antagonism, or does it genuinely reconcile? For Mark is a Gospel: its very title leads us to expect something that is both new and beneficial. Transitions of power are continuous; if that is all that the rise of Christianity represents, it is nothing new. Only the possibility of freedom and its exercise can vindicate its novelty. Similarly one set of antagonisms is continually replacing another. If the benefits of the gospel can be acquired only at the price of hostility to others, the claim to bring peace and reconciliation will prove empty.

To approach a Gospel in this manner is not simply to succumb to some fashion in religious sociology, though the debt to that ill-famed discipline must be generously acknowledged. The uncritical reading of the New Testament manifests itself in different ways from the stubborn refusal to submit it to moral criticism, to its lazy adoption as an infallible book. It is that habit which is directly responsible for many of the horrors of Christian history. In the light of that history the gospel claims to freedom and peace have a new urgency. Only by reading the New Testament critically – believing in freedom and peace, and subjecting our most precious religious traditions to those demands – can we hope to transcend our own grievous Christian history, and in that experience of transcendence discover for ourselves the truth of the gospel.

PART TWO

The Gospel According to Mark

THE GOSPEL ACCORDING TO MARK

The Gospel according to Mark, probably the first of the four Gospels to be written, is certainly the most difficult but also the most important to understand. The intention of the author, the kind of audience he envisaged, the use to which it was originally put, have all to be established. It was, for instance, never intended to be printed, so that everyone might possess a copy. The stress on the esoteric within the book suggests that access to the text may itself at first have been a privilege which the reader could not take for granted. Although it very quickly acquired a public use in the new Christian community, amplifying and eventually challenging the supremacy of the Jewish Scriptures, a much more private use may have been the original intention. The injunction 'let the reader understand' (13.14) seems to envisage an individual rather than a collective audience. There is also a lack of those repeated exhortations to unity and social cohesion which are a mark of the Pauline letters. The simple maxim, 'Be at peace with one another' (9.50), is remarkably isolated in its concern for the community. Moreover we read Mark apart from the oral tradition which provided its context; this Gospel is not intended as an exhaustive account of the tradition it mediates. The phrase in ch. 13 already quoted assumes that the reader will come to the text well furnished with a knowledge of Christian lore. If Mark sees no need to explain the significance of that notorious young man (14.51f.) who 'slipped out of the linen cloth and ran away naked', that is probably because he could rely upon his first readers supplying the rest of the story.

Esoteric in tone, allusive to a tradition of which we are often ignorant, Mark tempts us to rely on the wealth of association with the Jewish Scriptures to provide an interpretation. Recent scholarship has explored the rich variety of meaning which can be found on that basis, but such associations cannot provide a convincing interpretative structure. A readership which needed to be told that 'the Pharisees and the Jews in general never eat without washing the hands, in obedience to an old-established tradition (7.3) can hardly be credited with the recondite knowledge of the Jewish Scriptures assumed by many scholars. This would indicate that the scriptural allusions, which are numerous, belong to a much earlier stage in the formation of the tradition, and are little help in understanding the Gospel in its present form. To insist therefore that Mark can only be understood as an exercise in Jewish midrash is to exclude most of his readers from his meaning on slender grounds of probability. This analysis will therefore concern itself with the surface of the text, which has recently been neglected in favour of speculative reconstructions of its prior history. Moreover in its historical impact it is the surface meaning which has been dominant and creative.

(a) The shape of the Gospel: baptism and its rationale

Much of the difficulty of understanding Mark lies in the sheer originality of its literary form. By contrast the letters of Paul follow long established conventions which clearly indicate their function. Mark may not be the originator of a genre, but he is most probably its earliest surviving instance. Thus while we can assess much of the meaning of Matthew and Luke by their use and departure from Mark, we have no literary precedent by which we can assess this Gospel. If the literary form of Paul's letters supplies no material for comparison, they do provide expectations about the form and content of a Gospel. Paul's gospel concerns the death and resurrection of Christ. The death of Christ is the condition for the forgiveness of sins. The resurrection of Christ provides the substance and the promise of the believer's privilege. It is striking that the shape of Mark is so different from the Pauline account of the gospel. Here the gospel is present prior to the death and resurrection of Jesus, and provides their context. In no sense is the gospel their consequence (1.1, 15; 3.14). Thus while Paul articulates the believer's privilege primarily in terms of future reward, Mark conceives of the gospel as conveying power in the present. The immediate exercise of power at which Paul's letters only hint (I Cor. 2.4; II Cor. 13.3f.; Rom. 15.19) occupies the centre of the Marcan stage. Secondly, there is no hint that the forgiveness of sins is in any way dependent on Christ's death. Only unspecified benefits are ascribed to Jesus' death in Mark (10.45; 14.24), while forgiveness is conveyed by Jesus from the outset of his work (2.1–17). Thirdly, there is a remarkable preoccupation with Jesus' death, rather than his resurrection, which upsets the balance of Paul's dialectic (see pp. 54–58, 101–106). This is not simply a matter of the abrupt ending (16.8), which may be unintended, for the prophecies of the passion (8.30–33; 9.11–13, 31; 10.33f.) betray the same lack of balance as the actual and possibly truncated text. The details of the passion are dwelt upon; the resurrection is barely alluded to. Moreover the parable of the wicked husbandmen is preoccupied with the death of the Son and its revenge – not its reversal – by the Father (12.1–9). The Gospel according to Mark is therefore very different from what reading Paul might lead us to expect both as to form and to content.

The enormous imaginative power of the Christmas stories and the inclusion of the virgin birth in the creeds easily prevent us from perceiving the significance of Mark's opening, which is most emphatically 'the beginning' (1.1). Matthew and Luke tell a story from birth to death to resurrection, rehearsing in this pattern the life of Christian everyman. John begins with God, and his metaphysical introduction indicates the end, which for him is the same as the beginning. To appreciate the intention of the Marcan prologue, the most helpful contrast is not with these later revisions, but with Paul, writing to the Romans: 'This gospel God announced beforehand in sacred Scriptures through his prophets. It is about his Son: on the human level he was born of David's stock, but on the level of the spirit – the Holy Spirit – he was declared Son of God by a mighty act in that he rose from the dead: it is about Jesus Christ our Lord' (1.2–4). The comparisons and the contrasts with Mark are instructive. Mark shares with Paul a perspective of Jewish prophecy (1.2–3, 6), the acclamation of Jesus as Son of God (1.1, 11), and an emphasis on the Holy Spirit (1.8, 10, 12); but given these similarities, the differences are remarkable. First, while Paul may disparage Jesus' Davidic descent by comparison with the level of the Spirit, Mark omits it entirely. Only in the words of blind Bartimaeus is it alluded to (10.47, 49), while the teaching about the Messiah attributed to Jesus explicitly denies Davidic descent as a qualification (12.36f.). No note of it obtrudes in the mention of his family (6.3) or his anonymous home town (6.1). Jesus comes to the Baptist, not from Bethlehem, but from Nazareth (1.9). Unlike Paul, Mark has no interest in Jesus' human origins: for practical purposes, Jesus' life begins with his baptism. Secondly, for Mark it is at Jesus' baptism, not his resurrection, that he is both 'declared Son of God' in the most direct manner (1.11) and also clearly associated with the Holy Spirit (1.10). It is difficult to believe that these three contrasts with Paul are accidental. They suggest that for Mark baptism has an importance even greater than is apparent in Paul (I Cor. 10.2; Rom. 6.3f.). As John's prologue supplies a metaphysical context which serves as a key to the whole shape of his Gospel, so for Mark Jesus is the exemplar of the baptized, and this provides the shape and guides the emphasis of his Gospel. While Paul argues from the privileges and obligations of the baptized Christian, Mark simply portrays Jesus. The control and the privilege are implicit in the description, for in presenting Jesus in this way he explores and indicates the baptized identity of his readers.

For Mark, baptism represents intially a sharp discontinuity with the family. The believer is encouraged to identify with a Jesus without a past and whose life begins at baptism. Compulsory education and urban anonymity make it difficult to imagine the overwhelming control that the family exercised in Jesus' world, directing behaviour by its expectations and enforcing conformity by constant supervision. Baptism offered a way of escape, a means of achieving an identity independent of the inflexible background of family relationships. Mark does not conceal the element of conflict in such freedom, and portrays Jesus as himself participating in it. His family share the view of his ministry as madness (3.21). His visit to his home elicits a wry comment which again associates his family with the misunderstanding of society: 'A prophet will always be held in honour except in his home town, and among his kinsmen and family' (6.4). Any reference to his mother among the women at the crucifixion seems uncertain (15.40). The discontinuity is portrayed most sharply in Jesus' apparent repudiation of mother and brothers, which extends this heady promise to the reader: 'Whoever does the will of God is my brother, my sister, my mother' (3.35). To belong to the new divine family means leaving one's human family behind. When Jesus called James and John, 'leaving their father Zebedee in the boat with the hired men, they went off to follow him' (1.20). Jesus envisages his disciples giving up 'home, brothers or sisters, mother, father or children or land' (10.29); this confusion of property and kin introduces the promise of receiving in this age a hundred times as much', which is far removed from the comforts and ideals of bourgeois domesticity. It is anticipated that the home is not a refuge from conflict, but its focus: 'Brother will betray brother to death, and the father his child; children will turn against their parents and send them to their death' (13.12). It is, however, the control of the family, rather than its obligations, which is repudiated. For the polemic against the Pharisees' alleged teaching on Corban explicitly appeals to Jewish traditions of family piety and reaffirms them (7.9–13). The perception of exaggerated and self-seeking devices in traditions other than one's own is a commonplace of religious antagonism; but already in Mark's community the transition has begun from baptism as a sign of separation from the family to baptism as a badge of filial piety. The sect which begins in exercising freedom from its parents demands the conformity of its own children.

The replacement of a family identity by a religious one inevitably risks suspicion and opposition, for in standing outside the family the Christian had evaded the most elementary unit of social communication and control. Thus the baptism which bestows a new beginning courts persecution from society and culminates in death. It is a sure instinct which relates conflict in the family and opposition from society (10.30; 13.9–13). Baptism is explicitly identified with the martyr's death in Jesus' prophetic question to the sons of Zebedee: 'Can you drink the cup that I drink, or be baptized with the baptism I am baptized with?' (10.38). More obliquely, the divine sonship accorded to Jesus at his baptism is finally recognized by the centurion at his death (15.39). Thus the reader is prepared to understand Jesus' crucifixion as the culmination of his baptism, and encouraged to see his own baptism as committing him to the same course. Mark presents at least one consistent view of Jesus' death, not as some atoning sacrifice, but as the climax of a long history in which the prophet servants of God had died for their message (12.1–9). Thus throughout the Gospel the antagonism of surrounding society and the prospect of eventual persecution are quietly assumed. In the parable of the sower, it blights the word (4.17). In Gethsemane, when Jesus tells the sleeping Peter, 'Pray that you may be spared the test' (14.38), he also indirectly warns the reader what to expect. It is not a destiny confined to an élite in the community: 'For everyone will be salted with fire' (9.49). Thus Jesus 'called the people to him, as well as his disciples, and said to them, "Anyone who wishes to be a follower of mine must leave self behind; he must take up his cross, and come with me. Whoever cares for his own safety is lost; but if a man will let himself be lost for my sake and for the Gospel, that man is safe. What does a man gain by winning the whole world at the cost of his true self? What can he give to buy that self back? If anyone is ashamed of me and mine in this wicked and godless age, the Son of Man will be ashamed of him, when he comes in the glory of his Father and of the holy angels" ' (8.34–38). The cross here has not yet been moralized as simple ethical self-denial, though that is also demanded. The disciple and master are united in suffering for the gospel. The actual loss of life is envisaged, though the incentive is curiously at odds with the directive. For the promise of ultimate safety appeals to a motive which the disciple has already been asked to renounce. The passage ends with a prophylactic against the power of the human audience to enforce conformity by shame. Against it is ranged the applause of the angels and the regard of the Son of Man. Thus in neither case are caution or shame repudiated; they continue to be permitted, but in an eschatological perspective. When the reader's turn comes to suffer persecution he is admonished to rely totally on the Holy Spirit in answering his judges (13.9–13). Doubtless the studied silence of Jesus (14.60f.; 15.5) was intended to cheer and guide his imitators. Any premature attempt at self-justification before the usurping judgment of man is thus firmly discountenanced.

Alienation from society and the expectation of persecution are deeply engrained in Paul's letters, but Mark gives them a quite different rationale, for Paul's rewards are in the future, whereas Mark promises a present gain: the gift of the Holy Spirit. At first it would seem that the Holy Spirit functions in the two writers in an identical way. For both it is conveyed in baptism, and is a sign of the baptized person's new status as a son of God (cf. Mark 1.8, 10; Rom. 8). In both communities the Spirit is associated with prophetic speech (Mark 13.11) and provides a continuity between the new community and the Jewish Scriptures (12.36), so that they are alert to hear the Spirit, which is at the heart of their new identity, speaking in those prestigious texts from the past. But while Paul teaches that the Spirit's gifts are many and varied, for Mark the Holy Spirit conveys a much more specific power, the benefits of which are immediate. The moment that Jesus has received the Holy Spirit he is pushed into direct confrontation with Satan (1.12f.). The first recognition of his power, as well as its first display, is in exorcism (1.21–28), and victory over the evil spirits is celebrated throughout the Gospel in story after story. The triumph of the Holy Spirit over the unclean spirits is not only implied by the opening narrative; it provokes the only absolute prohibition which Mark's Gospel contains: ' "No sin, no slander, is beyond forgiveness for men; but whoever slanders the Holy Spirit can never be forgiven; he is guilty of eternal sin". He said this because they had declared that he was possessed by an unclean spirit' (3.28–30). The confusion of the Holy Spirit with the demonic threatens the whole meaning of the gospel, and demands the sternest repression.

Mark's understanding of baptism therefore provides the key to the whole shape of his work. Its repudiation of the controlling family explains the nature and omissions of his prologue; its concomitant opposition underlies the development of his narrative, with its culmination in faithful death. Its access to the Spirit's power and the triumph over the evil spirits supplies both the motivation of the reader and a basic message of the book.

(b) The recognition of Jesus' identity and the reader's privilege
In the letters of Paul the unique status of the apostle is the pledge of the believer's privilege – the apostle accords to his followers certain advantages which they can secure only by assenting to Paul's special role. In Mark the reader is flattered, not by being called a son of God or by being promised a position of security at the day of judgment, but by the use of a quite simple narrative device. Although the opening words, 'Here begins

the gospel of Jesus Christ the Son of God', may be a slight expansion of the original preface, they accurately reflect the viewpoint from which the Gospel is to be read, which immediately places the reader in a position of superiority. Unlike the characters in the story, who take part in the slow disclosure of Jesus' true identity, the reader knows the truth from the beginning. He has the satisfaction of a God's-eye view. The same device which bestows this advantage on the reader gives the narrative its excitement and its irony. Secure in our knowledge of Jesus' identity, we can enjoy the many misunderstandings in the story: the dullness of the disciples, the blindness of the Jewish leaders, even the double irony of the soldiers' mockery. Sooner or later, like the disguised prince in the fairy story or the returning Odysseus, Jesus will show himself in his true colours.

Through most of this Gospel's stories Jesus passes incognito, the reflection of social roles and human expectations which misleadingly define him. Most frequently he is simply referred to by name as Jesus; when this is qualified further, it is by his place of origin – Nazareth (1.9, 24; 10.47; 14.67; 16.6). He appears without a father, as 'son of Mary' (6.3), and Mark may mean to tell us that he was a carpenter (6.3), but the text at that point is unclear. He is given a fairly definite social place: not only do his disciples and his supplicants address him as 'Master' (4.38; 9.17; 10.20, 35; 12.32; 13.1; 14.14), his opponents speak to him in the same way (12.14, 19). It is a term of limited social deference, not of religious self-abasement. When Jairus, the president of a synagogue, 'threw himself down at his feet, and pleaded with him' (5.22), he expressed the urgency of his request; he is not worshipping his Lord. (The debtors in the parable use the same gesture – Matt. 18.26, 29). In controversy and by his disciples Jesus is sometimes addressed as 'Rabbi' (5.35; 9.51; 14.45). In comparison with the consistently exalted language by which Paul refers to Jesus, this threatens to reduce him to the commonplace, but the risk is necessary to the Gospel's drama. Because Mark so often obscures Jesus' true identity by placing him in an everyday social context, subject to quite ordinary expectations, he creates the conditions for mystery and the possibility of mistake. When Jesus asks, 'Who do men say that I am?' (8.27), he is articulating an anxiety which the text has been at pains to create. Indeed it has already been explicitly voiced in Herod's response to Jesus' fame: 'People were saying, "John the Baptist has been raised to life, and that is why these miraculous powers are at work in him." Others said, "It is Elijah." Others again, "He is a prophet like one of the old prophets"' (6.14, 15). Anxiety about the recognition of the Messiah is a recurrent theme of Christian apocalyptic: 'Then, if anyone says to you, "Look, here is the Messiah," or, "Look, there he is," do not believe it. Imposters will come claiming to be messiahs or prophets, and they will produce signs and wonders to mislead God's chosen, if such a thing were possible' (13.21f.). It is part of Mark's art to play on that anxiety, so that the same Jesus whom the reader has learnt to recognize as the Messiah warns him: 'Take care that no one misleads you. Many will come claiming my name, and saying, "I am he"; and many will be misled by them' (13.5f.). The anxiety which flatters the reader's perceptiveness in recognizing Jesus is eventually used to rule out any subsequent revision of that estimate.

The drama of the Gospel is derived from the gradual disclosure of Jesus' true identity as the Messiah, the Son of God. Already in Mark's mind these two categories have begun to be fused together (1.1; 14.61), but they still articulate different interests in the text. As 'Christ' is ceasing to denote a particular function and is becoming a kind of surname for Jesus (1.1), so there is little obvious interest in presenting Jesus in the light of messianic proof-texts. In Mark the messianic status of Jesus is important, but not as the fulfilment of Jewish hopes. Peter's recognition of Jesus as the Messiah has long been regarded as the hinge on which much of the narrative turns, but what matters for Mark is not the substance of Jewish messianic hope; it is the recognition of Jesus' hidden identity. That is what distinguishes the disciple in the Gospel, as presumably in the community in which Mark was written. While glimpses of the divine Son shine throughout the Gospel, the messianic claim is treated with emphatic reserve. Only at the trial and its aftermath does the claim become public – no longer the property and distinction of Jesus' disciples – and immediately it produces opposition and mockery. Jesus dies for being 'King of the Jews', as his disciples may die for calling him Christ. In Mark the recognition of the Messiah is the believer's distinction, and its cost is conflict and persecution.

In contrast to the messianic motif, which is entirely concealed in the first part of the Gospel, and only comes to dominate the account of the trial and the crucifixion, the reader is offered constant reminders that Jesus is the Son of God. He is directly acclaimed as such by the disembodied heavenly voice (1.11; 9.8); the evil spirits repeatedly recognize him (1.25; 3.11; 5.7) before they are silenced by his power. While Jesus' messiahship is asserted but never exercised, the Son of God is exhibited in every mighty act. The demons may be admonished to keep silent, but they say enough to leave the reader in no doubt of the significance of what is taking place. In the closing chapters Jesus even begins to apply the term to himself. In the parable of the wicked husbandmen, the son is the final martyr (12.6). His apocalyptic teaching culminates with the caveat: 'About that day or that hour no one knows, not even the angels in heaven, not even the Son; only the Father' (13.32). The embarrassing ignorance of the Christian community on such an important topic is thus sanctioned by the highest authority – in such circumstances to claim knowledge would be presumptuous indeed. Although Jesus' divine sonship appears in the trial (14.61), it plays no further role in the account of the crucifixion until in a muted form it is acknowledged by the centurion (15.39). Thus while Jesus' identity as Messiah distinguishes his followers and immerses them in conflict, his status as the Son of God is much more manifest, and is associated with power rather than with persecution.

The Messiahship is a secret (8.30), the demons are silenced when they salute the Son of God – both titles are the focus of self-conscious anxiety within the story. They indicate Jesus' mysterious and precious hidden identity. No such anxiety surrounds the use of the phrase 'Son of Man'. Nowhere in Paul's letters is Jesus referred to in that way, yet in Mark the term is often on Jesus' lips. Modern historians preoccupied by the reconstruction of Jesus' self-consciousness have seized on this term and subjected it to the most minute analysis, but however puzzling and varied its origins, Mark has a consistent and straightforward usage. In Mark only Jesus uses the term; he uses it quite explicitly, in public (2.10, 28) as well as in private (8.31; 9.9, 31; 10.33, 45). In every case Mark intends the phrase to refer to Jesus himself. It is therefore a unique term of self-reference which underlines for the reader the importance of the speaker and his message, but apparently in itself it gives nothing away about Jesus' identity. That is why in Mark's narrative Jesus is able to use the phrase so freely. By referring to himself in that way he discloses nothing. Only some of the things that he uses the term to say which must be concealed, as when he talks of his future suffering (8.31; 9.9, 12, 31; 10.33, 45) or identifies himself as returning in power (8.38; 13.26). The apocalyptic associations of the phrase may have been appropriate to certain claims, but they hardly indicate a specific title or function. This can be seen in Jesus' reply to the High Priest's question: 'Are you the Messiah, the Son of the Blessed One?' 'I am; and you will see the Son of Man seated on the right hand of God and coming with the clouds of heaven' (14.61f.). In referring to the Son of Man, Jesus is not introducing an additional title to 'Messiah' and 'Son of the Blessed One'. He is outrageously introducing himself at God's right hand. If it was a reference to the prophecy in Daniel (7.13), it would only be a platitude of Jewish expectation. What makes it blasphemy is precisely its self-reference. It is, however, the context that makes the term offensive; in itself it may be grandiloquent, but Jesus uses it too frequently and indiscriminately in the text for it to be highly charged. The Son of Man is no object of expectation; no one else greets Jesus with the term. No one, we may deduce, was persecuted for referring to him in that way.

To conclude this study of the suggestions which are being conveyed to the reader by the way in which Jesus is addressed and speaks of himself in Mark, one further point should be made. The first reader would have recognized himself in Jesus. For the baptized person also possesses the same kind of dual identity: on the one hand he is the person perceived by society, with a name, a home, with parents and occupation; but like Jesus, he too has been anointed with the Spirit and is a son of God, and like Jesus he may suffer mockery and persecution if his true identity becomes known.

(c) The authentication of Jesus and the gospel: the assertion of theophany

Turning from Paul to Mark one concern seems strangely absent. Paul gives much attention to authenticating his own position as an apostle, commissioned by the risen Christ. It is that which defines his position as God-given, rather than a human creation (see pp. 41–44, 62–66, 94–99). In Mark the author is quite invisible, which will not be the case in Luke and John. Here there is apparently no self-assertion on the author's part: he is entirely submerged in the objective force of his story. While Paul hopes to make his claims credible by drawing attention to himself, Mark achieves a similar end by systematically concealing himself. He does, however, establish the authority of Jesus – and indirectly the authority of his text – by objective assertions as bold as any Pauline claims about resurrection. In the opening story of Jesus' baptism we are firmly told: 'A voice spoke from heaven: "Thou art my Son, my Beloved; on thee my favour rests"' (1.11). Similarly, as the prophecies of the passion prepare the reader for the crucifixion, Jesus is once again directly authenticated by God: 'Then a cloud appeared, casting its shadow over them, and out of the cloud came a voice: "This is my Son, my Beloved; listen to him"' (9.7). So strong is this prior divine authentication that at the close an angel, in the shape of a youth 'wearing a white robe', is sufficient proof of resurrection (16.5). The response of 'fear' (16.8) indicates that it is God who speaks, but this is less explicit than the incidents which mark the baptism and the transfiguration.

These assertions of theophany deserve careful attention. In both cases they are introduced without any fussy self-consciousness into an objective narrative. The author certainly places them with care where they will deeply influence the reader's perception of Jesus and the text, but there is no explicit attempt to ground the author's credibility on these stories; their truth is quietly and effectively assumed. It is a sign of the success of Mark's art that relatively little attention has been paid to the objective truth of such claims. Paul's defiant words, 'If Christ was not raised, then our gospel is null and void, and so is your faith' (I Cor. 15.14), have brought down the closest scrutiny upon the speaker. Mark's equally startling assertions of direct divine authority are usually neutralized by modern commentators with surprising insouciance. They may point to the Old Testament allusions of the language, implying that once they have examined the literary origins of the expressions used by Mark, they have in some sense disposed of the embarrassment of his claims. Sometimes there is an appeal to historical relativism, suggesting however implausibly that divine voices from the sky were merely a part of everyday life in ancient Palestine. The Jewish Scriptures may have provided the vocabulary and the cultural expectations which made such claims to direct divine authentication credible, but that in no way qualifies the importance of the claim that is being made, nor does it dispose of the problem of its truth.

Mark and his readers could distinguish as well as we can the force of saying 'I believe that Jesus is the Son of God' as opposed to 'God has said that Jesus is his Son'. In choosing to present his claims in the latter rather than the former way, Mark is not writing in a fit of absent-mindedness. He intends in the opening words of his Gospel to present the reader with the strongest possible claim to direct divine authority. Ostensibly this describes Jesus, and prepares the reader to understand the subsequent stories in a certain way. Indirectly it also serves to establish the authority of the text. For one of the first claims that the reader has to assimilate is that of direct divine communication, which is unlikely to be a part of his experience. If the reader acquiesces in such an improbable claim so early in the Gospel narrative, he has no effective ground for challenging any of the other surprising claims which he will encounter later. The matter-of-fact way in which the divine voice is referred to discourages question. The author has staked his credibility on it quite as crucially as Paul stakes his credibility on the resurrection. It is the genius of Mark's assertions that they are made with such total assurance that one hardly notices them, or gives a thought to their author.

12

MARK: THE POWER OF JESUS

(a) Attention and expectation

A dead man raised to life may be a convincing demonstration of the power of God, but the man himself inevitably appears somewhat passive. He may be the worthy object of God's intervention, but unless a kind of Jack-in-the-box quality is attributed to him he himself appears as weak. Thus in Paul's letters with their emphasis on resurrection, the weakness of man and power of God are complementary (cf. pp. 101–106). In Mark Jesus is directly associated with power. He gains attention not as the object of divine favour, but as the agent of divine power. His mighty acts establish his fame, and bring him the constant attention of the crowd. The crowd in Mark is not simply a device like the chorus of a Greek tragedy to inform us of the significance of what it witnesses. Mark understands that the crowd itself enhances Jesus' power and authority. In every exercise of human power there is first a bid for attention. The speaker will use humour or rhetoric. Ritual in religion, parades by an army, the ceremony of government all exert an imaginative power over our attention, quite apart from any intrinsic strength in the institutions themselves. Thus part of the malaise of the modern church is that its buildings and its leaders have become a part of the landscape – their very familiarity robs them of their power to compel attention. Instead they have become a reassuring background – the crowds that surround clergy today are occasional and contrived. Against such a situation the crowds which Jesus evokes in this Gospel are a significant contrast.

The same narrative which describes Jesus compelling the attention of his contemporaries also serves as an implicit promise to the reader. The stories of exorcism and healing, of the control of nature and the escape from scarcity, all foster specific expectations of Jesus and those who claim to represent him. While modern churchmen may read such stories with varying degrees of embarrassment as they contrast them with their own impotence, Mark conveys no sense that these are tales from a unique and vanished past. They do not discredit the actual Christian community he serves; they merely define its legitimate expectations. However concealed, religion promises a benefit. In these stories of Jesus' power we see the kind of advantages for which Christians in Mark's community were looking. Because so many of Mark's promises are conveyed, not as fantasy about the future, but simply as stories of what has happened, his work possesses a very particular confidence and assurance.

(b) Exorcism and the price of dualism

Nowhere is the link more emphatic between the power of Jesus and his representatives than in the case of exorcism. Of the Twelve we are told that Jesus 'would send (them) out to proclaim the Gospel, with a commission to drive out devils' (3.15; cf. 6.7, 13). This delegation is not merely a matter of general description: the Gospel contains guidance for the particular problems that such a delegated authority created. In one story a disappointed father complains to Jesus: 'Master, I brought my son to you. He is possessed by a spirit which makes him speechless . . . I asked your disciples to cast it out, but they failed' (9.17f.). Jesus resolves the immediate crisis, but the recognition within the Gospel text that the power of his representatives was not always effective must have been helpful in explaining occasional failure, without compromising Jesus' position or totally destroying their own. Moreover Jesus gives two explanations of failure. In the story itself it is implied that the father's lack of faith has previously been a constraint (9.19, 22–24) and prevented success. Privately Jesus addresses the would-be exorcists: 'There is no means of casting out this sort but prayer' (9.29). Later in the same chapter the problem is faced of the unauthorized use of Jesus' name in exorcism (9.38–40). This suggests that while Jesus simply utters effective words of command, his imitators invoked the authority of his name, and this is envisaged by Mark as having begun in his lifetime (contrast Phil. 2.9–11). Surprisingly the disciples are rebuked for trying to stop such unauthorized use which undermines their own status. Jesus' concern is not with their standing, but with his own: 'No one who does a work of divine power in my name will be able the next moment to speak evil of me. For he who is not against us is on our side' (9.39, 40). The precise significance of this will be considered later, but it is fascinating to find outside the letters of Paul a similar lack of concern for historically authorized tradition. This is not the unanimous early Christian viewpoint, but it certainly demands a modification of more rigid understandings of tradition.

In one sense it is misleading to separate exorcism from healing, as Mark clearly understands them to be closely associated. This is underlined in his resumés of Jesus' activity (1.32–39; 3.11) and of the Twelve (6.13). Nevertheless the two kinds of power – exorcism and healing – belong to very different conceptual worlds, and it is therefore necessary to treat them separately. For the emphasis on exorcism in Mark raises acute questions about the dependence of his vision of the gospel on cosmic dualism. We have already seen that Paul's gospel demands a divisive stance towards society to provide both privilege and sanction. How similar are the implications of Mark's dualism? It is a world-view with obvious social dangers and theoretical contradictions. The intellectual inability to produce a coherent account of the relation between good and evil except in terms of immediate conflict has devastating implications when translated into social attitudes. It envisages irreconcilable conflict, to which the only acceptable conclusion is total victory. It is therefore a recipe for the most aggressive social behaviour. In examining the account of exorcism in Mark the cost of its dualist context must be carefully assessed.

Mark certainly develops his description of Jesus' power in a dualistic framework. Jesus' baptism immediately thrusts him into encounter with Satan (1.11). The Baptist's testimony, 'After me comes one who is mightier than I', is echoed in explicit teaching on the significance of Jesus' power over the unclean spirits: 'No one can break into a strong man's house and make off with his goods unless he has first tied the strong man up; then he can ransack the house' (3.27). The implications if applied to the reality of demonic power itself are most disturbing, but the sense that Mark intends expresses total confidence that Satan has been bound. Accordingly, there is little anxiety about recurrence after Jesus' exorcisms. The deaf and dumb spirit is commanded, 'Come out of him, and never go back' (9.25). The Gerasene demoniac is trusted to return home (5.19). It is probably significant that this Gospel does not contain the sobering teaching on the return of the evil spirit (Matt. 12.43–45; Luke 11.24–26) with its deeply pessimistic implications about the possibility of lasting deliverance. Mark is unclouded by such doubts. Jesus' power is totally effective, which the vain opposition of the unclean spirits only serves to underline. In two of the three detailed stories of exorcism the spirits' fear of Jesus is made explicit. The full description of the destructive and anti-social behaviour of the Gerasene demoniac only highlights his apprehension of Jesus: 'What do you want with me, Jesus, son of the Most High God? In God's name do not torment me' (5.7). At Capernaum, where the demoniac shrieks, 'What do you want with us, Jesus of Nazareth? Have you come to destroy us?', there is the same note of perceived threat (1.24). As Jesus is the focus of demonic antagonism, so opposition to him is readily understood in the same lurid categories. In the interpretation of the parable of the sower, the intervention of Satan (4.15) removes the word. This tendency is given most vivid expression in Jesus' rebuke to Peter: 'Away with you, Satan; you think as men think, not as God thinks' (9.33). In such instances Mark provides clear evidence that the dualism implicit in the exorcisms pervades his whole social outlook.

In assessing this aspect of Mark's portrayal of Jesus, it is easy to underestimate the importance of what is at issue. Our post-Enlightenment perspective has successfully banished the demonic to a fictional realm of horror entertainment, but throughout the early Christian centuries the visible defeat of men's spiritual enemies, the demons in exorcism and miracles of healing was the key to the success of the missionaries. At first this is surprising for outside the church demons, evoked only occasional dread. More usually they provided a convenient casual explanation for a wide range of surprising and incongruous experiences. It seems that Christianity succeeded in imposing a dualistic understanding on popular demonology, which intensified men's fear of the demonic – a development which made the Christian remedy both urgent and attractive. Demons were widely invoked to explain a bewildering variety of phenomena – the unlooked for misfortune of plague, the disturbed behaviour of riot, the private intensity of unhappy love. Nevertheless Jesus' exorcisms have a very specific nature. They make no reference either to personal accident or collective disaster. The nearest we come to any hint of Jesus providing general protection is in the blessing of the children (10.13–16), where such superstitions may be implied, but are certainly not explicit. It may well be that in deeply superstitious societies, where belief in evil spirits and amulets was widespread, the instances of Jesus' exorcisms would be quickly assimilated to accord with much more questionable expectations. People who had heard of his exorcisms might naturally look to him to protect them from accident or avert disaster, but it is remarkable that Mark gives no encouragement to such developments. Instead, Jesus' exorcisms all have a definitely personal reference. In every case the presence of the evil spirit is manifested by behaviour which is destructive to the individual and often separates him from society. The social phenomena which Jesus addresses in his exorcisms are therefore both carefully defined and still recognizable. To speak of such phenomena as 'possession' is certainly to locate the difficulty in the person manifesting such behaviour in a way which is misleading. 'Possession' is as much the creation of its audience, which may well have provoked the behaviour in the first place and which confirms the 'possessed' by its expectations and gratifies him by its predictable response. It would, however, be wrong to claim that such phenomena are the product of demonology, for self-destructive, socially isolating behaviour has in no way diminished in societies which have jettisoned belief in possession and dualistic religious world-views. Moreover the effectiveness of authoritative personal intervention in such situations, changing the individual's perception of himself and society's attitude towards him, is far from implausible. The understanding of the phenomenon may be deficient, but the treatment may none the less be effective.

The suspicion that the exorcist and the evil spirits are in some kind of unholy collusion is very ancient, and indeed is present in Mark. It is perhaps implied in the encounter with 'Legion', who speaks to Jesus on almost equal terms, and with surprising familiarity invokes God in his defence. His destruction in the herd of pigs suggests that he has been outwitted rather than simply overpowered. The suspicion is voiced explicitly by the doctors of the law from Jersualem: 'He is possessed by Beelzebub' and 'He drives out devils by the prince of devils' (3.22). They are not answered directly but, as Mark correctly points out, by riddles. 'How can Satan drive out Satan?' (3.24). The implication of this is that Satan cannot contradict himself, and that if he is opposed it can only be by God. There then follows a proverb which rings strangely in the ears of divided Christendom, 'If a kingdom is divided against itself, that house will never stand' (3.24f.). Here the implications of the first riddle are forgotten and the charge of his opponents is accepted at its face value. For a moment Jesus forgets to defend himself in his eagerness to proclaim Satan's destruction: 'If Satan is in rebellion against himself, he is divided and cannot stand; and that is the end of him' (3.26). The saying about the strong man already quoted gives the answer most immediately acceptable to Christian ears. Such charges as Jesus faced are a recurrent part of religious polemic. As we have seen, Paul makes similar charges against his opponents (see p. 121), and the Christian church later succeeded in discrediting both declining paganism and mediaeval witchcraft with the same accusation. For once the reality of evil spirits has been admitted, power over them is inevitably ambiguous. To invoke the power of God only skirts the question why God permitted such evil beings in the first place. Here the contradictions within the theory of dualism threaten to undermine the *bona fides* of the exorcist. In one sense, therefore, Jesus' suggestion that Satan himself is in contradiction and self-condemned is both effective and perceptive. Far from seeking to heighten anxiety about Satan in order to exalt Jesus' power, this saying attacks the whole conception of dualism, even at the risk of compromising Jesus himself.

Any assessment, therefore, of the exorcisms in Mark and the expectations they encouraged among his readers must be carefully qualified. They do not explicitly link Jesus with the whole range of superstitions regarding evil spirits, nor do they unambiguously endorse dualism, as the saying just examined clearly demonstrates. Nevertheless they do contain several dangerous contradictions. First, they do not appreciate the extent to which the exorcist is parasitic on the demonology he counters. The transmission of belief in evil spirits is not only a reflection of continuing human anxieties; it has also much to do with the continuing self-interest of those groups who meet those fears. In order to survive, the makers of amulets and the weavers of spells must excite fears as well as overcome them. The difficulty is that any dualistically conceived religion either offers total victory, which undermines the anxiety it allays, or it must perpetuate that anxiety while ostensibly proclaiming its end. Mark offers no clear resolution of this difficulty. With one voice he speaks of Satan's end; with another he fosters the practice of exorcism, which implies that Satan is very much alive. Thus paradoxically it was the Enlightenment of the eighteenth century rather than the emergence of Christendom that effectively extinguished the fear of the demonic, and since then the church has been faced with a cruel dilemma. Either Jesus' very achievement has made him redundant in this respect, or the church is tempted to be a carrier of the demonic world-view in order to have the satisfaction of providing its antidote. Secondly, the stress on conflict, which is intrinsic to dualism, has divisive social implications. The glorying in persecution which has already been noticed in this Gospel is the practical cost of the dualism it propagates. Unlike Paul, Mark has no concept of learning in religion; instead he can only envisage a reaction of total obstinacy, provoking irreconcilable conflict, which must be resolved by the ultimate intervention of God. In the words of his apocalypse: 'All will hate you for your allegiance to me; but the man who holds out to the end will be saved' (13.13).

There are therefore undeniable drawbacks to Mark's presentation of Jesus' power in terms of exorcism, but when we compare this with the Pauline picture there are also some advantages. There is no hint in the stories that Jesus is creating the conditions he then proceeds to remove. While in our society the religious tradition itself is directly responsible for transmitting the categories of demon possession, which it then alleviates, it would be anachronistic to attribute such a process to Mark. Jesus in the stories and Mark in the Gospel are responding to anxieties which are already present in their societies. They do not have to summon the unclean spirits before they can dispose of them. By contrast, Paul has to create the anxieties he allays, as is painfully obvious in the opening chapters of Romans. Only an audience whose confidence and self-esteem have first been subjected to his preaching of judgment can respond to his gospel of grace. This gives to his approach an aggressiveness and a hostility to human autonomy which is quite absent from Mark. It is intelligible that the crowds should of their own volition be attracted to Mark's Jesus: only those with strong motives of self-hatred would seek out Paul's proclamation. They might be subjected to it, but it is far from attractive. Mark is therefore more sympathetic to the autonomy of his audience, which is a precondition of their freedom. Moreover his vision of the gospel in terms of the removal of unclean spirits is able to respect the integrity of people in a way which eludes Paul. The personifications of sin and death which Paul creates serve to dramatize and intensify the internal conflicts of his audience in a way which mercilessly exploits their guilt and insecurity. By contrast the demoniacs in Mark are not treated as guilty, but as victims. The ideology of demon possession entirely relieves them of responsibility for their destructive and deviant behaviour. The release which Mark celebrates is untainted by any attempt to play on the hidden guilt of his readers.

This respect for individual autonomy and integrity gives to Mark's stories of exorcism real credibility as instances of deliverance and freedom. The demoniacs are freed from situations which are undeniably self-destructive and confining: convulsions (1.26; 9.18, 20), self-mutilation (5.5), impulsions to suicide (9.22). The stories proclaim a definite change and foster specific expectations in the reader. There is little evasiveness or ambiguity about the promise that is being extended. The reader's experience may falsify the claim, but the gospel in these terms can at least be evaluated and is open to criticism. Moreover the deliverance of the demoniacs does appear to bestow freedom rather than create obligations. Those who are restored to themselves in this way are released. They return to their homes or are restored to their families. There is no sense that they have to show their gratitude by conforming to Jesus' expectations. Equally, despite the propensity of dualism to conflict, the focus on evil spirits rather than evil human beings makes it easy to avoid recrimination, while the self-pity is voiced by the demons rather than by the demoniacs themselves. The demoniacs are reconciled to Jesus (1.21–28; 5.1–20) and also to society. It might of course be argued that in compelling the deviant to conform to the expectations of society at which they are protesting, Jesus is only exercising a misguided kind of social control: smothering the symptoms of conflict without regard to their causes. At this distance of time such a charge is impossible to answer historically, but it may be that

Jesus was able to heal the relationship between demoniac and society just because he stood at a slight distance from society and was not identified with either its goals or its disciplines. It is interesting that in two of the three demoniac stories the response of the social audience is challenged no less than the behaviour of the demoniac. Those 'who begged Jesus to leave the district' (5.18) after the cure of the Gerasene demoniac evidently did not identify themselves with the social discipline he purveyed. It is part of the realism of such stories that it is not simply the demoniac who is transformed, but the perceptions of his audience. As a picture of the gospel bringing freedom and reconciliation, the exorcisms in Mark, for all their difficulties, deserve considerable respect.

(c) The healing of the body

Turning from exorcism to healing in Mark's Gospel, one is immediately struck by the weight of emphasis which is placed on it; although it does not have quite the same theological significance as exorcism, with its overtones of dualism, it is the centre of much greater interest. There are twice as many detailed stories of healing, and repeated brief references to Jesus' healing activity (1.34; 3.10; 6.5, 55f.). The reason for this is not far to seek. In no instance does the demoniac take the initiative in seeking Jesus' aid; the encounter is either accidental, or Jesus' attention is directed to the demoniac as someone else's problem. In virtually every case the sick take the initiative in seeking out Jesus: the individual discovers the answer to his own prayer. As with exorcism, the delegation of Jesus' power to heal is explicit (6.13), and it seems a distinguishing mark of the church's healing that it uses oil. The significance of using some material agent in the process of healing will become apparent when we consider the process of Jesus' healing. It has long been recognized that the preservation of such Aramaic phrases as 'talitha cum' (5.41) and 'Ephphatha' (7.33) reflects the continuing use in its own work of healing that the early church made of such phrases. The range of illness that Jesus cures in Mark's short Gospel is astonishing: fever (1.29–31), leprosy (1.40–45), paralysis (2.1–12), a withered arm (3.1–6), the issue of blood (5.22–43), the threat of death (7.31–37), deafness, speech defect (8.22–26) and blindness (10.46–52). If this is any indication of the range of ailments of which the early church took cognizance, then in a world which was insecure and where remedies were rare and uncertain, we can readily understand the attraction of Jesus and his gospel. Advanced industrial society has only become preoccupied by economic inequalities because attention is no longer deflected by the gross inequalities in health which marked its predecessors. Jesus in Mark's Gospel is offering release from one of the most tyrannical constraints of all pre-nineteenth century societies.

There is an underlying assumption that sickness and sin are in some way related, so that the healing of the paralysed man is a sign that the forgiveness of his sins is real (2.10). The parallelism in one of Jesus' analogies is revealing: 'It is not the healthy that need a doctor, but the sick; I did not come to invite virtuous people, but sinners' (2.17). The role of the doctor in healing the sick is apparently acknowledged, but Jesus is not really perceived as a practitioner. Mark's view of healing belongs to an uneasy period of tension between the origins of empirical medicine and much more ancient religious diagnoses and prescriptions. The contradictions in attitude which such a situation produced can be seen in Ecclesiasticus, which attempts to hold together the prestige of traditional and more recent approaches. Its quotation will help place Jesus' activity:

> 9   My son, if you have an illness, do not neglect it,
>   but pray to the Lord, and he will heal you.
> 10 Renounce your faults, amend your ways,
>   and cleanse your heart from all sin.
> 11 Bring a savoury offering and bring flour for a token
>   and pour oil on the sacrifice; be as generous as you can.
> 12 Then call in the doctor, for the Lord created him;
>   do not let him leave you, for you need him.
> 13 There may come a time when your recovery is in their hands;
> 14 then they too will pray to the Lord
>   to give them success in relieving pain
>   and finding a cure to save their patient's life.
> 15 When a man has sinned against his Maker,
>   let him put himself in the doctor's hands (38.9–15).

In this situation Jesus is clearly aligned with the traditional understanding of illness as sin, with prayer as the remedy (Ecclus. 38.9). Significantly his healing of the leper ends with the instruction: 'Go and show yourself to the priest, and make the offering laid down by Moses for your cleansing; that will certify the cure' (Mark 1.44; cf. Ecclus. 38.11). In the story of the healing of the woman with the issue of blood Mark goes out of his way to tell the story so that it exalts Jesus at the doctors' expense. The woman 'had suffered from haemorrhages for twelve years; and in spite of long treatment by many doctors, on which she had spent all she had, there had been no improvement; on the contrary, she had grown worse' (5.25f.). This emphasizes not only Jesus' effectiveness, but his immediacy and his cheapness. Mark thus reflects a much more polemical attitude towards doctors than is exhibited in the muddled but conciliatory teaching of Ecclesiasticus.

Ecclesiasticus envisages prayer, sacrifice and the doctor's remedies. Mark, however, places great emphasis on a medium which the other author could not have anticipated – the body of Jesus. Repeatedly it is the physical touch of Jesus which is emphasized in the account of cures (1.31, 41; 3.10; 5.27–31, 41; 6.5, 56; 7.33; 8.23, 25). This goes far beyond legitimating the semi-liturgical gesture of laying on of hands (6.5; 8.23, 25). Indeed such an emphasis on the healing properties of Jesus' body must have created problems for his later representatives; the use of oil may have been an attempt to provide some objective substitute for the physical presence of the master. Paul's understanding of the sacrament of the eucharist (I Cor. 15.27–32) is presumably another. Mark ascribes to the body of Jesus an intrinsic healing power. This is most graphically expressed in the story of the healing of the woman with the issue of blood: 'She came up from behind in the crowd and touched his cloak; for she said to herself, "If I touch even his clothes, I shall be cured." And there and then the source of her haemorrhages dried up and she knew in herself that she was cured of her trouble. At the same time Jesus, aware that power had gone out of him, turned round in the crowd and asked, "Who touched my clothes?"' (5.27–30). This suggests origins of the doctrine of the incarnation, not in the myth of some descending and ascending heavenly being, but in the immediate healing properties of Jesus' body. The contrast between the Pauline view of the flesh and Mark's is dramatic. In Paul the flesh and the spirit are in unending conflict. In Mark the nearest we come to such a view are Jesus' sad words in Gethsemane to the sleeping Peter: 'The spirit is willing, but the flesh is weak' (14.38). In Mark the flesh may fail, but it does not possess the kind of active, perverting power (cf. pp. 164f.) which Paul attributes to it. Even when Mark enjoins the most dramatic surgery, he does so to preserve the body's life, not to safeguard the endangered spirit: 'If your hand is your undoing, cut it off; it is better for you to enter into life maimed than to keep both hands and go to hell and the unquenchable fire. And if your foot is your undoing, cut it off; it is better to enter into life a cripple than to keep both your feet and be thrown into hell. And if it is your eye tear it out; it is better to enter into the kingdom of God with one eye than to keep both eyes and be thrown into hell, where the devouring worm never dies and the fire is not quenched' (9.43–48). Such metaphors, however violent the behaviour they sanction, have not repudiated the body. It is a very different attitude from Paul's, 'flesh and blood can never possess the kingdom of God' (I Cor. 15.50).

Christendom paid a bitter price for the rivalry with the medical profession which is found in Mark. For nearly a millennium the traditions of ancient medicine and public health, in so far as they survived at all, were preserved by Islamic rather than by Christian hands. There is a curious justice that it should have been the shock of the Black Death and the powerlessness of the church to overcome it that led directly to the disintegration of mediaeval Christendom. In one sense, therefore, however attractive the picture of the healing Jesus, it represents a disastrous step – for Christianized magic proved no substitute for the slow accumulation of medical learning. But at another level Mark performed an invaluable service. Paul's distrust of the flesh is only part of a much wider sense of dislocation in the ancient world which came to be voiced in the words of Plotinus: 'When I come to myself, I wonder how it is that I have a body . . . by what deterioration did this happen?' Mark's emphasis on healing, on the legitimacy of the body's healthy functioning, his hopeful celebration of the life-imparting body of Jesus, provides an antidote to much sick resignation. Paradoxically the same writer who did such damage to the development of medicine had a unique influence in keeping before men's eyes the goal of physical health.

(d) The control of nature

In all the stories considered so far, human beings have been the focus and the beneficiaries of Jesus' activity, in release and healing. There are, however, three stories in Mark which are concerned much more impersonally with Jesus' control over the powers of nature. Two of them have some human concern: the ship's passengers are rescued from danger (4.37–41) and the labouring sailors are relieved by the dying down of the wind (6.47–52), but the chief interest of both stories lies in Jesus' mastery of the elements: 'Who can this be? Even the wind and the sea obey him' (4.41). In the second story his mastery is given literal expression in his walking on the waters. While Jesus' ability to exorcize and heal is carefully delegated to his chosen companions, no such expectations are encouraged about these powers. Even so, certain promises are communicated. In a specific sense these stories must have conveyed a consciousness of divine protection to travellers, so that Jesus must have appeared a kind of naval St Christopher. Much of the success of early Christianity derives from its association with people who were mobile: travellers, merchants and slaves. In the ancient world the predominant means of heavy transport was the Mediterranean; its dangers were not inconsiderable (Act 27).

It would, however, be misleading to give these stories too narrow a context. The sinister little tale of the cursed fig tree (11.12–14, 20–23) provokes Jesus to utter the most extravagant promises to the Christian reader: 'I tell you this: if anyone says to this mountain, "Be lifted from your place and hurled into the sea", and has no inward doubts, but believes that what he says is happening, it will be done for him' (11.23). Such faith will be examined later. Here two points suffice. First, it is given the most widespread reference: the promise is open, it is not confined to some élite group. Secondly, Jesus uses the massive immobility of the natural world to project an image of extensive power. Jesus thus acquires a strength and stability compared with which the most evident certainties of the natural world become questionable. This helps to make plausible the contrast between the Son of Man coming in power and glory and a disintegrating world: 'The sun will be darkened, the moon will not give her light; the stars will come falling from the sky, the celestial powers will be shaken' (13.24f.). But beyond the specific apocalyptic use to which Mark puts Jesus' cosmic power, he also opens the way to a much broader and more important exploitation of that power. By clothing Jesus with the power of the natural world, the way is open to interpret its accidents as expressions of his will. Plague, earthquake and every kind of natural calamity could be interpreted as signs of his wrath, incentives to repent. In this respect the menace of the withered fig tree is a portent of how Jesus' control over nature quickly came to be interpreted. On the one hand the lucky individual might thank Jesus for fortunate escape; on the other hand the church acquired a massive if unpredictable means of bludgeoning unbelievers into submission, and pointing lessons to the wavering. As late as the eighteenth century Protestant congregations in England were being assured that the Lisbon earthquake was God's punishment of Popish idolatry. Only the church's loss of nerve in discerning divine punishment and purpose in natural calamity has converted a most impressive sanction into the intellectual liability of theodicy.

(e) The escape from scarcity

Two miraculous feedings of the multitude are described in Mark's Gospel (6.34–44; 8.1–10), with details which suggest respectively Jewish and Gentile allusions. Often these are taken as variants of nature miracles, and indeed Mark himself links the first feeding with the walking on the water, explaining the amazed response of the disciples by the words, 'for they had not understood the incident of the loaves; their minds were closed' (6.52). Mark's awareness of the wealth of scriptural allusion in these stories is difficult to determine; certainly they have a hidden meaning for him, of which the first disciples remain strangely ignorant (8.14–21), and which he only partially indicates to his readers, in his emphasis on the particular numbers involved. The significance of the esoteric will be considered elsewhere. Here what is of interest is the kind of expectations they foster and reflect. The deliberate assimilation of both stories to the pattern of the last supper, where Jesus again takes the bread, says the blessing, breaks it and gives it to his disciples, suggests that these stories had more than simply historical importance for Mark. They seem closely related in his mind to his understanding and practice of the eucharist. They have therefore an immediate relevance to the present experience of his community; they are not simply another clue to the christological mystery.

The context of both stories is one of scarcity. In the first story we are told that Jesus' 'heart went out to them, because they were like sheep without a shepherd' (6.34). In the second, Mark provides this introduction: 'A huge crowd had collected, and, as they had no food, Jesus called his disciples and said to them, "I feel sorry for all these people; they have been with me now for three days and have nothing to eat. If I send them home unfed, they will faint on the way; some of them have come from a distance"' (8.1–3). Although the tendency to interpret the hunger as a need for Jesus' teaching arose early in Christian history, there is little hint that Mark understands the stories in this way. Jesus' concern at their shepherdless condition is followed by the comment, 'and he had much to teach them' (6.34), but it would be fanciful to suggest that Mark is primarily concerned with spiritual hunger. Both stories stress the satisfaction of physical appetite, and the enormous quantity of left-overs (6.42f., 8.8). It is important not to forget that physical hunger would have been a familiar, if occasional, experience of any ancient audience, and such language must have created vehement expectations which it would have been dangerous to disappoint. Jesus is unambiguously portrayed as a provider of material plenty. I Corinthians reveals that the primitive eucharist could focus greed and hunger. Paul comments that 'while one goes hungry another has too much to drink', and ends with the advice, 'when you meet for a meal, wait for one another. If you are hungry, eat at home, so that in meeting together you may not fall under judgment' (I Cor. 11.21, 33f.). The links between the feeding of the multitudes and the eucharist in Mark seem to represent a rather different solution to the same problem. Mark's stories emphasize the collective commandeering of food in Jesus' name and its redistribution at his direction, which results in miraculous plenty. While Paul sets the Corinthian community on a course which will ritualize the eucharist and relegate the satisfaction of hunger to the privacy of the home, Mark's community continued to satisfy real hunger at the eucharist by demanding the sharing and redistribution of food. Mark's stories of the satisfied multitudes both legitimate that practice and reassure potential participants that their physical needs will not be neglected. For those on the edge of destitution such a eucharist would have conveyed material as well as spiritual benefits. In this respect it is significant that the Acts of the

Apostles intertwines the collective use of property, the breaking of bread and the shared meal (2.42–47). The feeding of the multitudes seems to belong to the same world, and suggests that many in Mark's community would have had tangible experience of Christ's power to satisfy their hunger.

(f) Prayer and the inculcation of faith

The stories which tell of Jesus' power attract the attention of his audience, and educate the expectations of Mark's readers. They also contain explicit guidance towards the response which they are intended to elicit: faith. Jesus rebukes the disciples after the stilling of the storm by saying, 'Why are you such cowards? Have you no faith even now?' (4.41), which conveys a lesson to the reader. Faith is envisaged as the appropriate response to what they have witnessed and what the reader has read, but the response is also the condition for further expectations. Repeatedly, faith in the supplicant is seen as the prior condition for the exercise of Jesus' power; for while it is God and not Jesus who is the object of this faith, the coincidence of God's power with Jesus' activity inevitably tends to blur the distinction. Jesus is represented as responding to the faith of the paralysed man and those who brought him by forgiving his sins (2.5). He tells the woman with the issue of blood, 'My daughter, your faith has cured you' (5.34), and dismisses Bartimaeus with the words, 'Go, your faith has cured you' (10.52). The exorcism after the transfiguration contains explicit teaching about the necessity of faith. The pattern which Mark seems to envisage is as follows: Jesus' initial acts of power create expectations. Those who appropriate those expectations with confidence are gratified. Thus while the emphasis on the faith of those cured ostensibly mitigates the absolute character of Jesus' dominance, it conveys a rather different message to the reader. For the implication is that you will only be gratified if you respond uncritically to Mark's proclamation of Jesus. Moreover Mark provides negative lessons which make the same point. Jesus' return to his home contains the remarkable admission: 'He could work no miracle there, except that he put his hands on a few sick people and healed them; and he was taken aback by their want of faith' (6.5f.). His passion is introduced with the prophecy to his disciples, 'You will all fall from your faith' (14.27), and the crucifixion is associated with downright disbelief: 'The chief priests and lawyers jested with one another: "He saved others," they said, "but he cannot save himself. Let the Messiah, the king of Israel, come down now from the cross. If we see that, we shall believe"' (15.31f.).

In Paul the context of faith is obedience to the apostle; in Mark it is prayer. Jesus himself thus becomes the example rather than the object of faith. Repeatedly his mighty works in public are the foil for private solitary prayer. Between stories of exorcism and healing we are told that 'very early next morning he got up and went out. He went to a lonely spot and remained there in prayer' (1.35). Between feeding the multitude and walking on the water, 'after taking leave of them, he went up the hill-side to pray' (6.46). The implication of the narrative that Jesus' power is derived from his prayer is made explicit in his own teaching about exorcism: 'There is no means of casting out this sort but prayer' (9.29). In Paul's letters the content of his prayer is made public as a means of flattery and control; by contrast, Jesus' prayer in Mark is private, its content a secret. The source of his power is indicated, but remains mysterious. Only in one instance is this privacy broken – at Gethsemane. Historically the intrusion is absurd, for the narrative makes it clear that there can have been no witnesses; the necessity for the disclosure derives from Mark's own understanding of faith and prayer. For Mark these are concerned with the exploration and realization of the possible. Faith is not so much a passive acquiescence in reports of miracles or a submission to divinely ordained authority; instead, Mark envisages faith as the activity of redefining the possible, the imaginative transcendence in prayer of actual limitations. His teaching on faith and prayer is designed to evoke a new awareness of what is possible. The father of the demoniac is rebuked for too narrow a conception of the possible. He ends his approach to Jesus with the words, 'If it is at all possible for you, take pity upon us and help us', and receives a rebuke which is clearly intended to be instructive, 'If it is possible!' said Jesus. 'Everything is possible to one who has faith.' 'I have faith', cried the boy's father; 'help me where faith falls short' (9.22–24). For Mark, God represents a realm of transcendent possibility, which questions and qualifies self-inflicted human limitation. Thus to the astonishment of the disciples at the plight of the rich, and their question, 'Then who can be saved?', Jesus answers: 'For men it is impossible, but not for God; everything is possible for God' (10.26f.). This receives its most uncompromising statement after the withering of the fig tree, where faith and prayer are clearly related to the redefinition of what is possible: 'Have faith in God. I tell you this: if anyone says to this mountain, "Be lifted from your place and hurled into the sea", and has no inward doubts, but believes that what he says is happening, it will be done for him. I tell you, then, whatever you ask for in prayer, believe that you have received it and it will be yours' (11.22f.).

Such teaching appears unequivocal. The freedom from constraint which it offers is dramatic. It is also grossly unrealistic, and must cruelly disappoint those who accept it. It is less frequently noticed that the story

Mark tells contradicts such teaching. Jesus has faith in God and prays, but he is not delivered. By a strange irony Mark the narrator finds himself echoing the disbelief of the young demoniac's father; he tells us that Jesus 'went forward a little, threw himself on the ground, and prayed that, if it were possible, this hour might pass him by' (14.35). Jesus himself, however, is represented as using other words: 'Abba, Father, all things are possible to thee; take this cup away from me. Yet not what I will, but what thou wilt' (14.36). The wording would seem to be deliberate. The transcendence of God is reasserted, but it is qualified by the acknowledgment of the constraint of God's will. Our wills are limited by our power; God's will is not limited by weakness, but it is specific, definite. In prayer we cease to be hypnotized by our sense of impotence, and in that sense we are freed; but the prayer which liberates us from a preoccupation with power makes us conscious of a different constraint: the will of God. We do not discover our freedom in a vacuum; we learn to exercise it within certain real constraints, not of human impotence, but of the divine will. The claims, therefore, that Mark is making for faith and prayer are more chaste and less sensational than at first appear. They do not exonerate the believer from having to discover for himself the constraints of the divine will. Jesus' example is compelling. In Gethsemane he still does not know God's will. He discovers it only on the cross: 'My God, My God, why hast thou forsaken me?' (15.35). Teaching which at first seems heartless in the credulity it fosters is subjected to the discipline of its own disappointment. We are encouraged to explore the freedom we have; Mark does not pretend that that freedom is total.

13

MARK: THE AUTHORITY OF JESUS

(a) The gospel as teaching
The heart of Mark's Gospel lies in the teaching of Jesus with which the gospel is equated. For Mark, Jesus' preaching of the gospel provides the organizing principle of his whole picture. At the outset Jesus is presented as 'proclaiming the Gospel of God: "The time has come; the kingdom of God is upon you; repent and believe the Gospel"' (1.14f.). Repeatedly Jesus is referred to as teaching: in the synagogues of Capernaum (1.21) and Nazareth (6.2), in the temple in Jerusalem (12.35; 14.49), and much more generally (2.2; 4.34; 10.1). The preaching of his message is identified with his purpose and destiny: 'Let us move on to the country towns in the neighbourhood; I have to proclaim my message there also; that is what I came out to do' (1.38). More subtly the rejection of his message provides the dramatic conflict which the book articulates; it provokes the shedding of blood by which it is sealed.

As the miracles of Jesus convey the expectations of Mark's community and the promises which are held out to the reader, so the picture of Jesus as the teacher of a message legitimates and exemplifies the leadership of that community. In Mark Jesus provides the paradigm of the Twelve, whom he explicitly commissions both to exorcise and to preach (3.14). It is not therefore an exaggeration to see in the picture of the itinerant preacher a reflection of that group within the community which produced this literature and whose interests it served. This is most obvious in the selection of Jesus' parables in ch. 4. By comparison with the Sermon on the Mount in Matthew their range and interest are narrow. However, they display a literary ambiguity which is not without its benefits. On the one hand Jesus is represented as speaking in person to a specific audience, but repeatedly he appears to address the reader directly. As Paul confuses his own identity with Jesus to enhance his authority, so here the author has used a literary device to appropriate to himself something of Jesus' persona. Thus the concerns and anxieties of the travelling teacher acquire the most august precedent.

On the one hand the parables serve to sustain the preacher's morale, which is always undermined by the realities of indifference and rejection. His privilege is contrasted with the condition of his audience: 'To you the secret of the kingdom of God has been given; but to those who are outside everything comes by way of parables, so that (as Scripture says) they may look and look, but see nothing; they may hear and hear, but understand nothing; otherwise they might turn to God and be forgiven' (4.11f.). The unmistakable note of menace gratifies the aggression of the preacher and concentrates the minds of his audience. The self-exposure of the preacher is vindicated by the analogy of the lamp (4.21f.); his threatened self-esteem is preserved by the ultimate splendour of the mustard seed (4.32). The parables of the sower (4.3–7) and of the seed growing secretly (4.26–29) and the minuteness of the mustard seed (4.30) serve to allay the anxiety of the preacher at his lack of obvious response or status. The same selection that buttresses the morale of the preacher inculcates anxious attention in his audience (4.9, 23, 24f.) and underlines the danger of a short-lived response (4.13–20).

(b) The authority of Jesus in relation to Judaism

There are two passages in Mark where Jesus' authority is openly asserted, though in both instances the assertion is conveyed to the reader by the reaction of the audience. As Paul's assertion of the Lordship of Jesus is intertwined with his own dominance, so the elevation of Jesus in Mark's writing must have benefited his immediate representatives. In both passages there is an obvious polemical intention: 'The people were astounded at his teaching, for, unlike the doctors of the law, he taught with a note of authority' (1.22). It is difficult to avoid the impression that the negative contrast with the doctors of the law is a large element in the content of the claim. Mark thus sets the scene for Jesus' public career by successfully discrediting those rivals which the subject and the author are united in opposing. Mark's description of that authority is associated with two striking ideas: 'a new kind of teaching' and the obedience of the unclean spirits (1.27). It is significant that it is the demons rather than human beings who feel the weight of his authority (cf. 10.42–44). This should deter us from assuming that the authority which Mark attributes to Jesus is necessarily repressive. In this instance it seems concerned to secure human freedom rather than to suppress it. Equally important is the way in which the novelty of Jesus' teaching is so freely acknowledged. There is no attempt here to represent him as the restorer of traditional values. Indeed another saying which Mark attributes to Jesus gives him the most radical aspect: 'No one sews a patch of unshrunk cloth to an old coat; if he does, the patch tears away from it, the new from the old, and leaves a bigger hole. No one puts new wine into old wine-skins; if he does, the wine will burst the skins, and then wine and skins are both lost. Fresh skins for new wine!' (2.21f.). While Paul for all his criticism of the Law still legitimates positions by a straight appeal to the Jewish scriptures, Mark's use of them is consistently contentious rather than submissive.

Direct reference to the Jewish scriptures is quite frequent in Mark. In the opening passage the Baptist is presented as the fulfilment of a prophecy from Isaiah (1.2). Jesus summarizes Jewish law in terms derived directly from the Jewish scriptures (10.19; 12.29–31) and dies with the words of a psalm on his lips (15.34). There is no attempt to conceal his use of scripture or his observance of Jewish ritual (1.44; 14.12–16), but in Mark's hands the Old Testament acquires a specific and negative character. It is Jesus' delight in this Gospel to use the authority of scripture against its guardians. His breaking of the Sabbath is vindicated by David's eating of the shewbread (2.25). The commandment of Moses to honour parents is endorsed in order to attack the abuse of Corban (7.10). The permission of divorce by Moses is rejected on the grounds of the Genesis account of creation (10.1–9). The violent cleansing of the temple is justified by words from scripture (11.7). The Sadducees are refuted by a general appeal to 'the scriptures and the power of God', and then by an exposition of Exodus 3.15, as proof of the resurrection of the dead (12.18–27). The insistence on the Davidic descent of the Messiah is repudiated on the basis of Psalm 110.1 (12.35–37). In all these instances Jesus uses the Jewish scriptures in a purely *ad hominem* manner. Their authority is acknowledged only in so far as it serves to undermine the positions of those who might appeal to them. An equally negative use of the Jewish scriptures emerges in Mark's handling of prophecy. It is in keeping with his stress on the novelty of Jesus that while the Baptist is authenticated by prophecy, the Messiah is not. Instead prophecy is quoted to vindicate the opacity of the parables (4.12), and the concern of the Jews for traditions of ritual is condemned on the basis of a prophecy from Isaiah (7.7). In the account of the passion it is the betrayal of Jesus that is repeatedly referred to scriptural precedent (14.21, 27, 49). For Mark the key prophetic text of the Old Testament seems to be: 'The stone which the builders rejected has become the main corner-stone. This is the Lord's doing, and it is wonderful in our eyes' (12.10f.). By a curiously back-handed exegesis, Jesus is authenticated by the rejection of those who would appeal to the scriptures.

This attitude to the Jewish scriptures is reflected in the entire relationship between Jew and Gentile which Mark's Gospel assumes and celebrates. Paul's 'for the Jew first, and also for the Greek' (Rom. 2.10) is still present in the structure of the narrative. In a series of miracles Jesus first manifests his power among the Jews (1.21–28, 40–45; 2.1–12; 3.1–6; 4.35–41; 5.21–43) and only later among the Gentiles (5.1–20; 7.24–37). The two accounts of the feeding of the multitudes which are usually taken to refer to the Jews and Gentiles respectively display the same Jewish precedence which is also voiced in Jesus' reply to the Syro-Phoenician woman: 'Let the children be satisfied first; it is not fair to take the children's bread and throw it to the dogs' (7.27). But it is also a telling moment when the Gentile woman answers back: 'Sir, even the dogs under the table eat the children's scraps' (7.28). The words may be submissive, but the attitude is challenging, and the book is written from a consistently Gentile point of view. Jewish supremacy is not directly repudiated, but while lip-service is still paid to it, it is being effectively modified. Paul's attempts to organize Gentile tribute to Jerusalem find their equivalent in this Gospel in Jesus' teaching authorizing the payment of Jewish tribute to Caesar (12.13–17). Of the twelve loaves of the shew-bread (cf. 2.26), five are distributed to the Jews (6.38), but seven are distributed among the Gentiles (8.5). The Jerusalem temple is condemned for failing to be 'a house of prayer for all the nations' (11.17), which itself expresses an inclusive and all-embracing understanding of the new Christian community, which is Christ's body – the new spiritual temple. The end awaits not the conversion of the Jews, as in Paul's thought (Rom. 11.15f.), but the proclamation of the gospel to all nations (13.10). It is anticipated in the Gentile centurion's verdict: 'Truly this man was a son of God' (15.39). In the dissociation of Jewish and Christian identities, Mark's Gospel already reflects a very different viewpoint from that of Paul's letters.

(c) The authority of Jesus and John the Baptist

When later in the Gospel Mark returns to the authority of Jesus, the setting is overtly controversial. After the cleansing of the temple, as Jesus 'was walking in the temple court the chief priests, lawyers and elders came to him and said, "By what authority are you acting like this? Who gave you authority to act in this way?"' (11.27f.). Jesus parries the challenge with another question which both discomforts his questioners and relieves him of the need to answer them: '"The baptism of John: was it from God, or from men? Answer me." This set them arguing among themselves: "What shall we say? If we say, 'from God', he will say, 'Then why did you not believe him?' Shall we say, 'from men'?" – but they were afraid of the people, for all held that John was in fact a prophet. So they answered, "We do not know." And Jesus said to them, "Then neither will I tell you by what authority I act"' (11.30–33). The categories of the debate are identical to those of Paul in Galatians and I Corinthians, but Mark handles the issues with a reticence that is foreign to the apostle. With great delicacy the divine authority is clearly intimated, but not directly claimed. The use of John the Baptist in this respect sheds an interesting light on Mark's perception of that enigmatic figure. It is strange that Mark shows little interest in relating Jesus directly to the Old Testament, but has a great concern to define the relation of Jesus to the Baptist, who is unmentioned in the letters of Paul. It is far from clear whether Mark's community perceived the disciples of the Baptist as allies or rivals. They are linked with the Pharisees in their practice of fasting (2.18–20), but nevertheless Mark wishes to associate Jesus with the prestige of the Baptist. While a definitely subordinate role is assigned to him, there is an absence of that rancour which usually marks the competition of small and similar groups. One can, for instance, contrast the polemical attitude towards the Pharisees with whom the Christians also shared certain characteristics. Mark seems more concerned to claim continuity with the Baptist than to discredit his followers, and this is given its most eloquent expression in the derivation of baptism. For although it is of central importance in the definition of Mark's community, it is attributed to John and not to Jesus. It is John and not Jesus who is the Baptist.

The extent to which Mark aligns Jesus with the Baptist is considerable. John's proclamation introduces Jesus to the reader (1.7f.), and his preaching in Galilee only begins 'after John had been arrested' (1.14). When Herod says of Jesus that, 'This is John, whom I beheaded, raised from the dead' (6.16), he is only exaggerating a continuity which Mark himself wishes to emphasize. Like Jesus, John's message arouses enmity, and the reluctance of Herod to kill him (6.26) anticipates the hesitation of Pilate (15.10). He is like the servant in the parable (12.5), whose treatment the Son eventually shares. Most significantly in the debate on authority, Mark aligns Jesus with John in the internal conflicts of Judaism. The enemies of Jesus are discredited by their inability to make up their minds about John (11.32). The analysis of their silence which Mark provides for the reader underlines both their cowardice and their lack of perception. By contrast Jesus himself undergoes baptism, and so endorses John's subversion of a religious community defined by natural descent. The relationship which Mark wishes to convey is nevertheless an unequal one, as John's first words impress upon the reader: 'After me comes one who is mightier than I. I am not fit to unfasten his shoes' (1.7). The words with which the story of John ends have a finality which provides an effective counterpoint to the ending of the Gospel: 'When John's disciples heard the news, they came and took his body away and laid it in a tomb' (6.29).

The absence of bitterness in the account of John the Baptist despite the author's awareness of a distinct community of his disciples (2.18–20) suggests that for all the similiarities, there was no immediate competition. Why, then does the Baptist figure so prominently in Mark's Gospel, while he never merits a mention in Paul's writing? This cannot be explained simply by considerations of memory and narrative; for Mark, the Baptist is the answer to a very specific scriptural objection to Jesus' identity as the Messiah – where is Elijah? This expectation is referred to twice in the narrative (6.15; 8.38), and the appearance of Moses and Elijah at the Transfiguration (9.4) is not regarded by Mark as an adequate answer to that objection. This is shown by the conversation which immediately follows it: 'They put a question to him: "Why do our teachers say that Elijah must come first?"' (9.11). Jesus' reply is obviously intended to alert the audience to John's true significance: 'I tell you, Elijah has already come and they have worked their will upon him, as the Scriptures say of him' (9.13). The care which Mark has previously taken to make this cryptic remark intelligible to the reader indicates the importance of the point in his mind. It is the nearest that he approaches to articulating an argument from prophecy, and it only serves to refute an objection.

(d) The use of authority: anxiety and retribution

Mark projects Jesus as a figure of divine authority, but unlike Paul he does not need to draw attention to himself; in part this is because he secures his ends by attributing them to his Master, in part because his ends are different. However, the use which is made of Jesus' authority is in one respect very similar. Both writers manipulate eschatological fantasy to heighten anxiety and to provide sanctions. At his mildest, Mark uses the notion of future judgment to secure attention. In the explanation of the parable of the sower, the word rather than the listener is destroyed, but the threat is still effectively conveyed. More directly menacing is the tone assumed in the instructions to the Twelve: 'At any place where they will not receive you or listen to you, shake the dust off your feet as you leave, as a warning to them' (6.11). If the warning is unspecific, no reader of Mark's Gospel would long remain in doubt as to what is at stake. Judgment is not simply a spur to attention, it is also a sanction to enforce obedience. Those doctors of the law who disguise greed and injustice with piety are assured of 'the severest sentence' (12.40). Those who deny Jesus in this life will be denied by the Son of Man, 'when he comes in the glory of his Father and of the holy angels' (8.38). If the penalties are largely left to the imagination, a certain amount of guidance is supplied: 'It would be better for him to be thrown into the sea with a millstone round his neck' (9.42). Hell is referred to as the place, 'where the devouring worm never dies and the fire is not quenched (9.48), and is presented as less preferable than the short sharp shock of self-mutilation.

The assumptions which underlie such language are made plain in the little apocalypse of ch. 13. To read Mark's apocalypse is to perceive the background of much of his thought, but it is also to enter a world with preoccupations which are not otherwise present in the Gospel. This strongly reinforces the suggestion that it is a pre-existing literary entity, which Mark has simply incorporated within his own work. That is not to say that he would have disowned its beliefs, but that it reflects the interests and needs of a community other than his own, and the parallels in concept and intention with the writing of Paul are remarkable. As in Paul, anxiety about the timing of the end is deliberately fostered. Jesus is questioned by Peter, James, John and Andrew: 'Tell us . . . when will this happen? What will be the sign when the fulfilment of all this is at hand?' (13.4). The ultimate reply tempers urgency with agnosticism: 'When you see all this happening, you may know that the end is near, at the very door. I tell you this: the present generation will live to see it all . . . But about that day or that hour no one knows, not even the angels in heaven, not even the Son; only the Father' (13.29, 32). Having wound up his audience to the highest pitch of tension, he proceeds to exploit it in words which echo Rom. 13.11–13: 'Be alert, be wakeful. You do not know when the moment comes. It is like a man away from home; he has left his house and put his servants in charge, each with his own work to do, and he has ordered the door-keeper to stay awake. Keep awake, then, for you do not know when the master of the house is coming. Evening or midnight, cock-crow or early dawn – if he comes suddenly, he must not find you asleep. And what I say to you, I say to everyone: Keep awake' (13.33–37). This looks ahead to Gethsemane, and provides a sharp commentary on the behaviour of Jesus' closest disciples, but the emphasis upon the work of the servants and the responsibility of the door-keeper reflects exactly the preoccupations of Paul's letter to the Thessalonians. Its precise significance for Mark's community will be explored later.

'Take care that no one misleads you. Many will come claiming my name, and saying "I am he"; and many will be misled by them' (13.5f.). The tone is that of Paul writing to the Philippians on the threat of internal dissension, while the further description of false Messiahs (13.21–23) is reminiscent of II Thessalonians. In just the same way that Paul tries to

defuse the danger by reminding his readers that he has foreseen it
(II Thess. 2.5), the Jesus of the apocalypse congratulates himself on his
protective anticipation: 'You be on your guard; I have forewarned you of
it all' (13.23). Similarly the exploitation of secular anxieties (13.7–12)
echoes the approach of the opening chapters of Romans. The alienation
from society and the paranoid courting of persecution (13.9–13) reflect
the mood of Philippians and II Corinthians. The praise of perseverance
(13.13) and the flattering description of the elect (13.20, 27) is the
substance of Paul's prayers. There is even the same direct assertion of
absolute authority with which Paul has made us familiar. While Mark's
Jesus is usually modest in his claims about himself, he here proclaims:
'Heaven and earth will pass away; my words will never pass away'
(13.31).

Although Mark's concerns are different from those of the little
Apocalypse, he cannot be totally dissociated from it, for the theme of
retribution is deeply engrained in his account of the gospel. His promises
of power may be more immediate than Paul's, his projection of the
sinfulness of mankind may be less exuberant, but it would be sentimental
to obscure the role of divine vengeance in his thought. The crucial parable
of the wicked vineyard keepers ends with the words: 'He will come and put
the tenants to death and give the vineyards to others' (12.9). The death of
the Son heralds the end of divine patience. The gospel exists so to speak in
the interim between the cursing of the fig-tree and its withering
(11.14, 20). In this sense, the lament over Judas is prophetic of the fate
which awaits all those who are implicated in the Son's death: 'The Son of
Man is going the way appointed for him in the Scriptures; but alas for that
man by whom the Son of Man is betrayed! It would be better for that man
if he had never been born' (14.21). Just because Mark understands the
enormity of the crime, he is confident that the divine reply will not be long
delayed. His Jesus can unequivocally say: 'There are some of those
standing here who will not taste death before they have seen the kingdom
of God already come in power' (9.1). At the climax of the trial Jesus
threatens the High Priest with words which reflect Mark's own expectations: 'You will see the Son of Man seated at the right hand of God and
coming with the clouds of heaven' (14.62). Whether Mark's Gospel is
written in excited anticipation of the destruction of the temple, or
represents its triumphant celebration, he writes at a time of heady
expectation. He associates Jesus with the prophecy that the temple will be
destroyed (13.2; cf. 14.58), and sees in its desecration the signal that
deliverance is near. This sense of looming retribution both provides the
unique excitement of Mark's Gospel and imparts to Jesus' resurrection its

distinctive significance. While John is safely dead and buried, Jesus is alive, preparing for a victorious and violent return; he is mustering the heavenly hosts. In Mark's eyes the women at the empty grave did well to be afraid (16.8): they tell us what is to be expected.

(e) Authority in conflict

(i)   The challenge to moral and social prestige
The persistent note of revenge in Mark reflects social antagonisms and assertions of authority which are only partially acknowledged; but despite superficial resemblances his viewpoint is very different from Paul's. The savage repudiation of the opening chapters of Romans has no Marcan parallel. Paul needs to condemn Jew and Gentile alike in order to construct his own position of sovereignty. Mark is less ambitious and more specific. The cosmic authority and drama in which Paul delights is here replaced by a much more human picture. In Mark, Jesus' authority emerges in conflict with the prevailing forces – social and moral – of contemporary Palestine. He represents a contrast and challenge which provokes two kinds of response: wonder or offence, obedience or rejection. The reader's reaction is carefully educated, for Mark insists on the context of conflict as the key to understanding. The whole book is bound together by the unfolding struggle which begins when the crowd first contrasts Jesus' authority with the doctors of the law (1.22) and ends with the mockery of the chief priests and the lawyers as Jesus dies on the cross (15.31f.).

The points at issue are many, and his enemies varied. Lawyers construe the forgiveness of sins as blasphemy, and are rebuked by spectacular healing (2.6–12). Lawyers who were Pharisees complain of Jesus' table-fellowship with tax-gatherers and sinners (2.16) and of breaches of the Sabbath (2.23–28; 3.1–6). At this early stage the Pharisees join forces with their partisans of Herod, 'to see how they could make away with him' (3.6), and Mark thus conveys to the reader intimations both of Jesus' death and of its significance. Doctors of the law from Jerusalem accuse Jesus of complicity with Satan and in return are placed beyond forgiveness (3.22–30). Pharisees and doctors of the law from Jerusalem complain of Jesus' failure to observe ritual cleanliness, and are themselves rebuked for the abuse of Corban (7.1–13). The Pharisees are refused a sign from heaven (8.11–13), as later Jesus will refuse to vindicate his authority (11.27–33). Repeatedly Jesus prophesies his own destruction at the hands of the elders, chief priests and doctors of the law (8.31; 10.33); they are identified with the 'power of men' which, like disobedient Peter, stands against God (9.31). From the cleansing of the temple the pace of conflict quickens: 'The chief priests and the doctors of the law heard of this and sought some means of making away with him; for they were afraid of him, because the whole crowd was spellbound by his teaching' (11.18). Jesus is now represented as deliberately angering his opponents by pointing the parable of the wicked tenants of the vineyard directly against them (12.12). The Pharisees and the men of Herod's party endeavour to trick him in questions on tribute to Caesar (12.13–17), and when this device fails, he proceeds to silence the Sadducees on the resurrection of the dead (12.18–27). After a conciliatory interlude in which a lawyer is told, 'You are not far from the kingdom of God' (12.34), Jesus, having silenced all his critics (12.35), takes the initiative. First, he denies the Davidic descent of the Messiah (12.35–37), and then he satirizes the doctors of the law (12.38–40). The arrest follows swiftly (14.43f.), and the trial before the High Priest reassembles most of Jesus's opponents as his judges (14.53). They hand over Jesus to Pilate (15.1), and the chief priests play their last trick by inciting the crowd to ask for Barabbas (15.11). Pilate is nothing more than their reluctant instrument (15.10). It is not a flattering picture of imperial rule, but it is carefully not antagonistic.

The importance of this sequence is that it provides a comprehensive explanation of Jesus' death in a way which holds together religious controversy and social conflict. The vigour of the struggle never allows Mark to present Jesus' teaching in abstraction, and the conflict both explains Jesus' death and provides a religious rationale for it. Mark's account is singularly persuasive because of its realism about the nature of religious antagonism. He never permits us simply to interpret it as a conflict over doctrines. From the outset the prestige of a particular social morality – traditional Judaism as represented by lawyers and Pharisees, priests, Sadducees and Herodians – is identified with the social prestige of those who maintain it and profit from it. This combination of social status and moral prestige provides Mark's account of Jesus' life and death with a singular vitality. Mark enables us to perceive, as Paul does not, why Jesus was so subversive that crucifixion was the inevitable outcome. Paul's cosmic figure can condescend, but cannot overturn. Just because he is so commanding, he cannot afford to be too disturbing; he himself has too much to lose. So however much Paul may use the language of freedom, both he and his Lord find it difficult to tolerate. By contrast Jesus is portrayed in Mark as an immediate threat to the prestige of established morality and the whole social structure that gains its legitimacy by policing it. The challenge is so drastic that it naturally provokes violent reaction. Throughout, the exercise of his authority is critical rather than conservative: far from attempting to preserve a threatened order – social and religious, his criticism is presented as the instrument of its destruction. His authority is used not to bind others; it sanctions his own freedom, which brings freedom to others.

The method adopted in this study of recognizing and appraising religious authority may at times have seemed intrinsically hostile to the whole of the Christian phenomenon. It is a method which was immediately derived from a critical evaluation of Christian history. It is only possible for this ruthless and often destructive criticism to remain believing criticism, because of its affinity to the criticism which is ascribed to Jesus in the New Testament, and most obviously in Mark's Gospel. The examination of that criticism is the pivot on which this whole study turns: it provides the vindication of the method on which this study has been based.

(ii) The perception of oppression

Western industrial society has become so obsessed by economic inequality that we find it difficult to perceive society in terms other than those provided by a socialist analysis. When we enter a world where such over-simplification is discouraged, we are at first disoriented. Mark's perception of oppression is not primarily economic, though he is not blind to its economic expression. The doctors of the law are condemned because 'they eat up the property of widows' (12.40), and the representatives of Jesus are authenticated by their almost total lack of property (6.8f.). Moreover, the miracles of feeding the multitudes suggest an element of redistribution within Mark's community. Nevertheless, his perception of wealth is too ambivalent to allow it to become the criterion of injustice. The stress on the poverty of Jesus' authentic representatives should not be confused with a concern either to identify Jesus with the poor or to condemn the inequity of wealth. The viewpoint of Mark is not that of the poor who envy or need the wealth of the rich. Indeed he satirizes the awe of the disciples before a wealth which they do not possess, when they greet Jesus' stern teaching on the difficulty of the rich entering the kingdom of God with the astonished words: 'Then who can be saved? (10.26). Jesus himself does not speak for the poor; instead he conveys the contempt of the voluntary poor for the misguided rich: 'How hard it will be for the wealthy to enter the kingdom of God!' (10.23). That is an incentive not to the wider distribution of property, but to its rapid divestment. The freedom which Jesus commends is attained by ascetic abstinence, not by bourgeois self-sufficiency. His followers are not recruited to alleviate the lot of the poor; they are attracted by the prospect of an ultimate reversal of roles (10.28–31) in which they and not other people will be richly compensated for present deprivations. Mark's Jesus is little concerned with the damage that the rich do to the poor, nor can he envisage a world where poverty has been abolished (14.7). Wealth is not a good to be distributed, but a barrier to be overcome. Significantly the barrier is perceived from the viewpoint of those encumbered by property, rather than of those dispossessed by injustice. This is confirmed by the assumptions implicit in Jesus' teaching as Mark records it: God is represented as an absentee landlord (12.1–9; 13.34–35) and thus silently endorses the sanctity of property in one of its most blatant and irresponsible manifestations.

For Mark the origins of injustice are in the use and abuse of religion. Jesus' enemies are predominantly religious: he may inherit the Baptist's conflict with the Herodians (8.15) and be actually crucified by the Romans, but the main protagonists are doctors of the law, Pharisees, elders and chief priests. These occupy the dominant role in the society that Mark describes; compared to them the secular figures are quite secondary. It is a recurrence of the dismissive attitudes towards secular power which is found in Paul. Jesus remains silent and uncooperative before Pilate's judgment (15.5). The celebrated reply to the question of tribute to Caesar is deceptive in the apparent deference of the words: 'Pay Caesar what is due to Caesar, and pay God what is due to God' (12.17). For this is spoken by one who has forbidden his representatives to possess money (6.8). The poverty of Jesus is deliberately insubordinate: it makes possible the most radical repudiation of imperial claims. Paul and Mark share the assumption that government exists to discipline other people. 'Government, a terror to crime, has no terrors for good behaviour' (Rom. 13.3), is echoed in Jesus' words at his arrest: 'Do you take me for a bandit, that you have come out with swords and cudgels to arrest me?' (14.48). Despite the fact that Herod and Pilate are directly responsible for the two deaths that dominate the Gospel, they are almost exonerated by their combination of sympathy for their victims and powerlessness to avert their fate. Herod recognizes John as a good and holy man and endeavours to protect him: 'So he kept him in custody. He liked to listen to him, although the listening left him greatly perplexed' (6.20). Similarly Pilate is represented as anxious to secure Jesus' release (15.9). In much the same way that Paul delights in the weakness and ineffectiveness of his persecutors when writing to the Philippians, Mark derides Herod and Pilate. They may be able to command violence, but they are pathetic in their inability to withstand the clamour of their audience. Herod consigns John to death to gratify a dancing-girl: he is represented as 'greatly distressed, but out of regard for his oath and for his guests he could not bring himself to refuse her' (6.26). Similarly Pilate weakly gives in to the demands of the crowd: 'Pilate, in his desire to satisfy the mob, released Barabbas to them; and he had Jesus

flogged and handed him over to be crucified' (15.15). Even the most brutal
aspects of Roman military rule are portrayed as the unwitting fulfilment of
a divine purpose: the mockery of the soldiers recognizes the Messiah
(15.18); the forced service of Simon bears Jesus' cross (15.21); the
inscription giving the charge proclaims the truth for all to read (15.26).

In Mark's society effective power and real privilege belong to the
religious leaders. These do not depend primarily on economic dominance,
though they may use their position for economic advantage. They take no
responsibility for secular government, though they may at times use it for
their own ends. Their power is derived from the religious practice by which
they control and define society. The Jewish identity, which is primarily one
of birth, is reinforced by practice and conformity, which they supervise.
The prestige of the community and its morality are vested in its leaders,
who are themselves vulnerable to any attack on that community and its
practices. The most subversive activity of Jesus in Mark's Gospel is that he
points to the victims of that definition of the community: the sinners and
the tax-gatherers. The prestige of the religious is purchased at the cost of
the stigma of those against whom they discriminate, and with whom Jesus
identifies himself in the most public and effective manner: 'As he went
along, he saw Levi son of Alphaeus at his seat in the custom-house, and
said to him, 'Follow me'; and Levi rose and followed him. When Jesus was
at the table in his house, many bad characters – tax-gatherers and others –
were seated with him and his disciples; for there were many who followed
him. Some doctors of the law who were Pharisees noticed him eating in this
bad company, and said to his disciples, "He eats with tax-gatherers and
sinners!"' (2.13–16). The doctors of the law do not have to justify their
response, or add any further condemnation: they appeal to an audience in
whose eyes Jesus should be automatically discredited by such an observation, and attempt to shame his disciples into disowning him. For the
religious leaders have established their position by just such an act of
continuous distancing. What confirms them in their position is that they
do not mix indiscriminately, and thus preserve their own purity and that of
their community. To break that taboo is to challenge them and disrupt
their community. The force of Jesus' reply is neither apologetic nor
defensive: 'It is not the healthy that need a doctor, but the sick; I did not
come to invite virtuous people, but sinners' (2.17). He denies neither that
he eats with such people, nor that they are sinners, but uses irony to
subvert the distinction between those who see themselves as virtuous and
those they categorize as sinners. By accepting the definition of sinners
which his accusers put forward, he is able to expose their own complacency. In place of the judgmental separation which defends their status, he

suggests a restorative association which inevitably undermines it. His enemies correctly perceive that this threatens both the society which they have created and their own position within that society.

This conflict with authority provides the context in which to understand the slogan of Jesus' subversive message – 'The kingdom of God' (1.15; 4.26, 30). He is of course using a common-place of Jewish religion, which was widely current in contemporary eschatology. Most modern discussion of the term has revolved round the nature of Jesus' expectation. Did he look forward to the intervention of God in the immediate future? Is the realized eschatology of some of the New Testament a faithful account of his hope, or an attempt to deal with later diappointment? Such questions are a tribute to the enduring impact of Schweitzer's presentation of Jesus as an eschatological prophet – a portrayal which destroyed the Jesus of the liberal theologians of the last century. The importance of eschatology in providing promises and sanctions in Mark's Gospel has already been noticed, and at one level the kingdom of God is simply equated with such manifest reward and retribution (9.1; 10.24; 12.34; 14.25). Yet it also serves a political and polemical purpose, for the language of 'kingdom' is an explicit claim to authority and power. The kingdom of God in Mark's Gospel is distinguished and defined by the opposition it encounters. It is the ultimate means of challenging all competing claims. The kingdom of God provides the legitimation for opposing not only Herod and Pilate, but also the religious leaders, the Pharisees and the chief priests. In the mouth of the Patriarch of Constantinople or the Archbishop of Canterbury, 'the kingdom of God' is likely to sanctify the social order that has elevated them. In the mouth of Mark's Jesus it is no such demand for conformity, but the means of refusing obedience. Pilate and Caiaphas would readily have understood themselves as being in some sense the instruments of divine power: such rhetoric was a platitude both of imperial rule and priestly eminence. The kingdom of God, which so often before and since has been identified with human systems of dominance and control, acquires a quite new meaning when it is appropriated by the victims of those structures. It is this transformation which Mark's Gospel witnesses and celebrates. The kingdom of God no longer demands man's subordination – it has become the means of asserting human freedom.

(iii) The forgiveness of sins

Jesus' identification with the victims of Jewish society and its morality is not merely an emotional stance of sympathy; it has deeply destructive social implications, which are expressed in his teaching of forgiveness. We tend to take the doctrine for granted and fail to appreciate its disreputable character. In part this is because we understand forgiveness as a purely psychological transaction, a matter confined to inner consciousness. The sinner in Mark's Gospel is not defined by the acuteness of his feelings of guilt; he is socially visible, defined by the repudiation of others, orchestrated by their religious leaders. The sinner is a social pariah, manoeuvred into isolation, contaminating by his presence. In English terms the sin of which Mark speaks has more resemblance to the consequences of class division and the stigma of snobbery than to any of our religious classifications. In such a context the forgiveness of sins is not simply a private act of emotional generosity; it involves painful and costly public gestures. In eating with sinners Jesus put his own status and prestige at risk.

The radical message of forgiveness which Mark's Gospel contains is also obscured by the manner in which the doctrine of forgiveness has usually been interpreted. In its Roman Catholic form forgiveness is conditional on contrition: the recognition of the heinousness of the offence. In evangelical preaching forgiveness demands the prior conviction of sin; not until the proper state of self-hatred has been created can the healing words be spoken. It is therefore imaginatively difficult for us to disentangle the doctrine of forgiveness from the propagation of guilt which usually accompanies it. Moreover in that form the doctrine functions as an instrument of conservative re-affirmation: dissent from moral convention is consistently undermined by the offer of amnesty. The price of that amnesty is the recognition of the justice of the sentence, the individual's act of submission to the morality which condemns him. Furthermore, to speak of 'morality' in such an abstract fashion is misleading, for behind the 'morality' stands the social structure which creates it. So, for instance, if a Roman Catholic practises contraception he is not only 'breaking the natural law', he is also challenging the authority of the priesthood which has propounded that natural law. Ecclesiastical structures can reconcile themselves to intermittent or partial obedience so long as the prestige of the morality and those who are identified with it remains uncompromised. Repentance thus becomes the surrender of the deviant individual, who admits the appropriateness of his condemnation despite his own contrary experience. Behaviour which might otherwise threaten the social dominance of particular religious leaders is presented as a moral lapse, a shortcoming of the individual which requires the re-affirmation of moral standards and the self-abasement of the deviant. It is a process which deprives the individual of dignity and integrity and limits the extent to which it is possible to learn from experience. The only lessons which are admissable are those which require neither the revision of moral convention nor any loss of face for the ecclesiastical authorities. In this respect there is no significant difference between obduracy on the part of the Roman Catholic priesthood and the moral conservatism of evangelical preachers. Both can attempt to preserve their authority by the aggressive manipulation of shame and feelings of guilt.

It has to be admitted that the first steps of this development can already be seen in Mark's Gospel, so that forgiveness is beginning to be represented as the unique property of Jesus. In the story of the healing of the paralytic Jesus' words of forgiveness are met with the charge: 'Why does the fellow talk like that? This is blasphemy! Who but God alone can forgive sins?' (2.6f.). The reply which Mark attributes to Jesus has a specific self-reference: 'To convince you that the Son of Man has the right on earth to forgive sins' (2.10). It may be that in its original form 'the Son of Man' in that saying was intended to have a universal reference to mankind, but that is not Mark's intention. The motive for this christological restriction of forgiveness is doubtless to be found in the claims of the leadership in Mark's community. They were presumably already discovering the power which could be exercised once the claim to forgive had been suitably restricted to Jesus and then delegated to his representatives, a development which can be traced in subsequent gospel writing (Matt. 16.19; John 20.23). Similarly Mark shows signs of the introduction of a category of sin which is beyond forgiveness: 'Whoever slanders the Holy Spirit can never be forgiven; he is guilty of eternal sin' (3.29). Once the step has been taken of distinguishing what can be forgiven from what cannot be forgiven, the way is open to the complete distortion of the message. Such a distinction necessarily implies the existence of an élite within the community which can make such decisions, and once the authority of such an élite has been admitted, the community has no defence against the domination of that élite. In Mark's Gospel we can see the preliminary stages of such a development; the letters of Paul demonstrate its ultimate implications.

That Mark represents a period of transition in his understanding of forgiveness is indicated by traces of a very different attitude towards forgiveness from the one which has characterized most subsequent Christian history. In Mark, John the Baptist's message is not a call to rigorous obedience and conservative reaffirmation; he proclaims 'a baptism in token of repentance, for the forgiveness of sins' (1.4). Repentance expresses itself not in contrition, nor in submission to the established authorities of Judaism. Instead it involves a rite which questions the Jewish community based on circumcision, and which the Jewish Law neither anticipates nor demands. Jesus' continuity with John is represented not by the practice of baptism, but by the promise of forgiveness; however, Jesus' teaching on forgiveness in Mark's Gospel is distinguished by four innovations. First, the Gospel retains an astonishingly permissive account of Jesus' life and teaching. Even when allowance has been made for the qualification just referred to about the sin against the Holy Spirit, the preceding words are striking: 'I tell you this: no sin, no slander, is beyond forgiveness for men' (3.28). Equally telling is the total absence of the reiterated prohibitions which appear in Paul's letters. While the apostle is continually trying to control the behaviour of his readers in minute detail, the Master appears almost indifferent to such questions. Mark's Gospel is therefore the despair of those who seek to use it for the moral education of the young; it is not surprising that churches have always felt the need to supplement the Gospels with their own catechisms, which supply such deficiencies.

Secondly, although forgiveness is beginning to be understood as the specific possession of Jesus, unlike the power of exorcism and healing in this Gospel it is not delegated to his representatives. Quite the contrary, forgiveness is something which is exercised reciprocally, not hierarchically: 'When you stand praying, if you have a grievance against anyone, forgive him, so that your Father in heaven may forgive you the wrongs you have done' (11.25). There is an intrinsic connection between the liberality of proffered forgiveness in the permissive tone of Jesus' teaching and the absence of professional forgivers. So long as the exercise of forgiveness is mutual and undiscriminating they are redundant: the moment distinctions are made, forgiveness becomes the possession of those who make the distinctions. For they control it.

Thirdly, the condition of forgiveness is quite different from anything which has been insisted upon in subsequent Christian history. Instead of contrition, or confession to a priest, or faith in the redeeming blood of Christ, the condition of receiving forgiveness is simply the practice of forgiveness. This insistence on practice rather than benefit is the greatest safeguard of a community of mutual relations. Such a condition renders the whole hierarchy of later Christendom redundant, and questions the importance of the dogmatic tradition which that same hierarchy both promulgated and insisted upon.

Finally, forgiveness in Mark is conveyed by a Jesus who himself conspicuously breaks conventions. A significant part of the outrage he causes is that a Sabbath-breaker should take upon himself to forgive. The customary ascription of sinlessness to Jesus found elsewhere in the New Testament has served to conceal Mark's acceptance that Jesus extends forgiveness to others from a position which is itself questionable. In this

Gospel Jesus explicitly declines to be called good (10.18). This is in marked contrast to the priestly mediators of forgiveness, who endeavour to give plausibility to their absolution by not appearing to need it themselves. This recipe for hypocrisy is unavoidable where forgiveness is mediated hierarchically. Because in Mark forgiveness is reciprocal, Jesus is free to associate with the sinners he forgives.

It is on this incisive teaching about forgiveness that the credibility of the Christian gospel depends, for it indicates with precision the freedom and reconciliation that the gospel brings and the way in which they are communicated. The refusal to distinguish between the forgivable and the unforgivable removes the ultimate sanction of conformity, and in so doing creates the possibility of free, autonomous action. The insistence that forgiveness and the freedom which is its consequence are only dependent on their extension to others removes the source of both social antagonism and of religious domination. Moreover the reciprocal exercise of forgiveness mitigates the disruptive and isolated individualism which the possibility of autonomy might otherwise create, so that Jesus' teaching of forgiveness vindicates the hope that freedom and reconciliation are compatible. They are realized both as gift and as task. Liberal exponents of an ethical Christianity are always in danger of transforming the excitement of liberation into a daunting and dreary labour, but they are correct in stressing that the freedom and reconciliation which Jesus brings have to be exercised rather than passively possessed. More orthodox Christians who celebrate the achievement of victory are right to perceive our immediate dependence on others, and our ultimate dependence on Jesus, if we are to attain freedom and peace. We need first to be delivered and to be reconciled. Jesus' life and teaching represent the initiative which brought a new freedom and peace into the world, an opportunity which is only available to us through the continuing mediation of other people. We have to be loved into loving, and our freedom is made possible by the trust of others. In the gospel stories of Mark, Jesus reaches out to the leper and the Syro-Phoenician woman; he eats with tax-gatherers and sinners. He trusts himself to the representation of his disciples. He is vulnerable to the treachery of Judas and the betrayal of Peter. But the grace of Jesus' gospel, far from obliterating the need for further action, initiates it. The freedom which he displayed in his attitude to the Sabbath is not simply imitated, it is extended by his followers to the food-laws and circumcision. Similarly, his association with sinners is subsequently extended to the Gentiles. The gift he brings conveys no benefit in its possession except the possibility of using it. The only privilege his gospel bestows is the opportunity to exercise our freedom and to achieve our peace.

(f) Sexuality and the forgiveness of sins

Mark's presentation of this message of forgiveness is ambivalent. The predominant account is radical in its permissiveness and mutuality, but there are some features which point towards the control of forgiveness, characteristic of the later church. A similar ambiguity is discernible in the sexual teaching and attitudes which Mark ascribes to Jesus. While Paul verges on hysteria in his sexual prohibitions, Mark represents Jesus as being the object of intense female loyalty and devotion. Unlike the disciples they witness the crucifixion: 'Watching from a distance. Among them were Mary of Magdala, Mary the mother of James the younger and of Joseph, and Salome, who had all followed him and waited on him when he was in Galilee, and there were several others who had come up to Jerusalem with him' (15.40f.). While the women of Paul's letters stay passively and obediently in their own communities waiting for his letters, the women in the Gospel share its subject's mobility and are the witnesses of his resurrection (16.1). This is in striking contrast to I Corinthians 15.5–7, where every witness listed is male. Equally the story of the anointing at Bethany has insistent sexual overtones. The extravagance of the gesture and its physical intimacy have an unmistakable erotic suggestion. The gratification of Jesus, however morbidly preoccupied with his death, is explicit. Mark does not therefore isolate Jesus from women, as Paul would seem to commend (I Cor. 7.1), nor does he share Paul's preoccupation with promiscuity. Yet there is something of Paul's disparagement of human sexuality in Jesus' reply to the Sadducees: 'When they rise from the dead, men and women do not marry; they are like angels in heaven' (12.25). A view of sexual difference as transitory and superficial contrasts strangely with Jesus' insistence elsewhere that 'in the beginning, at the creation, God made them male and female' (10.5).

It is equally surprising to find that the bold proponent of forgiveness does not hesitate to equate remarriage after divorce with adultery (10.10f.), and Moses' permission of divorce is represented as a perversion of God's intention in creation (10.1–9). This hostility to divorce and remarriage is the only detailed point of continuity which Mark provides between the teaching of Jesus and the Baptist (6.17–20), but its significance is not easy to determine. In the Baptist's preaching it is a crime of depraved royalty, and there is a sense of John playing Nathan to Herod's David. To some extent it represents popular prophetic criticism of the shortcomings of a privileged élite, not dissimilar from the moral strictures on the famous of today's tabloid newspapers. Censoriousness remains a close cousin to envy. It must also indicate to us the sexual rules to which

Mark's community subscribed, strict obedience to which defined it from other groups. We see here a similar paradox to that noted about the practice of Corban (cf. p. 192): the same community which sits lightly to family identity insists upon strong family obligations. It is tempting to absolve Jesus of inconsistency by attributing such teaching to the new demands of a more settled and domestic community; but Paul's insistence that such teaching derives from Jesus (I Cor. 7.10f.) prevents any such simple solution. It cannot therefore be ruled out that the inconsistency is traceable to Jesus himself, and that like other men he was not always able to see the full implications of his attitudes.

As the regulation of sexual activity has played such a crucial part in the subsequent history of Christianity, the teaching on divorce deserves the closest scrutiny. In historical terms, conformity to a pattern of sexual behaviour has given the church its social visibility and identity. In blessing, regulating and policing that conformity the clergy have exercised control at the most intimate level of human experience; and they themselves have derived much of their prestige by exemplifying the conformity they demand. By a cruel irony Christianity has thus created its own parody of that Jewish religious authority with which Jesus struggled. In contemporary terms Jesus' teaching on divorce presents the church with a most delicate dilemma in societies where divorce and remarriage have become widespread. The evidence is overwhelming that the refusal by the church to remarry those who have been divorced is experienced as judgmental, discriminatory and shaming by people who are already painfully vulnerable and insecure. After much heart-searching even the Church of England has been persuaded of 'the pastoral necessity' for change, but the implications are disturbing. On abortion and homosexuality, on sexism, racism and unilateral disarmament the Jesus of the New Testament is disconcertingly silent. On the subject of divorce and the nature of later liaisons he is by contrast distressingly direct. He leaves room neither for pious conjecture nor for any complaint of irrelevance. None of the teaching on divorce and remarriage ascribed to Jesus in the Gospels could be read at the proposed ceremony without embarrassment to the couple concerned, and a condemnation of the minister proceding from his own mouth. If we approach Jesus' teaching as recounted in Mark with Paul's prohibitions ringing in our ears, there seems no escape from the difficulty. Jesus' teaching then appears to sanction the strictest marriage discipline, and any modification of that teaching is an effective repudiation of his authority, and hence self-destructive of the church's own position. Close attention to the Marcan text, however, suggests an alternative.

Mark uses words we recognize like 'husband', 'wife', 'divorce' and 'marriage', but we must be cautious in assuming that he is referring to the same kind of social relations and arrangements with which we are familiar in our own society. For instance the form of divorce which Jesus condemns is a very specific one, and is not necessarily to be equated with all forms of divorce as practised today. 'Moses permitted a man to divorce his wife by note of dismissal' (10.4). The divorce which Jesus declares to be contrary to God's intention in creation is envisaged as being the mere fiat of one of the parties; there is no expectation of the possibility of mutual consent. To condemn the arbitrary or unilateral practice of divorce is not necessarily to condemn every kind of divorce. Even more important is the difficulty of doing justice to the very unusual character of Jesus' understanding of marriage. It would of course be quite anachronistic to suppose that he had any conception akin to our modern notion of marriage based on romantic love, which is both comparatively recent and of largely Western European origin. Much more challenging to the Christian reader is the difference between the teaching on marriage ascribed to Jesus and the traditional attitudes of the church: it is innocent of any mention of vows, contract or ecclesiastical blessing. In view of the immense emphasis which subsequent Christianity has laid on the marriage vow, it is breathtaking to realize that Jesus himself makes no mention of it in relation to marriage, and such teaching as is ascribed to him on vows hardly encourages such a development (Matt. 5.33–37).

Equally embarrassing to the Christian tradition is the omission of any blessing or sanctification by religious representatives. Jesus delegates no authority to solemnize weddings. He himself does not even seek to regulate marriage: it is a role foisted on him by the malice of his enemies (10.2). Instead the man and his wife are left to get on with it, so to speak, without interference or licensing by any third party, and that freedom is apparently God-given in a way which needs no further reinforcement: 'In the beginning, at the creation, God made them male and female. For this reason a man shall leave his father and mother, and be made one with his wife; and the two shall become one flesh. It follows that they are no longer two individuals: they are one flesh' (10.6–8). Jesus' teaching has an almost brutal simplicity: physical sexual intimacy, sealed by the existence of children – the 'one flesh' of which he speaks – creates a relationship with irreversible implications and obligations. Contrary to the impertinence of the marriage service, the solemn words, 'What God has joined together, man must not separate' (10.9), do not envisage the intervention of a priestly hand, and this raises the most radical questions about the propriety of using church authority to bless and sanctify marriages of any kind. The emotional investment which this challenges is daunting. The church articulates the acceptance of society: those who are married receive status and offer observance, while the position of the clergy is reinforced in both prestige and finance by the transaction; but on Jesus' teaching it is all redundant. Moreover it encourages a practice, which is quite contrary to his intent, of distinguishing between 'unhallowed' sexual liaisons which carry no permanent obligations, and publicly recognized liaisons which alone involve commitment. It also inhibits the freedom and autonomy given to men and women by God, and introduces notions of recognition and blessing which have been a fruitful source of ecclesiastical tyranny. While the church likes to speak of blessing, it is also conferring respectability, and it is difficult to distinguish the content of that blessing from its attendant social expression and advantages. One may suspect that it is the refusal of respectability which is most resented by those who otherwise seem to have little time or interest in the church's teaching of forgiveness. To associate the church in this way with public approval is a betrayal of Jesus' teaching and practice.

We are now in a position to understand rather differently the stark equation of remarriage and divorce: 'Whoever divorces his wife and marries another commits adultery against her: so too, if she divorces her husband and marries another, she commits adultery' (10.11f.). Because Jesus does not make the validity of a marriage dependent on its recognition by a religious authority, his words are addressed to men and women contemplating divorce – he does not envisage rules for the ecclesiastical blessing of marriage, let alone legislation for a society to make divorce impossible. As we have seen, in his teaching marriage is self-administered, and in that context he is understandably concerned that divorce should not be a unilateral matter. Obviously such teaching can give no grounds for refusing to recognize a divorce that has been mutually agreed, nor is it even clear that he intends to discourage such mutual agreement, at least where there are no children. It has to be remembered that when Jesus says, 'What God has joined together, man must not separate' (10.9), God is conceived as working not through an ecclesiastical organization, but through the man, the woman and their children. In the absence of children it is difficult to see that there is any objection to their mutual separation. Inevitably divorce represents some absence of forgiveness, a failure to achieve reconciliation, and the reconciling freedom which Christ brings is only travestied if it becomes a pretext for selfish, unilateral behaviour. But separation is sometimes mutual, and where there are no children the church should respect the freedom that God gives to men and women, and might find this easier to do if it obtruded into such matters less.

A comparison with the Pauline form of this teaching is illuminating (I Cor. 7.10f.). For while Paul uses the form of direct prohibition, Jesus here invokes the distinction between marriage and adultery which was crucial to the maintenance of Jewish marriage discipline, as it has been in Christianity. If Jesus was represented in Mark as a divisive, ascetic figure, we would have to understand such language as a call to strict moral rigour. But Jesus is represented even here, not as upholding convention, but as flouting it; so a more subversive interpretation is demanded. He punctures the complacency of his contemporaries by first appearing to adopt their categories of marriage and adultery, and then turning them against their guardians by dangerously confusing the distinction – attaching the stigma of adultery to a condition they happily regarded as marriage. In much the same way his teaching shocks us by suggesting that many of the weddings already solemnized in our churches are themselves adulterous. A gospel of forgiveness is not being untrue to itself in making such points unless it means to convey an ultimate condemnation: for our smugness sometimes needs to be offended if we are to learn a new humility and tolerance.

14

MARK: THE DYNAMICS OF SECRECY

The most notorious problem in interpreting Mark's Gospel is its emphasis on secrecy. Ever since Wrede drew attention to the secrecy with which Jesus' messianic identity is surrounded, the subject has aroused perplexity, but if we are to understand Mark on this point it is important not to isolate 'the messianic secret', as if it were confined to this Gospel or exclusively related to Jesus' identity as Messiah. Earlier sections in this book on the veil (cf. p. 112) and on the secret (cf. p. 128) have shown that the preoccupation with secrecy is no Marcan prerogative. In Paul it interprets dissent, and conveys and defines privilege. These aspects are also present in Mark, but they take on a rather different form. Where the Pauline parallels are particularly helpful is in reminding us that secrecy had a much wider association in the early church than in relation to the messiahship of Jesus; in that respect Wrede's phrase can be deeply misleading. The specific injunctions to secrecy that the Gospel contains can only be kept in perspective if they are interpreted in the light of a dominant part of the teaching ascribed to Jesus: the repudiation of visibility.

(a) The repudiation of visibility

Not surprisingly, the radical implications of Jesus' teaching and practice of forgiveness were not immediately or consistently perceived and implemented. The consequences were only gradually realized and hesitantly extended, so that we cannot assume that all the attitudes attributed to Jesus in the Gospel are authentic reminiscences; nor that when correctly remembered they have been properly understood. There is, however, an underlying coherence in the kind of criticisms with which Jesus is associated – in a variety of ways he is represented as repudiating aspects of religious visibility. It is a characteristic of much religious tradition that it commends certain public practices which reinforce the religious identity of the participants and distinguish them from other people. The divisive consequence of such practices is not incidental or fortuitous – it is deeply associated with their rationale. Alienation from other people is thus legitimated as religious obedience, a strategy to which Christians themselves have often resorted in the course of their history. Moreover, external religious authority and visible practice mutually strengthen each other. When the stress in a religion is on inner consciousness and attitude, religious authorities external to the believer are immediately weakened – they simply do not have access to the believer's religious life without his consent. By contrast, visible observance gives public expression to religious power, and the prestige of religious leaders is dependent on the conformity which they can secure.

All this is faithfully described in the incident which introduces Jesus' teaching on defilement: 'A group of Pharisees, with some doctors of the law who had come from Jerusalem, met him and noticed that some of his disciples were eating their food with "defiled" hands – in other words, without washing them' (7.1f.). The lack of observance which the Jerusalem leaders notice cannot pass without comment, for their status is dependent on extracting such conformity, and once a society has repudiated that it has also made them redundant. By indicating the social context of the dispute Mark has succeeded in conveying something of this to the reader: 'Accordingly, these Pharisees and lawyers asked him, "Why do your disciples not conform to the ancient tradition, but eat their food with defiled hands?"' (7.5). Their notice is disapproving, but they refrain from immediate condemnation, and try to avoid open conflict. The form of their question is carefully phrased in order to leave open to Jesus a means of retreat. He could, for instance, disown his disciples in some way, or present a circumstantial justification for their behaviour. In either case a lack of observance which appeared to challenge the position of the Pharisees might be explained in such a way as to leave the prestige of their tradition unimpaired, and with it their own. It is fascinating that the debate is articulated in terms of a challenge to 'ancient tradition', which anyone familiar with English public schools will quickly recognize as a specious justification for the *status quo*. The appeal to tradition is usually a tacit refusal to specify any rational grounds for present arrangements which have been challenged; instead they are asserted to be unchanging, because no one can remember anything different.

Jesus' reply rejects any face-saving formula, and echoes Paul in Galatians and I Corinthians (cf. pp. 41ff., 62ff.): 'Isaiah was right when he prophesied about you hypocrites in these words: "This people pays me lip-service, but their heart is far from me: their worship of me is in vain, for they teach as doctrines the commandments of men." You neglect the commandment of God, in order to maintain the tradition of men' (7.6–8).

As in Paul, the appeal from men to God is associated with the evasion of criticism, for Jesus does not answer the criticisms of his opponents; he replies with a vigorous attack. Jesus' critique here might appear as merely a conservative protest against human oral tradition, as opposed to the divinely sanctioned Scriptures; but Mark's Jesus is also identified with revisions of scriptural teaching itself, in relation to the Sabbath, defilement and divorce. Thus the distinctive character of the Marcan appeal from man to God is that it is radical and innovative, not simply a reaffirmation of Scripture. While the early church quickly developed a liking for tradition which began with Paul's stress on his role as founding father, and proceeded to justify present practice by such appeals, Jesus here invokes God to challenge tradition and dispute the prestige of custom. It is a clear example of the way in which the appeal to God, far from sanctifying the given, is used to sanction irreverence; if it strikes us as unfamiliar, that is itself an indication of the extent to which the sting of his Gospel has been lost, and replaced by a new pious conformity.

The criticism of religious visibility is crucial to the attainment of human freedom; its application to the observance of Jewish food laws in Paul's letters made possible both a new freedom, and also a new community which transcended old barriers. Mark's community has the same concern to be freed from the observance of food taboos. The author's little comment on Jesus' teaching, 'Thus he declared all foods clean' (7.19), indicates both his own application of that teaching, and also some uneasy awareness that the application goes beyond Jesus' immediate intention. It is a tribute to the integrity of his reminiscence that he does not put into Jesus' mouth a direct statement related to his own interests, but instead transmits much more general teaching about defilement. The style of Jesus' teaching here is significant. He makes no appeal to any unique status, nor does he buttress his message with acts of miraculous power. Instead he tries to explain his teaching on the basis of common sense. He asks for attention and understanding, 'Listen to me, all of you, and understand this' (7.14), and appeals to shared experience and observation: 'Are you as dull as the rest? Do you not see that nothing that goes from outside into a man can defile him, because it does not enter his heart but into his stomach, and so passes out into the drain?' (7.18f.). He may flatter his disciples with the expectation that they will be more perceptive than others, but he is hardly resorting here to esoteric information. Sadly it has also to be admitted that the argument is weak: drunkenness and drug abuse both suggest that the principle is too simple to be convincing.

The general rationale for Jesus' teaching on defilement is presented in two rather different forms. First, 'Nothing that goes into a man from outside can defile him; no, it is the things that come out of him that defile him' (7.15). The distinction here reflects repugnance at the body's secretions. By comparison external dirt is only accidental; it has no religious significance. That Jesus was understood in this fairly straightforward physical sense is strongly suggested by the carelessness of his disciples in washing with which the passage begins. This teaching is then developed in pyschologized and interiorized terms that are much closer to Paul's contrast between flesh and spirit: 'For from inside, out of a man's heart, come evil thoughts, acts of fornication, of theft, murder, adultery, ruthless greed, and malice; fraud, indecency, envy, slander, arrogance, and folly; these evil things all come from inside, and they defile the man' (7.21–23). There is here a clear distinction between the body and the heart; if they are not in conflict like Paul's flesh and spirit, the harmony is only possible because they are envisaged as being quite separate. The implicit dualism is disconcerting, and its basis in reality is weak. Once again the Christian traditions are marked by an acute inability to recognize the interdependence of body and spirit. Nor is it any gain to human freedom if ritual observances are replaced by various forms of moral behaviour. Jesus is here represented as redefining defilement by a mixed list of misdemeanours similar to those used by Paul (Gal. 5.19f.; Rom. 1.29f.). This is only to substitute a much more intimate and pervasive social control for anything which religions of ritual might attempt, and is quite incompatible with Jesus' teaching on forgiveness as outlined in the previous chapter. Once again Mark represents here a community which is in the process of transforming that teaching in a way which will produce those intolerant and divisive communities of subsequent Christian history.

The use of some version of the body/spirit distinction for religious purposes is not, of course, an invention of Jesus; it has a long history in Jewish and Hellenistic religion, and is almost invariably used for critical purposes. It first makes it possible to articulate a distinction between the external forms of a religion and its internal substance; and then by refusing to admit the dependence of the spirit on the body, it facilitates the denigration of external observance as an expression of the highest religious devotion. Thus the Old Testament prophets ridiculed the sacrifices of the cult and exalted such religious dispositions as mercy. Similarly the Stoic interpreters of Homer gave a spiritualized account of the worst depravities which that robust poet depicts. As a device for criticizing religion, while claiming to defend it, the body/spirit distinction is formidable, but it easily masks social alienation. The reason for this is simply that I naturally tend to perceive *my* religion as spiritual and *your* religion as a matter of external forms. We only see the exterior of other people's religion, and can thus easily indulge in parody and caricature; by contrast we have immediate access in our consciousness to the spiritual dimension of our own religion, and therefore are in no doubt as to its sincerity and truth. Such a distortion of our religious perception is always likely, unless we are prepared to reject the demand for visibility with rigorous consistency. In this respect neither of the attempts to evade such consistency are effective. The conservative Jewish and Hellenistic response was not to dispense with the public cult, but to spiritualize it, to insist on the importance of inner disposition while at the same time retaining ancient ritual forms. The difficulty with that position is its contradiction. Although it appears to recognize the force of criticism, it refuses to change its practice and can give no coherent account of why such practice continues to be important. In reality the continuance of the sacrificial cult throughout the Mediterranean world long after it had been religiously discredited doubtless reflects the interests – social and economic – of the priesthoods who organized it; in much the same way that Christianity survives in Western Europe, despite its widespread intellectual and popular repudiation. Clerical structures have an inertia, a capacity for self-preservation and an interest in obscuring the extent of religious change which easily serves to conceal fundamental shifts of attitude. Equally unconvincing is the widespread Christian strategy of dismissing the visibility of other religions as absurd and worthless, but still insisting on various forms of Christian visibility, such as going to Mass or Sabbath observance, which are then defended as 'spiritual' observances. The dissatisfaction which is voiced in 'spiritual' criticisms of religion is recurrent. The difficulties involved in a purely spiritual religion which endeavours to secure invisibility by secrecy will be explored in this chapter.

Very similar issues are raised in Mark's earlier stories about Sabbath observance. Again the first incident is provoked by the refusal of Jesus' disciples to conform to the satisfaction of the Pharisees: 'One Sabbath he was going through the cornfields; and his disciples, as they went, began to pluck ears of corn' (2.23). In flouting Sabbath lore they were challenging a crucial form of religious visibility which had given post-exilic Judaism its distinctive identity. By means of strict enforcement of Sabbath rules, any assimilation of the Jewish community which would have diluted its identity was effectively prevented. As in the teaching on defilement, the Pharisees intervene defensively and cautiously, addressing their question not to the offenders, but to the teacher who is assumed to have responsibility for them: 'Look, why are they doing what is forbidden on the Sabbath?' (2.24). Once again Jesus replies with a distinctive boldness and freedom. He does not simply attempt to exculpate himself or excuse his followers; he vindicates their behaviour by attacking the assumptions of his questioners: 'Have you never read what David did when he and his men were hungry and had nothing to eat? He went into the House of God, in the time of Abiathar the High Priest, and ate the sacred bread, though no one but a priest is allowed to eat it, and even gave it to his men' (2.25f.). While the offensiveness of the answer is deliberate, its rationale is less clear. Already there are indications that it has acquired a certain christological flavour: in this reading the stress lies on the Davidic nature of the precedent, and it becomes a disguised form of messianic claim. We have already observed a similar form of christological reference in the teaching on forgiveness, and once that restrictive reading has become dominant it neutralizes any subversive echoes in Christian minds. It is no longer a saying which claims freedom for men, but elevates instead the uniqueness and authority of Jesus. The other rationale has quite different implications: this would lay stress on the hunger and need of those who broke the taboo as being an adequate justification of their action. Far from sanctioning christological hierarchy, the saying would then insist on the accountability of religious practices and rules to human needs, even at the price of apparent irreverence.

A similar ambiguity recurs in the saying which follows it: 'The Sabbath was made for the sake of man and not man for the Sabbath: therefore the Son of Man is sovereign even over the Sabbath' (2.27f.). The first half of the saying gives the broadest and most humane rationale for modifications of the Sabbath; the second suggests that there is something distinctive about Jesus which justifies his action. This is particularly the case once the term 'Son of Man' is understood as some kind of messianic title; however, in this instance the tension does seem clearly resolved by the implications of the 'therefore' which connects the two clauses. If the unique sovereignty of Jesus over the Sabbath is the main content of the assertion, the 'therefore' becomes inexplicable. Consequently the humane rationale must be primary, and Jesus' freedom in relation to the Sabbath only an instance of it. In such a reading the words 'Son of Man' are to be taken, as I have suggested earlier (cf. p. 97), simply as Jesus' term of self-reference, without any unique or messianic connotations. Moreover it is this possibility of humane modification of Sabbath observance which is emphasized in the healing story which follows. Here it is Jesus' own behaviour which scandalizes, and he carefully defines the grounds of his action: 'Is it permitted to do good or to do evil on the Sabbath, to save life or to kill?' (3.4). Mark skilfully attributes to this episode in Jesus' career the beginning of the conspiracy that ends in his death: 'The Pharisees, on leaving the synagogue, began plotting against him with the partisans of

Herod to see how they could make away with him' (3.6). The juxtaposition of events is carefully contrived to display Jesus' opponents in the worst possible light: but it does make plain the social consequences of radical religious criticism. The structure of religious control proceeds to defend itself.

Fasting, like food-laws and Sabbath observance, was a standard way in which the religious of Jesus' time distinguished themselves from other people; his teaching follows a now familiar pattern. It is introduced by the failure of his disciples to conform: 'Once, when John's disciples and the Pharisees were keeping a fast, some people came to him and said, "Why is it that John's disciples and the disciples of the Pharisees are fasting, but yours are not?"' (2.18). Jesus, when taxed in this way with the behaviour of his followers, is again represented as replying with words which suggest more than one rationale: 'Can you expect the bridegroom's friends to fast while the bridegroom is with them? As long as they have the bridegroom with them, there can be no fasting. But the time will come when the bridegroom will be taken away from them, and on that day they will fast' (2.19f.). At first it seems that the echoes of the eschatological bridegroom, whose coming brings the end of time, demand a messianic interpretation which draws attention to the unique status of Jesus and makes the behaviour of his disciples dependent on that status. The comparison with the disciples of John the Baptist, however, suggests a rather different meaning. Mark has already told his readers that 'John had been arrested' (1.14). His disciples had lost their bridegroom, Jesus' disciples still had theirs with them. Then the rationale for not fasting becomes one of surprising freedom: it is enough that Jesus' disciples are happy to justify their behaviour. The closing words foresee a very different time, and are an early prophecy of the passion. In themselves they certainly do not sanction the introduction of specifically Christian fasts, carefully distinguished by the days on which they occurred from Jewish fasts, which soon marked the early church; though perhaps already Mark's community was beginning to develop in such a way. At the least it suggests how the repudiation of fasting implied by Paul (Gal. 4.10) in his criticism of the sacred calendar could soon be modified with some apparent support from Jesus' own teaching.

The teaching on food laws, Sabbath observance and fasting all portray Jesus as in conflict with established forms of religious visibility by which the religious leaders maintained their dominance. What is most revealing about all these stories is the very different relationship between Jesus and his disciples which they display. In every case it seems to be the disciples who exercise the initiative. It is their lack of observance which precipitates the collision between their teacher and his opponents. Jesus consistently refuses to discipline them, nor does he try to protect himself by dissociating himself from them. The moralizing interpreter would merely insist that this reflects the moral rectitude of the disciples' behaviour, and that Jesus had no option but to support them. The fascinating point, however, is that they are not represented as implementing a moral programme which Jesus had previously laid down. Instead they are perceived as acting spontaneously, using their own judgment; and Jesus respects and fosters this freedom. But the stories also portray a fundamental contradiction in the religious viewpoint they convey. For paradoxically the refusal to conform to demands for public religious observance is itself intensely visible; so that the criticism of religious visibility acquires many of the characteristics of exhibitionism. Repeatedly they attract hostile attention to themselves and their master. Invisible spiritual religion thus proves to have a highly public face.

(b) Human fabrication and the destruction of the temple

Whether Mark's Gospel anticipates or celebrates the destruction of the Jerusalem temple, it is the temple which provides the backcloth to the passion, and from the beginning of ch. 11 it becomes the focus of the final controversies which surround Jesus' death. It is the physical location of conflict (11.12–20, 27–33; 12.1of.; 14.49), it is the object of dire condemnation (11.12–20; 13.1f.), it features prominently in Jesus' trial (14.58), and pursues him in the mockery on the cross (15.29). The dereliction of the temple and his death (15.38) are simultaneous and are clearly intended to interpret each other. We have already observed in Paul's letters the desire to replace the physical temple by the bodies of believers (I Cor. 3.1f.; 6.19; II Cor. 6.16), and to substitute conformity of behaviour for the sacrificial cult (Rom. 12.1f.). In Mark the long-established prophetic criticism of sacrifice within Judaism is voiced not by Jesus but by a sympathetic lawyer (12.33). Equally Mark quite unselfconsciously dates events by reference to the Jewish holy calendar, and shows Jesus carefully observing a festival which is intimately connected with the function of the temple (14.1f., 12, 16). It is not the temple ritual which is attacked in Mark, but the building itself, and this represents another and radical dimension of Jesus' criticism of religious visibility. In matters of conformity to public standards of behaviour we have seen that the initiative lies often with Jesus' disciples, and that he merely confirms what they have done. In relation to the temple he himself is the author of the attack. He curses the fig-tree (11.14), he cleanses the temple (11.15f.), and while the disciples are impressed by the size and apparent permanence of the temple, he foresees its destruction (13.1f.). Embarrassment about the temple reaches deeply into the Old Testament Scriptures. It is even written into Solomon's prayer of consecration: 'Can God indeed dwell on earth? Heaven itself, the highest heaven, cannot contain thee; how much less this house that I have built' (I Kings 8.27). Repeatedly this unease produces attempts to bring about, if not the temple's ruin, at least its aggressive reform (II Kings 23.4f.), and Jesus' cleansing of the temple is a continuation of that tradition. His criticism is, however, much more devastating than the mere creation of a disturbance. He was heard by his enemies and remembered by his followers as calling in question the very existence of temples, even of the temple itself.

To this day nothing speaks more eloquently of the dominance of a religious leadership than its physical expression in building; while the exercise of social control through the regulation of behaviour is always liable to stimulate conflict, impressive religious buildings appear to speak a more objective and harmonious language. Human beings are refractory. Stones, if properly arranged, stay in place. The connection between social dominance and conspicuous building, demonstrated by Karnak and the Vatican, continues even in a secularized modern world, exemplified by the country houses of the English aristocracy, by Stalin's palaces of culture, and the tributes to Western capitalism of Mies van der Rohe. The sanctions and the rhetoric may be different, but the reinforcement of supremacy is continuous. The transactions of power and prestige which the temple articulated were subtle and various. It provided a focus of Jewish identity, dispersed through the Mediterranean world, reminding them that wherever they might temporarily find themselves, they belonged elsewhere. It thus helped the Jew in Rome or Alexandria to reject his immediate environment as any suitable object of loyalty. Its size proclaimed the significance of those who worshipped there and the prestige and power of the priesthood which controlled it. Its vulnerability and expense made them subservient to those secular powers which provided its security and finance. This human fabrication, exploiting a familiar sleight of hand which confuses antiquity with permanence, was made more plausible and impressive by the uniqueness of its claims. In a world where the multiplicity of religious building had bred not only piety but contempt, the awesome uniqueness of the one place with which the one God had associated himself forebade any irreverent comparisons. A politically compromised priesthood disguised their financial dependence on the offerings of the faithful by demanding sacrifice to that one God whose attention they commanded. The anxiety at the heart of all theological assertion is only allayed, not resolved, by building; the construction, which is intended to express reality, betrays illusion by its very fabrication, an inability to reverence the given without selection or exclusion. However majestic and beautiful the temple walls, they must shut out a wider view which might question and undermine their significance. This theoretical contradiction is expressed in practical terms by the stratagems of the priesthood. Having focused all the prestige of an invisible world on a definite location, they are nevertheless forced to defend it. They cannot afford to let God speak for himself, but must impertinently defend his majesty by purely human measures; for it is only by defending God in this way that they can protect themselves from being discredited.

The criticism of the temple which Mark's Gospel ascribes to Jesus is curiously uneven. For instance, in the teaching on the end of the world, the menacing phrase about ' "the abomination of desolation" usurping a place which is not his' (13.14) is usually understood as referring to the defilement of the temple. The abhorrence of the language for such an act conveys assumptions of continuing reverence and respect. Similarly, although the story of the widow's mite (12.41–44) draws attention to an element of financial exploitation in the temple's constitution, there is no suggestion that the widow is misguided in her generosity. At first sight it would also seem that the rationale for the cleansing of the temple is ultimately affirmative rather than critical: 'Does not Scripture say, "My house shall be called a house of prayer for all the nations"? But you have made it a robbers' cave' (11.17). Jesus appears to be suggesting a way in which the temple might be reformed and established on a proper footing and the threatened end of the temple is only the verdict on a refusal to listen. It is a punishment on a particular temple; it does not express any intrinsic divine rejection of building temples in his name. The cursing of the fig-tree reinforces this point: there is a structural disequilibrium in fig-trees between leaves and fruit; but it is not fig-trees in general which are being cursed, but this particular unsatisfactory fig-tree (11.12–14). Thus Mark has begun to mitigate something of the harshness of Jesus' condemnation, but he retains evidence of a much more devastating critique. As modern English cathedrals make only too plain, grand religious buildings do not exist on thin air. Some kind of financial transaction has to take place in order to maintain them, as the postcards which have replaced the pigeons embarrassingly remind us. To attack the financial basis of the temple is not a programme for reform, but a recipe for destruction.

As Mark's text stands, Jesus is the uncompromising prophet of the temple's end: 'Not one stone will be left upon another; all will be thrown down' (13.2). Understandably his enemies identified the prophet with his message, and perceived him as a far from unwilling messenger of doom: 'We heard him say, "I will pull down this temple, made with human hands, and in three days I will build another, not made with hands"' (14.58). Although Mark carefully classifies this as false evidence (14.57), the charge is echoed in the mockery on the cross: 'You would pull the temple down, would you, and build it in three days?' (15.29). At the very least Mark seems to retain here a memory of a rather different account of Jesus' attitude towards the temple from the one he adopts in his text. It cannot simply be dismissed as a hostile version, for a variety of reasons. First, the self-conscious irony which anticipates the resurrection in three days suggests that this version of the charge has itself a Christian origin. This is confirmed by the very similar saying which is directly attributed to Jesus in John's Gospel: 'Destroy this temple . . . and in three days I will raise it again' (John 2.19). Thirdly it is associated with an analogy and a contrast between the temple made with hands and the temple made without hands (i.e. the human body), which is again of Christian origin and is reflected in other, particularly Pauline, sources (I Cor. 3.16f.; 6.19; cf. Heb. 10.19f.). Apart from this hostile testimony, it is strangely not attributed in Mark's Gospel to Jesus. Yet it is so crucially a part of his tradition, that when he writes of Jesus' death, he immediately interprets it by reference to the temple: 'Then Jesus gave a loud cry and died. And the curtain of the temple was torn in two from top to bottom' (15.37f.). As the Spirit departs from Jesus' body, the divine presence forsakes the temple.

An attitude of unqualified opposition to the temple is not only in keeping with the repudiation of other forms of religious visibility which has been detected in Mark's Gospel; it also makes intelligible the bitter opposition of the priests, who are otherwise rather unlikely allies for the Pharisees. The opposition of the chief priests is emphatic (11.28). They are represented as deviously arranging his death (14.1f.), and it is to them that Judas Iscariot resorts with his offer of betrayal: 'When they heard what he had come for, they were greatly pleased, and promised him money' (14.11). The trial takes place in the High Priest's house (14.53–65), the High Priest controls the proceedings, and utters the verdict of blasphemy (14.63). The chief priests intervene decisively before Pilate, inciting the mob to prefer Barabbas (15.11). A radical and negative attitude towards the temple may also explain a puzzling contradiction in the account of the passion. Although we can no longer talk of the amazing volatility of the crowd, which first welcomes Jesus and then turns against him, because that would make assumptions about the historical accuracy of the closing chapters of the Gospel which may be unfounded, there yet remains a dramatic and unexplained shift of attitude amongst the mob. Quite consistently the crowd are represented as Jesus' supporters (11.18; 12.38), their potential unrest is pledge of his security (14.2), and the priests are afraid of popular disaffection: 'They were afraid of the people, so they left him alone and went away' (12.12). Yet in the scene before Pilate the priests and the people have achieved an amazing realignment, for which there has been no preparation. It is a commonplace of modern Christian experience that church buildings are usually more popular than clergymen. It would appear from Mark's account that so long as Jesus was criticizing forms of social control policed by the religious leaders, he could rely upon widespread popular support; but once that same teaching was applied critically to the temple itself, the religious leaders saw their opportunity to discredit Jesus and seized it. As the fanatical scenes at its eventual destruction remind us, the temple not only represented a focus of priestly power; it was the object of intense emotional investment among a much wider section of Jews. To challenge its prestige only served to discredit the critic; the honour of the place was maintained by his crucifixion. It enabled everyone to see the man who uttered such godless words in his properly cursed condition. Once again we are faced by the paradox that the opponent of religious visibility only succeeds in exposing himself – isolated and ignominious – but still compelling attention.

(c) *The context of secrecy: an eye to the audience*

The significance of secrecy in Mark's Gospel cannot be understood apart from his understanding of Jesus' audience, which always has an eye to the manipulation of his readers. Jesus' challenge to religious visibility has, as we have seen, deeply contradictory implications for his audience. On the one hand he has to oppose the concern for a human audience, if he is to break the power of the religious establishment with which he is in conflict: the lawyers and the Pharisees use their prestige to direct the opinion of the crowd and shame dissenters into conformity, as ultimately the priests succeed in isolating Jesus from the mob and turning it against him. Yet Jesus himself is in competition with them for the ear of the people. He cannot hope to persuade the religious leaders; he must therefore appeal to the crowd. Hence the contradictions of the saying, 'If anyone is ashamed of me and mine in this wicked and godless age, the Son of Man will be ashamed of him, when he comes in the glory of his Father and of the holy angels' (8.38). On the one hand the power of the immediate audience to control by shame is being vigorously challenged, but only by appeal to another audience, however hypothetical, which will ultimately vindicate the speaker. For Jesus' repudiation of the uses of religious visibility is not the passive path of the quietist. He does not conform outwardly, while

maintaining an inner indifference. His refusal to conform is as visible as
the conformity it rejects. So the freedom which he practises and advocates
is scandalous, not face-saving, and therefore it readily creates spectators:
excited and consequently volatile.

In some parts of Mark's Gospel Jesus is portrayed, as we have just seen,
in a frankly populist light: the darling of the crowd, against whom the
religious élite is powerless. The excitement and attention of the crowd is a
continuous feature of Mark's portrait. After Jesus' first exorcism, 'the
news spread rapidly, and he was soon spoken of all over the district of
Galilee' (1.28). After the cleansing of the leper, 'the man went out and
made the whole story public; he spread it far and wide, until Jesus could no
longer show himself in any town, but stayed outside in the open country.
Even so, people kept coming to him from all quarters' (1.45). Thereafter
the crowd is a persistent presence (2.13; 3.7–10; 4.1, 35f.; 5.21; 6.30–33,
54f.; 7.24f.; 9.25; 11.8–10). Doubtless there is something of the itinerant
preacher's wish-fulfilment in such a picture. It is the kind of immediate and
dramatic impact for which they hungered, and which by recounting they
hoped to re-create; but the reality is much more complicated than any such
reductionist account recognizes.

The parable of the sower says of one group of listeners that 'as soon as
they hear the word, they accept it with joy' (4.16), but this immediate
welcome is quickly followed by falling away. If Mark underlines the
readiness with which Jesus was heard, he is also contemptuous of leaders
who are afraid of their audience, be it Herod (6.26), or the chief priests
(11.18, 32; 12.12), or Pilate (15.15). Each incident is carefully noted and
serves to interpret the others. Mark is not sentimental about the crowd,
and cannot allow himself to present Jesus simply as the mouthpiece of its
aspirations. Authority and status which are conferred by the people can be
removed by the same hand, and Mark is insistent that Jesus' authority is
not derived from other human beings. So throughout the Gospel there is a
game of holy hide-and-seek, whereby Jesus flirts with the crowd, attracts
their attention, but refuses to become their creature. In one sense the
carefully calculated public appearance and the staged withdrawal is a
device to elicit the attention it appears to disdain, and this manipulative
aspect of secrecy will receive further notice. What it most powerfully
conveys is the conviction that Jesus does not derive his power and
authority from men, however numerous and applauding, but from God.
We have already touched on this (see p. 214) when examining faith and
prayer. Consistently withdrawal from men is the condition for access to
God. After the public scene of the baptism 'the Spirit sent him away into
the wilderness, and there he remained for forty days tempted by Satan. He

was among the wild beasts; and the angels waited on him' (1.12f.). While the crowd seeks him, he endeavours to find solitude (1.32–39), anonymity (7.24f.), escape from their demands (6.30–33). Any suggestion that Jesus needs his audience is vigorously repressed.

At first sight this is reminiscent of Paul in Galatians (see pp. 41f.) and I Corinthians (see pp. 62–66), both in its repudiation of human authentication in the name of divine authority, and also in a passionate concern for the human response which it dare not own. In understanding Paul, political analogies are difficult to resist: the desire to control is so insistent, the pursuit of power so naked. Some element of the political refusal to acknowledge dependence is at work here, and will be explored in the next chapter, but it is not an adequate or sufficient interpretation. The Jesus of this Gospel is not the dominating Pauline 'Lord'; indeed only once is he greeted with the word (8.28). Instead, Jesus is a much more genuinely free and liberating figure. The dynamics of secrecy are not therefore to be dismissed as a mere political device; they illuminate the exercise of imaginative freedom. In the opening chapter it was suggested that 'the use of imagination to attain freedom inevitably distances human beings from each other' (see p. 13). If Jesus simply identified himself with the crowd, he would merely have conformed to its wishes, and lost the power to exercise his freedom by transcending its expectations. The insistence on withdrawal underlines the primacy of the individual's imagination in the practice and attainment of freedom, but the withdrawal is not ultimate; the renewed encounter with others guards against fantasy: unless the dream can be communicated it is fruitless. In all this, Jesus is far more like an artist than a politician. If he simply gives his audience what it wants, he will lose his own self-respect and that of his audience in the timid surrender to conformity. If he retreats into a fastidiously selected élite, his art will lose its vitality. He has both to stand apart in order to exercise his imagination freely, and then to submit himself to the public. He must be vulnerable to rejection, if there is to be a possibility of reintegration. As with the life of the creative artist, intense isolation and a passionate desire and need to communicate alternate with each other.

Distrust of the human audience is well illustrated by the satire on the doctors of the law attributed to Jesus: 'Beware of the doctors of the law, who love to walk up and down in long robes, receiving respectful greetings in the street; and to have the chief seats in synagogues, and places of honour at feasts. These are the men who eat up the property of widows, while they say long prayers for appearance' sake, and they will receive the severest sentence' (12.38–40). The religious pursuit of prestige is carefully described and ruthlessly exposed. It betrays its real nature in the exploitation of the poor, but the concern to cultivate an appreciative audience gives the satire a much wider application, which will endure as long as cassocks and rules of precedence are with us. Indeed the greeting of Jesus at his entry to Jerusalem, so lovingly regaled by the author, falls under the same ambiguity. Jesus is represented confronting a society based on subtle transactions of esteem and possible only through various forms of discrimination. The doctor of the law distinguishes himself by his clothing, which marks him off from other men. His status is publicly recognized: he gains status from the greetings he receives, and confirms the social standing of others by the way he responds. 'Chief seats' also put others in their place. The carefully orchestrated public performance always has its victims. To conform to the audience is to consent both to the society which gives such men approval and to the discrimination by which that approval is expressed; it is also to submit to the leaders who exploit that society. Only withdrawal from such an audience makes criticism possible. As long as one merely identifies with it, one accepts it. Not that Jesus is portrayed as acting without any regard to an audience. In the healing of the man with the withered arm he looks round at his enemies 'with anger and sorrow at their obstinate stupidity' (3.5). He does not divorce himself from his audience, even when it is hostile, but he deliberately refuses to be bound by it.

Equally telling is Jesus' defence of his vision of his own destiny: 'He began to teach them that the Son of Man had to undergo great sufferings, and to be rejected by the elders, chief priests, and doctors of the law; to be put to death, and to rise again three days afterwards. He spoke about it plainly. At this Peter took him by the arm and began to rebuke him. But Jesus turned round, and, looking at his disciples, rebuked Peter. "Away with you, Satan," he said; "you think as men think, not as God thinks"' (8.31–33). As in Paul the appeal to God against men protects the otherwise vulnerable 'I'. To imagine a destiny at such variance with the expectations and hopes of his followers and in such conflict with his wider audience would have been impossible if his attention had been preoccupied by either. He is free to transcend their expectations, precisely because he has not identified with them. He is able to imagine an achievement which is not dependent on the approval of his enemies or even of his friends, and is not compromised by endeavouring to secure it.

(d) The ambivalence of secrecy: the exercise of freedom

I have attempted to place the injunctions to secrecy which occur in Mark's Gospel in the wider context of the whole New Testament, and particularly in relation to the concern for the secret in Paul's writing and his ambivalent attitude towards his audience. Within Mark's Gospel the paradoxes of Jesus' repudiation of religious visibility have been explored and the caution of Jesus towards his audience has been analysed. When approached in this way the injunctions to secrecy in Mark begin to look rather different, for the secret has a much wider significance than the messianic identity of Jesus. It is associated with the content of his religious teaching and the style of his own authority. Moreover to talk about the messianic secret in Mark is immediately to oversimplify the evidence, for what is characteristic of this secret is the ambivalence of Jesus himself towards it. He may refuse the Pharisees' request for a sign from heaven with the words, 'Why does this generation ask for a sign? I tell you this: no sign shall be given to this generation' (8.12), but he has by his own admission given just such a sign in the healing of the paralytic, 'to convince you that the Son of Man has the right on earth to forgive sins' (2.10).

Such contradictory attitudes might be tamely defused by suggesting that Mark is only passing on conflicting traditions which he cannot resolve; but the contradiction is much more structural than such an account recognizes. Jesus may silence the demons (1.25, 34; 3.11), but the exorcisms themselves speak louder than the evil spirits. The injunctions to secrecy after spectacular cures (1.42; 5.43; 7.36; 8.26) are not intended to qualify their extraordinary nature, but to underline the disinterest of the healer. He acts in a way which secures the attention he refuses to admit that he seeks. Most fascinating of all is the delicate way in which Jesus first elicits the confession of Peter (8.27–33) and then gives 'them strict orders not to tell anyone about him'. His questions thus serve to open their eyes; he himself has no need of their answers. As will be clear in the next chapter, Mark is well aware of the immensely powerful picture of Jesus that this conveys, and the opportunities which this creates for his present representatives. But the ambivalence is also necessary to the exercise of Jesus' freedom: refusing either to conform to an audience or yet to turn his back on it, his freedom is scandalous. It is neither hidden nor ignored. Conformity would have deprived him of his freedom and others of their deliverance. Separation would have removed the possibility of offence. If he had sought to please his audience he would have ended in conformity. If he had secured the secrecy for which he asked he would have avoided scandal. It is precisely the ambivalence of his injunctions to secrecy that made him a scandal and his gospel subversive.

15

MARK: THE SERVANTS AND BENEFICIARIES OF THE GOSPEL

The subversive gospel which has been outlined in the preceding chapters has no need to perpetuate secrecy. At most, secrecy makes possible the creative distance and hence the imaginative freedom of Jesus; but of its nature it is self-dissolving, as one of the proverbs ascribed to Jesus makes plain: 'Do you bring in the lamp to put it under the meal-tub, or under the bed? Surely it is brought to be set on the lamp-stand. For nothing is hidden unless it is to be disclosed, and nothing put under cover unless it is to come into the open' (4.2f.). Here is no attempt to preserve mystery or the amour-propre of its guardian; instead the transience of secret knowledge is explicitly acknowledged, and with it the impermanence of any privilege which the esoteric confers. For unless it is communicated, it dies with the recipient; but if it is passed on, the privilege is diluted. Generous disclosure, far from fostering distinctions and divisions, undermines them. If this was the only theme in Mark's Gospel, it would celebrate the end of religious mystification, a paean of enlightenment, culminating appropriately in the rending of the temple veil (15.38). All the human fabrications which conceal and hide and separate would be cast aside, and truth, like the young man, would slip out of the linen cloth and run away naked (14.52).

(a) The political exploitation of secrecy

The excitement and novelty of Mark, and in this respect its credibility as gospel, good news, demand that the communication be effective and that the revelation be real, but the same communication which is necessary to the gospel threatens the status of its messengers. Total success would make them redundant. Mark does not therefore represent simply the destruction of secrecy, but also its construction. As was recognized at the outset (see p. 194), reader and writer are bound together by the privilege of sharing knowledge which is hidden from the participants in the narrative, as it is also to the contemporary world. This aspect of secrecy has an unmistakably political dimension.

Secrecy is repeatedly exploited, to establish not the authority and prestige of Jesus – that is done by the account of his power – but the authority and prestige of his present representatives. The connection between privileged knowledge and privileged people is most apparent in the passage which introduces the explanation of the parable of the sower: 'When he was alone, the Twelve and others who were round him questioned him about the parables. He replied, "To you the secret of the kingdom of God has been given; but to those who are outside everything comes by way of parables, so that (as Scripture says) they may look and look, but see nothing; they may hear and hear, but understand nothing; otherwise they might turn to God and be forgiven"' (4.10f.). The information that Jesus is 'alone' underlines the privileged intimacy of the Twelve. It is a technique which recurs frequently to distinguish the Twelve (10.32), the apostles (6.30f.) the disciples (7.17f.; 9.33; 10.10) and more particularly Peter, James and John (5.37; 9.2; 13.3f.; 14.32f.). Mark creates a sense of privacy, so that the reader has the frequent experience of eavesdropping on conversations behind closed doors. The privilege of esoteric knowledge is quite explicitly conferred upon a select group – 'to you the secret of the kingdom of God has been given' – and this is envisaged as intrinsically divisive. So that for Mark the parable is not a moment of open opportunity, but a secret riddle, a badge of division: 'With many such parables he would give them his message, so far as they were able to receive it. He never spoke to them except in parables; but privately to his disciples he explained everything' (4.33f.). Accordingly Mark enjoys writing in hints (13.14). Indeed he is so coy in disclosing his meaning that the key to his most self-conscious riddle seems to have died with him. With heavy hand he draws attention to the significance of the numbers involved in the feedings, the loaves and the baskets (6.51f.; 7.17f.; 8.17); the nudging of the reader is unmistakable, but the meaning defies plausible reconstruction. It is an important warning that the undistinguished character of his literary style is no pledge of a straightforward and transparent mind.

Mark clearly implies that some of Jesus's followers had a privileged access to his teaching. They knew before other people of his Messianic identity (8.29), his transfiguration (9.9) and of his suffering and resurrection (9.9, 30f.; 10.32). They are also able to anticipate accurately the time of the temple's destruction (13.3f.). Indeed it may well be that Mark regarded their proven accuracy in that last respect as a most important proof of the reliability of their other special information. Mark therefore confers a very particular distinction on Jesus' present representatives. Subsequent theories of the episcopate have secured an undue emphasis on the elements of appointment and selection in relation to the Twelve. Mark does not deny that there were authorities who were appointed by Jesus; but he does not simply provide a list of vouched-for names. In an astonishing anticipation of Irenaeus, the authentic representative has access to the hidden teaching. It is this which provides the proof and the benefit of such appointment. Intimacy is required not, as the modern historian might wish, to ensure accurate reminiscence, but rather to have access to Jesus' secret thoughts. Mark's Gospel may appear preoccupied with Jesus, but it is also concerned to advance the claims of his more immediate representatives: the stress on delegation and intimacy allows no other conclusion. Our interest in reading Mark may lie with Jesus; we look for evidence about him and readily assume that Mark's priorities are identical to our own. It is a misunderstanding that the Gospel is perhaps concerned to create, for its beneficiaries have much to gain from not attracting premature or critical attention. When we ask who were the intended beneficiaries of Mark's Gospel, however, we enter a very confusing landscape. We may even look back rather wistfully at the undisguised egotism of Paul's letters: the self-assertion in Mark's Gospel is considerably more devious.

(b) A polemical view of Jesus' representatives

It is a commonplace of Marcan studies that his Gospel contains a very unflattering view of the disciples in general, and of Peter and the Twelve in particular. This is usually seen as a sign of the primitive simplicity of the earliest Gospel, which is still prepared to show Jesus' first followers in all their human frailty; by contrast the later Gospels idealize the picture. This is a naive view of the matter. First, an enormous amount of the Gospel is devoted to portraying Jesus' representatives and to qualifying their status and authority; at least sixty verses of this quite small book are given over to the subject. Now as long as the interest of the reader is concentrated on Jesus, this may only appear as a digression; I would suggest, however, that it is a central part of Mark's purpose in writing his Gospel, that the viewpoint is consistent, and the element of polemic unmistakable. We know that there were many sources of prestige and authority in the early church, and Mark represents an attempt to order and evaluate quite a number of them. For instance, we know from Paul that James, the Lord's brother, quickly came to have a leading role in the early church (Gal. 1.19; 2.9, 12; I Cor. 15.7), and this is also reflected in Acts (12.17).

It is not, therefore, fanciful to suggest that Jesus' repudiation of family ties has a polemical intention. Jesus asks,'"Who is my mother? Who are my brothers?" And looking round at those who were sitting in the circle about him he said, "Here are my mother and my brothers. Whoever does the will of God is my brother, my sister, my mother"' (3.34f.). If Jesus' family had played no further part in the leadership of the early church, this would be merely a striking extension of privilege and identity. When Jesus here disowns kinship and deprives it of any privileged standing in his community, it is difficult to think that such teaching is not intended to put James and the Lord's family very firmly in their place.

Mark's chief concern is not, however, with Jesus' family, but with the Twelve and their leaders. We have seen how they are distinguished by intimacy and access to Jesus, and how Peter and Andrew, James and John are particularly marked out as Jesus' privileged companions. Just as Paul has no option in Galatians but to acknowledge the pre-eminence of Cephas and James, Mark cannot conceal the special position of the four disciples, whose call is the first public act of Jesus' ministry (1.16–21), of which they are the constant witnesses. As the potential catch we may demur at the predatory implications of the invitation to James and John to become 'fishers of men,' but Mark does not seem to share such misgivings. In the account of the Twelve's commissioning (3.13–19) these four are given the places of prominence in the list of names. Mark, like Paul, cannot directly attack their standing: the tension is not indicated by denial, but by qualification. Paul speaks of them as 'those reputed pillars of our society' (Gal. 2.9); Mark diminishes their credibility by a series of carefully judged stories. The treatment of Peter is well known: no praise for him at his confession of Jesus as the Christ, instead the epithet of 'Satan' (8.33); his folly and bewilderment at the transfiguration (9.5f.); his boasts at the last supper, contrasting himself with others and promising faithfulness to death (14.29–31), culminate in ignominious betrayal (14.66–72). In Gethsemane he is singled out by name, when Jesus taunts him for his sleep (14.37). Every specific mention of Peter after his call is thus designed to discredit him. The attitude is so consistently damaging that it must be intended to counter actual claims put forward for the chief of the apostles. Similarly James and John, whose call comes immediately after that of Peter and Andrew (1.20f.), are portrayed by Mark in a most discreditable light. The exclusive attitude towards authority which Jesus specifically repudiates is voiced by John (9.38–41). The brothers appear self-seeking in their ambition to sit in state with Jesus, and uncomprehending of the nature of their destiny (10.35–40). Any claims to primacy are explicitly ruled out by

Jesus himself: 'To sit at my right or left is not for me to grant; it is for those to whom it has already been assigned' (10.40).

If Peter, James and John receive especially hostile treatment, the prestige of the Twelve is also deliberately undermined. In a work which places a high value on knowledge and understanding, they are consistently shown as slow to grasp the significance of what they hear (4.10; 9.32) and see (6.51f.; 8.14, 21). Like James and John, they are presented as consumed by anxieties about their own status (9.33–37). Their fall from faith is prophesied by Jesus (14.27), and its fulfilment carefully noted by the evangelist: 'Then the disciples all deserted him and ran away' (14.50). Moreover Mark never misses an opportunity to remind the reader that Judas Iscariot, the betrayer of Jesus, was one of the Twelve (3.19; 14.10, 43). In part this is probably designed to underline the heinousness of the crime, in fulfilment of Scripture: 'Even the friend whom I trusted, who ate at my table, exults over my misfortune' (Ps. 41.9); but in view of the strongly negative attitude towards the Twelve in the Gospel as a whole, there is probably an element of malice in highlighting Judas' privileged identity. A body that had behaved as Mark portrays them behaving, and had numbered amongst itself Jesus' betrayers, can hardly have been listened to with uncritical respect in the church for which Mark was written.

Through most of Christian history, the emphasis on poverty has had a polemical intention, either to dismiss the power of secular wealth, or to discredit the pretensions of rich ecclesiastics. Mark lays great stress on the poverty of the Twelve. Simon and Andrew, James and John, are all represented as leaving their assets behind them (1.18, 20) at the call of Jesus. Levi simply forsakes the custom-house (2.14). Peter underlines the point when he reminds Jesus and the reader that 'we have left everything to become your followers' (10.28). The authority of the Twelve is so associated with the injunction to poverty and there is a strong impression that the one is conditional on the other: 'He gave them authority over unclean spirits, and instructed them to take nothing for the journey beyond a stick: no bread, no pack, no money in their belts. They might wear sandals, but not a second coat' (6.7–9). This insistence on poverty as the mark of Jesus' authentic representatives is repeated in the story of the rich young man, who is told by Jesus: 'One thing you lack: go, sell everything you have, and give to the poor, and you will have riches in heaven; and come, follow me' (10.21). This picture has become so integral a part of our imaginative vision of the early church that we easily fail to perceive that it is not self-evident. For Paul in his letters does not present the Twelve as ascetics, and makes it clear that they did not forsake their families (I Cor. 9.5). Moreover he infers that his self-supporting style of work is not only financially disinterested, but also disadvantaged when compared with those who made a living by preaching. This serves as a reminder that from one point of view the insistence in Mark that Jesus' representatives should have no property of any kind is also a justification for their living at other people's expense. The religious man's refusal to look after himself is always a mute demand that other people should do this for him. At the very least it reflects that the leadership in Mark's church adopted a stance of total poverty which was also a tacit claim to financial support from the faithful. But the injunction to poverty which confirmed their own status may also have functioned as a means of criticizing either the Twelve or their later representatives. The corruption of Judas by the promise of money (14.11) would add point to such a criticism of the Twelve. They are therefore accorded a very fragile status: it is entirely dependent on ascetic poverty. To insist on such a qualification seems both to have legitimated the leadership of Mark's church and voiced their criticism of the Twelve.

I have spoken earlier of the apparent invisibility of Mark (cf. p. 198). Certainly one is not made aware of him in the striking manner that Paul obtrudes upon the reader. Nevertheless his Gospel does express the outlook and claims of a particular group of believers. The leadership of Mark's church did not primarily identify itself with the Twelve. They claimed the same powers of exorcism as were given to the Twelve; they belonged to a community in which the claims of the Twelve could not be entirely ignored; but their own status was not dependent on any recognition by the Twelve. Instead they appear to have prided themselves on their self-authenticating poverty; on their pre-eminence in prayer (9.29), which contrasted gratifyingly with the scene described in Gethsemane; and on their willingness as faithful servants to share the fate of the Son (12.2–5). If there was no sign of any competing interests in the Gospel, the modesty and self-criticism of the portrayal of the Twelve and their leaders would be a most remarkable tribute to their reversal of dominance, their concern not to establish a position of authority at the expense of others' freedom. Close examination of the text, however, suggests a less self-effacing interpretation, for the authority of the Twelve is carefully limited for the benefit of a particular if less obtrusive group.

The leaders of Mark's church seem to have referred to themselves, by a play on words which Greek makes possible, as 'servants' or 'children'. Significantly, they enjoy an unqualified identity with Jesus that is never granted to the Twelve. For instance, while the latter speculate about their relative prestige, Jesus replies: '"If anyone wants to be first, he must make himself last of all and servant of all." Then he took a child, set him in front of them, and put his arm round him. "Whoever receives one of these children in my name", he said, "receives me; and whoever receives me, receives not me, but the One who sent me"' (9.35–37). The significance of this text for understanding the community in which Mark was written cannot be overestimated. The authority of the child and servant is thus set over the Twelve, and given the highest possible importance. The assertion of claims to leadership by deceptively modest rhetoric has already been discerned in Paul, the slave of Christ Jesus (Rom. 1.1). and is developed most elaborately in the letter to the Colossians (cf. pp. 126f.). The awareness that 'the children' of Mark's Gospel are not necessarily the sentimental creatures of Margaret Tarrant's art makes intelligible the jealousy of the disciples for such privileged beings.

Mark shows the two groups in conflict with each other, and portrays Jesus as unequivocally on the side of the children: 'They brought children for him to touch. The disciples rebuked them, but when Jesus saw this he was indignant, and said to them, "Let the children come to me; do not try to stop them; for the kingdom of God belongs to such as these. I tell you, whoever does not accept the kingdom of God like a child will never enter it." And he put his arms round them, laid his hands upon them, and blessed them' (10.38–41). The community of the children is here equated with the kingdom of God; only children may enter it, and it is by no means clear whether the Twelve qualify. We can see the criticism in Mark's community of the claims to dominance put forward by the Twelve or their successors most forcefully stated after the abortive request of James and John for promotion: 'Jesus called to them and said, "You know that in the world the recognized rulers lord it over their subjects, and their great men make them feel the weight of authority. That is not the way with you; among you, whoever wants to be great must be your servant, and whoever wants to be first must be the willing slave of all. For even the Son of Man did not come to be served but to serve, and to give up his life as a ransom for many"' (10.42–45). Here the claims to primacy of the Twelve, which Paul half accepts even in Galatians, are specifically denied by Jesus; instead he establishes the position, not of the Twelve, but of the servants. In those words the leadership of Mark's own church would have heard a reassuring reference to themselves. In the same way the closing words of the apocalypse describe very clearly the structure of authority, which governed Mark's church: 'It is like a man away from home: he has left his house and put his servants in charge, each with his own work to do, and he has ordered the door-keeper to stay awake' (13.34). Jesus, the absent source of authority, is represented by servants, to whom he has delegated his power.

The equivocation between the humility of the designation 'servant' and the assertion of authority is here quite explicit. Moreover 'the servant' establishes his credentials by 'staying awake', which interweaves anxiety about the end with perseverance in prayer. It is a telling profile of ecclesiastical prestige.

When therefore Mark tells the story of the unauthorized exorcist, we should not rush to the conclusion that this represents a generous disclaimer of monopoly powers; it is most probably self-defence. John's words, 'Master, we saw a man driving out devils in your name, and as he was not one of us, we tried to stop him' (9.38) may well describe how the Twelve regarded the leadership of Mark's community: unauthorized, not properly belonging, to be opposed. Jesus' reply which appears simply permissive may actually be legitimating: 'Do not stop him; no one who does a work of divine power in my name will be able the next moment to speak evil of me. For he who is not against us is on our side' (9.39f.). If this understanding of Mark is correct, then like Paul he is writing to justify an identity and authority which was suspect in the eyes of other Christian leaders. His position is not derived from the Twelve, but in tension to them. His is the church of the children, the servants who establish their position by their manifest poverty and unrelenting prayer, and who prove their credentials by their exorcisms. We now see why Mark responds so bitterly to the suggestion of the lawyers that Satan can cast out Satan. It is not simply Jesus' *bona fides* which are thus placed in doubt, but their own.

If this reading of Mark is correct, then it sheds light on the treatment of the resurrection and the shape of the original Gospel. The Pauline emphasis on cross and resurrection would lead us to expect that any Gospel would contain a very strong section on the resurrection of Jesus, detailing his appearances and actions, but surprisingly the Gospel text originally ended at 16.8, though quite possibly that end was not intended. Yet the resurrection of Jesus is important to Mark: so for instance on two occasions he takes care to explain that healing miracles do not themselves anticipate the resurrection. When the report is given that Jairus' daughter is dead, Jesus replies: 'The child is not dead: she is asleep' (5.39). The demoniac boy only 'looked like a corpse; in fact, many said, "He is dead". But Jesus took his hand and raised him to his feet, and he stood up' (9.27). Moreover Mark ascribes to Jesus teaching which defends the concept of resurrection. He attacks the Sadducees for knowing neither the Scriptures nor the power of God on this matter (12.18–25), and then cites Exodus (3.6) as evidence. Like all other New Testament writers, Mark must have a resurrection to make possible the reward which he both offers and seeks: 'in the age to come to eternal life' (10.30). It might therefore seem that the shape of the Gospel as it stands must represent an accidental truncation; if, however, the interpretation of Mark as containing a sustained polemic against the Twelve is correct, then the present shape of the Gospel becomes intelligible. It may not actually have ended with v. 8 as it stands, but it may well be that the original ending added very little further material.

For as the Gospel stands, it perfectly fits Mark's satire of the Twelve in general and Peter in particular. Jesus repeatedly prophesies not only his death but also his resurrection (8.32; 9.31; 10.34), which serves to underline the incredulity and lack of understanding of the Twelve. Even after the transfiguration, Peter and Andrew, James and John cannot grasp what Jesus is talking about: 'On their way down the mountain, he enjoined them not to tell anyone what they had seen until the Son of Man had risen from the dead. They seized upon those words, and discussed among themselves what this "rising from the dead" could mean' (9.9f.). This suggests that for Mark the resurrection did not give the Twelve any new authority as its witnesses, but merely overcame their stupidity and at last enlightened them as to what Jesus had continually been telling them. At the last supper Jesus first prophesies the desertion of the Twelve and then speaks of his resurrection: 'Nevertheless, after I am raised again I will go on before you into Galilee' (14.28). This last prophecy is associated by its context with the general desertion of the Twelve and the particular treachery of Peter. The message of the youth at the tomb therefore has a sting in the tail: 'Fear nothing; you are looking for Jesus of Nazareth, who was crucified. He has been raised again; he is not here; look, there is the place where they laid him. But go and give this message to his disciples and Peter: "He is going on before you into Galilee; there you will see him, as he told you"' (16.6f.). The reference to the prophecy at the last supper is explicit, and represents a final rebuke to the Peter to whom it is specifically addressed. It is not unfitting for this reading of the Gospel that its last words should be directed against one whom many regarded as the first of the apostles. Moreover, by ending on a note which reminds the reader of the blindness and unreliability of the Twelve, Mark avoids any rehabilitation of Peter and the Twelve. Far from the resurrection vesting them with unique authority in the church, it simply proves them wrong: Christ rises, so to speak, to spite them.

The theology of the longer ending of the Gospel (16.9–20) suggests that very early the church perceived the deficiencies of Mark's Gospel in the way that has been indicated. A mind brought up with either a Pauline insistence on resurrection or a sceptical historian's doubt of that event would expect the conclusion to remedy the omission of the resurrection appearances. Instead it has only a brief summary of appearances to Mary of Magdala and to two of his followers reminiscent of Luke's story of the road to Emmaus. Both incidents are received with disbelief by the others. Thus when Jesus appears to the Eleven it is first to reproach them 'for their incredulity and dullness' (16.14). That aspect of the summary seems entirely in character with Mark's own interests; however, the weight of the longer ending is not in the resurrection appearances but in the final commission and endorsement of the Twelve: 'Then he said to them: "Go forth to every part of the world, and proclaim the Good News to the whole creation. Those who believe it and receive baptism will find salvation; those who do not believe will be condemned. Faith will bring with it these miracles: believers will cast out devils in my name and speak in strange tongues; if they handle snakes or drink any deadly poison, they will come to no harm; and the sick on whom they lay their hands will recover." So after talking with them the Lord Jesus was taken up into heaven, and he took his seat at the right hand of God; but they went out to make their proclamation everywhere, and the Lord worked with them and confirmed their words by the miracles that followed' (16.15–20). It is exactly the viewpoint of which Luke/Acts has been successful propagandist; it also supplies a point which Mark himself fails to make. The Twelve are rehabilitated and explicitly authorized. If this reading of Mark is correct, that is not simply supplying a deficiency, but contradicting his intention. This is made more plausible by the length and explicitness of the commission.

(c) The servants use of their authority

The liberating message of forgiveness, mutually practised and received; the repudiation of religious visibility and the social control it made possible; the exercise of freedom in the face of repressive religious authority; identification with the victims of hierarchy expressed ultimately in crucifixion – all these themes are present in Mark, and give to his account of the gospel a force and credibility that Paul seldom achieves. It is tempting to leave the matter on that high note, but that would represent a failure of critical rigour. For Mark's Gospel is to a considerable degree in the grip of the same contradictions that mar Paul's letters. Behind the celebration of freedom and peace there plays a sinister counterpoint, which we fail to discern at our peril. For unless it is recognized and checked it will distort the impact of the Gospel, as surely as Paul's emphasis on his apostolate.

This is not to say that the servants themselves do not represent a spectacular reversal of dominance: 'You know that in the world the recognized rulers lord it over their subjects, and their great men make them feel the weight of authority' (10.42). To detect in those words an element of self-affirmation against the claims of the Twelve is in no way to diminish their liberating significance – it merely defines their cutting edge. Moreover, the servants who directed such words against the Twelve seem to have moderated their own stance in order to make it plausible. There is a relative absence of the attempt to specify behaviour which is so character-istic of Paul's writing, and to that extent Mark represents a more chastened and limited style of Christian leadership. It is noticeable that the idea of the Lordship of Jesus which is so intimately associated with the self-assertion of the apostle is only muted in the original text of Mark's Gospel (1.3; 2.28; 7.28; 10.51; 11.3; 12.36; 13.35) The style of leadership is not, however, entirely different. The powers of exorcism and healing establish a starkly non-reciprocal relationship. As was indicated in the chapter on the power of Jesus, the emphasis on faith is designed to control the reader; it does little to mitigate the disequilibrium of the relation between the healer and the sick. While doctors, as Mark reminds us (5.26), live off their fees, no such transactions compromise Jesus' sovereign independence. It is a trait of religious leaders to be more obviously concerned with power and prestige than with profit; not that this is necessarily disinterested, because in so far as they achieve the former goals they will also secure the latter.

In Paul's letters we discerned a continuous financial sub-plot. If Mark does not contain the detailed financial concerns and directives of the Pauline letters, that is because his leaders are less ambitious in their undertakings. Yet the insistence on renouncing wealth which distin-guished its leaders both secured considerable funds and also reinforced their exactions from the faithful; for total dependence creates an unanswerable claim to support. Not surprisingly, religious giving is strongly encouraged: the extravagance of the widow's mite (12.41–44) and of the anointing at Bethany (14.3–9) are unequivocally commended. The woman is assured that 'wherever in all the world the gospel is proclaimed, what she has done will be told as her memorial' (14.9). There will always be those for whom occasional spectacular generosity will be the most attractive form of religious observance. That such a response is so immoderately praised is doubtless a reflection of Mark's own dependence on the repetition of such behaviour. As in Paul's financial teaching, there are distinct incentives to generosity. The rich young man is offered the compensation of 'riches in heaven' (10.21), and the smallest donation is assured of its reward: 'I tell you this: if anyone gives you a cup of water to drink because you are followers of the Messiah, that man assuredly will not go unrewarded' (9.41). The financial profile of Mark's community is clear. On the one hand total renunciation of wealth by its leaders creates opportunities for attracting the poor; but the leaders then themselves become a charge on the community as a whole, with rights to support and hospitality which are sanctioned by promises of reward and threats of judgment (6.10f.). Jesus commandeers his transport to enter Jerusalem (11.1–10), and the arrangements for the large upstairs room to celebrate the Passover (14.12–16) doubtless reflect the kind of arrangements which the leaders of Mark's community might expect for their reception. The appropriate care of the 'servants' is a lesson the reader is not intended to overlook.

If the 'servants' of Mark's Gospel share something of Paul's character-istics, the community which they create is even more distressingly familiar. In the first place, it is, as we have seen (cf. pp. 190–194) identified by baptism and reinforced by persecution. In this respect it recalls Paul's letters to the Philippians (cf. pp. 54–58), the Colossians (cf. pp. 132–135) and the Romans (cf. pp. 158–161). As in Paul's letters to the Thessalonians (cf. pp. 33f.), the community is marked by eschatological anxiety (cf. pp. 38f.), and its alienation from surrounding society is expressed in a yearning for retribution (cf. p. 221), which is almost as powerful as the opening chapters of Romans (cf. p. 223). The very effectiveness of the community in redistributing wealth to which the miracles of feeding point (cf. pp. 142–149) would have fostered a tightly-knit group, held together by mutual benefit and aware of quite tangible advantages from their association which distinguished them from other people. Moreover, the stress on exorcism, which is so intrinsically dualistic in its understanding of man and society, has implications which are quite as divisive as Paul's gospel of salvation from wrath to come. Thus the peace of the gospel easily turns to threat, as Jesus makes clear in his instructions to the Twelve: '"When you are admitted to a house", he added, "stay there until you leave those parts. At any place where they will not receive you or listen to you, shake the dust off your feet as you leave, as a warning to them"' (6.10f.). The menace is no less effective for being vague: significantly it is designed not only to compel attention, but to extract hospitality.

(d) The understanding of dissent and rejection

The authority of the 'servants' and the character of the community they created are displayed as most destructive of autonomy in the response to criticism and disagreement which Mark's Gospel conveys. The predomi-nant dualism easily acquires a polemical character, discrediting criticism by identifying it with Satan (4.15; 8.33). The assertion of the miraculous from the first voice from heaven to the eventual resurrection serves to establish the unquestionable authority of the text and its author (see pp. 198f.). Similarly, the inculcation of faith (see pp. 213f.) encourages the uncritical response, as some of the teaching on prayer deliberately represses inner doubt (11.23). As in Paul (see pp. 94–99), the silencing of criticism is a tacit acknowledgment of the insecurity of the claims. There is also the same fear of revision: 'Take care that no one misleads you. Many will come claiming my name, and saying, "I am he"; and many will be misled by them' (13.5f.). It is exactly the same nervous tone we find in II Thessalonians (see cf. p. 36), Galatians (cf. see pp. 44, 47), Philippians (see p. 54) and I Corinthians (see pp. 66f.). As in Paul, the response which has already been obtained is used to prohibit any repetition of the process. It is in keeping with this distrust that Mark is ambivalent in his attitude to opposition. He loves to rehearse the wonder and surprise of the crowd, but only as it serves to enhance his message. He easily lapses into contempt for the audience if it fails to respond in the way which he desires. In the parable of the sower any failure of communication is entirely the fault of the soil; no sense of inadequacy clouds either the sower or the seed. Jesus utters the author's impatience: 'What an unbelieving and perverse generation! How long shall I be with you? How long must I endure you?' (9.19). This hardly builds up the self-esteem of the reader; nor does it foster respect for questioning voices. This element of contempt can easily develop into straightforward paranoia – the joyous expectation of persecution (see pp. 192f.).

All this culminates in deep inconsistencies of attitude towards the death of Jesus. At a narrative level Mark succeeds in giving a compelling explanation and account of that death. It is portrayed as the outcome of a long struggle with hostile religious authorities in which it is both the price of Jesus' own freedom and the measure of his identification with the victims of Jewish society. Moreover, as the examination of prayer suggested, there are features which recognize an element of divine constraint in such a situation (see pp. 214f.). This is most eloquently expressed in Jesus' entirely accepting attitude towards his death: 'He began to teach them that the Son of Man had to undergo great sufferings, and to be rejected by the elders, chief priests, and doctors of the law' (8.31). It is a measure of the dramatic genius of Mark that the reader readily acquiesces in that enigmatic 'must'. Quite apart from any theory of atonement, the story has created and communicated its own necessity. Yet it has to be acknowledged that the author seems curiously embarrassed by his own success. The prophecies of Jesus' death which begin with the words, 'the bridegroom will be taken away from them' (2.20), and proceed through the prophecies of the passion to the parable of the wicked husbandmen, the anointing at Bethany (14.8) and the words of the last supper (14.22f.), not only convey the calm acceptance of his death by Jesus, they also reconcile the reader to the eventual outcome. It is the same device that Paul uses in I Thessalonians (see p. 29), through which adversity is disarmed by foresight. Similarly Mark reiterates Paul's equivocations (see pp. 38f., 147f.), needing to assert both the sovereign responsibility of God and also the culpability of man. Thus Mark ascribes Jesus' death to divine destiny appointed by Scripture (9.12; 12.10f.; 14.21); but Judas' inexplicable treachery is still worthy of punishment: 'The Son of Man is going the way appointed for him in the Scriptures; but alas for that man by whom the Son of Man is betrayed! It would be better for that man if he had never been born' (14.21). Mark's incoherence at this point is identical to Paul's, so that Judas' action is described and judged, but cannot be understood. While the opposition of the Jewish authorities, however reprehensible, is quite intelligible, Judas remains beyond analysis or redemption.

The final sign that Mark remains unreconciled to his own account of Jesus' death is, of course, his insistence on its reversal by resurrection. Every prophecy of the passion is countered by the promise of resurrection (8.31; 9.9, 31; 10.34; 14.28), and it is with the assurance that Jesus' death has been reversed that the Gospel ends. Like Paul (see pp. 94–99), Mark is impelled to invoke the illusory in a vain attempt to mitigate the stark finality of Jesus' death. It has long been pointed out that the addition of the resurrection to the prophecies of the passion renders them innocuous, and makes the horror with which they were greeted incomprehensible. It is equally striking that apart from the brief controversy with the Sadducees (12.18–25), which has no prior preparation in the Gospel, the reversal of death plays little part in the teaching ascribed to Jesus in the Gospel narrative. Unlike the benefits of exorcism, healing and forgiveness, which are grounded in his life and teaching, this most spectacular of promises has all the appearance of an after-thought, grafted on to a life which neither anticipated it nor requires it. Such an improbable event could only be affirmed if one first attributed a privileged status to the evidence for it. It functions, therefore, as a covert elevation of the witnesses, and once assent has been given to such a position, no further criticism is possible. It is also a sad testimony to the inability of Jesus' followers, in contrast to their Master, to acknowledge and adjust to reality. Christians will continue to pay a heavy price in terms both of arbitrary authority and of inner anxiety until we have the rigour to acknowledge that positions of privileged epistemology are indefensible, and the courage to affirm the truth.

CONCLUSION

COUNTING THE COST

'He who begins by loving Christianity better than truth, will proceed by loving his own sect or church better than Christianity, and end in loving himself better than all,' said Coleridge.

> Quoted by Tolstoy in his reply to the Holy Synod's Edict of Excommunication.

(a) Towards a new approach to Scripture

This has been a limited study of the New Testament, confined to the letters of Paul and the Gospel of Mark. There is therefore some danger of coming to a premature conclusion on a partial view of the material. These texts are, however, the earliest Christian documents, and though a more extended survey would yield many surprises the overall impression would probably be little different. The rehabilitation of Peter in Matthew and the harmonizing account of Paul's relation to Peter in Luke/Acts are familiar topics seen, so to speak, in reverse. The stress on the role of the Spirit in Acts supplements the picture of charismatic leadership in I Corinthians and Romans, but it does not substantially modify it. The august language of the letter to the Hebrews probably contains the most significant omissions from this study – the challenge of the angels, the prestige of the priesthood, the play of shadow and reality. By contrast it is astonishing to find how many of the Pauline accents are echoed by the ecstatic prophet who wrote John's Gospel. There is the same confusion of identity between the writer and Christ, the same concern to assert an authority which transcends human accountability, a commitment to a dualistic anthropology and a deeply divisive attitude towards society. It would have been much more difficult to end this study on a constructive note if 'the spiritual gospel' had provided its climax, for John is vulnerable to nearly every criticism which has been directed at Paul. The two may appear very different in style, but in strategy they are astonishingly alike.

The purpose of this study has not been to provide a comprehensive

survey of the New Testament but to suggest, and I hope to vindicate, a new
approach to scripture, by asking a rather different set of questions from
those which have recently dominated New Testament study. Few things
are more depressing in teaching theology than the observation that even
those who enjoy the disciplines of scriptural criticism often lose any
appetite to read the texts by the time they have concluded their course.
Historical criticism has not necessarily destroyed their faith, but it does
seem to rob the texts of their holiness, their fascination, their power to
surprise and to sustain attention and love. In the religious imaginations of
the theologically educated the scriptures seem to have been replaced by
music, by later Christian writing, and by an emphasis on the eucharist
associated with the liturgical movement; indeed the popularity of the latter
in Protestant churches owes much to the confusion about scripture from
which their ministers suffer.

The rise of historical criticism has created not one, but three approaches
to the Bible: the radicals adopt a sceptical agnosticism, the conservatives
are driven to reactionary assertion, and the moderates attempt an
academic restatement. Most of the hostile criticism of New Testament
scholarship is directed at its allegedly destructive impact, for such writers
as Dennis Nineham, James Barr and some of the contributors to *The Myth
of God Incarnate* have been deeply subversive of traditional certainty. The
texts have been relativized and deprived of their mystique and authority.
Historical inquiry demands an open-mindedness and tentativeness which
sits ill with dogma. In that sense the historian has been far more disturbing
to Christianity than the scientist. Scepticism is not, however, the only child
of historical criticism: the conservative reaffirmation which marks Protestant fundamentalism and that ambiguous phenomenon in Roman Catholicism described as 'Biblical Renewal' are quite as much the outcome of
historical study as their sceptical and agnostic counterparts. The defensive
assertiveness, the distrust of reason, the increasingly shrill claims for the
authority of scripture itself are not simply the product of some Protestant
principle of *sola scriptura*; they are the fearful attempt to guard an
inherited position from a new enemy. Conservatives have the vast weight
of the Christian historical consensus on their side when they embrace the
inerrancy of scripture; liberals who overlook that are being evasive. But
the inflexibility and the self-consciousness are new, and can only be
understood as the creation of that very influence which they most bitterly
decry. It is the same paradox which must ascribe modern conservatism to
the impact of the French Revolution.

Those schooled by the Church of England and the BBC might well
suppose that truth lay somewhere in the middle, and the cause of academic

restatement is by no means dead. In Germany it has produced the New Quest for the historical Jesus; in England it has tempered scepticism, and produced the optimistic restatements of C. H. Dodd and John Austin Baker. It is a tendency which has received considerable new strength from the fresh awareness of the Jewish background of Jesus. Judicious, liberal and reasonable, it is understandably a little complacent about its qualities. Eschewing extremes in either direction, it is perhaps a peculiarly English theological approach. It is the outcome that Anglican bishops hope for in their ordinands; it is bracing in some of the readjustments it demands and is considered the path of intellectual honesty. Yet the God of truth is expected to see that orthodoxy comes out on top in the end. Attractive as this approach may be, it gives insufficient attention to the criticism of its competitors. The conservatives rightly detect a certain coldness, an inability to motivate, a compromising of authority which is inherently unstable. It will either lapse into unbelief, or ultimately settle for conformity rather than honesty. The radicals suspect it of timidity, and a refusal to face the implications of its own insights.

This has created a heritage of mutual recrimination. The sceptical agnostic rejoices in his own honesty and courage, and despises the conservatives because they lack the one and the moderates because they lack the other. The Christian world, outside their slender but enlightened ranks, appears obscurantist; if they are isolated within the church, it is often because they are comfortably insulated by university appointments. The conservatives see the sceptics as traitors, undermining the faith from within, and the moderates as fellow-travellers who cannot be trusted. The moderates tend to complain that the church suffers from a lack of theological education, and see the answer in study courses and adult instruction. Both conservatives and moderates complain of the isolation of the theologians from the church. The conservatives complain that they are destructive and sheltered and should be more subject to ecclesiastical discipline. The moderates are slightly hurt that the church seems to go on its way without giving them quite the attention which they feel they deserve. They are acutely embarrassed by the attitudes of the conservatives who are impatient of their cautious qualifications, and of the sceptics who tend to give their own position a bad name.

This mutual recrimination stretches across most religious denominations, but it is not the only destructive consequence of historical criticism: the very accessibility of scripture has been threatened. It was no accident that the Protestant reformation coincided with a technology which for the first time made the Bible widely available, and clergy and laity were united in a common conviction of inerrancy, so that the Bible was intellectually accessible to all. It might need the authority of the church for its true interpretation and understanding. It might require the intervention of the Holy Spirit to be effective for salvation in the heart of the believer; but the scriptures were fundamentally accessible to all on the same terms. Prayer and a holy life might be preconditions for reading the Bible. At most a knowledge of the sacred languages might be a proper distinction for the clergy; but the Bible of Protestants possessed power precisely because it was available to everyman. Historical criticism has meant that the Bible of scholars is no longer available to the ordinary believer, in a way that modern translations cannot overcome. He feels himself to be at a disadvantage. He knows that he has not had the opportunity to study, or to work out his beliefs. For most people it is not the distance of time which separates them from the New Testament; indeed, once equipped with fundamentalist preconceptions, modern man has very little difficulty in immersing himself in that first-century world and finding all the relevance he needs. The distance comes from a puzzled awareness that to understand the Bible properly far more knowledge is necessary than is at his disposal. Once he has digested the shock that Paul did not necessarily write all the letters attributed to him, or that the historical Jesus and the Jesus of the Johannine Gospel may not have spoken with the same voice, his confidence in his ability to assess and interpret the text has been decisively undermined.

Amongst the radicals and the moderates scripture has become the preserve of a small theologically educated élite, almost invariably clerical, and the very isolation of the texts from most believers has made them weaker and less interesting. Where clergy and laity still maintain a common attitude to scripture, as in fundamentalist Christianity, a very self-conscious attitude towards the Bible has to be adopted before it can be approached 'safely'. Scripture is then accessible to the uneducated, but demands that they remain uneducated if it is to remain accessible to them. In practical terms, the study of the Bible among Christians has become extremely difficult. The introduction of historical criticism will wrong-foot those who are not versed in it, limiting them to a passive or at best a questioning role, but depriving them of any confidence in their own judgment. The presence of fundamentalists will ensure that discussion is focused on the appropriateness of their particular attitude to scripture. Not surprisingly, there is a strong temptation to reserve the Bible for formal liturgical occasions, and to direct individual piety to spirituality or social action. It is not an atmosphere conducive to the study of scripture.

An equally damaging consequence of the historical approach is that the holiness of scripture has become equivocal. The book has lost its mystique.

More prosaically, it fails to excite. The dutiful repetition of the response, 'This is the word of the Lord . . . Thanks be to God', at the end of scripture readings in church will not rehabilitate the divine quality of the texts. It is depressing that the church has responded to uncertainty about the authority of scripture, not by argument or by supplementing it with other writing, but by mere reassertion. For the radical who remains a Christian, the vacuum may be filled by spirituality or the liturgy. For the moderate, scripture will still possess, rightly understood, the value of being the unique historical evidence for the life of Jesus; but the irreplaceability of historical evidence is different from a holy text. In practice the moderate has tended to find refuge from the bleakness of his scriptural position in the certainties of the dogmatic tradition, which is why Maurice Wiles' criticism of doctrinal fundamentalism is both so apt and so devastating. At first sight the conservatives might still seem to possess a holy Bible, but the appearance is misleading. Their interpretation is too wooden, too bound and prescribed by their own carefully adopted presuppositions, to have any convincing surprise or vitality. Indeed they do the ultimate injury to scripture by depriving it of any power to change their minds. Reading scripture becomes no longer an act of discovery, but a repetition of the familiar, which evades any change of mind or heart. For the fundamentalist, scripture has become an instrument of the believer's obstinacy, and the price has been well described by Tolstoy:

> Having acknowledged it all as sacred truth, it was necessary to justify everything, to shut one's eyes, to hide, to manipulate, to fall into contradictions, and, alas, often to say what was not true ('An Examination of the Gospels' in *A Confession*, The World's Classics, p. 105).

It must be pointed out that radical, conservative and moderate have all shared a common commitment to Christianity as an 'historical religion'. Modern theology has been preoccupied with the idea of revelation, seeing in this the distinctiveness of Christianity and the crux of all its dogmatic claims. The unique significance ascribed to Jesus in the doctrinal tradition has concentrated Christian anxiety about its own viability on its basis in the New Testament. The symbiotic relationship between the truth of the New Testament and the future of orthodoxy has been obvious in many forms since the eighteenth-century argument for the truth of Christianity from the evidence of miracles. The doctrinal claim of Christ's historical uniqueness inevitably made Christians anxious about the evidence for its basis and content. With increasing urgency Christians asked what historical events could vindicate the metaphysical uniqueness of Christ, tending to place ever greater weight on the resurrection. The result was that the poverty of the factual basis for such claims only became more obvious. The outcome of the exercise is that the doctrinal convictions which gave rise to the historical quest and contributed such urgency to its conclusions have themselves now been discredited. It has therefore to be pointed out firmly that the preoccupation with history was not simply scientific. It was the consequence of particular doctrinal commitments which it has been unable to sustain. In some sense, therefore, the whole 'historical' preoccupation of modern theology has proved a mistake. This does not mean that we must jettison the historical method, but that we can afford a new detachment towards historical conclusions.

In suggesting an alternative approach to the Bible my first concern has been to give a rather different account of its holiness: its distinctively religious quality. With Tolstoy,

> I do not regard the Gospels as sacred books that have down to us from the Holy Ghost, even less do I regard them as mere historical monuments of religious literature. ('The Gospels in Brief' in *A Confession*, p. 122).

The books of the New Testament deserve our attention, not because they are inerrant or because they are a unique historical record, but because they have proved to be books of immense power. Only the writings of Mohammed and Marx can be compared in their social, personal and imaginative impact. The New Testament has exercised power over human life and society for an unparalleled period of time, and in a bewildering variety of cultures. This power is not therefore incidental, or something which follows as a conclusion from doctrinal premises. It is its substance; it is what distinguishes a holy book from ordinary literature. Traditionally, however, this power has been envisaged in terms of unchanging authority. The crucial difference, which I am advocating, is that holiness is not a matter of submission to authority, but of exercising freedom. The authoritarian note in scripture, which cannot be ignored, is only a foil to the invitation to freedom, which is its substance.

From this I have argued that Christians should jettison any attempt to rehabilitate traditional christology in reading scripture. There are two reasons for this. In the first place, traditional accounts of the unique significance of Jesus can only be substantiated by conceding to the text a special status, which is inimical to human freedom. Secondly, it gives to historical reconstruction a self-destructive significance. On the one hand historical method is intrinsically hostile to claims of metaphysical uniqueness, while such claims give to historical considerations a distinctive urgency. For if Christ is indeed unique, then it matters profoundly that we are able to distinguish his life and teaching accurately, for no substitute will be adequate. If freedom is our first principle, then it is with claims of salvation that we must be primarily concerned when we read the Bible as Christians. To repeat words from the first chapter: 'It is enough that the reader admits the possibility of human freedom and of reconciliation between men, and does not regard those possibilities as mutually incompatible' (cf. p. 13). Such a concern demands a much more active reading. The text is no short cut; it is neither infallible itself, nor a witness to an infallible person. As long as the concern was with the person and significance of Jesus, the text might represent an objective truth which the reader has only passively to acknowledge. Salvation as the possibility of freedom and peace has not only to be acknowledged, it has also to be grasped and practised by the reader. The text only helps to create possibilities; it is for the reader to realize them in life. Precisely because the New Testament only creates possibilities, it does not convey benefits. The only privilege it bestows is the opportunity to exercise our freedom and to achieve our peace. At most the Gospels represent a particular initiative in the achievement of continuing human goals. They are no substitute for our achievement, but a liberating reminder of what is possible.

To turn from anxiety about the status of Christ to this search for salvation opens the way to the most rigorous rational, historical and moral criticism of the text, because we are no longer trying to rehabilitate by critical means privileged structures which are incompatible with them. Readers of this book are most likely to complain of the ruthlessness of the criticism which such an approach makes possible. I have not shirked from pointing to incoherences of argument, to fantasy, manipulation and illusion in the texts. Moreover, I have insisted that the reader should have the confidence of his own moral judgment, and have not hesitated to convey a direct emotional response, not only to the writing of Paul, but also to the teaching ascribed to Jesus. If sometimes I have used rather violent adjectives, it is because too often the appropriate emotional response to the text has been inhibited by its religious prestige. The irreverence has been a deliberate attempt to remove distorting varnish. For unless some immediate emotional response to the text is permitted, one ends by adopting the moral viewpoint of the author without question. So often in the past the reading of scripture has been an exercise in conformity and the evasion of responsibility. As long as it is associated with some kind of infallible speaker, the reader is being invited to silence his own judgment and adopt a superior position. Inevitably the approach I have followed is subjective, but it has the virtue that it takes full responsibility for its judgments and encourages others to do the same. If it seems too subjective, that is most safely qualified, not by repudiating responsibility for our own moral judgment, but by insisting that it is subjected to the discipline of public communication and debate.

This encouragement of rigorous criticism of the Bible, and its extension beyond matters of historical fact to include the examination of the accompanying moral attitudes, is primarily designed to restore the Bible to the reader, and to rescue it from control by scholars. In this respect I see little difference between the confusing reconstructions of historical speculation and the contorted theological fabrications of fundamentalists. So long as the reader is expected to arrive at some prejudged conclusion, he will stand in awe of his guide, be he critical historian or conservative preacher. The benefit of reading scripture does not lie in arriving at a particular set of conclusions, but in the nature of the exercise. It is the stimulus to use our minds, to trust our judgment, to respond with our own emotions and moral vision. In that exercise and in no other way scripture conveys its benefit to the reader. Like the riddle of the Zen master its value lies not in possessing one privileged meaning, but in wrestling with its perplexities. The disciple has no other reward apart from the struggle. What matters in religion is not the knowledge of any particular truth, but the process of learning. In searching the scriptures for what sustains freedom and promotes peace, we begin to realize that for which we seek.

(b) *Where does this leave the truth of Christianity?*

In the preface I tried to place this book in the religious tradition to which it belongs. Its implications are uncomfortable for most of the dominant schools of modern theology. I have tried to write a genuinely evangelical theology, which makes a concern for the gospel the key to the scriptures. I do not, however, believe that this can be done unless evangelical Christianity itself is prepared to practise repentance, and that is costly because repentance for Christians demands the revision of beliefs, not merely their reiteration. In the stress on reconciliation I have tried to do justice to the catholic dimension of Christianity, but I have to admit that I regard the universal claims of the Roman church as aggressive imperial-ism. It will be a tragedy if all the search for renewal only leads to a new self-assertion. By sympathy I am closest to the liberal and latitudinarian traditions of English theology, but I recognize that often these have been too complacent about the implications of their own criticisms. A liberal method is incompatible with the preservation of privileged structures either in doctrine or in society. Perhaps this will be most easily perceived as a contribution to the fashionable theology of liberation; but if that is the case, it must also be a warning of the difficulty of that enterprise. It will certainly give little comfort to the recent tendency to invoke the foolishness of God to vindicate the silliness of clergymen.

To some readers this will appear not merely a subversive gospel, but a subversion of the gospel. They are likely to be especially impatient with me for refusing to raise the question of the truth of Christianity. Surely, it might be argued, if Paul did in fact receive a commission from the risen Christ, if Jesus really is Lord, if the Thessalonians actually were fornicating, if the miracles of Mark's Gospel did take place, then the stance that I have adopted has simply refused to take seriously the claims it pretends to be examining. Do not such claims demand an examination of their truth? Have I not consistently betrayed a closed mind on this vital issue? The refusal has been deliberate, and rests on two grounds. The first is a moral objection, that the possession of the truth provides no justification for either the arbitrary and oppressive use of authority or the encouragement of divisive social attitudes. I regard the force of that moral objection as very strong, but it is partly dependent on a view of the truth of Christianity which I have not so far fully articulated. Quite simply, every claim to truth which I have tacitly dismissed can only be established either by conceding a privileged status to a particular type of evidence, or by adopting uncritically the viewpoint of a certain social group. The whole weakness of traditional Christian teaching is that it rests on these two unsatisfactory foundations, which are of course in collusion with each other. On the one hand, acceptance of the special position of the Bible or the hierarchy defines the Christian community. On the other hand, the community insists on proclaiming as true propositions which it is claimed can only be properly understood and appreciated from within the group that is so defined. When, for instance, in the first volume of his *Systematic Theology*, Paul Tillich speaks complacently of 'the theological circle', and claims that 'every understanding of spiritual things is circular', he is making the most damning admission. For a truth which can only be affirmed by espousing the viewpoint of a particular community is necessarily socially divisive. Truth which is dependent on belonging to a group can only be defended by refusing all social assimilation.

I cannot conceal that many of the distinctive claims of Christianity are vulnerable to this criticism. This is particularly true of the miraculous and the dogmas of Jesus' divine nature and atoning work. At this stage I only want to draw attention to three kinds of concept which have been widely used in the Christian tradition and which I believe must be firmly repudiated. The first is paradox. Some striking examples of this were examined in the writings of Paul (cf. pp. 98, 102): Tertullian, Luther, and Kierkegaard have all given it a substantial role in their presentations of Christianity. It is a device which readily attracts attention, exciting by its contrasts and teasing in its incoherence. It is difficult, however, in Paul to regard it as anything other than a brilliant but empty piece of rhetoric, which only has one unambiguous function – to prohibit criticism. Very much the same has to be said about the invocation of mystery, not to justify silence, but to defend statements which are incoherent (cf. pp. 128f.). While Austen Farrer used to insist that we carefully distinguish between mystery and muddle, he would appear to have been too optimistic. The notion of a mystery which has been revealed and is now manifest is intelligible (cf. p. 255). Equally one might use the word to refer to the unutterable, which is otherwise respected by silence; but once confusing statements are accorded the status of mystery, all that is being acknowledged is the power of those who proclaim them to extort conformity from others. In view of the attention it has received in modern theology, perhaps my most damaging criticism is in respect of the term 'act of God'. Before writing this book I imagined that the fact that acts of God could only be acclaimed from within particular communities was regrettable but not otherwise significant. I would now argue that the very notion of an act of God is only intelligible in terms of the social identity and divisions that it articulates, which is why the impact of the critical historian has been so devastating. For it is one of the roles of the critical historian to scrutinize the traditions of a community, which inevitably reflect a partial viewpoint, by placing them in a wider social context. It is precisely this that distinguishes the critical historian from the purveyor of propaganda. To call an event 'an act of God', be it the Exodus, the resurrection, or the defeat of the Armada, is to indicate the importance of an event to a particular community and to affirm one's participation in that community. This consciousness of divine intervention on behalf of an individual or a society is nothing other than self-assertion over against other individuals or societies which have not been so significantly blessed. Such claims do not merely fail to overcome social alienation; they articulate and transmit it.

The first requirement for establishing the truth of Christianity is that it be presented in such a way that it does not demand the contradiction of truth established on other grounds. The truth of Christianity cannot therefore be established without an element of self-criticism on the part of the church as well as the individual. The believer has a responsibility for exercising his own critical judgment, and the church must exercise a similar self-criticism. All the criticisms of Christian doctrine which I have put forward are not designed to negate Christianity; instead they represent a contribution to that process of self-criticism – a necessary but constructive revision. For this examination of freedom and authority in the New Testament has ultimately an apologetic intention. Suspecting that traditional christology could not be convincingly rehabilitated, and that historical criticism would not establish but destroy it, I have tried to present a rather different account of Christianity which would do greater justice to its identity as gospel and might also be shown to be convincing. To insist that the truth of Christianity cannot be considered apart from the way in which it is used ultimately implies that the truth of Christianity can only be established in practice. In this account of Christianity you discover its truth not by believing it but by trying to practise it. Nevertheless, there is a necessary preliminary, and that is the examination of the way in which the religion has functioned in the past, and particularly the way in which it functions in its basic texts. I have used notions of freedom and reconciliation to define and clarify the understanding of salvation. In the first place they were derived negatively in response to the phenomena of Christian history, and to that extent they represent a criticism of the faith. But being a hopeful and believing person I trusted that ultimately they were values which had been derived from the Christian texts. I began by regarding that conviction as problematic: certainly the texts contained much that was oppressive and divisive, but they also provided the means of their own criticism. In that respect they represent a convincing initiative in the achievement of freedom and peace, and foster a similar achievement in their readers. That was the limit of my apologetic intention.

(c) Death: reversal or transcendence?

The most controversial modification of the traditional Christian picture put forward in this study is probably the positive repudiation of resurrection. For I am not merely advocating a spiritual reinterpretation of the belief as one possible approach to a difficult and perplexing subject. The examination of Paul's testimony to the resurrection (cf. p. 94) was painful to write, because if it is correct, its implications for the belief in the reversal of death are devastating. If it was only a matter of rehearsing Hume's familiar arguments on the improbability of miracles one might take refuge in a reverent agnosticism in which discreet silence demanded that the more exuberant beliefs of others went unchallenged. But to the intellectual difficulties of credibility I have added moral objections which do not leave open the path of quiet compromise. The Christian claim of resurrection is not harmless. It is intimately connected with the assertion of absolute authority by one group of human beings over another. Its basis in fantasy demands both the vigorous repression of doubt and the aggressive conversion of others. I am well aware that historically it is the reversal of physical death that Christianity has proclaimed, and many generations of believers have found courage in that message. Their ability to overcome the fear of death seems directly related to their belief that its power had been broken. One has only to read the letters of the early Christian martyr Ignatius to appreciate the strength which such a vision imparted:

> I am the wheat of God, and let me be ground by the teeth of the wild beasts, that I may be found the pure bread of Christ . . . When I suffer, I shall be the freedman of Jesus, and shall rise again emancipated in him. (*Epistle to the Romans*, iv).

Yet for all its heroism it is a vision founded in illusion and fantasy, and as the Pauline teaching shows so clearly, it produces as much anxiety as it allays, for it is dogged by the insecurity of its basis.

I do not underestimate the disturbing implications of this argument, for the pattern of cross and resurrection is not only central to the doctrine of Paul, it is one of the dominant symbols of the Christian imagination. There is, however, another reason why at least in its Pauline form this pattern has to be radically revised, for it gained its intellectual coherence from the alleged link between sin and death. So long as physical death could be seen as God's punishment of sinful mankind, the Pauline picture possessed immense psychological power. But to the historical doubts about the reality of Jesus' resurrection must be added the equally destructive awareness that physical death is an integral part of organic life, and long predates the appearance of man. Man did not introduce death into an uncorrupted world; he evolved in an environment in which death was a necessary part of its organic processes. The assertion of a link, therefore, between human sin and actual death cannot be true; and Paul's theology of cross and resurrection, the conquest of sin and death, is thus deprived of any coherence.

Without death there can be no life; we cannot glibly abstract death and regard it as a punishment imposed upon a living world to which it is alien. Nevertheless, any gospel which speaks of human freedom must take account of death, because it represents for us the ultimate constraint. Death cannot be a punishment for any human attitude or behaviour, though we can quite easily be persuaded to the contrary. Death has therefore no moral significance, nor can its reversal be interpreted as an appropriate sign of divine favour. But the fear of death has the most pervasive influence on all our adult actions. It lends an urgency to our selfishness and is a constituent of all our lust and greed. Anxiety that we have only one short life impels us to violence and is a major element in our unhappiness, so that human beings who are afraid of death are deprived by their fear of much of their freedom. Traditionally Christians have always asserted that this fear could only be overcome by their promise of reversal; but we have already noticed how small a part this promise plays in Mark's account of Jesus' life, and we have only to look around us to discover that there is no necessary relation between Christian conviction and indifference to death.

I look forward to a revision of Christianity which will no longer encourage men to make fragile and insecure affirmations that conceal our ignorance and often only mask our fear, but will instead celebrate the conquest not of physical death, but of the fear of death in life. The message may not immediately sound a Christian one, but if we listen to one of its great nineteenth-century exponents, there are surprising echoes of a familiar voice:

> Human beings have an instinctive passion to preserve anything they like. Man is born and therefore wishes to live for ever. Man falls in love and wishes to be loved, and loved for ever as in the very first moment of his avowal . . . but life . . . gives no guarantees . . . Every period is new, fresh, filled with its own hopes and carries within itself its own joys and sorrows. The present belongs to it. But human beings are not content with this, they must needs own the future too . . . What is the purpose of the song the singer sings? . . . If you look beyond your pleasure in it for something else, for some other goal, the moment will come when the singer stops and then you will only have memories and vain regrets . . . because, instead of listening, you were waiting for something else . . . You are confused by categories that are not fitted to catch the flow of life (Alexander Herzen, 'From the Other Shore').

In these words Herzen does perhaps more justice to the man who taught us to take no thought for the morrow and to consider the birds of the air than our churches which preach a future life in his name. Again it would seem that it is from Jesus that Herzen has acquired one of his most haunting images:

> We think that the purpose of the child is to grow up because it does grow up. But its purpose is to play, to enjoy itself, to be a child. If we merely look to the end of the process, the purpose of all life is death.

Victory over the fear of death is an intrinsic part of the Christian gospel: today it is not strengthened, it is only obscured, by the promise that death can be reversed.

(d) A God for whom we are responsible to each other

The demand for a change in Christian claims about death has been clear
and unmistakable, but this reading of Paul's letters and Mark's Gospel,
also suggests a much more pervasive change in my understanding of God.
The emphasis on the function of doctrines, on asking questions about the
use to which human beings are putting their religious claims and language,
makes possible a new understanding of the reality of God, modified and
more intelligible. For the logical consequence of this approach to scripture
is that the only reality of God lies in the use of that word by human beings.
It does not refer to some supernatural or mysterious or special being; it is
instead a word of the creative imagination by which we construct first in
imagination and ultimately in reality a new and different world. The only
significance of the word 'God' is its purely verbal function; that is not
necessarily disparaging, for its function is uniquely precious: it is an
integral part of human freedom, a means by which we transcend the
given and transform ourselves and the world.

All attempts to objectify God, to attribute to God an assured metaphysical reality, have therefore to be abandoned; and that for religious as well
as for philosophical reasons. The intellectual difficulties of such objecti-
fication are a commonplace of the modern philosophy of religion. The
religious objections are rather different, and lie in the acceptance and
evasion of responsibility. A God objectively or supernaturally conceived
connives too easily with our attempts to evade responsibility for our
constructions, which are thus removed from the possibility of criticism.
Moreover the unchanging metaphysical God, whose relationship to the
world is fundamentally non-reciprocal, has always been associated with
the construction and preservation of equally unbalanced social relationships. Tolstoy describes a vivid example of this process:

> As equality among men never has existed anywhere in actual life and
> does not now exist, it has happened that as soon as a new religious
> teaching appeared (always including a confession of equality among all
> men) then at once those people for whom inequality was profitable tried
> to hide this essential feature by perverting the teaching itself. This has
> always happened wherever a new religious teaching has appeared. And it
> has been done for the most part not consciously, but merely because those
> to whom inequality was profitable – the rulers and the rich – in order to
> feel themselves justified by the teaching without having to alter their
> position have tried by all means to attach to the religious teaching an

interpretation sanctioning inequality ('What is Religion?' in *On Life and Essays on Religion*, The World's Classics, p. 236).

The God implied by the gospel of the New Testament is necessarily a criticism of other possibilities. Such a God cannot simply sanctify the given and celebrate the world as it is, as the best possible world; for that God is quite redundant, just because he makes no difference. Indeed the only function of that God is to deter change; he is the classic ally of the privileged and powerful, for whom alone such a vision of reality is plausible. His praise represents the triumphant expression of their own power and dominance. By contrast, the God of the New Testament is abused the moment he is identified with human structures of authority and social control. Far from legitimating those structures, the Christian account of God emerged in bloody conflict with them. It is true that in the New Testament itself the process has begun by which Jesus merely sanctions one system of social control as opposed to another, but I hope I have convincingly demonstrated that that is a betrayal of the possibilities which the gospel creates, and to which the New Testament itself also witnesses.

The God of the gospel sustains human freedom first of all by providing a vocabulary which readily challenges all human structures of authority and control. This subversive character is not temporary and circumstantial, something which is relevant to one society but not to another; it is one of the intrinsically Christian uses of the word God. The appeal to God negates all existing human claims – it places them in question, and thus enables the individual to resist them. Secondly, it provides a language which enables human beings to transcend the given, to achieve imaginative detachment. Without such a possibility, the scientific description of reality will only reinforce present oppression and inequality. By contrast the language of religion facilitates the creative redescription of reality. Thirdly, this is no substitute for action, but a preparation for it. A religion confined to the imagination, be it the awareness of the mystic or the consciousness of grace, remains in the most negative sense unreal. Once the imagination has been detached from action, the way is open to religious fantasy and every kind of dishonest compensation. The God of the Christian gospel frees precisely because he calls to action. Objective benefits which are passively received easily rob their beneficaries of initiative. By contrast, the gifts of the Christian gospel are obtained only in use.

Such a God gives no sanction for a timid retreat into arbitrary and isolated subjectivity. The exercise of freedom is private in origin, but ultimately it is accessible and public. The believer in the Christian God must subject himself to the discipline of communication, which involves listening as well as speaking. The believer must therefore always be prepared to give reasons, to share his understanding, to listen to criticism and thus to achieve a greater intelligibility; for once he takes refuge in a believing circle his freedom is divisive and becomes an expression and instrument of alienation. The privileged proclamation of the pulpit is no satisfactory substitute for mutual discussion. The exercise of our freedom, which is also our discovery of the will of God, is necessarily co-operative with others. Ultimately, however, it is the need to exercise freedom in action which ensures that religion cannot be a matter of private fancy. The believer may challenge the world as he finds it, and use his imagination to construct a different world, but when he proceeds to act on that vision he cannot evade the recognition of constraint. The need for action ensures that beliefs about God are incarnated, and in that incarnation they are tested and explored. For the writers of the Gospels, the actual fate of Jesus in suffering and death was clearly intolerable; they could only affirm it if it was vindicated and reversed by a miraculous resurrection; but it is far from clear that Jesus himself shared their assessment of his freedom. By contrast he appears to have acknowledged and accepted the risks of his own action, and thus invites us to do the same.

We may use God to challenge other men and the world as we perceive it, but we cannot use the word to evade our ultimate engagement with them. God enables us to defy social constraint and to remould reality: he does not enable us to deny our dependence on others or to lie about what is true. A God who sustains our freedom is also a God for whom we have to recognize our responsibility. We have to acknowledge our creativity in his construction, and our responsibility to each other for the ways in which we invoke him.

(e) The plausibility of the church as a reconciling community

I have only begun to think through the implications of this study for the style and organization of a church. If many of the consequences seem critical or destructive of our present ecclesiastical arrangements, that is only because I place such crucial importance on the church. A gospel which proclaims reconciliation cannot be a matter of solitary, isolated achievement, however important the individual's role in the achievement and exercise of freedom may be. If it is to be plausible, it must be associated with a community which fosters such achievement; for wherever divided human beings have been reconciled, such a community must be the outcome. The reconciliation which Christians are invited to achieve has a distinctive openness to the outside world; it is travestied if it becomes a group of the like-minded huddling together for shelter and mutual comfort in a hostile world. On this view of the gospel the church is not a community which confers a privileged identity on its members. Its purpose is not to convey benefits to those who belong to it, but to function in such a way that all mankind is freed and reconciled. The universal dimension of the church is no justification for the aggressive imperialism of much mission- ary activity; it is a reminder not of the church's claims to the obedience of others, but of the church's dependence on the affirmation of others. Its credibility is entirely dependent on those who are outside it. What Christians say about themselves is mere self-assertion: it is in the verdict of those who are not Christians that the truth and effectiveness of the Christian faith is proved.

All this suggests a very specific function for the Christian community and only underlines its importance. Nevertheless, this examination of the New Testament, not to say some knowledge of church history, indicates that this is a very tender area of credibility. At all times Christian communities have exhibited markedly divisive traits. They have seldom been distinguished by their ability to associate with the surrounding world. They have also demonstrated a disconcerting inability to live with each other. This has led many Christians to make a heavy investment in the ecumenical enterprise, the attempt to express in practice the unity of which the church speaks. This has been the most distinctive aspect of Christianity in this century, and to some extent it is the ambiguous fruit of secularization. Flourishing and confident Christian organizations have usually found it more attractive to forget compromising competition: faced by indifference and uncertainty it is tempting to seek reassurance in the embrace of those we have learned to call 'the separated brethren'. The only danger in seeking reconciliation between Christians of different traditions is that we may forget that the gospel is not simply a call to live in harmony with each other; its goal is the peace of mankind. The crucial uncertainty which can only be resolved by practice and experience does not concern the relation between Christians of antagonistic traditions. It is over whether it is possible for a community to maintain an identity without aggression and self-assertion towards surrounding society. It is quite possible to envisage a successful outcome to the ecumenical endeavour which will only have created a more tightly organized and self-confident community, the better to do battle with the world. Such a church would only be a reconstruction of mediaeval Christendom; it would add nothing to the plausibility of the church as a reconciling community. For a unity of Christians which is achieved at the price of hostility to the world has not transcended our divided and conflicting life – it has merely redrawn the boundaries. Such fragile and antagonistic unity is no different from what we know already.

The most far-reaching implications of this study come from its understanding of forgiveness, and it is this which represents the most abrupt challenge to the stance of the churches. The existence of the church is not defined by its sacraments, or by an authorized ministry, or by doctrinal orthodoxy, but by the practice and exercise of forgiveness. Such a definition of the church must be disturbing, because it contrasts so sharply with the churches as they exist. This is not primarily because most churches place great emphasis on sacraments, ministry and doctrine. The real unease stems from the awareness that the churches seem much more successful in purveying guilt than in conveying forgiveness, and are so frequently identified with censorious and judgmental attitudes. This is particularly true of their impact on those who are outside them. This is not a matter which can be resolved by brighter packaging or greater personal sensitivity. The contradiction at the root of the church's difficulties can only be resolved by painful decisions. For the church which is entrusted with a message of forgiveness wishes at the same time to have the prestige which comes from being the guardian of an allegedly unchanging moral law. It is not possible for the same institution to perform convincingly both those functions, because the one is subversive of the other. Moreover because the message of forgiveness is always scandalous and brings its messengers into disrepute, the church in practice only retains the rhetoric of forgivenesss, while implementing a policy of conformity. No one has perceived this with greater clarity than William Blake in his poem, *The Garden of Love*,

> I went to the Garden of Love,
> And saw what I never had seen:
> A Chapel was built in the midst,
> Where I used to play on the green.
>
> And the gates of this Chapel were shut,
> And 'Thou shalt not' writ over the door;
> So I turn'd to the Garden of Love
> That so many sweet flowers bore;
>
> And I saw it was filled with graves,
> And tomb-stones where flowers should be;
> And Priests in black gowns were walking their rounds,
> And binding with briars my joys and desires.

His perception of the contradiction in the church's practice is matched by the power with which he communicates *The Everlasting Gospel*:

> It was when Jesus said to Me,
> 'Thy Sins are all forgiven thee.'
> The Christian trumpets loud proclaim
> Thro' all the World in Jesus' name
> Mutual forgiveness of each Vice,
> And oped the Gates of Paradise.
> The Moral Virtues in Great fear
> Formed the Cross and Nails and Spear,
> And the Accuser standing by
> Cried out, 'Crucify! Crucify!'

I doubt whether this account of the gospel will enable many readers whole-heartedly to endorse the denomination to which they belong; but the moral must be a more creative one than withdrawal. That would be as divisive as anything in a church from which one might wish to dissociate oneself. It would therefore be entirely self-defeating. I write as a member of the Church of England, and am aware that many of its aspects are quite incompatible with the gospel as it has been understood in this book. Very often, particularly in schools, the Christian message is totally identified with social conformity and control. Virtually every congregation is marked by a subtle interplay with a class structure which is more faithfully reflected by the church than effectively transformed by it. The hostility to foreigners and more recently to immigrants is something which the national constitution of the church directly re-inforces. The extent to which the prestige of the clergy is tied up with the preservation of buildings mirrors the relationship of the priesthood to the temple in Jerusalem. These are but a few respects in which the book invites critical reflection: to leave is too easy; by contrast change is tedious, painful and confusing. Paradoxically the merits of the Church of England are accidents of history. Its liberal tradition in theology was made possible by the weakness of its machinery of discipline. Its comprehensiveness owes as much to its endowments as to any native tolerance. If its hierarchy has been subjected to constitutional reform and limitation, that is not unconnected with its ramshackle mediaeval legal inheritance. Perversely it is the establishment which compels it to embrace the community, and the privileged connection with the state ensures that it cannot even use the sacrament of baptism in the effectively divisive manner that some of its purer members might wish. I find the Church of England by turns infuriating and endearing: it is a curious and local phenomenon, and few of its virtues travel. It cannot therefore plausibly claim to represent the church of the future.

The present impasse in ecumenical relations underlines the importance to those concerned of ecclesiastical structures. The suggestion which has recurred throughout this book, that christological claims are only disguised forms of clerical self-assertion, receives strong support from observing the fundamental and divisive impact of claims to authority on the relations between denominations. Thus even where they are largely agreed in terms of doctrine, they find it difficult to compromise their separate structural identity. This indicates an unmistakable and disturbing sense of priorities. It is therefore as well to remember that the achievement by Christians of reconciliation with one another is not primarily a reconciliation of clergymen, though it must eventually include them. Equally it is important that it is a peace which respects freedom. If Christian unity at the cost of social antagonism will have achieved nothing, neither will a realignment of clergy at the expense of lay freedom. Free churchmen have therefore some right to be cautious of the self-aggrandizement of the episcopate, and Anglicans would be wise to remember that behind the papal figurehead there works a formidable and largely unreconstructed bureaucracy. Laymen of all denominations might benefit if the ecumenical movement paid greater attention to the Religious Society of Friends, for it is perhaps the Quakers who represent the most straightforward path out of our difficulties. More than any other denomination they exemplify in their structures a critical and subversive understanding of the gospel: freedom from doctrinal preoccupations, an awareness of the divisive impact of sacramental practice, the fostering of mutual rather than hierarchical relations, and not least an absence of clergy. The question which that society addresses to the churches is in many respects the same as that asked by this book.

(f) A clergyman's vocation

I am conscious of having written with a certain sharpness and a strong use of anti-clerical salt. In part this reflects the tone of those lay theologians from whom I have learned most: Blake, Kierkegaard, Simone Weil and Tolstoy. It is not the most comfortable stance for a clerical writer, and it has only been reinforced by this study of the New Testament. For the conclusion is unavoidable that the failure of the church to reconcile is intimately connected with the desire of the clergy to domineer. Anti-clericalism is sometimes cheap. It is easy to compensate for one's own religious inadequacies by making impossible demands of others. Nevertheless it has often been salutary and not undeserved. For if Christian leaders have not positively created alienation to strengthen their position, they have certainly been in frequent collusion with it: using it to make their promises interesting and their discipline effective. As a clergyman, I have felt that this book has been like sawing off the branch on which I myself am sitting. It has not been an essay in satire, but in self-criticism. I have found many of its conclusions threatening.

It is therefore appropriate to write a few words about how I now see my own vocation. Fundamental to Christianity is a message of mutual forgiveness, of which every Christian is called to be an agent. In this respect the clergyman's power to forgive is no different from that of any other Christian. A clergyman's position is inevitably ambiguous, temporary, of its nature working towards its own redundancy: for his function is not to control but to free. The success of a clergyman lies not in the flattering dependence but in the autonomy of other believers, creating a community which is loving and affirmative. A clergyman has no monopoly of initiative, and it is important for the health of the community that he does not create a position where he has the power to inhibit the initiative of others. For the person who seeks to encourage initiative can subtly acquire the power to veto. Too often it is the only satisfaction that clergymen allow themselves – so that impotent to create, we compensate ourselves by saying no. In two respects, however, it is important that a clergyman has the authority to challenge the community he serves and represents. If clergy have a tendency to make themselves indispensable, communities are not without their own limitations of vision and sympathy. It is a natural tendency of all groups to reinforce their identity by exclusion and antipathy. It is a clergyman's particular responsibility to counter such developments by accepting responsibility for the extension of forgiveness and for association with the outsider. That is not to give him the authority to decide who should be forgiven and who belongs; it is to give him the rather ungrateful task of insisting on the forgiveness of the unpopular and the welcome of the unattractive. We will only be credible and effective in that role, however, if we can secure the consent and understanding of our communities. It is a dependence which successfully mitigates clerical arrogance.

I hope that this understanding of a clergyman's vocation is clear and also consistent with my account of the gospel. It does not, of course, immediately dispose of all the problems, for the traditions and expectations of the clergy reflect a very different understanding, from which no clergyman can entirely dissociate himself. A degree of embarrassment is therefore unavoidable, but the most damaging compromise is the extent to which every clergyman connives with strategies that are primarily concerned with the maintenance of his own prestige. This is seen most obviously, but also most innocently, in a preoccupation with church buildings. Its most sinister aspect is the encouragement in clergymen of deceit. For while clergy need forgiveness in exactly the same way as their congregations, so long as forgiveness is mediated by them, so long as the models of forgiveness are hierarchical rather than mutual, that need must be disguised. In a way which Christian doctrine finds difficult to admit, the plausibility of priestly absolution is maintained by the deceptive appearance of a clergyman who confers that of which he apparently stands in no need. This creates the paradox that the member of the community who calls others to honesty is himself in the most difficult position to practise it. This is not a harmless process, because it continually creates its own victims. Significantly, even when the Church of England no longer has the courage to discriminate against the divorced in general, it still needs to stigmatize divorce among the clergy. To be a clergyman is to collude with a system of clerical discipline which is in direct conflict with the gospel with which we are entrusted. That is a decision which must remain problematic.

(g) The Christian affirmation

The novelty of Christianity has continually to be rediscovered. Faith is not a matter of repeating the beliefs of others; that is only a recipe for reducing the gospel to boredom. Faith involves a careful listening to the past, and honest revision in the light of present experience. A clergyman can often avoid embarrassment by resorting to equivocation, which disguises the extent of change, but quickly robs Christianity of its content. I have done nothing to conceal the radical nature of the changes required if Christianity is to be honest with itself and to speak with conviction to the world beyond its boundaries. It would therefore be easy to extract from this book a series of spectacular denials, and represent them as the substance of the argument: one more stage in the erosion of such traditional beliefs as the incarnation or the physical resurrection of Jesus. It has not, however, been my intention to make another contribution to the pathology of Christianity. The denials are only necessary to clarify the affirmation. My purpose has been to draw attention to a message of forgiveness contained in the New Testament, and to explore its positive implications in terms of freedom and reconciliation. If I have neglected the metaphysical status of Jesus, that is because I regard it as a distracting speculation, which risks distorting the call to forgiveness. That call invites us to practise forgiveness, to learn to forgive, to acknowledge our own experience of being forgiven. If human happiness depends upon the opportunity to hear that message, it is necessary to question any belief which might obscure it, and to jettison any doctrinal commitment which might compromise it.

Today the affirmation of Christianity is greeted with widespread indifference, which makes it tempting to respond defensively by stressing the contrast between the church and the world, proclaiming a strict discipline and a clear identity. Secular indifference and religious sectarianism are not as opposed as their proponents believe. The different successes of both the repackaged papacy and of fundamentalist simplicity are no sign of a new age of faith, but the measure of general disinterest. Sectarian religion and secular indifference each lend plausibility to the attitudes of the other. If the practice of forgiveness is placed at the heart of Christianity this deadlock is broken. First, it enables Christianity to rediscover its distinctive generosity. The sectarian stance must stress clear authority, public observance, the disciplines of visibility which effectively divide men. Forgiveness respects and fosters individual freedom, recognizes the necessity of a certain privacy, and questions the bitterness of human antagonism. Secondly, it points the way in which Christianity can recover the initiative in the world at large. Christians need neither conform to a puzzled contempt for religious belief, nor disown the disturbing insights of secular man. We are able instead to listen to his criticisms and to salute his aspirations towards freedom and solidarity. A church which is truthful about its own failure to realize those aspirations encourages a similar realism elsewhere.

Christian and non-Christian both live in a world of much violence and injustice. To speak of freedom and peace is not to reflect the world as it is. Such language risks disappointment and invites pain. The words easily become empty slogans, or cease to be uttered as they are replaced by a tired and silent cynicism. Forgiveness, the refusal to discriminate, the acceptance of suffering without recrimination and retaliation, are the necessary forms of freedom and peace in a violent and unequal world. The figure who speaks to us of forgiveness not only reminds us of the victims of our society; he speaks as one of them. His message is our gospel, not because it immediately secures the freedom and peace which it promises. His followers have repeatedly experienced constraint and antagonism, but they prove that they are his followers by not perpetuating such experiences, which means not inflicting them on others. His message is good news, because it enables us to break the recurring pattern of violence and injustice, and assures us that such change is possible. Only the practice of forgiveness makes it possible to be hopeful in our kind of world.

Learning to forgive is the programme of the Christian life. As we cease to impose our demands on others, we no longer need to turn away from those who disappoint us. Our identity is discovered not in the disapproval which distinguishes, but in learning to affirm what at first seems threatening. As we ourselves are treated with forgiveness we grow in confidence and courage. In this way we learn to be thankful people. We begin by only being grateful for what gratifies us, which is usually something which distinguishes us from others – security, prosperity, good health, family happiness. Unless we learn a greater generosity, such narrow gratitude condemns us to a life of bitterness, which is inevitably dominated by resentment at being hurt and recrimination against those we blame. The goal of the Christian life is learning to thank God 'at all times and in all places'. We learn to affirm what at first seems painful and thereby are enabled to affirm what at first seems alien. Such thanksgiving is no longer the complacent reflection of particular good fortune, but invites us to celebrate the existence of others and to affirm an ever wider range of our own experience. In this way the eucharistic prayer transforms the vision of the worshippers, and in that transformation they discover that they themselves are changed.

DATE